The Shield of Achilles

Le Bouclier d'Achille

The Shield of Achilles

Aspects of Canada in the Victorian Age

EDITED BY W.L. MORTON

McClelland and Stewart Limited
Toronto/Montreal

Le Bouclier d'Achille

Regards sur le Canada de l'ère victorienne

W.L. MORTON, EDITEUR

The Canadian Publishers
McClelland and Stewart Limited
25 Hollinger Road, Toronto 16

Hephæstus began by making a large and powerful shield, adorned all over, finished with a bright triple rim of gleaming metal, and fitted with a silver baldric. The shield consisted of five layers, and he decorated the face of it with a number of designs, executed with consummate skill and representing, first of all, Earth, Sky and Sea, the indefatigable Sun, the Moon at the full, and all the Constellations with which the heavens are crowned, the Pleiads, the Hyads, the great Orion, and the Bear, nicknamed the Wain, the only constellation which never bathes in Ocean Stream, but always wheels round in the same place and looks across at Orion the Hunter with a wary eye.

Next he showed two beautiful cities full of people . . . Next he depicted a large field of soft, rich fallow, which was being ploughed for the third time . . . He also showed a king's estate, where hired reapers were at work with sharp sickles in their hands . . . The next scene was a vineyard laden with grapes . . . He also showed a herd of straight-horned cattle, making the cows of gold and tin . . . Next the god depicted a dancing-floor like the one that Dædalus designed in the spacious town of Cnossus for Ariadne of the lovely looks . . . Finally round the very rim of the wonderful shield he put the mighty Stream of Ocean.

I see in the not remote distance, one great nationality bound like the shield of Achilles, by the blue rim of ocean—I see it quartered into many communities—each disposing of its internal affairs but all bound together by free institutions, free intercourse, and free commerce; I see within the round of that shield, the peaks of the Western mountains, and the crests of the Eastern waves—the winding Assiniboine, the five-fold lakes, the St. Lawrence, the Ottawa, the Saguenay, the St. John, and the Basin of Minas—by all these flowing waters, in all the valleys they fertilize, in all the cities they visit in their courses, I see a generation of industrious, contented, moral men, free in name and in fact—men capable of maintaining, in peace and in war, a constitution worthy of such a country.

THOMAS D'ARCY McGEE, 1860

Contents

List of Illustrations

Reverend Joshua Marsden. *Toronto Public Libraries.*

Reverend E. H. Dewart. *Toronto Public Libraries.*

Alexandre Vattemare. *George Bante Publishing Company.*

Une annonce dans *La Gazette de Québec.* jeudi, le 18 février, 1841.

Louis Veuillot. *Réplique.*

Mgr Ignace Bourget. *Archives des Diocèses de Montréal.*

Prince Roland Bonaparte. *Réplique.*

Louis-Antoine Dessaulles. *Studio B. J. Hébert, St. Hyacinthe.*

Railway accident at Beloeil, 1864. *The Public Archives of Canada.*

The Old Victoria Bridge. *The Public Archives of Canada.*

E. Churchill & Sons' ship "Marlborough". *Maurice Crosby Photograph.*

Steamer *Quebec. The Public Archives of Canada.*

" 'Gavazzi Riot' at Montreal". *The Public Archives of Canada.*

Illumination of Montreal. *Toronto Public Libraries.*

The Honourable Henry Sherwood. *Toronto Public Libraries.*

The Honourable J. W. Johnston D.C.L. *The Public Archives of Canada.*

Lord Dufferin. *Photo: Notman and Fraser, The Public Archives of Canada.*

Lord and Lady Aberdeen. *Photo: W. J. Topley, Ottawa, 1898, The Public Archives of Canada.*

Thomas Fuller. *The Public Archives of Canada.*

Frederick William Cumberland. *The Public Archives of Canada.*

Drawing of the proposed University College. *Toronto Public Libraries.*

East view of University College in the 1860's. *Toronto Public Libraries.*

The Parliament Buildings (Centre Block), Ottawa, c.1869. *The Public Archives of Canada.*

Cathédrale Marie-Reine du Monde, "St. James Cathedral," Montreal. *The Public Archives of Canada.*

La Basilique, Québec. *Archives du Québec.*

Baronde Gauldrée Boilleau. *Archives du Semenaire de Québec.*

Abel-Frédéric Gautier. *Archives du Semenaire de Québec.*

Metlakatla, British Columbia. *Provincial Archives, Victoria, B.C.*

Church and Indian Band, Metlakatla. *Provincial Archives, Victoria, B.C.*

The Inauguration of Dufferin Terrace, Quebec. *The Public Archives of Canada.*

"Muffining." *The Public Archives of Canada.*

The Dufferins at the Curling rink at Rideau Hall. *The Public Archives of Canada.*

At the foot of the Toboggan Slide. *The Public Archives of Canada.*

Rideau Hall in the Lorne period. Wood-engraving from *Canadian Illustrated News*, Dec. 7, 1878. *The Public Archives of Canada.*

Lord Lorne. *Photo: Notman and Sandham, The Public Archives of Canada.*

Lord Monck. *Photo: W. J. Topley, The Public Archives of Canada.*

Lord Grey. *The Public Archives of Canada.*

Editor's Preface

The completion of this volume of essays and its title from Thomas D'Arcy McGee's famous oration, were suggested by one of the authors, Mr. Laurence Sidney Fallis, Jr. The editor's reply to the suggestion was that he would attempt to edit such a volume if Mr. Fallis would do one of the essays.

The authors who contributed so generously of their knowledge of the period were recruited by writing to various friends in Canadian universities and to those whose names were suggested. To those who helped in that way, as well as to the authors themselves, it is a pleasure to repeat my thanks publicly.

The essays, beyond such a procedure, and a general statement that they were to be concerned with intellectual and social history, were not planned, and are not written to any definite theme. The period discussed centres on Confederation, and the interests of the authors decided what application they might have. Such being the case, it is surprising how recurrent certain themes and names are.

It will be noted that many themes and some regions are not explicitly dealt with; this is an acknowledged matter for regret, but it was necessary to proceed with such authors as had time to prepare a contribution.

It is the editor's hope, to which the contributions of his associates give much substance, that the volume will assist what other work of the kind has been done to enable its readers to glimpse what great areas of knowledge of the beliefs and motives of Canadians await research and analysis. In these essays it is possible to begin to see what past Canadians really thought and were.

It is hoped also that this modest venture in publication in both Canadian languages may challenge Canadian readers to awaken the widespread, but latent, bilingualism of Canada.

The authors are responsible for their contributions, the editor for his, and for the general editing of the volume.

Thanks are owing also to the Canada Council for a grant which made the undertaking possible, and to the publishers for their great helpfulness and especially for undertaking to publish one volume in both English and French.

The Shield of Achilles

Le Bouclier d'Achille

The Evangelical Creed in Canada

Goldwin French, University College, McMaster University

If, in the words of an eminent historian, "religion is the substance of culture, and culture the form of religion,"[1] the centre of Canadian history should be the history of the Christian religion. To Canadian scholars and to the Canadian popular mind alike, this would appear to be a meaningful generalization. S.D. Clark has remarked that "in few countries in the western world has religion exerted as great an influence upon the development of the community as it has in Canada."[2] To Roy Daniells "religion . . . not the class struggle [is] our chief problem and the true enigma of our society."[3] Equally, critics of our society and culture are wont to attribute our deficiencies and such habits as they consider disagreeable, to the baneful effect of the "Puritan" tradition – a tradition that is alleged to be singularly powerful in this country.

Whether one agrees with the analyst or the critic there can be little doubt that Christianity has been a powerful formative factor in the growth of this nation. With rare exceptions, however, this relationship has been described in assertions that reflect the prejudices either of the hagiographer or of the jaundiced assailant. Its real nature remains obscure and little understood.

Needless to say, in what follows this mystery will not be fully revealed or its contours definitively explored. The most that one can do is to seek to illuminate some of its complex features at a specific point in time. The period that has been chosen is the two decades immediately preceding Confederation, a generation in which ostensibly British North Americans were overwhelmingly Christian, not having succumbed as yet to the materialist delights of a later age. Furthermore, attention will be focused upon evangelical Protestantism, rather than upon the whole range of Canadian Christianity.

To define evangelical Protestantism and culture is outwardly simple, but in reality extraordinarily difficult. Can one not argue, for example, that all the Canadian Protestant churches were evangelical in that they were constituted by the voluntary ingathering of individuals sharing specific religious beliefs and practices? Was there not in all the Protestant churches an awareness of the need to proselytize, and a continuing concern for the quality of their inner life? The term should be confined, none the less, to those denominations consisting essentially of those who professed conversion and accepted forms of discipline designed to strengthen their faith and to shew forth its implications. The two groups which fell most clearly into this category were the Methodists and Baptists, but the evangelical temper was present among substantial numbers of Anglicans and Presbyterians.

If evangelical is an elusive word, culture is even more imprecise. Ideally, a cultured society is one in which literature and the arts are fully developed; in this sense British North American society had little culture in the 1850's.[4] But literate Canadians were well supplied with books and artistic objects; they were acquainted with a variety of architectural styles; the press purveyed literature and literary criticism; the young were being educated in increasing numbers in schools, academies and colleges. Through all these media a distinctive climate of opinion and a set of attitudes were emerging that, in their turn, would shape the growth of Canadian culture and the reactions of Canadians to it.

Since British North Americans took their religion so seriously, it necessarily affected the cultural atmosphere. What they read, what they saw, what they heard, were influenced by, or filtered through, the tissue of their religious beliefs and practices. The history of religion is indeed an essential clue to the mode and language of Canadian thought about human nature and human destiny, and hence about Canadian culture. To comprehend the relationship between evangelical religion and culture one must begin, then, by trying to understand the mood of the evangelical Christian.

Our ability to understand the religious ideas of our forebears is limited significantly by popular and scholarly stereotypes, and by our inadequate knowledge of those factors which shaped their growth. In our secular and humanist generation it is singularly difficult to enter imaginatively and sympathetically into the world of religious concepts and imagery within which many Canadians lived a century ago. We assume without hesitation that it must have been akin to that of contemporary revivalist groups. Conceiving as we do that these are the haven of mostly illiterate, lower-class fanatics, we dismiss them as of little consequence in our sophisticated society, and unwittingly we conclude that the convictions of our predecessors were similarly lacking in relevance. In reality, the evangelical Protestantism of the last century was in the mainstream of the Reformed tradition. The difference between it and "orthodoxy" was one of emphasis and a sense of urgency, not as today, the chasm resulting from the massive theological and philosophical revolution of the last seventy-five years.

A second notion that is firmly fixed in many minds is the identification of evangelicalism and Puritanism. Too often the word Puritan evokes unpleasant memories of bigotry, persecution, and the regulation of morals by ecclesiastical and secular means. In North America, the term "Puritan" should be used only in reference to the religious tradition that crystallized in New England, – a tradition whose outstanding feature was the determination to create "a city upon a hill," a "godly commonwealth" to which the eyes of all people would turn in admiration and imitation. The authentic heirs of this great expectation are not the denominations, but such groups as the Mormons – communities that arose in the social and intellectual debris of the New England Way.[5] To identify Puritanism and mid-nineteenth century evangelicalism is generally to substitute pejorative language for serious analysis.

Among historians two other concepts have contributed to our misunderstanding as well as to our understanding of evangelical Protestantism. Our religious history is said to have been permeated by conflict between church and sect forms; the gradual disappearance of the frontier is seen as the principal reason for the progressive shift from sectarian to churchly religion.[6] In effect, social instability has stimulated the development of otherworldly or sectarian religious organizations; social stability has led to the growth of churches which have adapted themselves to the needs and interests of society.

That the church-sect antithesis and the frontier thesis are useful conceptual tools is certain; but their relevance to the understanding of Canadian conditions is questionable. In British North America as in the United States, a number of denominations developed – religious communities whose members were held together in each case by their pursuit of a common objective. Their differences arose out of the distinctive character of their aims, and these in turn were determined as much by their historical backgrounds as by immediate circumstances. Hence the ends sought remained much the same long after the period of settlement had passed. Similarly, the shifting frontier was not so much a challenge to theological and liturgical adaptation as the symbol of a new society in which religious and other institutions had to be established. The distinctive aspect of British North America was that this new society was less pagan and less detached from its past than in the United States. Metropolitan pressures were stronger and the antipathy toward them less acute – a factor of the greatest importance in producing the specific flavour of Canadian Protestantism.

In 1850, after a half-century of strenuous effort, only 15.5% of the American people claimed church membership, but the majority of the admittedly smaller Canadian population professed affiliation with some denomination.[7] Roman Catholics constituted the largest single group; the Methodists, Anglicans and Presbyterians comprised the bulk of the Protestant community.[8] Twenty years later, the proportions had not changed greatly. But this obscured the fact that the Anglicans and Presbyterians were increasing and would increase most consistently in future. One may agree with F.H. Underhill that the Methodists "set the imprint of their character upon the life of [Ontario],"[9] but any assessment of the range and depth of evangelical influence in British North America as a whole must take into account the prevalence of such convictions among Anglicans and Presbyterians. That these were widespread was indicated by the protracted controversy between high and low churchmen within the Anglican fold and by the importance of dissenters from the Kirk in the Presbyterian camp. Indeed one might argue that the dominant strand in Canadian Protestantism was evangelical.

All other obstacles aside, our membership in a generation in which God is, if not dead, at least unemployed hinders us from entering readily into the religious atmosphere of the 1850's. At its core was an overwhelming conviction of the existence, the presence and the power of God in human affairs. Christians might differ about the manner in which God worked, but they were persuaded that He was continuously active, guiding the course of events, rewarding and protecting His supporters, admonishing and punishing those who deviated from His path. Thus an Anglican newspaper insisted that a serious railway accident was a judgement of God on those who built and operated railways on Sunday. Anson Green, an enlightened Methodist, set out at length a dreadful tale about the simultaneous deaths of two brothers who had refused his entreaties to repent and had gone on "cracking nuts in the house of God."[10] God, he asserted, had hardened His heart as they had hardened theirs against Him! In his old age, Green and his English brethren were certain that God, working through his tailor, had saved him from death in a train wreck. "Let those doubt a special providence who may, I cannot. The Lord's eyes art always upon his children and his powerful arm is around them. Guided by such an eye and protected by such an arm we are safe, whether on land or water."[11] To his younger colleague, Albert Carman, it was clear that "if one plant brings forth the wild grapes, it can be plucked up and a new seed dropped by the rivers of water."[12] Much of the work of God consisted in the destruction of useless plants and the planting of fresh ones.

This providential view of history was, of course, neither new or specifically Protestant. Its implications strike us as absurd, immoral, or singularly disquieting. Then, as now, it often encouraged complacency, smugness and the misinterpretation of chance or coincidence. Positively, however, it was a compelling factor, especially for the evangelical Christian. To believe that the whole of existence stood under judgement was to ensure that the moral significance of all actions would be admitted and assessed. The primary criterion for evaluating any action or decision was not expediency, but its correspondence with what appeared to be God's will for man.

The evangelicals' assessment of human nature was as conservative as their doctrine of Providence. If they were aware of the psychological and ethical revolution of the eighteenth century, they rejected its insights. They accepted the fruits of technological progress (except on Sundays), but they were insensitive to their philosophical implications. Rather they subscribed without hesitation to the idea of original sin. William Gregg, writing in the 1880's, stated that the Presbyterians "maintain the doctrines of original guilt and depravity."[13] To a man they were certain that men, left to their own devices, could not and would not resist temptation, which to them meant either willingness to thwart the evident purposes of God or to resist those who sought to set them upon the true way. Sin, moreover, would bring retribution: a visitation of the divine wrath in this life; and eternal punishment in the next, where "the unwashed spirit" would be "ushered into the presence of a sin-avenging God."[14] The vivid assurance of the faithful that this fate awaited all sinners, produced that intense concern for spiritual health so characteristic of the evangelical mentality.

Since time was always running out for millions of souls, it was the church's duty to preach the Gospel without ceasing and without fear. From this conviction arose the spirit of revival. Revivalism had two important aspects: the substance of preaching, and the manner in which the word was purveyed. Each of these was culturally as well as religiously significant.

Among the Canadian denominations, the Methodists were the most enthusiastic exponents of the evangelical position. Their activities serve to illustrate its principal features. Methodist preaching and practice derived from the writings and example of John Wesley. "Our main doctrines," said Wesley, "which include all the rest, are three – that of repentance, of faith and of holiness. The first of these we account, as it were, the porch of religion; the next, the door; the third, religion itself."[15] One of the first Methodist sermons preached in Canada was on the text: "Repent ye, therefore and be converted," a theme that would become the trademark of "the thundering legion." Repentance consisted "not merely of regret and remorse for past deeds," but an overwhelming "consciousness of the sinfulness of the heart," and of "the burden and misery" of sin, and a determination to be delivered from it. This, in itself, was the work of God, but men had the ability and the right to choose whether they would enter the "porch" of the religious life. "The repentant heart turns to God, as the needle to the pole."[16]

The Methodist believed that true repentance was accompanied invariably by faith – "the resting of the soul upon Christ alone for salvation."

Faith was the free gift of God, available not as the Calvinists asserted only to the elect, but to all who sought it in humility and spiritual agony. Through faith the convert received evidence that he was relieved of the penalties of sin, that he had become a true member of God's family, and that the Holy Spirit had begun a process of regeneration in his soul, by which he would be restored to the moral image of God. A genuine conversion, moreover, would bring with it a sense of certainty, a positive assurance that God had opened His heart to the anguished sinner. He need not have the qualms and the hesitations of those who thought themselves "elect."

Repentance and conversion were, however, but the prelude to a religious life; the attainment of holiness was its essence, because ultimately the imperfect man cannot perceive God fully. Christian perfection to the Methodist meant purity of motive and an awareness of entire dependence upon God; it did not mean that men could free themselves of the limitations and frailties of this earthly existence. The believer could enter upon this glorious phase of his spiritual career only by so disciplining himself that he became a fit subject for the "second blessing," or the experience of sanctification. The beginning and the end of the religious life thus rested upon the individual's admission that he does not belong to himself but to God, and the positive action of the Holy Spirit in transforming this into a living reality.

Convinced as they were that the doctrines of justification, assurance, and holiness were the crucial elements in Christian teaching, the Methodists sought to present them simply, cogently, urgently, and in the kind of emotional context that would impart to the listener a vivid awareness of his shortcomings and his potentialities. The sinner's resistance was broken down by the use of hymns, by impassioned oratory, by the testimony of those in or entering the fold, by interminable services, and by the fervour generated in crowded assemblies. The atmosphere of such a gathering is strikingly conveyed by Charles Churchill, a Wesleyan missionary in Nova Scotia. So dense was the crowd in the chapel that "it was with the utmost difficulty they could give way sufficiently for me to pass through to the pulpit." While he was speaking "a breathless silence, interrupted only by deep sobs, hung over the assembly; but when this part of the service was succeeded by exhortation and appeal . . . a heaving was visible in the whole assembly." Soon the disturbed "were bowed three deep around the altar, kneeling in prayer, and weeping bitterly." The next evening, "at one time ten or twelve persons arose at once, as though one gust of the Holy Spirit's quickening power had simultaneously burst their bonds, their places being quickly filled with others as they retired."[17] For many the religious life began in this way; the Methodists generally asserted that an emotional conversion was the only entrance to the Christian experience.

Too much, however, has been made of this aspect of evangelical and especially Methodist Christianity. Equal attention was paid to the practice of faith and the achievement of perfection. Canadian Methodists, following Wesley's example, established a set of rules designed to secure this objective. Not only were Methodists to live simply, to keep the Sabbath, to abstain from alcohol, and to avoid frivolous amusements such as card-playing and dancing, but also they were to find time for private and public devotions, especially attendance at love-feasts and the Holy Communion. Above all, they had to participate in the weekly class-meeting, a gathering in which each individual was to describe his spiritual condition, his successes and failures, and to seek the counsel of his brethren concerning his religious development. Ideally, by this means, the convert would learn what God expected of him and was enabled to lean upon his brethren in carrying out God's will.

The Methodist doctrine of perfection as such was not acceptable to other evangelicals, but the religious temper of Methodism embodied many of the essential elements in their view of life. One would find it difficult to distinguish the Presbyterian from the Methodist in these birthday reflections: "I could not help wondering at the goodness of God to me, both in temporal and spiritual things. May my life, if it is to be longer spared, be devoted to the advancement of His glory and service. I would so number my days as to apply my heart to heavenly wisdom."[18] Or: "I feel ashamed when I think how little I have done for God, for the church, for the world. . . . Souls have perished while I have been slumbering and still a merciful Redeemer bears with my infirmities and multiplies my years. . . . " To "eternity I am hastening, and soon its mysterious light will dawn upon me."[19] In effect, the authentic evangelical was characterized almost invariably by his constant awareness of the presence of God in human affairs and by his belief in the reality of human evil. He was certain that through divine intervention men could be saved from themselves, and that the process of conversion was marked by humiliation and exaltation. The true Christian was an ascetic, who sought constantly to strengthen his faith by participation in private and public worship, and who demonstrated his love of God by charitable deeds and upright behaviour. Honesty, sincerity, sobriety, seriousness, a sense of purpose, and the acceptance of responsibility for others were the proper outer attributes of the transformed inner man.

If this was the substance of the evangelical conception of human nature and human destiny, in what manner did it affect the climate of opinion of British North American society? Any satisfactory answer to this question must take into account not only the nuances of outlook within the evangelical camp, produced by the historical development of the various denominations, but also the diverse implications of their religious ideals. Furthermore, it should include intangible pressures and the institutional activities of the evangelical churches.

Critics of the social and cultural impact of evangelical Christianity have regularly fastened upon the emotionalism, the anti-intellectualism, the un-awareness of historical continuity, and the moral inflexibility that are said to have accompanied the spread of its influence. Richard Hofstadter, for example, has argued recently that "to the extent that it becomes accepted in any culture that religion is largely an affair of the heart or of the intuitive qualities of mind, and that the rational mind is irrelevant or worse, so far will it be believed that the rational faculties are barren or perhaps dangerous. . . . In modern culture the evangelical movement has been the most powerful carrier of this kind of religious anti-intellectualism. . . ."[20]

This generalization is doubtless relevant to the study of nineteenth-century American culture; but it, like many others drawn from American history, is not fully applicable to Canadian conditions. Although the temper of Canadian Protestantism was predominantly evangelical, it was distinctly different from that of the American variety. In the United States, the religious foundations were laid by Congregationalism, Presbyterianism, and Anglicanism, each of which was repudiated in the late eighteenth century by many, perhaps the majority of its adherents. In so far as any of these churches subsequently recovered, it did so through theological and liturgical capitulation to the force of revivalist or extreme evangelical Christianity. Religious leadership in America was assumed by the Methodists and Baptists, and to a lesser degree by Presbyterians who deserted the old cause. But, while Methodism especially had live metropolitan roots, these were largely ignored. The successful denominations accommodated themselves to their circumstances and to the needs of their society, and in so doing became highly simplistic in doctrine and practice. Richard Cartwright ex-pressed a common attitude when he said: "I do not wish to undervalue education, but really I have seen so many of those educated preachers who forcibly reminded me of lettuce growing under the shade of a peach-tree . . . that I turn away sick and faint."[21] Similarly, C.G.Finney, a Presby-terian, based his theology on the Bible and "the philosophy and workings of his own mind." "I cannot believe," he said, "that a person who has ever known the love of God can relish a secular novel." He would have agreed with a Methodist preacher's assertion that "it is grace and gifts that furnish the real live coals from off the altar."[21]

Doubtless one could readily match these statements with similar effu-sions from Canadian evangelicals in the 1850's, but this would be to mis-construe the delicate balance in their total outlook. In marked contrast to the American denominations, the Canadian churches were the products of the intimate interplay of traditions, derived partly from Britain, and partly from the history of British North America. At no point did any denomina-tion dominate the Canadian religious scene in the degree that the Metho-dists and Baptists dominated American Protestantism. The Anglicans and Presbyterians in Canada, after a difficult start, attracted increasing numbers of adherents. To a significant extent, they imitated their rivals, but much more crucial was their maintenance of close relations with their British brethren and their retention of standards derived from the parent churches. Anglican and Presbyterian evangelicalism were not cut off from their respective theological and liturgical traditions; each developed in some measure in the context of the intellectual evolution of British culture.

What is not so well appreciated is the extent to which the Methodists and Baptists were similarly influenced. At the outset, British North American Methodism was simply an extension of the emerging American Methodist Church, and in Upper Canada it retained some of the quality of its origin. But the real foundations of Methodism in the Maritime Provinces were laid by the English Methodist Conference, and after 1830, representatives of that Conference played an influential role in the development of Canadian Methodism. In both cases, the Wesleyans acted as a conservative force: they strengthened respect and sympathy for the Anglican communion; raised the intellectual stature of the ministry; and encouraged restraint in preaching and worship. Furthermore, the constant interchange of representatives between the two conferences gave a new and wider horizon to Canadian Methodism.

The early Baptist churches were similarly offshoots of the religious life of New England and New York; but, unlike the Methodist churches, they derived from the Puritan and not the Anglican community. Hence, their theological orientation was Calvinistic, modified by Arminianism, particularly the conviction that the church consists only of those converted souls who will submit to baptism. This evangelical emphasis was strengthened greatly by the New Light movement and by the subsequent growth of revivalism in the United States. In the Maritime Provinces however, the primitive simplicity of the early Baptist churches and ministers was altered greatly by a strong infusion of Anglicans, who imparted a remarkable intellectual stimulus to the Baptist association. In Upper Canada, too, the Scottish Baptists who settled in the Ottawa Valley were unusually successful, both in strengthening the evangelical orientation of their brethren, and in raising their standards of leadership.

The consequence of this interplay of traditions was a gradation in attitudes toward the training of clergy and ministers. The Anglicans and Presbyterians insisted upon an educated and cultured ministry, and to that end made provision at an early date for theological, as well as general education. By contrast all varieties of Methodism believed that the indispensable prerequisite for a minister was God's call to that vocation. Grace, not gifts, made the preacher; God's mandate was revealed by the response to his preaching. Hence, formal theological instruction was not introduced by the Methodists until late in the century. On the other hand, the number of educated ministers rose steadily after 1840, especially in the Wesleyan conferences which represented the largest group of Methodists. In this category were men trained in English Wesleyan colleges, in the rising Canadian Methodist institutions and less commonly, in the United States. As one moved across the spectrum of Methodism, from the Wesleyans to the Primitive Methodists, the proportion of trained ministers fell, but so likewise did the importance of these bodies. More revealing, perhaps, was the apparent absence of conflict (especially among Wesleyans and Methodist Episcopals) about the relative weight to be attached to grace and gifts, to the work of the Spirit, and to the benefits of education.

Undoubtedly there were many Canadian Methodists and Baptists who believed that "an intellectual clergyman is deficient in piety"; but many conservative churchmen thought that "an eminently pious minister is deficient in intellect." The former opinion had been widespread in an earlier generation (and still appears occasionally in the twentieth century, especially in rural churches); but by 1860 a degree of stability had been achieved in the evangelical community, and the atmosphere was not antagonistic to scholarship and intellectual attainments. By that time, the leaders of the evangelical churches, if not the rank-and-file, were highly receptive to the association of learning and religion, and to the encouragement of cultural growth.

The critic might well reply that, although the evangelical churches were not formally anti-intellectual, the nature of their convictions was such as to inhibit and pervert the growth of literature and the arts. Specifically he might contend that an irrational, other-worldly form of religion cannot be effectively linked with the emergence of a rational and humanist culture. He could go further: "[Evangelical Protestantism] turned its face deliberately toward the past instead of toward the future in its interpretation of man and his need. . . . Its narrowness and mediaevalism, its emotionalism . . . its crass supernaturalism and Biblical literalism; its want of sympathy with art and science and secular culture in general, turned them permanently against religion."[23] This is not an issue peculiar to Canada, but, because of the authority of the evangelical ideal, it is of especial relevance to our cultural history.

It would be implausible to suggest that such criticism has no validity; but it can be argued that the relationship was not as simple as has been supposed. To begin with, at the core of the evangelical theology there was tension between the Calvinist and Arminian positions. Ostensibly the latter was the voice of the future, but it had absorbed, none the less, some of the qualities of the former. Methodists referred frequently and indignantly to the wickedness of the doctrine of election; yet they could not free themselves from the Calvinist concern for the glory and honour of God in human affairs. Indeed, this concern reinforced their own conviction that the convert must be constantly alert to the application of the Holy Spirit to his own improvement. This, in association with the strongly Calvinist orientation of

Presbyterians and Baptists, made it difficult for Canadian culture to develop autonomously. Rather there was an inherent tendency to regard its growth as of less import than the fulfilment of God's design, and to assess its manifestations in the light of their contribution to that design. It was inconceivable to the evangelical mentality that any kind of knowledge or cultural activity should be furthered unless it served this useful objective. Since it was easier to define the objectionable and the useless than the constructive, the evangelical temper encouraged a kind of nagging suspicion of literary, artistic, and scientific pursuits – an attitude that was countered in some measure by the more sophisticated ministers and laymen.

Less tangible, but perhaps more decisive in the long run, was the conflict between reason and emotion, the claims of the mind and of the heart, – a conflict that assumed different guises in the Calvinist and Arminian households. For those who held firmly to election, emotional religion had little appeal. It could be demonstrated rationally that God claimed the sinner; hence, preaching consisted of the clear presentation of God's aims and methods, which could be understood and appropriated only by faith instilled by Him. There was little need to play upon the emotions of the hearers, because God evidently disliked uproar, and the liturgical adornment of worship. Thus a devoted Presbyterian could assert: "I have not much to tell you about my experience, but I can tell you of my *faith*."[24] Austerity and solemnity were the distinctive features of Presbyterian architecture and religious services. A profound religious experience undoubtedly lay concealed behind this outer shell, as was inadvertently revealed by the editor of the *Christian Examiner*: "The poetry of [the Psalmody] is suited to the subjects, masculine and vigorous, dignified and sublime"; "the ancient Scottish music is beyond all doubt, the best that can be found. There is a peculiar kind of wild rich pathos about it."[25] Its effects none the less were contradictory and ambiguous. The Calvinist at his most enthusiastic was more receptive to reasoned argument than were many evangelicals, and hence he was susceptible to the claims of education and scholarship. But the suppression and constriction of the emotions, and the barrenness of his environment, served to narrow his cultural responses. He found it difficult, if not impossible, to enjoy himself wholeheartedly, to conceive that not every object, idea, or action has, or ought to have, a purpose and that the creation and contemplation of beauty is a legitimate activity.

"It is a fundamental principle with us," John Wesley declared, "that to renounce reason is to renounce religion, that religion and reason go hand in hand, and that all irrational religion is false religion."[26] To many, nevertheless, Methodist and Baptist evangelicalism was a denial of this principle; Methodist preaching and worship was in their view essentially irrational, and therein lay its threat to true religion and culture. The legacy that Wesley bequeathed to his followers was in reality singularly confused. Although Wesley was a product of Oxford, a voracious reader, and an indefatigable writer, he was capable of Bibliomancy and prone to interpret ordinary occurrences in Providential terms. Conversely, he was remarkably modern in his reliance upon the evidence of experience in assessing the testimony of his followers. His doctrinal and liturgical teaching was an ingenious combination of pietist and Anglican concepts. In the hands of his Canadian disciples, these characteristic emphases became attenuated but did not disappear. Wesley's unsophisticated approach to theology was reproduced faithfully, as was his doctrinal eclecticism. This approach could and did lead to the blurring of vital issues and to the substitution of sentimental moralizing for serious thought; however, it could and would facilitate an accommodation between theology and the changing thought-patterns later in the nineteenth century. Methodist emotionalism, the necessary concomitant of Wesley's teaching, justly earned its exponents a reputation for excessive zeal. Methodists were likely to mistake temporary exaltation for moral transformation; and, whatever their pastors might say, they were not above supposing that, because more cultured persons were less enthusiastic than themselves, their manners and their works were suspect and probably immoral. Ultimately, though, the most important aspect of the Methodists' experimental approach to religion was that, in a very real sense, the sinner "got religion" rather than being taken by it. They were sufficiently orthodox to deny this, yet it was implicit in Wesley's whole approach. This would result eventually in the humanizing of Christianity and in a *rapprochement* between religion and culture.

Leaving aside these possible long term trends, many would contend fervently that the surroundings of Methodist and Baptist worship were as hostile to the arts as were those of the Presbyterians. Methodism has come to be synonymous with bad taste and vulgarity – a charge that can be verified if only on architectural grounds, because so many structures dating from the late nineteenth century still survive. Obviously Methodist services were conducted in a simple physical context and were themselves disordered and colourless – at least to those familiar with the great architectural and liturgical traditions of the Roman and Anglican churches. Evangelicals opposed formal procedures, such as written prayers and sermons. They prayed and spoke as they were moved, often at short notice; their hearers were required to participate fully in song and to demonstrate their feelings in other ways. This was not a milieu congenial to form and style and to the contemplation of the mystery of reality. None the less, if it is to be seen in perspective, its other dimensions must be understood. Methodists and Baptists had no inherent antipathy to beauty, that is, to good architecture, to colour, to the effective use of music; and some of them were sensitive to the glories of the natural order. Their very reliance on the emotions unconsciously predisposed them to appreciate artistic experience. Indeed, much of the tastelessness and informality of evangelical worship derived not so much from their own convictions as from their prejudices – a morbid suspicion of the older churches – and from the class and geographical composition of the membership. Rural dwellers and poorly educated persons were heavily represented in the evangelical denominations; and their habits of mind cannot be simply ascribed to their religious beliefs. The artistic standards of a later generation were the natural concomitants of a vulgar society, not all of whose features can be blamed on the churches.

Possibly the most forceful charge leveled against the evangelicals is that the moral constraints attendant upon membership in these denominations imposed restrictions on the development of Canadian culture. The basic intent of such regulations was to make the Christian consider the implications of his actions, and, above all, to focus his mind on his eternal, not his temporal destiny. Carried to its logical conclusion, this attitude really involved complete separation from the world, a course that most evangelical Christians were unwilling to adopt. Unfortunately, in settling for life *in* the world, but not *of* it, they frequently passed over those forms of immorality, such as intolerance, selfishness, egotism and hypocrisy, that were most antipathetic to the spirit of the Gospel, and fastened on artistic and social activities whose immorality is not so readily perceived. Religious newspapers and ministerial reminiscences regularly dwelt on the same themes. Card-playing was a deplorable waste of time that could be better employed in spreading the Gospel or improving the mind. Dancing, as popular an occupation as cards, was the subject of fierce condemnation. In 1861 one finds Anson Green aroused by the festivities attendant upon the Prince of Wales' visit to Canada. "These fantastic vanities," he assured an argumentative lady, expel "good impressions," extinguish "feelings of piety," and hinder prayers. Devotees of dancing incurred "fearful responsibilties" by setting a bad example to their brethren.[27] He and others gleefully retailed accounts of parties broken up by those who, suddenly stricken with their sinfulness, knelt in the midst of their "pleasure-lusting" companions. From its inception, too, the *Christian Guardian* inveighed against the theatre. Drama could not be reconciled with any Christian standard of morals, for on the stage crimes were so tastefully presented that their wickedness went unnoticed. A Christian should never countenance what he would not do, or would not want to see done by his family. Above all, play-going was a distraction from sound learning, to which insufficient attention was paid. Who, the editor triumphantly concluded, would wish to be summoned from the theatre by death? – ill-informed, his passions aroused, and his mind distracted from the truths of the Gospel.[28] Who, evangelicals also demanded, would wish to be caught reading fiction? Novels, too, stimulated immorality and falsehood; their "withering influence" discouraged the reading of morally constructive literature.

Childish as this kind of comment appears to us today, it is only fair to emphasize that it was motivated not so much by a "spoil-sport" habit of mind, as by a vivid awareness of life's ephemeral quality and by a rigorous determination to use the available time for "serious" pursuits. Regrettably this positive, if limited, objective was often lost to sight. A clear line was not drawn between frivolity and innocent amusement, between great literature, tawdry writing, and solemn, pretentious sentimentalism. The cathartic effect of the drama was ignored or unknown; the aesthetic value of the creation and observation of rhythmic movement was completely hidden. Prohibition was simpler and provided a ready means for separating the saved from the damned, but in the end it produced a strand of intolerance, meanness, and myopia whose effects were remarkably lasting.

Customarily, opponents of the "Puritan" mentality are wont to stop at this point, having described the narrow legacy of that view of life. In fact any assessment would not be approximately complete, if no reference were made to the evangelicals' conception of historical continuity, their nationalism and their educational philosophy.

Students of American denominations have commented on their "history-lessness," that is a distinct tendency "to ignore the developments which had taken place in the old world after the first century."[29] They conceived that in the Bible could be discerned normative beginnings; that "the intervening history was largely that of aberrations and corruptions" and that in America new structures could be built on the truths now rediscovered.[30] Those who shared this outlook eschewed historical perspective and an awareness of tradition – a habit of mind that encouraged Biblical literalism and pragmatism, and discouraged discrimination between types of doctrine and practice.

In some measure, this viewpoint was shared by Canadian evangelicals. Especially during the formative years, the Bible was the inevitable source and standard of religious ideas, and practice was decidedly experimental. Once a degree of maturity had been attained, a more balanced position emerged, – an attitude that differed subtly from that prevailing in America and which necessarily had a distinctive cultural impact. Perhaps the most effective presentation of the evangelical case was made by Dr. Albert Carman. "How otherwise than by Holy Scripture," he asked, "do we know anything of the true Church of God?" "Some things [are] very clear and plain." The claim that God's connection with his Church throughout history is a "mere chronological bond" is a vain pretension. He agreed that "there may have been epochs of revelation," and "decisive acts of government in this century or that," but Christ did not at one point "give all goodness and spiritual power into a few hands" and then depart from the world. Rather "the perpetuity, power, and progress" of history "are found in the constant flow of mighty forces far beneath the surface of events and far down out of ordinary human sight." The reality behind history is the living Christ, possessed from before time "of infinite wisdom and power," the "centre of the Christian system, the spring of the Lutheran reformation and the source of the Christian revival." Throughout history, God has broken into it to restore life to the Church after it had been destroyed by men's "faithlessness and shame." The true church is any company of Christians in which life and energy are derived from Christ and which demonstrates His spirit in honest dealing and godly living. "Losing our hold of the present living Christ our glory is departed, as surely as if we lose our hold of a past creating, a past atoning Lord and Saviour."[31]

Carman, a representative and scholarly Methodist, clearly did not believe that any religious group could reach back to the Bible and to the early church as a primitive standard of excellence. History is not meaningless. Rather it is a flowing stream in which God's purpose is more clearly revealed from time to time, because men persistently lose contact with the directing power of the Holy Spirit. What matters in the church is not adherence to forms, but a constant awareness of the "developing scheme of human redemption." Although Carman and others of his mind were highly conservative, they were committed implicitly to an evolutionary view of church history and of theology – one which would take into account perspectives derived from tradition and the advance of human knowledge. For secular society and culture this conception at its best – which was not always in evidence – indicated the need to combine traditional and environmental influences, to adapt the past, rather than to set about the creation of utopia in the wilderness. In this light the destiny of Canada was not to figure as a great experiment, cut off from the history of its peoples, but to prolong and blend its traditions in a new context.

This outlook was doubtless related to another noteworthy element in the temper of Canadian evangelicalism, namely its incipient nationalism. Obviously the emergence of this attitude owed much to secular developments, but the churches themselves were very conscious of the national issue and sought to promote interest in the sources and ingredients of nationalism. Contrary to popular opinions, this was a concern of all the Protestant churches, yet it was rather more manifest among the evangelically minded.

The nationalist note was sounded as early as 1840 by Egerton Ryerson: "From whatever part . . . a man may emigrate, when he settles in Canada are not all his interests Canadian? . . . CANADA is . . . HOME . . . and any attempt to excite feelings from the 'place of their birth' against those who have been born in the 'place of their adopted residence' is unpatriotic, unchristian and unnatural."[32] A decade later, a Wesleyan missionary reminded his brethren that they were forming "a new church in a country possessing all the elements of a mighty empire."[33] In 1860, Ryerson told his daughter: "My plan is if spared from the age of 60 forward, as long as I have life and strength, to write books for the benefit of my country."[34]

Lest these comments should be thought unrepresentative, more striking evidence is provided by a later editor of the *Guardian*, E.H.Dewart, in his introduction to a volume of Canadian verse. "Only the illiterate and unreflecting," believe that enough books exist already, he began. "Whatever is discovered as new in the records of creation," should be embodied in literature. Equally reprehensible, however, was the widespread idea that "it is superfluous to make any attempt to build up a literature of our own." "A national literature is an essential element in the formation of national character. It is not merely the record of a country's mental progress; it is the expression of its intellectual life, the bond of national unity and the guide of national energy." No country in the world paid so little attention to native literature or was so indifferent to poetry. In Canada there was "almost universal absence of interest and faith in all indigenous literary productions;" this matter for national reproach was viewed with "undisturbed satisfaction." This state of things, he noted, was usually said to be the result of the primitive state of society and culture. The real reason was to be found in "the low and false conceptions" held by Canadians about the nature and importance of poetry. It is in fact "the offspring of the whole mind . . . in its highest moods of sympathy with the truths of the worlds of mind and matter." "The useful and the beautiful are both from God. Each has its appropriate sphere. They are not antagonistic: the one is the complement of the other." Assuredly, Canada's colonial position inhibited the growth of an indigenous literature, but, he concluded, Canadians must learn to look to their own land and their own future. "We have the inspiring spectacle of a great country, in her youthful might, girding herself for a race for an honourable place among the nations of the world." The "majestic forms" of nature, and "human nature in . . . its relation to the spiritual and divine – still presents an exhaustless mine of richest ore, worthy . . . of the deepest human and spiritual knowledge."[35]

The uncharitable might retort that, if Canadians had low and false conceptions of poetry, Dewart's own brethren had helped materially in shaping that poor taste. But, as significant as his keen appreciation of poetic values was his concern for the creation of a national culture, which he believed would contribute materially to the political and social unity of Canada. Not all evangelical ministers were as articulate as Ryerson and Dewart; but they voiced a common feeling of identification with Canada that arose naturally out of the experience of the churches in creating acceptable syntheses from imported and local materials. This underlying current of opinion probably helped to stimulate interest in federation and the attendant issues of a national sentiment and culture. When the churches themselves began to establish national organizations in the 1870's and 1880's, this intangible pressure would make itself felt much more effectively. To the extent, however, that the various denominations and the parts of some, such as the Methodists, had worked out distinctive internal compromises between metropolitan and indigenous pressures, they contributed to the cultural diversity as well as the unity of Canada.

Pervasive as were the indirect influences exerted by the evangelical churches on the social and cultural atmosphere of British North America, these were but a part of their contribution. In education, they played a direct and positive role at the primary and secondary levels. No attempt will be made here to describe this in detail, but rather to indicate some of the basic ingredients in their educational philosophy.

Broadly speaking, the evangelical churches did not attempt to establish primary schools. From the outset they supported public or national systems of education. Their viewpoint was perhaps best expressed by Egerton Ryerson. Education he defined as "that instruction and discipline which qualify and dispose the subjects of it for their appropriate duties and employments of life." The basis of "an Educational structure adapted to this end should be as broad as the population of the country . . . the whole based upon the principles of Christianity . . . ." Those subjects which were essential for all "should be brought within the reach of the most needy, and forced upon the attention of the most careless." It was absolutely necessary to make "Christianity the basis and cement" of the system. He added: "By Religion and Morality I do not mean sectarianism in any form, but the general system of truth and morals taught in the Holy Scriptures . . . . To inculcate the peculiarities of a Sect and to teach the fundamental principles of Religion and Morality are equally different." Sectarian teaching, he asserted, is "productive of ecclesiastical corruptions, superstition . . . social disputes and civil contentions . . . ."[36] Hence, in the legislation framed by Ryerson, only limited provision was made for separate schools, an arrangement supported by most evangelical Protestants.

The clear intent of this conception was not, as has been supposed, the separation of church and state in the field of education, but rather to use the schools as vehicles for the dissemination of Christian principles. Given the widespread contemporary acceptance of those principles in British North America, this was a legitimate objective, in so far as common agreement existed about the meaning of Christianity. Unfortunately, in practice "the general system of truth and morals taught in the Holy Scriptures" meant very different things to Protestants and Catholics; indeed, evangelical and conservative Protestants were by no means in agreement on certain vital issues. At best, therefore, the elementary schools became noteworthy means for the inculcation of Protestant values and so diffused these throughout British North American and Canadian society.

Apart from the inherent ambiguity of this device, its social and cultural impact would have been less objectionable if generous treatment had been accorded to the minority, specifically the Roman Catholics. To their credit Ryerson and other administrators endeavoured to secure this, but their brethren were less charitable. The *Christian Guardian* contended that to provide public funds for separate schools would be to further the interests of Romish and Puseyite intolerance. Those who preferred the "contracted purposes of a bigoted sectarianism to the more comprehensive and noble aims of national improvement" were "traitors to the best interests of posterity."[37] Five years later the Wesleyan Conference in the Maritime Provinces enjoined "its ministers and people to use their utmost endeavours to diffuse the principles of the Protestant Reformation and to counteract the pernicious tenets and practices of the Romish apostasy,"[38] an injunction that was repeated in sundry guises by evangelical churchmen throughout the latter half of the nineteenth century, and especially in connection with primary education.

The sordid details of this long battle need not be recalled here. From the standpoint of the evolution of Canadian culture, the sad fact is that the evangelical churches used their considerable authority to promote intolerance and bigotry. In so doing, they discouraged the formation of a liberal climate of opinion in which intellectual and cultural diversity would be cherished, and thereby delayed in some measure the attainment of cultural maturity in Canada.

In marked contrast, the evangelical contribution to higher education was more noble and more constructive. All the churches, evangelical and other, participated during the nineteenth century in providing colleges and universities for the training of the élite so urgently required in this country. This is not the place to recite the detailed history of new foundations or of the conflicts that marred their formative years. What is of interest are the assumptions from which the founders of such institutions as Victoria, Mount Allison, and Acadia universities proceeded.

Ryerson's inaugural address as principal of Victoria College, an institution in which no religious tests were required, but in which a liberal education based on Christian principles, was to be given, is particularly illuminating. "The grand object" of any educational agency, he suggested, was to develop, improve and perfect the "physical, mental and moral faculties." To this end emphasis would be laid on English, science, and philosophy. The usual objections to the study of English were based on prejudice, whereas Classics must not "be so taught and studied as to render the English language and the active industry of common life contemptible in the estimation and feelings of the student." The physical sciences required vigilant attention, if only because the knowledge of nature could be applied to useful purposes. As for philosophy, "to know our maker and ourselves . . . to employ our intellectual and moral powers according to the principles of reason and truth is the great end of our existence." Withal, "the great principles of our common Christianity" would not be abandoned "to the irreligiousness of scepticism or false philosophy."[39]

The same problem was examined twenty years later by the founders of

Mount Allison University. Higher education should aim at the development of the intellectual capacities through "the study of language, of literature, and of science." It would benefit the merchant, the legislator, the lawyer, the journalist, the teacher and the minister. "Piety has no preference for ignorance and barbarism." Religion has "a natural affinity for knowledge, refinement and mental training." "Man's education gives form and colour to the character of his life, and this in its moral aspects settles his eternal destiny." Thus it was imperative "to educate the moral faculty." An education "that abjures the culture of the moral nature is a monstrosity . . . a most presumptuous denial of the final God-decreed object of human training." Yet, morals could not be taught in isolation. "All courses of collegiate study should be pervaded, and rectified and vitalized by the sublime Christology of revelation," an objective which could be achieved most effectively by universities operating under denominational auspices.[40]

The aims then of the evangelical colleges and universities were three-fold. Their creators sought to provide a useful kind of higher education, that is, one adapted to the needs of a new and growing society. For this reason, less emphasis was placed on traditional and more on modern areas of study. A university should nevertheless be catholic in its interests. No area of investigation was to be excluded on moral or doctrinal grounds; on the contrary, reason and truth were to be pursued throughout. The whole range of knowledge was to be considered in the light of God's ultimate purpose for man. At the core of the university there would be "that fusion of the sacred and the secular . . . which is the spirit of the evangel."

Before Confederation, the denominational colleges were of course still in the formative stage. When they did reach maturity, they were not always true to the ideas with which they had begun, for it was by no means easy to reconcile their religious beliefs and their educational insights. The tension between evangelical religion and secular culture was often most acute in the educational process. There remains the significant fact that at the mid-century, the evangelical churches were beginning to produce a new generation of ministers and laymen, in whose preparation were combined the values of the Christian tradition, a receptivity to the great changes taking place in the sciences and philosophy, and an awareness of the significance of the sciences to nineteenth-century civilization. In a very real sense, this approach facilitated and eased the transition from the intellectual values of the past to those of the present, and helped to preserve at the same time an appreciation of the durable and valuable elements in the older system.

At the outset, it was suggested that anyone dealing with the intricate interplay of evangelical religion and culture in our society can at best hope to outline the most fruitful areas of contact. In searching for these one has to re-establish an intuitive and sympathetic understanding of a system of ideas, and a quality of mind that is foreign to the mental and moral atmosphere of our generation. When this is accomplished, one is still uncertain what kinds

of questions may and should be profitably asked. In this respect, the history of revivalist religion in the United States is illuminating, if only to establish the uniqueness of our experience in this, as in other fields. My intention has been to suggest the fruitfulness of this kind of comparative study, not to exploit it in detail.

That the impact of evangelical Protestantism on Canadian culture throughout the latter half of the nineteenth century was immense is certain; but a tentative evaluation of its range and depth is the most that can be given. Clearly it is not enough simply to describe and to condemn the restrictive attitudes of the churches towards many aspects of literature and the arts. The repressive and inhibiting effect of this outlook must be balanced by an appreciation of the distinct differences between the churches, and of the positive cultural implications of their beliefs and their forms of behaviour. In the end, possibly the most vital accomplishment of the evangelical denominations was to maintain the hold of the traditional Christian conception of God's design for man in an increasingly antagonistic environment. In so doing, they perpetuated in our culture a strong consciousness of the past foundations of our civilization, and of the width and depth of reality. By adopting a constructive attitude toward the emergence of new insights and new values, they made possible cultural evolution, rather than revolution in our society. The works of Hugh MacLennan, E.J.Pratt and Northrop Frye are the logical and characteristic outcome of the dilemmas and the values built into our cultural history by the power of the evangelical churches.

Notes: The Evangelical Creed in Canada

1. P.Tillich, *The Protestant Era* (Chicago, 1948), 57.
2. S.D.Clark, *The Developing Canadian Community* (Toronto, 1962), 168.
3. J.Park (ed.), *The Culture of Contemporary Canada* (Toronto, 1957), 29.
4. For assessments of the state of British North American culture see C.F.Klinck (ed.) *Literary History of Canada* (Toronto, 1965).
5. F.H.Littell, *From State Church to Pluralism* (New York, 1962), 57-62.
6. S.D.Clark has dealt most effectively with this theme. See, for example, his *Church and Sect in Canada* (Toronto, 1948).
7. Littell, *op. cit.*, 32.
8. In 1861, the Methodists comprised approximately 24% of the population of Canada West, the Anglicans 22%, the Presbyterians 21%.
9. F.H.Underhill, *In Search of Canadian Liberalism* (Toronto, 1961), 149.
10. A.Green, *The Life and Times of the Rev. Anson Green, D.D.* (Toronto, 1877), 22.
11. *Ibid.*, 347-348.
12. *Centennial of Canadian Methodism* (Toronto, 1891), 237.
13. W.Gregg, *History of the Presbyterian Church in the Dominion of Canada* (Toronto, 1885), 19.
14. Green, *op. cit.*, 21.
15. John Wesley, *Works*, v, 333.
16. E.Ryerson, *Canadian Methodism; Its Epochs and Characteristics* (Toronto, 1882), 78.
17. C.Churchill, *Memorials of Missionary Life in Nova Scotia* (London, 1845), 76-80.
18. United Church Archives *Bulletin* (1962), "Journal of William Bell," 31.
19. Green, *op. cit.*, 318-319.
20. R. Hofstadter, *Anti-Intellectualism in American Life* (New York, 1964), 47.
21. Quoted in Hofstadter, *op. cit.*, 102.
22. *Ibid.*, 94, 98.
23. A.C.McGiffert, *Protestant Thought Before Kant* (New York, 1911), 175.
24. W.H.Elgee, *The Social Teachings of the Christian Churches* (Toronto, 1964), 205.
25. *The Christian Examiner*, November, 1838.
26. R.W.Burtner and R.E.Chiles, (eds.) *A Compend of Wesley's Theology* (New York, 1954), 26.
27. Green, *op. cit.*, 383.
28. *Christian Guardian*, December 12, 1829.
29. K.S.Latourette, *A History of the Expansion of Christianity* (New York, 1937-45), iv, 424.
30. S.E.Mead, *The Lively Experiment* (New York, 1963), 111.
31. *Centennial of Canadian Methodism*, 230-238.
32. *Christian Guardian*, November 11, 1840.
33. *Records of the Wesleyan Missionary Society*, Beecham to Evans, April 10, 1852.
34. C.B.Sissons (ed.), *My Dearest Sophie* (Toronto, 1955), 12.
35. E.H.Dewart (ed.), *Selections From Canadian Poets* (Montreal, 1864), IX-XIX.
36. Ryerson's report from which these statements are taken was printed in the *Christian Guardian*, July 8, 15, 22, 1846.
37. *Christian Guardian*, November 10, 1852; April 13, 1853.
38. *Minutes of the Conference of Eastern British America* (1858), 24.
39. *Christian Guardian*, July 6, 13, 1842.
40 *The Provincial Wesleyan*, January 16, 23, 30, 1861.

God's Peculiar Peoples

S. F. Wise, Director of History, Department of National Defence

> *"For who hath known the mind of the Lord?*
> *or who hath been his counsellor?"*
>
> *Romans 11:34*

In every age men, in innocence or presumption, have brought the deity down into life and attributed divine sanction to their earthly ends. Wherever this has happened, and for whatever reason, the resulting psychological consequences have been extraordinarily powerful. The conviction of being in harmony with the purposes of God has set up strong inner drives that are manifested externally as a righteous sense of mission. Among Christian peoples, group myths of this kind have frequently been arrived at by way of the providential theology. The fact that the French-Canadian people were helped to a consciousness of themselves through the preaching of their special mission by the Catholic Church is well known, although the history of the idea of the unique French-Canadian witness in North America has not yet been traced. This essay is concerned with some unfamiliar variations on the same theme among the English-speaking inhabitants of British North America, and with the failure of the providential theory to furnish a unifying myth for English Canadians in the early Victorian era.

Looking for a sense of common purpose animating any of the societies of colonial British America in the later years of the eighteenth century is not the most rewarding of pursuits. Only when a society has come to consciousness of itself as a community, as a collectivity distinct from all others, with its unique interests and special place in the world, is it gripped by the idea of an overmastering destiny that transcends the short-term divisions of politics or class or locality. The more intense the feeling of communal distinctiveness, the sharper, more far-reaching and more exclusive will be the sense of common purpose.

In some of the societies of colonial America a sense of unique destiny, even of mission, took shape with astonishing rapidity. New England is the prime example. A homogenous people – united by a common misfortune, a common role in dramatic events, and sharing deep religious convictions – soon came to an intense belief in their special mission under God. "God sifted a whole nation that he might send choice grain over into this wilderness," said William Stoughton in 1668. And so miraculous did the survival and prosperity of New England appear, and so much in keeping with their reading of the manner in which God had prospered Israel, that the Puritans of Massachusetts Bay concluded that they had been singled out for special favour.

Look from one end of the heaven to another, whether the Lord hath assayed to do such a work as this in any nation, so to carry a people of His own from so flourishing a state to a wilderness so far distant, for such ends and for such a work. Yea, and in a few years hath done for them, as He hath here done for his poor despised people. . . . What shall we say of the singular providence of God in bringing so many shiploads of his people through so many dangers, as upon eagles' wings, with so much safety from year to year?[1]

The Puritan sense of being specially called lay at the root of American national feeling, and has always been an important part of the American's sense of national destiny. During the Second World War, the president of the Princeton Theological Seminary thought it not inappropriate to recur to this most venerable stream in the American consciousness, observing that the United States was "committed as a nation to accept the responsibility which God, in his providential economy, lays upon states such as ours to provide a political order in which principles of righteousness may receive concrete social expression. It becomes the responsibility of the American state, in a world in which the most elemental principles of human right are denied, to employ force for the restraint of evil and the establishment of an order of justice."[2]

There are certain similarities between the Puritan founders of New England and the peoples who moved into the colonies of northern British America in the last half of the eighteenth century. All were, in a sense, displaced peoples, whether fleeing from sixteenth or eighteenth-century religious persecution, or from severe social and economic dislocations in

Scotland, Yorkshire or New England, or as political refugees from the American Revolution. But unlike the Puritans, the refugee populations of early Canada had little to unite them. Each group had its own tragic myth to sustain it; even the New Brunswick loyalists (who would seem to have provided that province with a homogeneity lacking in the other colonies) were united only by the fact of their common loyalty. In terms of origin, class, religion, and politics they were divided. In each of the colonies, a sense of community and of communal purpose took generations to build; and a national consciousness was at least a century away. In the meantime, the idea of empire was the only myth providing some sense of unifying purpose which transcended the intense localisms of British North America – but by no means for all.

On one level, the politics of each colony consisted in conflicts between local executives and their opposition (impermanent alliances of religious and sectional interests); but, on another level, politics consisted in conflicts between imperfectly realized concepts of the proper future of the colony (often conflicts between idealized examples such as the government and society of Great Britain, and those of the United States). However, because few in all the colonies participated fully in politics, regarded politics as a central concern, or conceived of it as a meaningful way of achieving their aspirations, the politicians had no monopoly on visions of British North America's future.

In Canada, just as in early New England, the providential theology was a fruitful source of such visions; but rather than providing a unified intellectual framework into which the whole of colonial experience, past, present and future, could be fitted, it was appropriated to the needs and uses of various distinct groups, and the manner in which it was employed is a demonstration of the degree of difference among these groups.

Among the fishermen and pioneer farmers who had settled in Nova Scotia, New Brunswick and Prince Edward Island, the power of the gospel raced like wildfire as a result of the extraordinary preaching of Henry Alline. It was a fire not soon spent. For the next generation, outport and farm were kept in a state of religious fervour by itinerant New Lights, Methodists, Baptists and dissenting Presbyterians. Though politically mute during the last quarter of the eighteenth century, the folk of hinterland and seacoast underwent a religious experience as sustained and exalted as anything in the history of the Canadian church. In the eyes of the thousands of men, women and children won to grace, their leaders were like the prophets and patriarchs of the Old Testament (indeed, among the Baptists, the founding preachers were styled "Fathers"). To the preachers themselves, overwhelmed by the quenchless thirst of their flocks for the Word, it appeared that the Old Testament God was once more moving among his people in all His awful splendour, strengthening the hearts and lungs of His professors, and striking terror into the souls of the sinful. "I cannot refrain from letting you know," wrote Father Harris Harding to a brother Baptist, "that the Almighty God of Jeshurun has girded his sword on his thigh, and is riding the flaming chariot of Israel like a glorious conqueror; his majesty and power are seen among the inhabitants of Annapolis. . . . Colonel Delancey's daughter and some others . . . are under distress of soul."[3]

That God could be a real presence among the poor and meek of Nova Scotia, just as He had been among the oppressed people of Israel, was not a difficult idea for Bible Christians to accept. It was, in their view, only the vain professors of mechanical Christianity, who in the pride of wealth and station had interposed between themselves and the grace of God the earthbound institutions of men – who cast doubt upon the reality of the divine presence, and thus denied the promise of the Scriptures. "Some perhaps will now say," Henry Alline wrote in response to orthodox criticism of his ministry, "that all extraordinary calls are ceased, and therefore how is it possible for us to know, who God calls or intends to call for the work of the ministry any other way, than by their coming through such and such orders of men, &c. To which I answer that if extraordinary calls are ceased, yet the spirit of God hath not ceased to work with the children of men; neither is the spirit of God any more limited now, than it was seventeen hundred years ago." And who better to know the intentions of God than Alline, blessed with the supreme confidence that came from "a divine commission from heaven," or the many who through him had "experimentally" known grace, and "can call God to witness?"[4]

The world that Alline and his followers denied was the world of the wealthy and powerful, the world of the officers of government, the well-to-do merchants, the ministers of the formal churches. This was a world inhabited by men who believed in the laws of reason, and who attributed those events not explicable by reason to the operations of chance and fortune. To them, the existing political and social order was the product of natural forces that in the last analysis were identical with the ordinary providence of God, the ultimate rational disposer of things. Whatever was, was right.

Set against this world was that of the evangelical Christians of the maritime colonies. Their world, while indubitably the product of God's ordinary dealings with men, was one in which chance had no place. There was nothing random about the life of a man, or about the life of a society. All that occurred was the outcome of divine intent, even the most seemingly trivial of circumstances. Normally, it was true that the race went to the swift, and the battle to the strong; but God's transactions with men were not always at this level. In these isolated little colonies of British America, signs abounded of God's grace to the humble. So numerous and unusual were these manifestations that it was evident that the ordinary rules of providence were once again suspended, and that God was abroad among the people in a special and particular way, confounding the proud, casting down sinners, breaking up dead churches, and calling forth a host of witnesses to truth where before had been only "the dryness of the desert."

There was, in these convictions, a world-view powerful enough to open and sustain a political and social gulf between the upper and lower orders of maritime society. But while the sense of living in separate worlds unquestionably existed on both sides, those moved by evangelical Christianity were too diverse in origin, and soon too fragmented by sectarianism to achieve a consciousness of themselves as a separate "people"; although occasionally the rhetoric of political reformers owed much to righteous evangelicalism and to its sense that the common people were set apart from the self-serving and corruption of the great. Far more frequently expressed than the conception of a providence determining the destiny of a whole society, was the intense belief in the role of Providence in an individual's life.

Life on the frontier may be depicted as brutish and hard, and the frontier itself as a stage of cultural regression and of the democracy of common suffering. Yet the inner lives of those who endured its cruel testing were filled with the struggle of the spirit, and the life of the pioneer community was quick with signs, visitations, dispensations, and "times", and abounded with small miracles. Over every man was the hand of God. Each man's life was a record of his transactions with God and of God's purposes with him – for those who had the faith-given discernment to read it. The speechifying of assemblymen, the comings and goings of the governor and his lady, the echoes from Parliaments, Congresses and Conventions, even the distant thunder of the great clash of nations, were less real and far less important than the backwoods drama of eternity surrounding those touched by grace.

The dominant idea of the omnipresence of God received most eloquent expression in the sermons, writings and memoirs of the frontier preachers. "Providence is the glory of the missionary," Joshua Marsden exclaimed. "What man upon such an errand would leave his native shores and face peril and fatigue in distant climates without the hope of a reward, without the confidence of a protector, without the consolation of believing in an all-seeing God?" The biography of the Rev. James MacGregor, missionary of the General Associate Synod to the poor Scots of Pictou, is essentially a narrative of the gracious dealings of God with him and with his work. The education of young James for the church was the off-shoot of a trip taken by his father to the Lowlands; but what the mundane historian might regard as mere chance, MacGregor's biographer saw "as the means of the arrangements of Divine Providence of determining the character of his whole future life." (It was providential, too, that the money to send James to school came by his father "keeping a still, and manufacturing a little whiskey.") MacGregor never doubted that his mission to Nova Scotia was specially blessed, and that his successes were signs of God's tenderness towards him. As he said in urging young ministers to follow his example: "I shall not say that God is better in America than in Britain, but I mistake it if you shall not find him better to you." God prospered his work, and occasionally did so in the most direct way.

In July 1790, at Onslow meeting house, I had a speedy and remarkable answer of an ejaculatory prayer. Immediately after sermon, at my right hand stood up a man and intimated to the congregation that Mr. Chipman would preach there after half an hour's interval. Immediately I prayed in my heart, 'Lord, confound him, that he may not prevent the springing of the good seed sown', for I knew that Mr. Chipman, being a New Light preacher, would teach the people the grossest errors. About five minutes after he began to preach, Mr. Chipman fainted and continued senseless about ten minutes and though he recovered, yet he did not preach any that day.[5]

The Methodist literature enshrined a less partisan Providence. The memoirs of the Rev. Duncan McColl contain a number of gentle miracles, related with utter simplicity and earnestness. McColl was a former soldier who underwent a conversion experience while setting up as a merchant at St. Stephen's, and, feeling certain that "the Lord called me to the ministry," set up as preacher instead. Even before he formally joined the Methodists, he had built up a faithful congregation through the power of his preaching and the impressive example of his own life. The emotional pitch of this little society is conveyed by McColl's account of the recovery of his wife from desperate sickness in 1788. She had "lost her speech, and nearly her motion," and in a sickroom filled with the brethren, was sinking towards her end. McColl continues:

I was walking the room, when a feeling came over me which at first caused me uneasiness; I challenged that feeling, and wondered from whence it came, and instantly a thought came forcibly across my mind, saying, that Christ went into Peter's house, and saw his wife's mother lying in a fever, rebuked the fever, and she rose up. A thought followed, saying, which was it, his body or his spirit, that wrought the miracle? I said it was the spirit. Is he not here? Can he not raise up your wife as well as her? I said, yes, Lord. Go touch the clothes on her bed, and she shall recover. Nature trembled, but the spirit said go, nothing doubting. I went quietly and touched the clothes over her: she looked at me and called for a tea spoon to cleanse her mouth from phlegm. All wept when she spoke, and from that moment she recovered.[6]

Such things bred conviction; and conviction bred further miracles. The sense of election supplied by experiences such as these kept the Methodists a people apart.

Joshua Marsden's *Narrative of a mission to Nova Scotia, New Bruns-wick and the Somers Islands* is full of "precious seasons." He and a company of the faithful, journeying by sled across the Gulf ice to Tatama-gouche (where he proposed, somewhat audaciously, to level a sermon at the Acadians), were brought into extreme danger when their horses "as if possessed of a thousand devils," bolted and overturned the sleds. Although several sleds were smashed, "the providential hand of God was most visibly displayed," for not a single person was seriously hurt. On another occasion, Marsden vividly described the plight of himself and some companions lost in a blizzard while crossing the River St. John. The cold bit to the bone and night was coming on, when suddenly they stumbled upon the shoreline and entered the saving warmth of a house. "Thus divine providence (the infidel would say chance) interposed for our preservation."

Such experiences strengthened Marsden's faith, and prepared him for further tests. In 1804, the brigantine *Rover*, on which he was a passenger, was driven helplessly out to sea when in sight of Sambro Light. While the crew and his fellow passengers gave themselves up for lost he let his Bible fall open, he tells us, and "although I am no advocate for bibliomancy," was deeply struck when it opened upon Psalm 107.

I reasoned thus: "is not God the same as heretofore? has he not all power in heaven and on earth? do not the prayer of his people still come up before his throne? is not all nature under his control? even the winds and the waves obey him. Were not the things that were written aforetime written for our instruction, that we through patience and comfort of the scriptures might have hope?" From these reflections sprung an inward reliance on the divine veracity, faithfulness, and power; and I felt satisfied God would deliver us. The wind, which had blown from the north-east, lulled and came round to the south-west; and . . . we got into Halifax the next night.

Evidently Marsden was a man over whom a superintending eye was much needed. His knack for getting into tight corners (an infidel might have something to say about that) had not left him on another voyage – this time across the Bay of Fundy. He strayed into the path of the main boom as the vessel came about, and was knocked over the rail by the foresheet and launched towards the cold Fundy waters. In mid-arc he managed to lay hold of a convenient rope and swing himself back abroad, to the astonishment and edification of the crew. This remarkable piece of gymnastics Marsden chastely described as "a gracious deliverance coming through the gut of Annapolis."[7]

Kindly interventions of Providence to spare the lives of the faithful, whether upon the sick bed or when at the mercy of the elements, were by no means the only occasions upon which the ordinary course of nature was reversed. Quite as characteristic was the sudden visitation of the wrath of God upon the sinful, in so dramatic a way that no one could misunderstand the proper wages of sin. There were many such stories; but one will suffice. Marsden relates the fate of a particularly dissolute member of a dissolute and godless community. In the prime of his life and at the boisterous peak of a drinking bout amid his carousing fellows, this man was struck stone dead while fetching yet another jug of rum. This alarming providence "damped the mirth of his companions," but, as in all such sudden removals, God's purposes were fulfilled in the consequent reformation of the settlement.[8]

Another means by which God's intentions towards men were made manifest was through the dramatic conversion of some person who, perhaps because of his wealth or station, or because of his outstanding depravity, would be deemed a most unlikely recipient of grace. Such conversions were invariably given maximum publicity through the pulpit and in religious literature because of the promise of mercy they provided even to the most miserable of sinners. Perhaps the most remarkable instance of the kind was that narrated in the Rev. Charles Milton's *Narrative of the gracious dealings of God in the conversion of W. Mooney Fitzgerald and John Clark.*[9] Fitzgerald and Clark were convicted felons, each with a long criminal record of the blackest kind. Their trial, at Saint John, occurred during a revival being preached in the town by Milton, one of the Countess of Huntington's missionaries. Milton undertook not merely to bring them the consolations of religion in their last days, but actually to convert them before they went to the gallows. At the same time, he used their experience to heighten the success of the revival he was conducting.

Milton's account of his proceedings would have been as familiar to the seventeenth century as was his surname; it was the kind of thing that gladdened the hearts of the Saints and appalled the orthodox. He first visited Fitzgerald and Clark the morning after a jury had found them guilty, and discovered them loaded with chains, "like the damned in hell," in black despair. "This, together with the disagreeable stench which arose from them, so affected me, that I was speechless for some time." Once recovering his voice, he embarked upon his mission with great ardour; for it was at once apparent to him (and soon to the world to which he published the matter) that the condition of these men was an allegory of the human condition in general. All men were damned by the Fall, were loaded by the chains of their sins, and were utterly incapable by their own efforts of saving themselves. Fitzgerald and Clark were especially depraved: their violent crimes, their black hearts "hard as adamant," their boyhood religions (one "a rigid papist," the other "a churchman") would provide the most testing of challenges for the saving grace of God.

So, day by day (and often twice a day), Milton led his charges through the theology of salvation: read to them, argued with them, prayed with them, and joined them in hymns. Gradually Saint John itself and soon the country round about became aware of the wondrous work being wrought through Providence upon the souls of these hideous malefactors. As each familiar obstacle in the progress towards becoming "new men" was surmounted within the death cell, the tidings were conveyed beyond the prison walls. The penultimate event for popular edification came when Milton (standing upon a table) preached out of doors to "a great concourse of people," who divided their attention between him and the prisoners, exhibited upon a slope next the jail. By the thirteenth day of his visitation to them, Milton felt able to announce that Fitzgerald and Clark, through the blessings of Providence, "were ripening for the inheritance of the saints in light." That evening he went once more to them.

At five o'clock I was again locked up in the cell with them. This afternoon the death warrant was read to them by order of the judge; after which, by their own desire, their coffins were sent into the cell. To see them lying in their coffins was a sight which no feeling mind could behold without being affected. I endeavoured to comfort them with those cordials which the Physician of Souls appoints for a troubled soul. After the useful exercise of praying and singing I left them.

On the eve of their execution, the prisoners underwent the temporary lapse customary in the spiritual biographies of the Saints, when "Satan was let loose upon them," but their faith triumphed over this testing. Their execution was transfigured from a sordid hanging to an intense religious drama. The emotions of the condemned, of the folk of Saint John, and of Milton himself reached a state of ecstasy transcending the inexorable operations of secular law. Fitzgerald and Clark were led from the cell that had been "turned into a Bethel" for the common folk of the town. Clark said as they went, "Here I walk to glory," while Milton drew the attention of the reverent spectators to "the mystery and goodness of Divine Providence." "After they had warned others to escape the wrath of God, at half past twelve o'clock they were launched into eternity," having consummately acted their parts in a morality play directed, not by the skilful Milton but, so far as the spectators were concerned, by Providence.

It was exhibitions such as this that aroused the ridicule of the sects by the "respectable" classes and their churchmen. Though God might superintend the life of every man, it was unwarranted and excessive, according to them, to believe that one could interpret His intentions in the lives of individuals. Unbalanced attachment to such a doctrine led directly to extreme forms of behaviour, to the kind of absurd, tasteless and grotesque conduct that the eighteenth century knew as "enthusiasm." Alexander Pope epitomized this view:

> *Shall burning Etna, if a sage requires,*
> *Forget its thunders, and recall its fires;*
> *On earth and heaven new motion be imprest,*
> *O blameless Bethel! to relieve thy breast?*
> *. . . When the loose mountain trembles from on high.*
> *Shall gravitation cease if you go by?*

Indeed it will, said Joshua Marsden, "if this seem like enthusiasm I shall bear the stigma."[10]

Shall we, in compliment either to Pope, Hume, Middleton, or any other sceptical poet and philosopher, give up and deny a particular providence? – – – we might as safely give up the whole of religion altogether, and go back to the chance, atom, *and* fate *systems. What! overlook the many particular answers in prayer with which God favours his people; overlook the many promises that offer his interference in the hour of need; overlook his watchful care over his church, and say that Jehovah is only an unconcerned spectator of his children's afflictions?*

Vital religion, in the view of its adherents, must be shielded from the sceptics, the dry moralists, the rationalists and the episcopal latitudinarians; for otherwise its mystery, beauty, holiness and simplicity would be stripped away, and nothing be left but a lifeless code of moral regularity. Vital religion was too powerful and honest a thing for those who attached importance to respectability and mere forms, "so it often fares, O blessed Jesus, with thy pure gospel – 'the poor receive it, and the rich will not.' "[11]

II

While the orthodoxy clergy of the time scoffed at the absurdities into which the enthusiastic sectarians were led by the undue emphasis upon a particular providence, they themselves were prone, as the custodians of the nationally established churches, to an extensive application of the providential theology to the fortunes of nations rather than of individuals. Just as invocation of a special providence gave meaning and consolation to the hard life of the new settlements, so did fitting of the enormous convulsions of the French Revolution and ensuing wars into a divine plan of history provide a satisfying explanation for the more politically-oriented members of the national churches. From the pulpits of the Anglican and Presbyterian churches of British North America, the clergy attempted to impose system and order upon the extraordinary events overtaking the world, and to reconcile the part played in them by Britain and British North America with the larger purposes of God for man.

Quite the most detailed sermon on this subject was delivered, in 1794, by the Rev. Andrew Brown of the Church of Scotland, who was for a time minister of the Protestant Dissenting Church in Halifax. Entitled *The perils of the time, and the purposes for which they are appointed*, it is worth examining at some length because of the representative character of the argument employed, and because it provides a standard of orthodoxy against which other sermons of the time can be measured. Although he was not a political preacher, Brown said, "the present times challenge particular notice"; in such times, it was the duty of the Christian minister to extend his province to public affairs, since all history was "ordered by God for the correction and instruction of the nations." Who could doubt that the hand of God was behind the catastrophe of the French Revolution? Even for remote and insignificant Nova Scotia, the contest with France was a vital struggle, "the most important in its principle, and . . . the most divisive in its consequences of any national quarrel that ever demanded the unanimity and vigour of Britons since the foundation of the monarchy." Revolutionary France had released the energies of twenty-six million people for the purpose of extending to others, by propaganda and by conquest, its new-modelled government. But though its leaders spoke the language of liberty and fraternity, France stood for the principle of evil in history; "with a Daemon's purpose, the anarchy of France assumed an Angel's form." For the first time in modern European history, the nations opposing France risked not merely military defeat, but the actual destruction of their constitution, social order, and arrangements for religious worship, and their replacement by the novel principles of Condorcet and the strange gods of Robespierre. "Hence, in a general view, it is not the war of one country more than another, but of the whole body of mankind. It is the war of every country that has either a civil establisthment, a code of law, or a system of religious faith."[12]

Why had God made the times so perilous? What moral effects were his judgements intended to secure? Brown properly observed that "it would ill-become a short-sighted mortal to determine beforehand what may be the precise purposes which God is carrying forward"; yet, with singular precision, the divine plan of history had been revealed in Scripture and was there for all to read. According to that plan, it was no part of the intention of God that impiety and anarchy should conquer permanently, but rather that such afflictions were visited upon men to purify their hearts, and upon nations to restore their moral health. In this sense, God's judgements were monitory and corrective, and meant for trial. In another sense, they were penal, and meant to punish incorrigibility. It would be wrong, therefore, to interpret God's disasters as proof of the universality of guilt. Both the just and the unjust were involved in them, and it was impossible for man to discover what judgements were intended for trial, and what for punishment. To some extent, however, God's purposes had already been made plain.

Without doubt the terrible calamities which have lately been desolating France, and which by her instrumentality have been extended to other countries, were commissioned in part to scourge a guilty age for the gross corruptions which universally abound, and for the growing boldness of profaneness and immorality. Yet in the awful dispensations ordained by God for the cure of those disorders, the good suffer with the bad, and frequently merit and virtue themselves prove the occasions of ruin. Still the lesson is forcibly written, even in the blood of the righteous, that in the end national vices will draw down national punishments.[13]

Thus the faults of the Ancien Régime in France had been terribly corrected, while the punishments awaiting "the nameless atrocities of anarchy" were yet to come.

What mercies yet lay unrevealed behind these awful happenings? Brown was persuaded that Providence was admonishing the nations for their reception of the sceptical philosophy of the age, and of the tenets of deism. The social effects of the rationalist attack upon Christianity had been profound and destructive; so destructive, indeed, that men must surely apprehend the warning given, and return to the ancient guide of the gospel, "which moderates the passions of the rich, and supports the virtue of the poor." So this age of darkness, hopefully, would be followed by an age of light, in which public morality and private virtue would be restored. In addition, Brown believed, Providence had been demonstrating, through the exhibition in France of the "uncontrolled licentiousness of a savage democracy," how impracticable all abstract schemes of political reformation were, and had been warning the peoples of Europe to return to the acceptance of frames of government more in accord with the frailties of human nature. There could, after all, be no liberty without coercion, and as for equality – "that splended delusion of the present age, the vision of the weak, and the pretext of the wicked" – it was against the primal laws of creation, since "regularity and beauty, harmony and the universal whole, result from the existence of inequality."

Such, my brethren, in my humble opinion, are some of the purposes of correction and instruction for which the late disastrous revolutions have been ordained by God: And I am strongly inclined to believe that until these lessons be effectually inculcated, there will not be an end to the troubles of the earth. Should therefore the admonitions already given prove insufficient to subdue a licentious and intractable generation, justly may we fear that more grievous admonitions will be added to the number, until awakened by the divine judgments, and chastened by their own disorders, the residue of the nations shall listen to the voice of Providence, and learn submission to its appointments.

What was the place of the British nation in the providential scheme? God had shown "the most unmerited goodness to our nation." Despite the grossness, luxury and dissipation of British life, the nation had been exempted from the full fury of divine wrath. Nova Scotians had special cause for thankfulness, perhaps because they had some special merit.

No factions have divided our people, or distracted our government. Clubs and cabals are unknown in our settlements. No one has dared to accuse another of dissaffection. . . . No people were ever more highly favoured, or blessed with a better opportunity of becoming wise and good and happy. Let not the kindness of Providence plead with us in vain. Enjoying safety in the midst of danger, let us observe the dispensations of judgments to other lands, and apply the instructions which they deliver to our own improvement. In a particular manner let us beware of the prevailing vices which have produced the perils of the time – infidelity, licentiousness, and a spirit of innovation.[14]

Nowhere, however, did Brown claim for Britain or for Nova Scotia a select place in the workings of Providence. Unlike Henry Alline and his followers (who claimed supernatural sanction for their ministry), Brown asserted no "divine commission" for the British nation. What he did profess was sufficiently sweeping: that divine sanction upheld the political, religious and social arrangements of the countries arrayed against Revolutionary France, and that the perils of the times were warnings of the punishment that awaited those who fell away from them.

In this, he was at one with his Anglican contemporaries. Bishop Inglis had no doubt whatever that humanity had reached a great crisis in its history, in which the judgements of God were abroad.

The aspect of the present times appears to be big with events that are momentous and alarming – like a dark and gloomy cloud, overspreading the face of heaven, full charged with materials of ruin, and ready to burst with destructive violence. The prophecies contained in the book of God, which will assuredly be fulfilled in due time, authorise us to expect the most awful calamities in the latter times. The commissioned Angels stand ready with Vials of wrath. . . . *The judgments of God are actually abroad.*[15]

Inglis was quite as confident as Brown that regicide France merited the most condign punishment; and like Brown, though in much stronger language, Inglis described the war as "a contest in the cause of humanity against violence and blood, of order and government against anarchy and confusion, of right and justice against lawless rapacity, of real liberty against oppression and tyranny, of truth against falsehood, and of God against the most audacious Atheism." Long before the Revolution, France had invited calamity by embracing materialism and deism, and with them came the reign of "voluptuousness, sensuality, and lasciviousness." The Bishop's only specific charge in this formidable catalogue of sins is a little anticlimactic – the French had taken to card-playing on Sundays, and reprehensibly carried it on, "under an exterior of politeness . . . " which only served to disguise the poison.[16]

Yet how was it that the undisciplined armies of Revolutionary France had been permitted a series of smashing victories against the professional soldiery of monarchical Europe? Was it possible that God was using the French as his instrument to punish Britain and other nations for their transgressions? Inglis thought it quite possible. The history of the Jewish people showed that whenever they had fallen from the paths of righteousness, God had visited them with his sore judgements, and had used for his purpose such pagan idolators as the Egyptians and the Babylonians. "God Almighty permits wicked and tyrannical governments to prosper for a time . . . he makes them his scourge, the instruments of his justice upon others." The British people should therefore take their recent misfortunes as an express sign of God's displeasure. "Come, and let us return unto the Lord," Inglis enjoined his hearers in the words of Hosea, "for he hath torn, and he will heal us; he hath smitten, and he will bind us up." The course of events in France demonstrated that "a nation is no more exempted from madness and phrenzy than is an individual," and that the horrors of the Terror, the wanton destruction of the fabric of organized religion, and the invasion of ancient rights of rank and property were "the natural and necessary consequences of the levelling, atheistic principles which are adopted in that miserable country." The proponents of these principles in Britain, to Inglis, offended both God and the genius of English history. Had that history not come to a stop with the Reformation and the Glorious Revolution?

We enjoy the benefits resulting from those changes, we should be thankful to heaven for them; and look back with reverence to the fortitude and virtues of our ancestors who were instruments, in the hand of Providence, of conferring those signal blessings upon us. For we live in a period when the Religion of Jesus Christ is professed and taught in its native purity, as contained in holy Scripture. We live under the best of Civil Constitutions; where we enjoy as much Liberty as is consistent with a state of Civil Society. . . . In these circumstances, to think the business of changing should still go on, and never stop, must surely proceed from (a) spirit of innovation . . . or from something worse.[17]

Although Inglis' sermons sounded a more patriotic note than did those of Brown, the Bishop was nevertheless careful not to exalt British virtues. The real meaning of current history was that there was a need for a purifying repentance; without it, the British nation would be broken like a potter's vessel.

But as the war unfolded, and as the Royal Navy began to reach toward that control of the seas finally won at Trafalgar, the sermons of the Anglican clergy of British North America became progressively less humble and more patriotic in content. More and more the purposes of God were linked to the war effort of Britain; and more and more the national church preached the divinely ordered mission of Britain against the new Babylon.

Some interesting examples of this process occurred after Nelson's victory over the French fleet at Aboukir Bay in 1798. Nelson himself had announced to the Lords of the Admiralty that "Almighty God has blessed His Majesty's arms in the battle." In far-off Saint John, the Rev. Mather Byles, Loyalist and Harvard graduate, uttered a heartfelt "Amen." What man could question that Nelson's victory was the outcome of "the secret, irresistible scheme of Providence," and that it provided irrefutable proof that the British people were "the favourites of God," doing His work against "Satan" personified as France. "Satan was the first Rebel; the first who disdained subordination, despised Government, insulted his *King*, and renounced his God. He deceives and infatuates a distracted world, and under the specious names of *Liberty* and *Equality* introduces anarchy and confusion." Byles' sermon is one long, strident flight of national self-congratulation, in which the purposes of God are intermingled with the bloody triumphs of British arms.

When have our irresistible Navies, the floating bulwarks of the Kingdom, been more potent and more formidable? At what period of history have their victories been more illustrious, complete, and decisive? Some have spread the terror of the British Arms to the burning line, and others to the Northern Ocean. Some have rode [sic] with unrivalled Majesty on these American seas; others have controlled the Eastern World, and anticipated the first blush of the dawning day; and others have recalled to our memories the miracles of ancient times, by turning the waters of Egypt into Blood. In this uninterrupted series of prosperous events, is not the Almight Hand conspicuous?[18]

The sermon offered on the same subject by Bishop Jacob Mountain of Quebec presents a contrast in style. It lacks Byles' bumptiousness, and is pitched at a much higher level of Biblical scholarship. But Mountain's intellectuality and grasp of Old Testament historiography led him to a conclusion as extreme as that of Byles, and much more thoroughly worked out. His view of the role of Providence in history was that its judgements were, in effect, rewards and punishments for good and bad behaviour on the part of nations, a stand that was certainly a perversion of the orthodox theology on the question.

Nations undergo chastisement by various means, arising out of their own misconduct; by the irregular ambition, the factious intrigues, the seditious turbulence of their members, by the annihilation of order, and the subversion of government, by the destruction of their fleets and armies, . . . by the growing power of their enemies, and by the diminution of their own power, and the loss of their independence: these various calamities are the result, and under Providence, the punishment of public vices. Nations prosper by the concurrence of events which are the reverse of these: and their prosperity is the fruit, and the reward, of their public virtues.[19]

Although God had first used the French as His flail to "chastise the wickedness of an ungrateful world," the British people, having passed through the refiner's fire, were, "now, happily for ourselves, and for the world, made the instruments of chastising the arrogance and humbling the power of France." The public virtues of Great Britain were obvious to any discerning eye. Her constitution, "established on the broad basis of natural justice, matured by the experience of ages" was "calculated, beyond all others, to preserve the liberties, to engage the affections, and to promote the happiness of the people," whether in the homeland, or "extending to these Provinces, her highly favoured Children." Her arts, sciences and letters were distinguished by the accomplishments of genius. Above all, her established religion, "equally remote from Superstition and Fanaticism," was "sound in its Doctrine, correct yet liberal in its Discipline, simple yet dignified in its Ceremonies," and stood as a shining light to the world. Mountain denied that it was "National Pride" that enabled him to testify to the superiority of Britain, and conceded that her worthiness was a matter only of degree. "We may justly hope . . . that we are *comparatively* the objects of God's favour, for we have not yet denied him – and we are engaged against an enemy whom we may, without presumption, consider as much more wicked than ourselves." But such qualifications are unconvincing.

The heart of Mountain's message was not just that Providence was rewarding British virtues by success in arms, as Byles said, but that these marks of favour meant that Britain was elected by God not only to defeat the French, but also to fulfil a mission to all mankind, like Israel, her ancient counterpart.

What is it that our example, combined with our successes, might not do for the world? The noble stand which we have made, has been considered as effecting the salvation of Europe. . . . How glorious a distinction it would be for us, to be worthy of being made the instrument, in the hands of Providence, of restoring the tranquility of the world! of discrediting that spurious and pernicious Philosophy, which has deprived them at once of the benefits of Divine Instruction, and human Experience, and delivered them over to the darkness of scepticism, and the wild speculations of conjectural policy; which has dissolved all the bands of order and society; and under the specious names of Fraternity, Equality *and* Liberty, *let loose all the plagues of tyranny and oppression, of assassination and plunder, of debauchery and atheism!*[20]

Mountain was by no means alone among the colonial Anglican clergy in expressing this radical extension of the providential theology. His brother bishop, Charles Inglis, had concluded by the time of the false peace of Amiens that Britain had been set apart for a mission to all mankind. Her survival amidst the general ruin of kingdoms and empires, and specifically the miraculous thwarting of such infamous plots as the Nore mutiny and Colonel Despard's conspiracy, were "signal mercies of God to our nation," and proved that Great Britain was "the delegated instrument of Providence to arrest the progress of anarchy and impiety, and to vindicate the cause of Religion, social order, and regulated Government throughout this habitable earth."[21]

The conception that certain nations may be specially favoured by God in order to perform a providential role in history has a strong foundation in

Christian theology. It hinges upon the acceptance of the eternal validity of Old Testament historiography, the core of which was the covenant between God and Israel. God called the Jews, made them a peculiar people, and their history thus became a record of their vocation. Israel was elected of God, not to glorify itself, but because it was signally fit to stand as witness to God's intentions for man. The history of Israel was therefore a prolonged transaction between God and the Jews, in which the Jews, according to the Christian view, were ultimately condemned and dispersed. But during that epoch when Israel was favoured by God, its prophets, as Herbert Butterfield has pointed out,

> . . . *ascribed the successes of Israel not to virtue but to the favour of God; and instead of narrating the glories or demonstrating the righteousness of the nation, like our modern patriotic histories . . . denounced the infidelity of the people, denounced it not as an occasional thing but as the constant feature of the nation's conduct throughout the centuries; even proclaiming that the sins of Israel were worse, and their hearts more hardened against the light, than those of the other nations around them.*[22]

Far from emulating the prophets, Mountain, Inglis and other ministers of the state religion fell into the common error of accommodating the workings of Providence to the prevailing system of values, an error that has trapped so many of their counterparts in other ages. They dutifully ascribed British victories to God, but at the same time took them as proofs of special merit; and instead of denouncing the sins of the nation, became apostles of the divine mission of Britain to the world, a mission in which secular elements were inextricably intermingled with religious ones.[23]

No Anglican clergyman went farther in confusing the two than John Strachan, rector of York. His most noteworthy sermons on the subject were delivered in 1814, on an occasion of imperial triumph; and again at a time of crisis in the history of the provinces of Upper Canada, on December 14, 1838.[24] Though the two sermons were delivered nearly a quarter of a century apart, they are sufficiently alike to be considered together. They represent Strachan's deepest feelings and beliefs with respect to the proper place of Upper Canada in North America and in the Empire. Nothing he said in them is inconsistent with his behaviour in his years of power and influence, and the position he took in them explains a good deal about that behaviour.

In his speech in 1814, Strachan started from the historically sound position that the whole period from the decade of the 1770's onward should be regarded as a unity: "posterity will call this the age of revolution." It was a time unique in human history. Whereas it had taken humanity two thousand years to discern God's intentions when he gave the victory to the Greeks at Marathon, in the present age "never have so many unquestionable proofs of a superintending Providence appeared in so short a period."

The meaning of recent history was to be sought through an informed application of the lessons of the Old Testament.

The history of the Jews, tho' merely a fragment of that of the world, unfolds most distinctly the moral government of God and demonstrates that as he dealt with that people so does he deal with all nations. By this we are taught to contemplate profane as well as sacred history in a religious point of view, and though the finger of God may not always be distinctly seen, we may rest assured of his continual presence and superintendence. The Jewish history is therefore a lamp by which we can read passing events.[25]

What the lamp of Jewish history disclosed to Strachan was nothing less than that the British were the second Chosen People of God. "What the Israelites of old were to the surrounding nations, so the British appear to be the present inhabitants of the world." Just as God had entrusted his truth to the Jews, so had He entrusted it to another nation in the present day. "Here, My Brethren, I allude to the British nation, but not in the spirit of boasting or of ostentation." What proofs existed for this extraordinary assertion? Britain's miraculous triumph over the French Antichrist, and the qualities which, under God, had made it possible:

Now, although Great Britain has many sins to deplore; yet, on a comparison with other nations, it will be found that she possesses more true liberty, more solid morality, and more true religion, than they. Where is there a nation equal to the British in the number and extent of its charitable institutions? or possessing such a spirit of independence, such intrepid virtue; such a rational piety; these are the distinctions which have enabled her to continue successful against the world in arms![26]

The notion that the British are God's chosen people has never been very far beneath the surface of English patriotism, though seldom in comparatively recent times has it been quite so solemnly proclaimed as by Strachan. It is not sufficient to explain Strachan's relentless pushing of the providential theology to its ultimate conclusion by the fact that he was an ideologue, while his clerical colleagues on the whole were not. There is about his treatment of the subject a tone redolent of a more vigorous Protestantism, deriving perhaps from the unorthodoxies of his Scottish upbringing, and from a version of the national tradition more vital, positive and assertive than that of his English contemporaries.[27]

As William Haller recently has pointed out, the idea of England as the Elect Nation was a significant part of the nationalism of Elizabeth's time.[28] It was propagated chiefly through the national church and by popular religious writers like John Foxe. In the margin of his patriotic diatribe against the French, Bishop Aylmer condensed the notion into three words: "God is English," while Archbishop Parker had no difficulty in justifying persecution of nonconformists, since "where Almighty God is so much English as he is," Englishmen had a duty to protect His true religion from impious assault. The central theme of Foxe's martyrology was the election of the English nation as revealed in history; and Milton, in his well-known references to "God's Englishmen" and to England's mission "to give out reformation to the world," was but the most distinguished of his generation to draw heavily and with conviction upon Foxe's historiography.

John Strachan, temperamentally and perhaps through his schooling, was much closer to this tradition than were his brothers in the church. In the overblown prose of the 1838 sermon there are many echoes of the language of Foxe and of the *Areopagitica*, as in the following passage:

At the Reformation, the Holy Spirit seemed to be with our Fathers, & they separated no farther from Romanism than Romanism separated from Christian truth, & the Apostolic Church which they purified and renewed has ever stood forth as the bulwark of the Protestant or true Faith. Three centuries have elapsed since England was considered the seat of true Christianity. She arose from the slumber of ages and shook off the mass of heavy corruptions which had accumulated in darkness, and stood forth dauntlessly in her purity, the witness of God amidst a world lying in wickedness. She has stood since that period with the Bible in her hands, abiding firmly by the doctrines it reveals.

Although Strachan's sermons had as a chief theme the doctrine that the British were "God's peculiar people," they differ greatly in tone. It was not just that the first came at a time of victory, and the second during one of the most critical and disheartening periods of Canadian history. When Strachan preached his victory sermon, he was a young man who had just planted his feet firmly upon the lowest rungs of the ladder of colonial preferment, and could see opening ahead of him opportunities for influence and power not normally given to the poor son of a Scottish quarryman. The Rebellion sermon, on the other hand, was an embittered valedictory, a defiant vindication of the principles for which Strachan had stood during his years of political power, and which had been in retreat, both in England and in Upper Canada, for some years prior to 1837.

Thus the 1814 sermon is a political manifesto couched in the trappings of providentialism. In it Strachan laid down for his York congregation the lessons of the great war now ending. All flowed from the central fact that Great Britain, "the shield of afflicted humanity, the successful hope of a suffering world," had been God's chosen instrument in the punishment of atheistical France, and was now given the task of ordering a world restored to peace. Since Strachan held that the particular system of government, religion and society obtaining in Britain was an approximation of the providential order blessed by God, it naturally followed that the restored monarchs of Europe must re-shape their realms in accordance with the British model. This meant that the lot of the lower classes of Europe must be raised above that of 1789. "Wise reforms" must be introduced to ameliorate their condition; criminal codes must be revised so that "justice may be separated from ferocity, and punishment from revenge"; exclusive distinctions of rank must be broken down; and economic distress relieved by the abolition of oppressive systems of taxation. Even in England, a reformation of manners on the part of the upper orders of society was required, in order to prevent a recurrence of democratic unrest. "Public decorum, a reverence for religion, and attention to the feelings of inferiors, ought never to be separated from rank and station."

In calling for a more enlightened and humane leadership from the ruling classes of Britain and Europe, Strachan by no means intended to encourage a reforming spirit among the people. The core of his message is to be found in his reflections on what Providence wished to teach the masses. They must have learned that the "self-named Patriots" and abstract constitution-spinners who had led the world such a dance had been unmasked for the deceivers they were. The wars had taught that no government framed by fallible man was, or could be perfect. It was to be hoped that the peoples had learned to suspect the artifices of factious demagogues who, from demonic ambition, sought to turn them against their natural rulers. It was inescapably revealed that "the two great experiments in America and France to constitute governments productive of virtues and happiness only . . . have completely failed. Only by "peaceable and gradual steps, and not by revolutions" can "the most solid improvements in the Science of governments be obtained." The American Revolution had wrought a cruel delusion in the mind of the peoples of Europe; they had lost themselves in "golden dreams of transatlantic felicity." God's judgements had shattered such visions:

The present age has demonstrated that no great and decided amelioration of the lower classes of society can be reasonably expected: much improved they certainly may be, but that foolish perfectability with which they have been deluded can never be realized. . . . In times of tranquility the people may be better instructed, the laws may be made more equal and just, and many new avenues of enjoyment may be opened; but labour is the lot of man, and no system of policy can render it unnecessary, or relieve the greater portion of mankind from suffering many privations.

These lessons were not for Europeans alone, but for those Canadians who had been foolish enough to be attracted by American republicanism. For Strachan, there was really no difference at bottom between the United States and revolutionary France; the two societies were founded upon the same secular and egalitarian assumptions. In 1812, this fundamental identity was disclosed when the United States had "deserted the cause of humanity" and become the abettor of Napoleon. "No state but this became the ally of France by choice." The American people, "traitors to the peace and happiness of mankind," had made themselves "the Satellites of the Tyrant," yet had the arrogance to address Canadians as slaves, and to profess engagement in a war of liberation. Divine retribution would be visited upon the United States just as surely as it had been upon France.

In the blessed struggle against the powers of darkness, the Upper Canadians had taken a distinguished part. Their survival alone was miraculous. Like the Israelites of old, they had kept the faith against formidable odds, they had vindicated the memory of the Loyalists. They would emerge from the struggle a better and purer people, having been purged of those "traitors and false friends whom a short-sighted and mistaken policy had introduced among us." Among God's chosen people, therefore, the Upper Canadians had won a special place; "we have gained a name among our fellow-subjects which will be forever precious." Strachan appears to have conceived the future role of Upper Canada in the New World as a kind of leaven, or, to borrow a phrase from Prynne, though "but a Remnant, a seede, a little flocke," the Upper Canadians would stand as witness in North America to the truth of God in church and state. "Now," he proclaimed, "the dawn of the happiest times is rising upon us."[29]

It is at this point that the Anglican interpretation of the time of troubles ceases to be war-inspired propaganda and becomes the doctrinal basis for post-war conservative policy. As it happened, John Strachan, the most extreme exponent of the idea of the Elect Nation among the colonial clergy, was also in the best position after the war to translate the implications of that idea into the shaping of the future of a colony. Upper Canada was a remote and exposed colony, filled with inner tensions and deeply apprehensive of the United States; and it was the most receptive environment in British North America to extreme political solutions. As teacher to a whole generation of political leaders, as churchman, polemicist and political in-fighter, and as a member of the executive government, John Strachan, more than any other man was responsible for the framing of Tory policy in church and state, and for the rationale by which it was defended. Too frequently Strachan's career has been explained in terms of his great vanity and ambition, and his rhetoric has been dismissed as a kind of elaborate cover for self-seeking. But beneath that rhetoric there lay utter conviction. The ruthlessness and intolerance of his political style derived from the absolute belief that the prescriptions he defended in church, state and society were part of the providential order, that Upper Canada had a special mission to preserve them in North America, and that any opposition to them was a sign of the grossest and most blasphemous infidelity, and of a dangerous sympathy for the condemned revolutionary society of the United States.

By the time of the Rebellion of 1837, Strachan had all but failed in his attempt to build an ordered Christian society in Upper Canada. He himself had lost his position as executive councillor, had been passed over for advancement in the Church, and had been forsaken in his defence of the privileges of the Church by many of his pupils and protégés. The people of Upper Canada, or many of them, had turned to such false prophets as Mackenzie, the Bidwells and Peter Perry. In Great Britain the very Ark of the Covenant had been violated. Dissenters and Catholics had been emancipated; the Reform Bill had destroyed the delicate balance of the constitution; a Whig government had betrayed the faith by withdrawing support from the great mission societies of the Church. When Keble, Newman and Pusey denounced national apostasy, Strachan was strongly attracted; but as prominent members of the Oxford movement drifted towards what Strachan regarded as an outmoded superstition, he was filled with dismay. His cup of bitterness was filled to overflowing by the whole course of British colonial policy in the 1830's, which to Strachan seemed nothing but a series of betrayals of the appointed purposes of the Empire. Strachan's commitment to his personal vision for Upper Canada approached fanaticism, for only a fanatic could believe that the Rebellions of 1837-38 were God's punishment upon a sinful generation.

In the Rebellion Sermon, Strachan identified himself with Hosea, the prophet from whom he took his text. The paraphrase of Jewish history with which the sermon began was a transparent recapitulation of recent British and Upper Canadian history; when he spoke of Hosea reproaching "with stern intrepidity" the deplorable profligacy and licentiousness of the Jews, it was his own role and other targets that he had in mind. Much of the sermon was an indictment of the British government. Strachan deplored the spectacle of a nation "raised up for mighty purposes" proving false to its destiny, and, like Israel, quitting the service of Jehovah. "It is because the Protestant principle has been in less vigorous operation, and superstition and infidelity have raised their heads in high places." True, some signs of the great calling remained. The moral triumph of the emancipation of the slaves was a benefaction that stood "without a parallel in the history of the world." Perhaps it was not yet too late; perhaps "the illustrious part which Great Britain and Ireland have been so long appointed to take in the great theatre of this world is not yet accomplished; but that this great Empire is reserved to a suffering world to be the refuge of the afflicted and distressed, the asylum of liberty, the guardian of Morality, the bulwark of Christianity, and the impregnable barrier against that dreadful torrent of infidelity which so many of the nations are now drinking." Perhaps God's wonderful deliverances might still be recalled, and the warning judgement delivered upon the Canadas "may be confined to this extremity of the Empire and our Government may take warning and repent . . . as the Israelites sometimes did when punishment only reached their borders."

The original sin of the British government was in permitting a powerful nation to grow up in North America without providing it with an established church. The consequent "liberalism, fraud and infidelity" had brought the judgement of the American Revolution. But recent colonial policy demonstrated that the meaning of this providential warning had not been assimilated; Britain's remaining colonies had not been adequately protected from contamination, and therefore "the mass of corruption engendered in the neighbouring States, once our Sister Colonies . . . has rapidly increased and extended to these Provinces its venomous poison."

Great Britain was not alone in its guilt. Strachan had bitter words for those Anglicans who had withdrawn their support from his projects for education and for the Church. Even more bitterly he denounced provincial society at large for its unnatural preoccupation with party politics. When the Jews split into parties, they became soft and ennervated, at a time when "union and National energy were essential to render them a match for their more powerful Neighbours." With traitors within, and a malevolent enemy without, what need had Upper Canada of factions in order to achieve her simple destiny? "And," Strachan burst out, perhaps with his eye upon those regrettable parishioners, the Baldwins, "here suffer me to remark that there is not a single grievance or matter of contention in this Province, lately so tranquil, prosperous & happy, which three well-informed honest men might not, in a few days, settle to the satisfaction of all reasonable minds."

What might not have been accomplished had Britons and Canadians not sinned against the light?

What glorious things might have been effected in North America. The brightest Imagination is unable to picture the scenes of peace and happiness which it would have exhibited, and these Provinces, instead of being exposed to traitorous conspiracies within and without would have presented a Christian society built up in righteousness.

The Rebellion Sermon, for all its conventional summons to repentance and purification, was a cry of despair by a man who has all but given up hope of seeing "a Christian society built up in righteousness" come into being in Upper Canada. The idea of Upper Canada as a beacon or witness of religious and secular truth in North America, first broached by Simcoe and taken up so enthusiastically by Strachan, was an impossible one, at least in the terms in which Strachan conceived it. But the fact is that Strachan held this ideal; and that for many years it gave coherence to conservative policies, and had a most decided effect upon early Canadian development. It helps too to explain why the forms of conservatism which grew up in old Ontario appear so much more extreme than those found elsewhere in British North America. And it is surely paradoxical that John Strachan, the harsh critic of the fanaticism and enthusiasm of the sects, should at heart have been a zealot far more extreme than they. Were the sectarians, in their heartfelt trust in a particular providence, any more absurd than the clergy of the Church of England, and the higher enthusiasm of the providential mission of the Elect Nation?

Unlike Massachusetts Bay and nineteenth century French Canada, the societies of English-speaking British North America did not discover in the providential theology the materials for a myth that would unite them as a people apart, and supply them with a sense of inner cohesion and direction. Among the frontier folk of the Maritimes, the effect of the idea of a special Providence was to exalt the humble as against the worldly, and ultimately, when given a secular twist, to provide a basis for political dissent. The Anglican myth of British election was to have a long life, whether in the Upper Canadian expansionism of a Charles Mair, the Anglo-Saxon racism so prevalent among those Canadians caught by the vision of Empire at the century's end, or in the recent pathetic by-way of British Israelitism. But in the hands of Strachan and his fellows, the providential sense of mission was too narrowly conceived, too deeply rooted in the defence of a dying order to catch the imagination of the people, and to provide the basis for an emergent Canadian nationalism.

Notes: God's Peculiar Peoples

1. William Stoughton, "New England's true interest"; Thomas Shepherd, "A defence of the answer made unto the nine questions or positions sent from New England against the reply thereto by Mr. John Ball"; in Perry Miller (ed.), *The American Puritans: their prose and poetry"*, New York, 1956, 26-7, 116.
2. John A. Mackay, *Heritage and Destiny*, New York, 1943, 105.
3. John Davis, *Life and times of the Rev. Harris Harding*, Charlottetown, 1866, appendix.
4. Henry Alline, *Two mites cast into the offering of God for the benefit of mankind*, Dover, N.H., 1804, 127, 133, 134.
5. Joshua Marsden, *The narrative of a mission to Nova Scotia, New Brunswick, and the Somers Islands*, Plymouth, 1816, 72; George Patterson, *A memoir of Dr. James McGregor*, Edinburgh, 1859, Ch. 1, passim; James McGregor, *Letter . . . to the General Associate Synod*, Paisley, 1793, 12; Patterson, *Memoir*, 90.
6. Duncan McColl, "Memoir of the Rev. Duncan McColl," *Methodist Magazine*, 1841, 301.
7. Marsden, *Narrative*, 40, 62-3, 70, 95.
8. *Ibid.*, 39. The sectarians' belief in the immediate punishment of transgressors came under frequent attack from churchmen. Bishop Charles Inglis thought it was the result of a gross misreading of Scripture. During the Jewish theocracy, such situations occurred, but under the Christian dispensation, "when the whole will of God, and the plan of redemption, are explicitly revealed," punishment was reserved to a future state. See Charles Inglis, *A charge delivered to the Clergy of Nova Scotia at the triennial visitation holden in the Town of Halifax in the month of June, 1791*, Halifax, 1792, 33.
9. The narrative was published in London in 1790.
10. Marsden, *Narrative,* 63. According to Bishop Inglis, "enthusiasm, when applied to religion, signifies a belief in private revelations, calls, or some commission from the Deity. . . . In general, this proceeds from a heated or disordered imagination; the suggestions of which are mistaken for luminous communications from God." *Charge to the clergy*, 1791, 23. As will be seen, Anglicans were not immune to luminous communications.
11. Marsden, *Narrative*, 71, 93.
12. Andrew Brown, *The perils of the time, and the purposes for which they are appointed*, Halifax, 1795, 9, 11-13, 17.
13. *Ibid.*, 21.
14. *Ibid.*, 31-5, 36, 39.
15. Charles Inglis, *A sermon preached in the parish church of St. Paul at Halifax on Friday, April 25, 1794, being the day appointed by proclamation for a general fast and humiliation in His Majesty's Province of Nova Scotia*, Halifax, 1794, 30-1.
16. *Ibid.*, 23, 27-8.
17. *Ibid.*, 14, 24-5; Charles Inglis, *Steadfastness in religion and loyalty recommended*, London, 1793, 18.
18. Mather Byles, *The victory ascribed to God: a sermon delivered December 2d, 1798, on the late signal successes granted to His Majesty's arms*, Saint John, 1798, 5, 9, 12, 15.
19. Jacob Mountain, *Sermon preached at Quebec, January 10, 1799 . . . for general thanksgiving*, Quebec, 1799, 7-8.
20. *Ibid.*, 15-17, 26-30.
21. Charles Inglis, *A charge delivered to the Clergy of the Diocese of Nova Scotia . . . in 1803*, Halifax, 1804, 8, 22-3. By this time Inglis' mind had taken an apocalyptic turn. Since it was probable that the Seven Last Judgements had begun,

it was now necessary to establish the equivalences among the Little Horn of Daniel, the Whore of Babylon, the Roman Catholic Church, and Napoleon the Antichrist. *Ibid.*, 44-7.

22. Herbert Butterfield, *Christianity and History*, London, 1957, 73.

23. A sense of national mission arising from the experiences of the war was not confined to the ministers of the Anglican Church. Thomas McCulloch, who had joined McGregor at Pictou in 1803, was proud of Britain's role as "the bulwark of liberty and the refuge of oppressed nations." But to his mind, the time of troubles through which the world was passing had been marked out by Providence as the prelude to a great revival of religion. In this coming resurgence, Britain's glory was to be religious, not political. "Our native country is invested with honours more transcendant and glorious: it has 'a witness in heaven' and 'a record on high'. The churches of Britain are the glory of Christ, and, by divine grace, they have become the centre of a zeal for religion which is spreading like a torrent." Britain had been elected to carry the gospel "to the whole family of man." The providential theology thus provides a link between the imperial and missionary urges, Anglicans emphasizing the one, the dissenter McCulloch the other. See Thomas McCulloch, *The prosperity of the church in troublous times,* Halifax, 1814, 9-10, 23.

24. John Strachan, *A sermon preached at York, Upper Canada, on the third of June, being the day appointed for a general thanksgiving,* Montreal, 1814; *Ontario Archives, Strachan Papers,* MS sermon on the text "And thy judgements are as the light that goeth forth," Hosea 6:5. The MS sermon has the notation in Strachan's hand: "Toronto, 14 Decr. 1837. A Fast day by public proclamation on account of the rebellion & attacks from the U. States." Strachan was a year out in his reckoning. No attacks from the United States had occurred by December 14, 1837, nor had secret societies like the Sons of Liberty or the Patriot Hunters, to which Strachan refers in the body of the sermon, yet been organized. On Dec. 8, 1838, *The Church* published Lt. Gov. Arthur's proclamation fixing Friday, Dec. 14, 1838, as a day of public fasting and humiliation. Attacks from the United States took place very shortly before that date, on Nov. 11 at Prescott and on Dec. 4 at Windsor and Sandwich. Most of the superscriptions on Strachan's MS sermons appear to have been made by him in the 1850's.

25. *Sermon of 1838,* 4; *Sermon preached at York,* 5; *Sermon of 1838,* 2.

26. *Ibid.,* 7, 8; *Sermon preached at York,* 6.

27. The tradition has produced many forms of theological exotica in Scotland. The Gifford Lecturer at the University of Glasgow in 1897 made a gallant attempt to combine the notion of "elect race" with the new biology of Darwin, equating "fittest" with election. Why, he wondered, had "Providence . . . hitherto shown a preference for small nations as its instruments: Israel, Greece . . . the inhabitants of the British Isles?" Alexander Balmain Bruce, *The Providential Order of the World,* New York, 1897, 262.

28. William Haller, *Foxe's Book of Martyrs and the Elect Nation,* London, 1963.

29. "Times" is the scriptural term for changes of providence, as in *Acts* 1:7: "It is not for you to know the times and the seasons which the Father has put in his own power," a passage Strachan and his brethren seem to have overlooked.

The Personal and Living Bond 1839-1849

Jacques Monet, S. J., Loyola College

"Je me souviens." So, from proud armorial bearings, boast all French Canadians. And for many of them the best memories are those surrounded by the golden circle of the Crown. It is not always so; but so it is for the decade of the 1840's. Indeed, during those years, the most momentous perhaps in the long history of French Canada, four men came out "in the image and transcript" of their monarch to link together the Canadiens and the British Crown. And during those same years, the Canadien politicians, under the Crown and with the assistance of its representative, saved their national identity, and committed their future to what Louis-Hippolyte LaFontaine called "les institutions britanniques auxquelles nous sommes fortement attachés."

At the end of the 1830's, French Canada was in ferment. Under British domination for some seventy-five years, the Canadiens had succeeded in surviving, but not in developing by themselves a full, normal, national life. They had kept the essentials: their French language, their time-honoured and peculiar jurisprudence, and their particular system of education. But they needed new life. The economy lagged, the problems of education were such that in 1836 the schools closed, and the old civil code no longer applied to modern circumstances. Above all, the upward thrust of the growing professional middle class created a serious social situation of which the rebellions of 1837 and 1838 were only one expression. Clearly, if the struggle for national survival were to hold any meaning for the future, French-Canadian nationalists needed new solutions.

They were divided, however. Some thought *la survivance* could be assured only by political isolation in a territory over which French-Canadians would be undisputed masters. These were led by John Neilson and Denis-Benjamin Viger. The first was the famed editor of the *Quebec Gazette* and a veteran of every political campaign in Lower Canada since 1797; and the second was one of the really remarkable men of his generation, a gentleman accomplished in science, poetry, and above all in the law and the Constitution. Others, broader-minded and more practical, held to a doctrine which Louis-Hippolyte LaFontaine would translate into politics. They held that it was the flexibility of the British constitutional system that could best assure not only the permanence of their acquired national rights, but also (by means of responsible government) the certain hope of a broadening future for their language, their institutions and their nationality.

To achieve responsible government, however, LaFontaine needed to accomplish two things. He had to achieve the unified assent of his people to British parliamentary democracy; and, secondly, to persuade his people to unite with the Reformers of Upper Canada. Neither was easy. In the years immediately following the rebellion, French Canada's strongest sympathies were with the leaders of the Viger-Neilson group; and the terms of the Union with Upper Canada were especially designed to crush French Canada's national culture. Indeed, the bill passed by the British Parliament in 1840 outlawed any official use of the French language, and provided for a remodelling along British lines of both French Canada's particular legal system, and its traditional pattern of education. Still, LaFontaine espoused the Union, and campaigned for responsible government. And after a decade, he became in 1848 the first Canadian Prime Minister in the modern sense.

LaFontaine's triumph was greatly determined by the four Governors General who succeeded each other throughout the decade: Charles Poulett Thomson, Lord Sydenham; Sir Charles Bagot; Sir Charles Metcalfe, Lord Metcalfe; and the Earl of Elgin. They were varied in background and in the measure of their success; but, taken together, they played no small part in the reconciliation of French Canadians to the British connection: and by the end of the decade, they achieved to a remarkable degree the "victorious, happy, and glorious" demanded for them in the royal anthem.

*   *   *

In mid-afternoon on October 19, 1839, "toute la garnison était sur pied" in Quebec as Sir John Colborne, erect on his black charger and in the full gold and scarlet of a Major-General, "entouré d'un nombreux état-major," rode out of the old Chateau Saint-Louis to welcome his successor, Charles Poulett Thomson. The *Pique* carrying the new Governor General had rounded the historic Island of Orleans two days earlier, and docked in the ancient harbour; but Poulett Thomson had decided to remain aboard until Colborne arrived from Montreal. Then, short, slender, but supremely self-confident, he stepped briskly off the gangplank, and took the salute from his predecessor. After this simple ceremony, he drove to the castle to take his oath of office and issue a Proclamation announcing his assumption of power.

News of Thomson's appointment had reached Canada a month earlier; and with it, speculation had begun about his antecedents in both trade and reform. Though the latter might be a reassuring sign, the Canadiens wondered about the first. Was Thomson linked to the Quebec merchants' long-time rivals, the timber interests trading with the Baltic? And even if he did overcome this personal involvement, would his business interests not incline him, in any event, to favour the local oligarchy and its French-baiting policies? "Il se propose de se guider," the editor of the Quebec newspaper *Le Canadien* mused uneasily on October 18th, "sur l'opinion des hommes marquants de la race britannique dans les deux Canadas." He was also the first governor of the Canadas chosen from outside the aristocracy – a not-too-flattering gesture to a people so sensitive to appearances. He was a bourgeois, with such a funny name at that. Napoléon Aubin, the editor of *Le Fantasque,* a witty Quebec newspaper, underlined the barnyard aspect on September 17:

Notre nouveau gouverneur-général, le très honorable POULET Thomson est maintenant attendu journellement à Québec. Je fais matin et soir des voeux pour que ce poulet-là fasse de meilleur ouvrage que les coqs-d'inde qui l'ont précedé. A en croire ces poules mouillés de journaux tories ce n'est toujours pas un aigle. Le bon Dieu bénisse tous ces oiseaux-là.

Funny or not, merchant or not, the man, the Canadiens decided, should be given a chance. An address of welcome was prepared by the Quebec merchants, and in Montreal, a new newspaper called *L'Aurore des Canadas* declared its intention to be firm but fair.

Ne nous déshonorons pas par la flatterie, par des bassesses; mais présentons-nous à lui comme des gens qui ont foi dans la bonté de leur cause, comme des amis d'un gouvernement juste et honnête. Réclamons pour tous les citoyens des droits égaux. . . . Comme nous ne voudrions pas être jugés par Mr. Thompson [sic] sans être entendus, il ne faut pas, non plus, le juger sans l'entendre.[1]

"Le Soleil Levant" – so *L'Aurore* called him – arrived in Montreal on October 23, and won opinions which could have been much worse. Nature had conspired against him: as he sailed from Quebec aboard the steamboat *Canada,* an electric storm broke out; then, a bolt of lightning struck the main mast of the *Pique* which he had just left; then, on his way up the Saint Lawrence, one of his prize horses jumped overboard and drowned; finally, as he neared Montreal, another storm so tossed the steamboat that Thomson became too seasick to take part in the planned official reception. But when he held his first levée at the Chateau de Ramezay on October 26, he received more callers than any of his predecessors. He also made a good impression. As *L'Ami du Peuple* noted on October 30:

Son Excellence paraissait souffrante, ce qui donnait à sa figure une teinte d'austérité. . . . Ses traits annoncent l'homme qui a l'habitude des affaires et qui n'est pas étranger à l'impassibilité qui doit distinguer les personnages revêtus de hautes fonctions. Il est âgé de 37 à 38 ans, mais la maturité de son esprit perce dans toute sa contenance. . . . L'entourage de Son Excellence avait quelque chose de brillant et le riche costume d'apparat que le Gouverneur portait était fait pour en imposer.

Within weeks, however, the Canadiens' worst fears were confirmed. As 1839 turned into 1840, they saw Thomson, like so many previous governors, become more and more the prisoner of the anti-French interests in the Province. They had received happy assurances that he would base his policy on the principle of "equal justice," but they gradually came to understand how wide a distinction he could draw between thought, word, and deed. By August 3, 1840, *Le Canadien* could claim

. . . dans le Bas-Canada, depuis l'administration Dalhousie, il n'y en a pas eu d'aussi impopulaire que celle du gouverneur-général actuel.

The Canadiens reacted to the governor in an unusual way. In earlier decades they had answered governors Dalhousie and Aylmer by withholding supplies; to Gosford, Durham, and Colborne they had presented apathy and rebellion; but at Poulett Thomson, "que nous maudissons tous bien sincèrement,"[2] they simply laughed.

"Notre POULET" began to figure prominently in the press. Indeed, for the next two years, *Le Fantasque* hardly ever referred to the Governor General otherwise than as POULET. Aubin claimed, for example, on April 13, 1840, that it was no wonder that so many pigeons had been sighted this year over Lower Canada, for

Messieurs les pigeons, tout fier de savoir que les Canadas étaient gouvernés par un volatile, ont cru devoir venir déposer leurs hommages aux pieds ou plutôt aux pattes de notre POULET.

Later, on May 4, playing upon *voler*, to fly, and *voler*, to steal, Aubin reflected it was perfectly normal for the Governor to have advocated the Union.

Le bill d'Union dressé d'après les plans de notre gouverneur-général veut que le Bas-Canada paie les dettes du Haut. Les gens qui ne sont point versés dans les mystifications politiques appellent cela un vol. Moi, je trouve absolument rien là d'étonnant. Ne voit-on pas tous les jours des poulets essayer de voler.

Again, playing upon *cornichon*, a pickle, and *cornichon*, a greenhorn, he went on in the same issue: "Tous ceux qui ont vu Mr. Thompson [sic]

s'accordent à dire que c'est un POULET tout a fait appétissant. Je le crois bien, il est tout entouré de cornichons." Aubin kept this up for eighteen months, finding even more enjoyment still in the parsimonious, vain, and unscrupulous aspects of Thomson's personality.

The Governor – "cet avare" – counted his pennies like every merchant, Aubin averred on July 27, and how he prided himself on his domestic economy! (In fact Thomson lived very simply.) How handy, that he should only have to walk across Bonsecours Market Square to reach Government House: "Il est allé faire le marché lui-même et il aurait sans doute continué s'il n'avait su qu'on se moquait publiquement de lui." At home, he spent much of his time in the kitchen preparing the menu:

Il va gouter les sauces de ses cuisiniers; collationne le livre de son maître d'Hôtel; fait servir à ses aides-de-camp des viandes froides afin qu'ils en mangent moins. . . . Il querellait il y a quelque temps son cuisinier de ce qu'il n'avait su faire que trois crèmes avec un bouteille de marasquin, disant que lui-même aurait pu en faire une douzaine.

Aubin concluded on the advantages of being governed by a good house-wife. Parsimonious, Thomson was conceited as well.

Thomson enjoyed cheering crowds. And Aubin, in one of of his cleverest satires on July 6, pictured "le POULET" explaining at great pains and with accents of Spanish, Italian, Arabic, and very poor French, to the confused Montreal Chief of Police that it was his duty to gather and pay a noise-making crew for the Governor's every appearance, just as London police-men did to celebrate the outings of the Queen herself. To the objection about high costs, "le POULET" answered:

You fanatic ignorant canadian, *vous pas comprendre le spéculation. Les pauvres gens qui vont se prosterner devant le reine et les grandes person-nages recoivent du police, comme j'ai dit à vous, trois ou quatre shillings. Avec ça ils vont se saoûler au taverne, et le Police les prend le soir et fait payer à eux cinq shillings d'amende pour les corriger de l'ivrognerie, you see. voye-voys?*

In this passage Aubin also satirised Thomson's superb confidence in the art of bribing. Indeed, he says, the Governor liked to play grand master in the art of negotiation, break thousands of promises, and especially bribe all opponents of his policies. *Le Canadien* also referred to this characteristic on September 6, putting in Thomson's mouth the light verses:

> *Du haut de mon trône d'ivoire*
> *Je vois la situation*
> *Et mon ministère illusoire*
> *Peut marcher sans l'opinion*
>
> *Membres charmants, venez à moi*
> *Je suis une caisse sonore*
> *Qui s'ouvre aussitôt qu'on l'adore;*

Je suis le million qui luit;
Je suis la commission même.

Je suis un vieux commis de banque
Je connais la valeur de l'or;
Je serai pour celui qui manque
De principes, un vrai trésor.

But even with his alleged diplomacy, Thomson had deceived no one, Aubin declared. One day he pictured *Son Excellence*'s descent into the underworld. There as vain as ever when he was alive, he confidently joined Machiavelli, Talleyrand, and Fouché, only to be greeted with the sting: "Pauvre fou! tu pensais être aussi rusé que nous, mais tu n'étais que méchant."

Bourgeois, conceited, and crafty, the Governor was apparently also a ladies' man – or so the French Canadians thought him. *Le Fantasque* reported on August 3, that a frequent topic of conversation in the streets of Quebec during the summer of 1840 was "le célibat de M. POULET Thomson." And on hearing of a Palace revolution in Turkey, Aubin, on July 27, offered the exiled Prime Minister a new job as "premier eunuque du sérail de Monsieur POULET Thomson." The same type of rumour also circulated in Kingston after the vice-regal transfer there in May 1841. Witness the *Fantasque*'s very unequivocal note on the new capital city on September 23, 1841:

. . . la cage de milord POULET est situé au milieu d'un petit bois . . . là aussi est son sérail, dont l'une des demoiselles d'honneur, dit la chronique scandaleuse de Kingston, est passée aux Etats-Unis pour de grosses affaires.

In April 1841, the Governor General, who had been created Baron Sydenham in September 1840, almost died of an attack of gout. Aubin took advantage of the occasion to publish a "Testament de Charles POULET Thomson, mieux connu sous le sobriquet de Baron de Sydenham et de Toronto." In it he is at his mocking best. "Le POULET" bequeathed nothing to the poor, for stolen goods can only do them harm; and to his future biographer he gives

. . . ma bibliothèque consistant en un dictionnaire de commerce; un traité du calcul des intérêts. Je lui recommande de me flatter beaucoup dans sa description de ma vie publique parce que même avec cette précaution on la trouvera encore assez hideuse.

As to Colonel Gugy (a *vendu* politician and a gallant who served as another object of Aubin's satire and of French-Canadian dislike) he donates his horses and his . . . ladies of honour. He hesitates however to recommend a successor, for

On trouvera difficilement un homme possédant toutes les qualités requises pour continuer mon oeuvre. . . . Je recommande seulement à mes successeurs de se procurer de l'argent, beaucoup d'argent: l'argent fait la

*force! Je les prie bien d'abolir autant que possible la langue française,
d'attaquer tout de bon la religion Catholique. . . . de ne pas négliger l'emploi
de la police. . . . Ce corps nous procure un excellent canal pour l'écoulement
de l'argent surabondant du coffre publique.*

A few weeks later, on May 22, 1841, *Le Canadien*, less subtle, was no
less emphatic in summing up its own feelings:

Le Whig *de Kingston dit qu'on se propose d'illuminer en cette ville
lorsque le Gouverneur-Général y arrivera. On illuminerait bien ailleurs s'il
voulait bien partir du pays. Nous ne voyons pas quels ménagements a droit
d'attendre de notre part le chef de l'administration la plus inique et la plus
tyrannique qu'ait jamais eu le Bas-Canada. Chacun de ses actes est une
injustice et une spoliation contre un peuple sans défense.*

With feelings such as these reflected in the press, no wonder Lower
Canadians reacted with studied coolness at every official opportunity.
Indeed, on both occasions when the Governor General went out to meet
them, they took care to ration their courtesy. In early June 1840, on doctors'
orders, he sailed to Sorel, then up the Richelieu to Saint-Ours, Chambly,
Saint-Hyacinthe and St. John's, returning to Montreal by train. On June 15,
Le Canadien expressed the hope that

*Son Excellence aura sans doute dû se convaincre pendant cette excur-
sion dans nos campagnes, que les Canadiens n'étaient pas si noirs qu'on les
avait fait et que le représentant royal avait eu la bonté de les peindre lui-
même.*

In fact, *Son Excellence* received "des marques non équivoques d'empressement et de satisfaction" from those too well-mannered to give anything else, the Seigneuresse de Saint-Ours, and the priests at the Collège de
Saint-Hyacinthe. But the crowds he loved so well raised no cheers, and
Thomson's comment (in a private letter) may have betrayed his disappointment. "Those counties," he wrote, "present a melancholy picture:
the population rapidly increasing and the people unwilling to quit their
neighbourhood and settle on new land, until actually starved out. The
physical state of the people is, however, better than their moral condition.
Their ignorance and credulity are unbounded."[3] Three weeks later, at the
beginning of July 1840, Thomson took a second trip. He stopped in Quebec
and Kamouraska on his way to visit Halifax. In Quebec, as *L'Ami du
Peuple* reported on July 1, "il s'est trouvé bien peu de monde sur son
passage, et pas une acclamation n'est venue lui révéler qu'on s'occupât de
lui". But as he left his carriage to enter the ex-Assembly House, a few
English-speaking sympathisers let out an indiscreet hurrah, with the
immediate result that a concert of rather tactless whistles and catcalls came
from the French passers-by. "Le silence du peuple en pareil cas," noted
Le Canadien on July 1, "est aussi éloquent que des sifflets et il est plus
noble et commande le respect." During his stay the Governor remained
safely indoors, attending to the reorganization of the municipal council.

When the time to leave arrived, he decided to sail at midnight, an hour less likely to draw attention. Aubin commented on July 6:

Il paraît que le personnage n'aime point la musique, car il est reparti vendredi à minuit. Cela étonne beaucoup de gens de la campagne qui pensaient que le poulet n'est pas un oiseau nocturne quoique c'en soit un de mauvaise augure.

On his return trip in July and August, he also arrived and left in the middle of the night.

In Kamouraska – "n'osant plus compter sur l'enthousiasme des grandes villes, il se rabat sur les villages," commented *L'Ami du Peuple* on July 15 – he received an official welcome from the notables. On the wharf about one hundred spectators and an assortment of school children raised a cheer. Then the Governor retired to one of the principal homes to hold an informal levée. He was greeted in an atmosphere of strict correctness, and with the respect due any distinguished guest; but he could hardly claim a popular ovation. Thomson did receive an ovation a month later from English-speaking Sherbrooke where for two days he passed under triumphal arches and listened to addresses of thanks and praise. He might well be feted, commented the editor of *Le Canadien*, Etienne Parent, on August 21, for he had just gerrymandered the county of Three Rivers in favour of Sherbrooke.

Later, when Thomson was elevated to the peerage, the British party in Montreal resolved to honour him publicly. The three Saint societies (George, Andrew and Patrick) drew up plans for a mammoth procession to accompany the new Baron Sydenham from the gates of the city to Government House. The French, however, were in no mood for congratulations, and let it be known that the parade might turn out to be rather thin. Sydenham (perhaps conveniently) suffered another attack of gout; and, through Peter McGill, the mayor he had appointed, announced he could not bear the strain of a state occasion. He deceived no one, however, as *L'Aurore* commented on October 2:

Son Excellence avec cette finesse de tact qui la caractèrise, ayant pressenti que son triomphe à Montréal serait tellement maigre que ce ne serait pas un triomphe, a cru qu'il serait mieux pour elle d'être malade et de dire qu'elle ne voulait pas de triomphe! N'est-ce pas là être assez renard pour une poulette.

The French had scored again. Some months later, in May 1841, Sydenham left them for Kingston, the new capital of United Canada. There, on September 4, he stumbled from his horse and broke his right leg. Weakened by gout, nervous from sleepless nights and day-time anxieties, Sydenham never recovered. After lockjaw set in, he died on September 19, 1841. This time the French Canadians seemed to forget even the most elementary good manners. At first, they continued to laugh. On September 9, Aubin imagined Sydenham writing to Sir Robert Peel: "A propos, pour comble de détresse, mon cheval est tombé, moi dessus, je me suis cassé le cou près de la cheville du pied. . . . Les braves Canadiens ont montré la plus vive sympathie pour mon cheval!" Later, as reports from Kingston grew more serious, he stopped his banter to say very plainly on September 13, "Quand à nous, nous ne voulons de malheur à personne, mais si Son Excellence se cassait le col ou autre chose nous dirions: Que la volonté de Dieu soit faite. Tant pis pour lui, tant mieux pour nous."

After the Governor had died, Etienne Parent put out a single issue of *Le Canadien*, that of September 24, 1841, with the traditional thick-set lines of mourning, but not a single word about the Governor. On the back page of the next issue, (September 29), he published a short summary of the details of the funeral at Saint George's in Kingston. In Montreal, *L'Aurore* came out on September 25, with the thick black lines, but wrote bitterly:

Nos réflexions sur sa vie privée seraient injustifiables aujourd'hui que la tombe le sépare de nous. Mais sa vie publique appartient à l'histoire, elle appartient surtout à la presse libérale et indépendante d'un pays traité en province conquise et soumise au plus odieux despotisme par l'homme même dont le devoir était de la gouverner en père. . . . Comme Canadiens, comme libéraux, et même comme hommes, nous ne pouvons oublier ses crimes. Dieu auquel il s'est recommandé en mourant, nous l'espérons, l'a reçu au sein de sa miséricorde.

On the back page of *Le Fantasque* for September 20, Aubin announced the Governor's death between two thin little black lines (these too perhaps satirical) and the comment: "Nous avons rencontré plus de cent personnes qui savaient la nouvelle et pas un n'a dit un mot de regret." A week later he noted that the mayor of Montreal, Peter McGill, had ordered municipal mourning for one month, and he hoped that Quebec would not imitate "cet acte d'hypocrisie."

Wasting no tears on Lord Sydenham, the French Canadians soon began to speculate about his successor. Sir Charles Bagot's appointment was announced in London on September 27, 1841, and reported in Quebec on October 8. The Canadiens soon made him the centre of their discussions. What they knew of him did not impress them. In fact, they had never heard of him. "*L'Unicorn* qui vient d'arriver," commented Aubin on October 11 in *Le Fantasque,*

annonce comme définitive la nomination de Sir Charles . . . nous ne savons encore qui attendu que quelques journaux l'appellent Pagot, d'autres Bagot; nous croyons que c'est un Fagot.

They were told that he was a diplomat; and this they considered no recommendation, as *Le Canadien* noted on October 8: "C'est dire que d'une administration loup nous allons passer sous une administration renard." On October 21, *L'Aurore* declared its opinion that "dans la présente condition de cette colonie, toute autre chose qu'un diplomate eut convenu." And *Le*

Fantasque on October 25, addressing the Governor directly, echoed these sentiments:

On répand le bruit que vous êtes diplomate! Mais sachez donc que nous annoncer ainsi votre arrivée, c'est nous dire: Garde à vous, Canadiens, nous vous envoyons le plus rusé coquin dont nous puissions nous passer pour le moment; il a fait des prouesses en Russie et mille autres contrées étrangères; il a trompé au nom de l'Angleterre cinquante nations diverses; il a joué avec son visage, avec sa connaissance, avec sa parole; il n'a ni foi, ni loi, c'est un Talleyrand, un Fouché, moins l'illustration, moins la renommée.

But, they seem to have decided that perhaps they should await the outcome and hope for the best.

Meanwhile officials and politicians converged on Quebec to greet the new Governor General as he landed. The Administrator, Sir Richard Jackson, and several of his Councillors, arrived on November 3, to be followed a few days later by Bishop Ignace Bourget of Montreal. The Mayor of Quebec, René-Edouard Caron, and the city fathers had already drawn up the customary address of welcome. Was it their sentiments which Aubin reflected in an open letter in *Le Fantasque* on October 25 which he directed to Sir Charles? In it he presented the usual catalogue of the country's wants – free elections, impartial distribution of patronage, public funds spent only with public approval, and the right of each citizen to "parler la langue qui lui plaît le plus" – concluding with a dramatic appeal not to "suivre la trace de vos devanciers, couper, tailler dans nos institutions, nous écraser, nous torturer," but

liez nous ensemble et au char de votre souveraine par l'amitié, par la reconnaissance, et soyez sûr que l'intérêt, c'est à dire l'amour du bien-être, de la paix, fera le reste.

Be that as it may, State, Church, and Citizenry awaited in vain. The new Governor's ship was driven back by gales. By the end of November the officials had returned homewards, their feelings, perhaps, emphasized by *Le Fantasque* on November 29: "C'est ennuyeux. On ne pouvait pas, cependant, en y réfléchissant bien, attendre autre chose d'un si grand diplomate." Surely an inauspicious beginning.

Because it was winter, Sir Charles now had to come by the American route (New York, Albany, Utica) and duly arrived in Kingston on January 10, 1842. On that day some two hundred sleighs, their riders bundled in buffalo robes, jingled all together into Kingston from across Lake Ontario's deep snows. Along the shore, little informal groups waved their greetings as they caught sight of the handsome, courtly, old diplomat. Two days later, the sleighs were out again, this time along the road leading out to Alwington House on the outskirts. There, hundreds of people filled the drawing-rooms as Sir Charles, splendid in his decorations and with the red ribband of the Bath slashed across the silver-braid of his Court uniform, stood before this brilliant, bemedalled staff and personally greeted each one of the Capital's leading citizens. The regime had begun, and whatever feelings were hurt by the delay two months earlier, the new Governor was deluged with the Quebeckers' customary addresses of welcome. The Catholic Archbishop Signay wrote nostalgically, "Aujourd'hui les citoyens de Québec se trouvent privés d'un honneur qu'ils ont toujours grandement apprécié, celui c'être les premiers à offrir leurs hommages au Représentant de l'Autorité Royale," but he prayed that the new Governor "contribuera à établir sur des bases solides l'harmonie qu'il est si désirable de voir régner parmi les sujets de Sa Majesté."[4] Bishop Bourget sent an emissary to deliver personally his message of welcome. Addresses also came from the cities of Quebec, Montreal, Three Rivers, and from the different patriotic societies, all entertaining the brightest hopes for his successful administration.

Few of them realized then how successful it would be for the Canadiens. In fact, even before his departure from the mother country, the new Governor had meditated seriously upon the French-Canadian question, helped by a surprising number of letters on the subject from sources most varied but all in agreement on the solution they advised. From Sir John Colborne, who had put down the rebellion four years earlier and been so cordially hated for it in return, he received a penetrating analysis of the position of the French in Canada, and the advice that:

I think that the population of French origin are to be recovered by attention to their wants, and that they will prove less troublesome than the Yankee classes settled in the Western districts. A few of the young priests have been corrupted, but the ecclesiastics generally of the R. Catholic community are very respectable, and will be found ready to work with a Governor inclined to improve the condition of the Seigniories.[5]

One Henry Parish, an official of the British embassy in Washington, thought "the recovery of the affection of these people a matter of the deepest political and diplomatic importance."[6] And in a letter from the Earl of Westmorland, Bagot read a memorandum to the effect that

The Canadians as a nation had resisted LaFayette and Washington. They had remained uninvited through the great French Revolution & loyal to their new dynasty under every change until the wandering, unguided Emigrants from Great Britain . . . in the form of usurers, Missionaries, Demagogues, Paupers wandered without distinction, & introduced themselves amongst a people who were unable to cope with adventurers, as much their superiors in craft and subtility [sic] as in Industry and enterprise.

To secure a return of this traditional loyalty, Lord Westmorland suggested, Bagot must devote all his care to the Canadiens' "Ancestorial [sic] customs."[7] From these and many such messages, there could be only one conclusion: if the Governor seriously intended to preserve the British connection, as indeed by his office he must, then, his first duty should be to recover the loyalty and sympathy of the French Canadians. And the best means to achieve this, he was told, was to attend to their susceptibilities, to treat them as true British subjects.

Within a month after his arrival, having observed carefully for himself, Bagot had come to the same conclusions. He set out to heal the tensions and strains of the Union. At the end of January, he began with the first opportunity that presented itself. Receiving in audience Mayor Caron and other Quebec notables who had travelled to Kingston to present the old capital's address of welcome signed by 6997 *Québecois*, he departed from the usual custom of acknowledgement. Instead of repeating the words of the address, he proclaimed in a gracious and tactful speech "my determination to know no distinctions of National or Religious creed." And he made it a point to tell these proud men who still regretted that the capital had been moved from Quebec to Kingston how sorry he was that he had been unable to land in the ancient port. To Archbishop Signay, he wrote in elegant French, in his own hand, a long letter in which he reiterated his intention to

profiter *de la première occasion, à l'ouverture de la navigation de la rivière, de visiter la Province Orientale, quand j'aurai l'honneur, à ce que j'espère, de vous témoigner de vive voix comme je suis sensible à l'accueuil favorable que vous me faites, et de vous prouver mon désir ardent d'établir et de maintenir sur des bases les plus solides et les plus égales, cette harmonie qui doit toujours régner parmi les sujets de notre Auguste Souveraine, et de cimenter de plus en plus les liens qui les attachent à Son Trône.*[8]

Indeed, he intended to go down to Lower Canada as soon as possible, "visiting Montreal, Quebec, and other places," he wrote to the new Colonial Secretary, Lord Stanley, "making personal acquaintance with members for that part of the Colony, and using my endeavours to produce a good impression upon the French part of the population."[9] But even before his tour, he had begun to conciliate.

He made a number of appointments, each a minor one, but, in the context, of great symbolic value for the Canadiens. Bagot, deeply human, understood what he described to his friend Mr. Grenville as "the universal thirst for place, every man in this land, no matter who – comes to my excellency and hopes it will please it to give him a small (he always means large) place in some public office."[10] He seems to have understood the importance of even the smallest political appointment to a nation rendered (by what it considered a policy of exclusion) extremely sensitive to the proportion of its representation in the public place. "It is despairing," he wrote in the same letter to Grenville, "to see how they always take justice and kindness only as instalments of their own unreasonable pretensions wrung from our sense of their consequence, but it is none the less my duty and my policy to administer these ingredients to them as I propose to do as soon as I get amongst them." As well as appointing a large number of

French-sounding names to public posts, he conferred the title of Queen's Counsel on several prominent Canadien lawyers, and more fundamental to *la survivance*, made an unprecedented choice in selecting a French Canadian for the post of Chief Justice of Montreal, and another to head the Lower Canadian section of the Department of Education.

In the spring, he decided on direct diplomacy. His wife, Lady Mary Bagot, was scheduled to land at Quebec at the end of July; and, in going down to meet her, he would take the opportunity to continue personally what his measures had already begun to accomplish. As it turned out, he succeeded beyond his fondest hopes.

Sir Charles arrived in Montreal in the late spring. There, unfortunately, the British party sought to monopolize his visit. The Mayor, Peter McGill, had proclaimed plans for a procession of the three English-speaking benevolent and patriotic societies to escort the Governor from the city limits on Saint-Antoine Road to the Chateau de Ramezay. And, indeed, on the appointed day, which was the eve of the Queen's birthday, they formed a colourful sight, with their banners unfurled, and their flags, and the animated sound of regimental music. But the French happily refused to be left out; after all, they too must impress the Governor with the justice of their claims. *L'Aurore* noted on May 14:

On a tant de peur que les ignorants Canadiens trouvent une occasion de manifester leurs sentiments que ces ignobles loyaux font tout dans les ténèbrés afin que loyauté soit toujours métier et marchandise exclusifs. Nos concitoyens savent à quoi s'en tenir sur la réception qu'il leur convient de faire à Son Excellence.

Thus when the Governor arrived, and proceeded as *Le Canadien* reported on May 25 under triumphal arches "avec tout l'éclat qu'avaient fait ésperer les préparations," the French Canadians, though officially excluded, raised an universal shout of their own. And on the Queen's birthday, when Sir Charles held his first levée, the Canadien politicians made it a point to attend *en masse*. Bagot himself observed, "God knows what it may all be worth, but I am assured by those practised in such matters, that my levée was unprecedented."[11]

Bagot began to win more friends. He invited several locally important Canadiens to the Legislative Council, and offered to a number of politicians the offices of Commissioner for the Seigneurial Inquiry and the Solicitor-Generalship. When he renewed the Commissions of a number of French Justices of the Peace that had been suspended during the "troubles" in 1838, *L'Aurore* noted on June 14: "Sir Charles veut fort et ferme entrer tout de bon dans la voie de la justice."

Soon stories began to make the rounds. One reported in *L'Aurore* on June 11 went that "Son Excellence se promenait l'autre jour, en habits séculiers et n'avait rien pour le distinguer que la dignité de son maintien et la noblesse de sa physionomie." When a man met him on the street, a man of the people, "le type national du pays," the man, "frappé de l'air distingué du personnage," tipped his hat. Sir Charles stopped, and returned the greeting "avec tant de grace et d'urbanité" that the *habitant* ran to ask someone who the gentleman was. When told it was the Governor General, he exclaimed: "Celui-là, il nous trompera pas." Of such stuff are legends made.

By the time Bagot left Montreal on June 22, 1842, he might well be content with his month's work. His fame preceded him to the old capital. Here the Mayor, Caron, had tolerated no exclusion from the welcome ceremony on racial grounds. And the *Québecois* decided to do the honours on this royal occasion as they alone could. They had begun to consider this man as a friend.

Auspiciously on the morrow of Saint-Jean-Baptiste day, Bagot aboard the *S.S. Queen*, sailed past Cape Diamond and down an avenue of flag-decorated steamships lined up in the ancient harbour. He disembarked to the tune of "des airs canadiens," met the Mayor, and climbed into an open landau for the procession to the City Hall. It was a pleasant summer day, with much more sunshine than fog. He waved right and left as he rode through the streets paved that morning with pine needles and spruce branches, under rich triumphal arches of oak foliage, up the Côte de la Montagne, and on to Place d'Armes. There he reviewed the troops who stood like monuments resplendent in full dess, and the officers of the four benevolent societies gathered with flags flying. At the Hotel-de-Ville all was glad and gracious. Bagot stepped out onto the balcony. From there he could see the fifteen hundred members of the Société Saint-Jean-Baptiste (who had been following his carriage) wind their way up from the Basse Ville and pour into the square beneath him. Above them, along the three other sides of the square, he gave a courtly bow to "les dames qui dans leurs toilettes les plus élégantes, montrèrent leurs belles et riantes figures à toutes les fenêtres." At his feet, he watched the colours as workingmen and professionals, rich and poor, crowded behind the green and white banner of Saint-Jean-Baptiste, the glory of French Canada shining on every face. From the whole square he could hear the joyous airs of "Vive la Canadienne." He seemed deeply moved. Turning to Mayor Caron, he whispered "Mais, c'est un peuple de gentilhommes." After leaving the City Hall, he drove smiling through the crowd over to the apartments prepared for him in the north wing of the old Assembly House. In the narrow streets nearby, the students of the Séminaire de Québec, massed around their college band, broke into an enthusiastic "God Save the Queen." Then, away past the crowds, the flags, the music, he mounted the stairs, according to *Le Canadien* on June 27, "au milieu des applaudissements de la foule qui avaient été presque continuels depuis son arrivée." Surely a day he would never forget; and one which the ancient city, with nostalgia for the old, good days, has long remembered.

Lady Mary Bagot arrived three weeks later, and finished Bagot's conquest. On July 28, she invited to a "circle," all that Quebec held most elegant. *Le Canadien* reported the next day that:

Toutes les origines y étaient représentées par ce qu'elles avaient de plus notable. Nos dames sont revenues des plus enchantées des aimables qualités de Lady Bagot et des demoiselles Bagot qui toutes parlent le Français avec élégance et facilité.

Perhaps towards the end of his stay, Bagot read *Le Fantasque* for July 28, 1842. In it Aubin reminded him of "les trois routes politiques" left open to him now that he knew his people. First, he could hold to the old line of ostracism, or he could try to "s'aventurer sur un mer d'eau tiède, n'être ni chat ni rat, flatter tout le monde," and accomplish nothing. Thirdly, he could choose the way of honour, and

oublier et faire oublier les injures passées, régner par la justice; se persuader qu'il est politique de regarder les canadiens-français comme une nation adjointe à l'empire britannique et non subjuguée par lui; de leur garantir ce qui leur est cher, ce qui leur est dû; d'abandonner aux habitants du pays la direction de leurs propres affaires.

It was a tribute to Bagot's great gifts of charm that Aubin thought he would follow the third way.

By the end of the summer, both by his measures and by his own personal diplomacy, Sir Charles Bagot had obviously succeeded in his efforts to convince French Canadians, first, that they could trust him; and second, that some good could come out of the Union. Of course, young Louis-Hippolyte LaFontaine and his partisans had been arguing the second point since 1839, and within a few weeks, during the historic September days of 1842, the two men, the aging, gracious diplomat, and the intense, sharp-willed young politician, would join forces. Bagot, realizing that the changing pattern of politics in the Assembly forced him to turn to LaFontaine, and the French Canadian politician increasingly under pressure to prove his claim that the Union and the British connection could be made to serve French Canada, met to negotiate. After several days, made painful by Bagot's sense of what was due to his other Councillors and LaFontaine's eagerness to make it clear that he accepted office on his own, and not the Governor's terms, young LaFontaine and his associates became, on September 10, 1842, the first French Canadians since the Conquest to enter the executive branch of the government of their country, and thus enabled to express and direct their people's national aspirations.

Immediately an almost unanimous Hallelujah Chorus exploded across Lower Canada – and to Bagot went the glory. The first note came from LaFontaine's vivacious *aide-de-camp*, George-Etienne Cartier. He wrote how he had rushed to LaFontaine's law office on first hearing the news, and with the new Attorney-General's staff "avons bu ensemble le champagne à votre santé. Nous avons mis nos estomacs en unison avec nos coeurs."[12] The press echoed the sentiment. On September 20, 1842 *Le Canadien* put out an *extraordinaire* to announce in the biggest headlines its typographers could devise the "REMODELLEMENT DU MINISTERE"; then, on the next day, it added:

Des Canadiens français, des hommes de cette race proscrite vont faire partie du ministère, et par conséquent être appelés à diriger les affaires de l'état. N'est-ce-pas là une chose inattendue, inouie? . . . Nous pouvons dire que Sir Charles Bagot, en ralliant les Canadiens à son administration, a fait un acte de haute politique qui aura l'effet le plus salutaire. Que par de pareils actes, et il en aura beaucoup à faire, le gouvernment nous rende pleine et entière justice, nous ne demandons que de la justice, et nous garantissons la possession du Canada à l'Angleterre aussi longtemps qu'elle voudra la conserver.

And at *Le Fantasque*, Aubin agreed on September 22: "Après les gouvernements des Colborne et des Sydenham, ce simple retour vers une politique moins exclusive fait revivre le Canada d'une vie nouvelle et ramène la joie, la confiance, et, le dirons – nous, la loyauté dans le coeur si longtemps ulcéré de ses habitants."

LaFontaine's partisans (as all good politicians must) did more than hymn their joy; they translated it into action. In fact, they almost had no alternative. For one thing, they heard disturbing sounds from the British party. Secondly, they must master the last and lingering anti-Unionists in French Canada who still hesitated to rally to the party. And within three months they found an added reason to act quickly: fear that disease and death might rob them of their hero. They decided accordingly on a succession of public meetings in honour of the Governor. These, they hoped, would console Sir Charles for the insults heaped upon him by the anti-French (since September the latter had been writing about Bagot the same kind of invective the Canadiens had thrown at Sydenham). Perhaps these would also help him pyschologically to regain the physical strength he needed to remain at his post. For very soon after the new Council had been installed, Sir Charles had fallen mysteriously and seriously ill – enough for rumours to circulate that he had died. "La nouvelle de la mort du Gouverneur," a friend wrote to LaFontaine, "laquelle grâces au Ciel c'est trouvée fausse, avait jeté les amis du pays dans la consternation, et elle avait produit chez moi une impression vraiment pénible."[13] Prayers and expressions of sympathy, the good *habitants* decided, would restore him. "Les bons sujets canadiens," wrote Aubin in *Le Fantasque* on November 19, "tremblent pour les jours de l'homme qui leur apporte un peu de justice. La tranquilité, l'absence des tourments, un air pur et sec, des témoignages d'estime et de respect, voilà ce qu'il faut à Sir Charles Bagot." Since in most of the minds, the Governor symbolized the Union (Sydenham had been hated precisely because of this), each meeting and address of sympathy and congratulation, each prayer, would also drive an extra nail into the coffin of the anti-Unionists.

The press agreed. *Le Canadien* on December 12 envisaged the good results that would flow from the meetings:

Le mouvement va se propager d'un bout à l'autre de la province comme celui de la vague, et il s'élèvera en faveur de Sir Charles Bagot un concert de voix approbatrices qui l'empêchera d'entendre ou lui fera mépriser les insultes grossières que ses barbares ennemis ne cessent de lui adresser. Les voix des Canadiens français seront unanimes et tous les Anglais raisonnables, tous ceux qui désirent la paix et la prospérité permanente du Canada sous l'égide de l'Angleterre s'empresseront de se joindre à eux.

In Quebec a meeting was called in mid-afternoon on a week day, December 23, and was nevertheless very well attended. Mayor Caron presided, and politicians of divers hues sat side by side to vote a resolution that offered, as *Le Fantasque* reported the next day, "de ferventes prières" for the Governor's well-being and continued residence in the colony, "où votre présence ne peut que tendre à resser les liens qui nous unissent à la Grande-Bretagne."

The countryside almost improved on the old capital. By the end of November a meeting had been held in Portneuf where an address was adopted, proving, as *Le Canadien* mentioned on December 5, "un éclatant démenti à ceux qui prétendent que les Canadiens-français désirent une séparation d'avec l'Angleterre ou qu'ils demandent autre chose qu'à vivre en paix et en harmonie avec leurs concitoyens." In LaMalbaie, another meeting adopted the same address, and at Saint-Anne-de-la-Pérade and Rimouski, despite bad weather, large crowds cheered a similar one.

In Montreal, a triumphant rally took place on January 12, 1843 when three thousand Montrealers – the largest public meeting there since 1822 – gathered to sing the praises of Governor and Council, and pray Divine Providence, as *Le Canadien* reported on January 16, to "reserrer les liens qui unissent cette colonie à la métropole." Such was the enthusiasm that the *Mélanges Religieux* forgot its theoretical impartiality to write on January 17:

Cette démonstration solennelle de toute une ville, et à laquelle s'unissaient de coeur ceux qui ne purent y prendre part, est un des évènements les plus significatifs qui se soient passés ici depuis longtemps. Il doit avoir, il aura certainement un grand retentissement. Il dira donc à l'Angleterre ce que valent pour la mère-patrie des enfants qu'on lui a dénoncés si souvent comme dénaturés et indignes de toute affection; et par contrecoup ce que valent à leur tour ceux qui les ont ainsi constamment calomniés. . . . Espérons que Dieu conservera au pays un homme que le pays sait si bien apprécier, et qui comprend si bien lui-même ceux qui ont mis en lui leurs plus légitimes espérances. Les campagnes ont donné le même exemple de

loyale sympathie que la ville. De toutes partes sont envoyés des adresses de
félicitations à Son excellence. Il sera difficile après cela de mettre en doute
la loyauté canadienne. Que les gouverneurs soient toujours équitables et un
peuple comme le nôtre sera toujours soumis.

From the Montreal district, other addresses and resolutions poured in,
from Longueuil, and Saint-Denis, and Saint-Hyacinthe, everywhere, *Le*
Fantasque reported on December 21, "le ralliement autour du noble homme
d'état qui nous gouverne et de ses conseillers est unanime."

The editorials, the addresses, and the meetings, none could stop the
advance of Bagot's illness. He died on May 19, 1843, amid universal
French-Canadian requiems. Three months before, however, the Canadiens
had learned his tenure was at an end. On February 25, 1843, news reached
Quebec that Sir Charles Theophilus Metcalfe had been appointed to succeed
the dying Bagot. The government in Kingston had already heard the news,
and with it reports lavish with praise of the man. "Often have I lain in my
bed," the ailing Governor confided to the Colonial Secretary, "considering
whom I should most desire to have as my successor and to play out my hand
here. And Metcalfe has first invariably presented himself to me."[14]

In the press also, the appointment gave rise to the highest enthusiasm.
On April 11, the *Journal de Québec* told its readers that "les esprits les
plus soupçonneux, s'appuyant sur le passé, sont forcés, malgré eux, de
reconnaître en lui un homme d'une extrême justice et d'une grande habilité.
Ayons donc foi dans un avenir si proche." *Le Canadien* had commented on
February 25,

D'après ce que nous connaissons des antécédents de Sir Charles Met-
calfe, il y a peu d'hommes plus propres à remplacer Sir Charles Bagot. . . .
On assure que Sir Charles Bagot est très satisfait du choix qu'on a fait de
son successeur.

Napoléon Aubin grew lyrical. He wrote in *Le Fantasque* on March 4th,
that Metcalfe:

. . . aime à juger par lui-mème et ne se laisse jamais conduire.
Il ne souffre pas qu'on cherche à l'intimider.
Il ne se laisse jamais surprendre par la flatterie.
Il est modeste, point présomptueux, et ne s'aveugle pas sur lui-même.
Il est infatigable, et saisit habilement toutes le parties d'une question. . . .
Il est un homme équitable dans toute la force du terme.
Dites, Canadiens, avez-vous encore vu promesses aussi brillantes?

Meanwhile, on the very day of Aubin's article, Sir Charles Metcalfe
sailed from Liverpool on the *Columbia*. On March 29, he reached Kingston,
and through slushy streets lined with troops he rode to his hotel in an open
sleigh, at the head of a procession "qui avait une extension d'au moins un
mille," past cheering crowds. On the next day, he went to Government
House and met his Councillors. Portly, moon-faced, and balding, he looked

like Benjamin Franklin, noted *Le Canadien* on April 3, and he showed, besides, all the signs of a good, firm, and prudent character. Moreover, "la confrontation de son front indiquerait, suivant les phrénologistes, le siège d'une haute intelligence."

Then there began the usual testimonials, the rush to meetings of congratulation, and the hurried composition of loyal addresses. One of the first came from Quebec where, as *Le Canadien* reported on April 10, "une assemblée très nombreuse et respectable" chaired by Mayor Caron met on April 8, and cheered a text prepared by John Neilson – who had apparently forgotten his promise to Poulett Thomson that no French Canadian would ever co-operate with the Union. Another arrived from Montreal. There, on April 11, over five thousand people joined to sing the praises of the new Governor. The address itself, published in *La Minerve* on April 13, repeated the city's "satisfaction de voir qu'un gouverneur cher au pays est remplacé par un homme à la réputation si distinguée." And others came from Sainte-Elisabeth-de-Berthier, from Longueuil, from Saint-Hyacinthe.

As a matter of fact, Metcalfe deserved most of this. Born and trained in the Far East, he had developed into what Macaulay termed "the ablest civil servant that I ever knew in India." Later, as Governor of Jamaica, he had solved all problems and won all hearts by his kindness and generostiy, earning from the Colonial Society in London the tribute that "no colonial government could henceforward be conducted on any other principle than those [sic] of his administration." Now, in his late fifties, prematurely aged and afflicted with cancer of the face, he left his quiet retirement reluctantly and out of a stark sense of duty. And here in Canada, he continued, as ever, to make the best of impressions. Within the first five months of his tenure, he donated over £250 to various charitable (mostly religious) institutions in Lower Canada alone – thus initiating a habit which he would continue until his very last days, when, if there were two opinions of his policies, there still remained only one about his generosity.

French Canadians responded quickly. As early as June 19, on the occasion of the Governor's pardoning a prisoner, *La Minerve* commented:

Chaque jour nous apporte la nouvelle d'un acte de miséricorde de la part de Sir Charles Metcalfe. C'est une grande puissance d'attraction que la miséricorde en politique. . . . Honneur donc, nous n'avons pas besoin de dire courage, à celui qui est juste et miséricordieux par principe et par caractère.

And later, when Montreal celebrated its first restored Saint-Jean-Baptiste holiday, Metcalfe's coat-of-arms appeared among the principal decorations, while in the ancient capital, to the tune of "An old English gentleman," *Le Fantasque* reported on July 3, the Québecois toasted him at the banquet with: "Nos meilleurs voeux l'accompagnent dans la tâche noble mais difficile qu'il a entreprise et lui promettent notre sincère coopération." Then in August 1843, when he came down to Lower Canada, the French Canadians gave him a more cordial personal welcome than they had ever accorded any other governor.

In Montreal, where Sir Charles was due on August 21, 1843, men put up banners and bunting, women prepared their best dresses. The Temperance Society published marching orders; the firemen planned to parade in full regalia; and the militia made ready to station troops at regular intervals along the processional route. In front of the City Hall, Mayor Bourret ordered a huge triumphal arch to stand and proclaim the city's loyalty with big Union Jacks and allegorical designs of Britannia and Justice. And high in the newly-completed towers of Notre Dame, the Sulpicians installed a specially-designed keyboard which *La Minerve* reported on August 21, would connect with the great bells and "exécuter l'hymne national au passage de Son Excellence devant l'église paroissiale."

Accordingly, at three o'clock in the afternoon of the day appointed, August 21, 1843, despite strong winds and thunder showers, an imposing *cortège* composed of the Mayor and Aldermen, distinguished clerics, presidents of the older and recently-founded societies, and members of the Chamber of Commerce, proceeded some ten miles out to the steamship landing to await the Governor. Behind it followed "une foule de gens impatients de témoigner leurs respects à Son Excellence." And, back inside the walls, the soldiers in full dress stood poised, large crowds awaited impatiently in the wet streets, and "toutes les fenêtres sont garnies de dames." Unfortunately, they were all disappointed. *Son Excellence*, though he had been travelling since seven in the morning, was delayed by the storm. By six o'clock the tired troops had returned to their barracks; and the patient procession left Quesnel's. No one considered how much this might be an omen of future disappointments.

The Governor arrived quietly only after seven. He rode directly to the Hotel Rasco. On the morrow, he apologized for yesterday's delay, and with great fanfare, visited the Port, Saint Ann's Market, the Mercantile Library, the new Notre Dame "qu'il paraissait contempler avec beaucoup de satisfaction," McGill College, and the Hospital of the Grey Nuns. Everywhere, he received protests of devotion, and gave the best impression. Before sailing for Quebec, he finally conquered *le tout Montréal* by declaring as *La Minerve* reported on August 24 "que Montréal méritait de devenir le siège du Gouvernement."

In Quebec, the city council and citizens organized an even more magnificent parade, spurred on by Montreal's example and by their own press. *Le Fantasque,* in fact, underlined the main motive on August 19:

J'espère que les citoyens de notre ville sous la forme de la Société Saint-Jean-Baptiste se réuniront pour lui [Metcalfe] faire une réception sans pareille, afin de lui montrer qu'il y a quelques Canadiens à Québec, chose passablement notoire mais dont ne voulaient pas convenir les anciens gouverneurs.

They spangled the streets with colour, built two huge triumphal arches decorated with the Metcalfe armorial bearings, and called out three regiments of the garrison to form a double line along the route from the dock to the Hotel du Payne.

Then, on the evening of August 24, Mayor Caron and his Council, all suitably robed, the whole array of the city's magistrates, General Sir James Hope, the Commanding Officer, the regimental bands, the presidents of the societies of Saints Andrew and Patrick, the companies of firemen, all the members of the Saint-Jean-Baptiste Society "avec sa musique, ses décorations, ses superbes bannières et les drapeaux de la milice," and whatever else was left of citizenry, all descended to the "quai de Gillespie and Co" to greet the distinguished guest. He disembarked as a salvo of seventeen guns thundered high on the Citadel, and took his place in the Mayor's official carriage. With Mayor Caron he rode between rows of soldiers presenting arms, up Saint-Pierre Street and the Côte de la Montagne, under Prescott Gate "ornée de verdure et d'une couronne de baronet," and on to Place d'Armes where the Saint George Society stood cheering. Then, as he left the carriage, he received the usual addresses, and answered "par des paroles gracieuses." Afterwards, the Société Saint-Jean-Baptiste which had marched ahead "presqu'au complet et dans le meilleur ordre, bannières, flammes, étendards déployés," three times raised a universal shout of "Vive le Gouverneur." They had wanted, said *Le Canadien* the next day, to show honour "à celui qui, tant par son caractère personnel que comme représentant de Sa Majesté, mérite si justement leurs respects et leurs hommages."

In Three Rivers on August 28, there was the same story of salvos and pomp, of triumphal arches and streets lined with cheers. "Toute la ville était sur pied," wrote *Le Canadien* on August 30, and that night, when Sir Charles left to visit the Saint-Maurice ironworks, an excited crowd went out spontaneously to escort him back. On the next day, he travelled to Sherbrooke, went on to Stanstead, to Chambly, to Sorel, and in each, the Canadians repeated the same splendid, noisy, and popular welcome. They meant, of course, to impress him with the success of Bagot's policy, but they also admired in him the generous and dignified gentleman who continued on this trip, as usual, to shower them with kindness. As *La Minerve* noted on September 1:

Il n'y a pas de souverain en Europe, nous pouvons le dire sans exagération, qui se montre aussi peu ménager de sa bourse que notre gouverneur-général Sir Charles Metcalfe. . . . Son Excellence a semé sur son passage dans sa promenade actuelle les largesses.

"If grand receptions," Metcalfe himself confessed in a letter to his sister, "loyal addresses, banners displayed, and triumphal arches could afford comfort and assurance, I should have them."[15] The Canadiens meant that he should. They did not yet know that in the Council Chamber approval rang with less wholehearted a note. For during this time, Sir Charles and his Councillors were growing openly disputatious. And soon the personal and practical difficulties which divided them would explode from behind all the cheers to precipitate what French-Canadian opinion at the time termed *la crise Metcalfe.*

On November 27, 1843, all of Sir Charles' French-Canadian councillors resigned in a body. They explained publicly that the Governor General had made a number of appointments without consulting them; their real concern, however, was the fact that Metcalfe was gradually undermining the principle of responsible government on which they had accepted office from Sir Charles Bagot in September 1842. In their eyes the point was an essential one; for Metcalfe's actions, influenced as they appeared to be by anti-French intrigues, seemed to take back what Bagot had given. Accordingly, they resigned their commissions and appealed to the Assembly. The Assembly, as expected, gave them a majority. But to the astonishment of everyone in the capital, a small number of Canadien members voted for Metcalfe against LaFontaine and, apparently, against their own best national interests. At their head sat Denis-Benjamin Viger, and John Neilson. Could it be that these had turned their backs on their life's work?

On receiving the news, the lower province's first reaction was indeed one of surprise. In Montreal *La Minerve* was the first to receive the word. On November 30 it published a straightforward account of the resignation with the simple query: "Que fera Sir Charles dans une conjoncture aussi périlleuse? On l'ignore." In Quebec, French Canada's senior newspaper, *Le Canadien,* put out an *extraordinaire* on December 2; it printed *La Minerve*'s same bare facts, and added the laconic comment: "Nous croyons devoir nous borner à reproduire les bruits et faits mentionnés." Indeed for the next few weeks most of the editors seemed unable to work up an opinion.

They were hesitant, torn between astonishment and respect for the Governor's intentions. On the one hand, they realized he had just hounded to its resignation the first and only Executive Council of which French Canada had ever approved. On the other, they knew him to be deep in negotiation with such unimpeachables as René-Edouard Caron, the popular Mayor of Quebec, Denis-Benjamin Viger and John Neilson. Once surprise and wonder had abated, however, the more discerning among them began to see more clearly that *la crise Metcalfe* turned upon different interpretations of responsible government and as the debate raged throughout Lower Canada for the next three years, Sir Charles Metcalfe's personality and motives became a permanent sign of discord.

For LaFontaine and his followers, he was "Machiavel," "tyran," "Néron," "patron de l'Orangisme," "l'ennemi du peuple," and "le destructeur de la sécurité." Aubin also worked up a few satires in *Le Fantasque* against "old squaretoes," underscoring especially the Governor's devotion to "l'Orangisme" and his inffectiveness at Council meetings. Metcalfe, unfortunately, took the satires to heart, and even lowered himself to the point of writing to Aubin and denouncing, in vain of course, his "heartless vulgarity."[16] "I will always look upon him," LaFontaine himself wrote to his colleague Robert Baldwin, "as a man who had no respect for truth, not to use a harder word. I may forgive anything but a lie."[17]

For Viger, who had taken the oath of office as Metcalfe's main French-Canadian councillor on December 13, 1843, and for his party on the other hand, the character of Sir Charles was a valuable asset. They noted how, during that very month of December when he had been betrayed and insulted by his ministers, he had continued his princely gifts to charity, and taken the first steps in the repatriation of the capital to Lower Canada. And they added a count of the French-speaking *patriote* functionaries which he had appointed or maintained in office: some judges, the clerk of the Council, the Superintendent of Education, the Speaker of the Legislative Council, etc. As *L'Aurore* described him on June 12, 1844, "Le bon, l'honnête, l'excellent Sir Charles" deserved confidence because of "la pureté des ses intentions, l'heureux naturel qu'il a pour les doctrines libérales, et ses penchans [sic] particuliers pour la belle population franco-Canadienne alliée par le sang à l'un de ses aieux." He was also to be praised for his generostiy. Indeed it seemed that never could the Governor leave a worthy cause unaided. During the first eight months of 1844, for example, he sent £200 to "un monsieur lié à l'un des officiers de Kingston et se trouvant dans l'infortune," £20 to the French edition of the *Journal of Agriculture*, £10 to the Maison de la Providence at LaPrairie, £10 to the Maison d'éducation des filles de la Baie St. Paul, £10 to the Catholic Women of Kingston, £10 to Dr.W.Nelson for a sick patient, £10 each to the Catholic churches at Frompton, St. Bernard, St. Anicet, Hingsford, and others. Nor, of course, could Viger's press ever omit strategic publication of the same. As the charities multiplied, so did its acclaim for "cet homme bienfaisant et génèreux, l'ami et le protecteur du pauvre, de l'éducation, des sciences et des arts, un homme tolérant, prodigue." *L'Aurore* on December 31, 1844, brought this type of political adulation to its logical and laughable conclusion with some hundred Metcalfe-praising LaFontaine-hating alexandrines which began:

> *Philanthrope zélé dont la noble sagesse*
> *Au bien de ce pays qui l'occupe sans cesse*
> *Voudrait nous préparer un brillant avenir*
> *Puis à faire le bien trouve son vrai plaisir*
> *Ma muse en ses accents t'offre un sincère hommage*
> *Et c'est de tous ses voeux l'expression, le gage ...*
> *Ta conduite passée est un brillant tableau*

Où le vrai se présente en son jour le plus beau
Elle exprime sans art ce que vaut la droiture,
Détruit l'injuste erreur et confond l'imposture
Démontre que ta main abat ces vils tyrans
Seuls ennemis du peuple en leurs perfides plans. . . .

As admirable as they knew him to be in private virtues, the Viger group were still more impressed by the Governor's public acts, especially the moving of the capital, and the pardon of the political exiles of the rebellions of 1837 and 1838.

Ever since their banishment, hardly a week passed without some public mention of these "compatriotes gémissant dans l'exil," as *Le Canadien* called them on November 26, 1841. Hardly a month passed without some petition for their pardon. "The French Canadians," Metcalfe reported to London, "pant for the return of their countrymen and will not be satisfied without it."[18] Immediately after LaFontaine's resignation, therefore, the Governor and Viger published the news that an individual pardon would be granted to each of the exiles who would petition for it. A group of politicians from among Viger's partisans set to work. They circulated a quantity of petitions for each one of the exiles, and began a publicity compaign to gather funds to finance their passage home. Sir Charles, of course, headed the list of subscribers – he sent a much publicized £100. Actually the monies came quickly. By the end of March, 1844, the Association proudly announced that all fifty-five of the exiles who wanted to return had been pardoned, and *L'Aurore* on February 27 underlined the moral of the whole story: "Deux choses doivent frapper tous les yeux. 1. l'empressement de Sa Majesté de se rendre au voeu si ardent de notre patrie; . . . 2. c'est grâce à la recommandation de Sir Charles Metcalfe lui-même que ce pardon a été accordé."

In a general election in 1844, LaFontaine won handsome majorities in the French ridings, but the Governor's partisans carried a slight overall majority and *la crise Metcalfe* continued in Parliament for long months to come. Sir Charles Metcalfe himself, however, reached the end of his painful Canadian career in November, 1845. He was dying of cancer, unable to open his mouth except with great pain, and blind in his right eye. On November 10, *La Minerve* reported:

Si on croit les bruits qui circulent depuis hier il parait que lord Metcalfe est dans un état de faiblesse qui ne lui permet plus de s'occuper des affaires, par suite de la diète qu'il est obligé d'observer. On assure que Son Excellence n'a pris aucune nourriture solide depuis près de quinze jours.

La Minerve, of course, could hardly wait to see him go. Indeed, it seemed almost happy to print the daily chronicle of his decline, as if the last obstacle to responsible government were rotting there before it. To the bulletins from Government House, it added such cold comfort as, for example, on October 30, "on ne peut se justifier du retard qu'on a apporté à demander un successeur à Son Excellence."

On November 23, Metcalfe invited his faithful Councillors to Monklands, his new official residence in Montreal. Sitting in the dark, his head swathed in bandages, he asked them to decide his fate. Some burst into tears. But all agreed that, on the chance of saving his life at home, he must go. On the 24th, the second anniversary of *la crise,* troops lined the road, and so, according to *La Minerve* on November 27, did "les pompiers en costume et quelques uns des Old Fellows [sic]." Behind them a vast, hushed, tender crowd, made up, perhaps of the hundreds who had personally experienced the Governor's many kindnesses. Lord Metcalfe and his Councillors rode quietly past them; he was in agony, and they were close to tears. At the wharf, he descended "soutenu par deux personnes de sa suite," and, true to type, stood dutifully to hear the short, sad civic address from the Mayor. Despite the great wound gnawing through his cheek, he answered graciously. Then, "très affecté, et sa suite aussi, il a versé des larmes et n'a pas été le seul." He boarded the *Prince Albert* to cross the river, his Councillors insistent on attending him as far as the train. One of them, Denis-Benjamin Papineau, wept all the way. "Je n'en ai pas honte," he wrote to his wife,

et je n'en aurai jamais honte. Il faut avoir connu comme j'ai été à même de le faire la douceur et l'amitié de cet homme-là, son esprit de droiture, son tact dans les affaires, son affabilité, son esprit de condescendance, sa patience, et son assiduité dans les affaires, ses précautious et son attention pour ne pas s'en laisser imposer . . . pour pouvoir apprécier la perte que fait le pays en le perdant.

At LaPrairie, after another tender parting scene, Papineau, still emotionally upset, waited to bid the last good-bye: "Je lui ai donné la main et à sa suite le dernier de tous."[19]

"Lord Metcalfe," *L'Aurore* eulogised on November 27, "emporte avec lui tous les regrets de tous les hommes bien nés et sensibles à la reconnaissance." But *La Minerve* remained unimpressed:

Quelques poignées d'or jetés à la face de tous les demandants ne doivent pas faire oublier que la bienveillance sociale n'a rien à démêler avec les devoirs attachés à l'administration de toute une province. . . . Les actes de bienfaisance annoncés journellement au son de la trompette et qui ne sont pas accompagnés d'une conduite sans reproche peuvent devenir suspects, c'est un manteau qui a couvert bien des fautes.

After bidding his last farewell to Lord Metcalfe, Denis-Benjamin Papineau rode back to the Chateau de Ramezay. There at three o'clock in the afternoon of the same day, November 26, 1845, he attended the quiet installation as interim Administrator of the Province of Lieutenant-General Charles Murray Cathcart, eleventh Baron and third Earl Cathcart. Having taken his oath, the new Administrator spoke to his Councillors in a speech, as Papineau wrote to his wife, "remplie de bon sens et de sentiment. Il veut marcher sur les traces de son estimable prédécesseur, afin de gagner par là la part d'estime si bien méritée sous ses yeux à celui dont la santé précaire avait nécessité le départ si prompt." Lord Cathcart, a tall, dark aristocrat of military bearing, had come out to Canada in June, 1845, to serve as Commander-in-Chief of the Forces. With a great number of his contemporaries of his class (and former colonial governors), he shared the distinction both of an enviable record in the Napolenonic Wars, and of having horses shot from under him at Waterloo. Now with Britain and the United States close to war over Oregon, he had been sent out to impress the North Americans with the Empire's intention to fight.

After five months as Adminstrator, Lord Cathcart received, in April, 1846, his Commission as Governor General in his own right. But the Oregon threat having passed, he was recalled at the end of the year. A kindly, unassuming man, he had throughout his life taken little interest in politics; and when not absorbed by the army, had taken to science, among other accomplishments discovering a new mineral called Greenockite after his courtesy title, Lord Greenock. He paid no more attention to politics in Canada. He was repaid in kind by the Canadians who, in turn, gave him little notice.

The French press hardly ever mentioned Cathcart except in official bulletins, and he seems to have received none of the treatment given to his predecessors; no loyal addresses and gracious responses, no flag-waving receptions, not even an occasional bit of controversy or satire. It was soon enough absorbed in discussing Metcalfe's more permanent successor, the Earl of Elgin, the man they expected would repair Metcalfe's error.

As early as September 1845, LaFontaine had written: "Lord Metcalfe est le lord Sydenham et son successeur sera le Sir Charles Bagot." Thus with his keen intuition into the political struggle he was waging, the young leader had foreseen what in fact would happen. And, on September 7, 1846, *La Minerve* announced that "le successeur" who would be "le Sir Charles Bagot" had indeed been designated. "Lord Elgin," *La Minerve* wrote, "qui fut le successeur de sir Charles Metcalfe à la Jamaique a été nommé Gouverneur-Général."

Even in the manner of his arrival, Lord Elgin imitated Bagot. While the government and people prepared to receive him, he was delayed; and when he did arrive, again like Bagot, he did not immediately side with LaFontaine.

At first the Canadian press was guarded. "Lord Elgin sera longtemps regretté," wrote the *Mélanges* in a typical comment on September 11:

par les habitants de la Jamaique, à cause de ses bonnes qualités tant privées que civiles et de plus à cause de l'aide et de l'encouragement qu'il a donnés à l'agriculture; s'il en agit ainsi, il sera sans doute bien vu de la part des cultivateurs canadiens.

And *La Minerve* added on September 14: Nous pouvons sans doute espérer que tous ceux qui auront été gouverneurs à la Jamaique ne seront par nécessairement des tyrans." But most of LaFontaine's friends expected that Lord Elgin would dissolve Parliament as soon as he arrived. One of their newspapers, *La Revue Canadienne*, wrote on September 18:

Le Conseil Exécutif est l'âme du gouvernement constitutionnel (ministère responsable); notre gouvernement est donc un corps sans âme. Nous espérons que lord Elgin va de suite lui donner la vie, en refondant son ministère.

With other politicians they prepared publicly to receive the new Governor, and enthusiasm mounted. On November 3, 1846, Lord Cathcart vacated Monklands, then on December 21 *La Minerve* reported that the political leaders had petitioned Mayor Ferrier of Montreal to "convoquer une assemblée publique pour prendre en considération la convenance d'adopter une adresse de félicitation au comte d'Elgin." They held their meeting; but on December 28 they were disappointed to read in *La Minerve* that "Son Excellence le comte d'Elgin ne doit s'embarquer que le 4 de janvier." On January 13, 1847, they met again to adopt an address of welcome composed by A.N. Morin, LaFontaine's chief lieutenant. By now, in fact, after three months of waiting, they were very anxious.

Finally on January 25, 1847, James Bruce, Eighth Earl of Elgin and Twelfth of Kincardine, stepped off the *Hibernia* in Boston Harbour to begin a progress towards Montreal every bit as brilliant as Bagot's tour of Lower Canada. A cold coming he had had of it, buffeted by Atlantic gales and suffering "les fatigues et les privations" of a three-week journey in the worst time of the year. The Mayor welcomed the new Governor at the Porte-Saint-Antoine. The banners and emblems of the different societies had hastily been erected there after the storm to offer "un coup d'oeil magnifique," *La Minerve* continued.

Après la lecture de l'adresse et la réponse, le cortège se mit en route, Son Honneur le Maire ayant pris place dans la voiture de lord Elgin. A son passage où stationnaient les différentes sociétés Son Excellence fut saluée par de brillantes acclamations et les bandes de musique jouèrent le God Save the Queen.

Then the crowds lining the streets moved in to join the procession. They roared their cheers "avec des acclamations et des applaudissements sans cesse répétés." At the Chateau de Ramezay, Son Excellence descended, and the majority of the Canadians saw him for the first time. As *La Minerve* reported on February 14:

Sa taille est au-dessous de la moyenne et il parait prendre de l'embonpoint. Quoiqu'agé que de 37 ans il parait un peu chauve et a des cheveux

et des favoris très gris, le teint brun et méridional, les traits fins et délicats,
les yeux noirs et animés, une bouche petite et indiquant la fermeté et la
décision de caractère. Sur le tout, c'est une physionomie agréable et intel-
ligente, et on le dit doué de beaucoup d'éloquence.

The new Governor definitely made a good impression. "La réponse de
lord Elgin," *La Minerve* continued:

à l'adresse des habitants de Montréal a été appréciée comme elle devait
l'être, on ne pouvait désirer rien de mieux, et le Pilot *a raison lorsqu'il dit*
que cette réponse de Son Excellence nous permet d'anticiper que lord Elgin
sera le gouverneur du peuple Canadien et non celui d'un parti. Son discours
s'adressait à toute la population du pays, à toutes les nuances d'opinion,
et personne ne peut mettre en doute la sincérité de ses paroles.

"Il faut avouer," the *Journal de Québec* concluded on February 4, "qu'il
s'annonce par de bien favorables augures."

Still, the new Governor took over a year to call the French-Canadian
leaders to office. He found that the government Metcalfe had bequeathed
to him could still command a small majority, and thus, according even to
LaFontaine's interpretation of responsible government, that it was entitled
to remain. He must accordingly wait until the general election expected at
the end of 1847 to bring the French in. Meanwhile, he set out to persuade
them of his good will. And before long, he had quite succeeded.

Schooled as he was in every grace, he charmed the Montrealers as Bagot
had done. At Monklands over the crest of Westmount, or at the Chateau
de Ramezay downtown, he impressed everyone with his elegant French,
and with the "courtesy and attention paid to every sort of visitor." In June
1847, for instance, he marked the anniversary of the Coronation by "une
brillante réception à Monklands" that according to the report in *La Minerve*
on June 24, attracted, in pouring rain, "une foule immense au point qu'il
était difficile de circuler." They had come out to be captivated by "Son Excellence en grand uniforme" and by *Madame la comtesse d'Elgin* ("On ne
pouvait s'empêcher d'admirer ses manières pleines de dignité, sa pose
gracieuse, et son aimable sourire"). Later, in July, he entertained again, this
time for the politicians; and "we were successful," he wrote, "in bringing
men of all parties together and dismissing them well pleased."[20]

In the fall of 1847, he sailed down to carry his message to the Canadiens' first-born. With the Countess and her sister Lady Alice Lambton, he
left aboard the *Montreal* on September 23, and arrived the next day in
Quebec to celebrate a triumph even greater than Bagot's memorable Saint-
Jean-Baptiste visit in 1842. "On eut dit," wrote *La Minerve* on September
27, "que la vieille capitale reprenait son rôle naturel, retrouvait son
ancienne vie." He came up to the sound of cannon and under the traditional
spruce arches, "accompagné du maire dans la voiture à quatre chevaux aux
armes de Son Excellence." The streets overflowed with joyous, cheering

Québecois who turned out in the pouring rain. In front of the Hotel du Payne the Saint societies, "munis de leurs drapeaux et de riches insignes" stood in a solid mass, "the St George's and St Jean Baptiste societies turning out together for the first time and the president of the former wearing the maple leaf, the Canadian french emblem."[21] *Leurs Excellences* appeared on the rain-drenched balcony, and, that most renowned Québecois of them all, John Neilson, President of the Saint Andrew's Society, read their loyal address. The Governor and the Québecois understood each other perfectly. Had he betrayed to them his inner thought? "What a magnificent site for a seat of government!" he later wrote to the Colonial Secretary, "How wonderful that Montreal should ever have supplanted it!" What more gracious sentiments could he have found to win this ancient, sceptered city?

Thus by tactful personal interviews and by brilliant receptions, Elgin persuaded the Canadiens that he was on their side. And when at last the results of the general election placed the Governor General in the constitutional position from which he could properly bring in the French and, as he put it, commit to their trust "the flag of Britain," he became one of their heroes. On the night LaFontaine's election was proclaimed in Place d'Armes in Montreal, it was two prominent rebels of 1837, Dr. Wolfred Nelson and George-Etienne Cartier, who proposed to the "foule très nombreuse trois *cheers* pour le Reine et trois hourras en honneur de Son Excellence le Gouverneur-Général."[22]

A year later he put the crowning touch to his conquest of the Canadiens. He reinstated the official use of their mother tongue, and did so in the grand manner: at the supreme moment of the colony's ceremonial life, the Opening of Parliament.

On January 18, 1849, amid traditional panoply, and through rows of troops stationed bright scarlet against the snowbanks, Lord Elgin slid smartly in a large sleigh down Notre-Dame Street to the Marché Saint-Anne. There, white-plumed and splendid in his dark-blue and silver tunic, he proceeded to the Red Chamber, crowded for the occasion with dark, formal-coated Councillors with their wives in bright colours. Seated under the huge canopy, he read his speech. He paused, and, his courtly diction filling the Chamber, he repeated it once over in elegant French. Thus, in one fine, royal, unprecedented gesture, he wiped out forever and for all Canadiens to hear, the last national iniquity of the Union.

As the vice-regal procession receded, old Denis-Benjamin Viger in tears exclaimed: "Que je me sens soulagé d'entendre dans ma langue les paroles du trône!" And the young journalist-M.P. Joseph Cauchon rushed from the Legislative Council to his desk in the Assembly to write out a report for the *Journal de Québec*, praising "ce fait inouie dans les fastes de notre histoire parlementaire." Another journalist, Hector Langevin, who had attended as a guest, noted proudly for his readers that "Lord Elgin prononce le Français aussi élégamment qu'un Parisien." As Lord Elgin stepped out a few minutes later into the fresh and open air, the fanfare seemed to ring out with greater sound, and, in the distance, the bells of Notre Dame proclaimed in clearer tones, perhaps, their ceremonial *God Save the Queen.*

*   *   *

Thus it was that throughout the 1840's, four British Governors, varied in character and background, led French Canada's politicians, slowly and by degrees, from avowed hatred and hostility, through discussion and respect, to open confidence, esteem, and even reverence.

Lord Sydenham, the efficient and enterprising business man who had no patience for the economically backward, misunderstood the Canadiens, and all but told them so. He earned in return their hatred and, possibly worse still, their sarcasm. Lord Metcalfe, kindly, honourable, and trained to auto-cracy, was unable to accommodate himself to changing political circum-stances. Nevertheless, he respected the French. He gave financial support to their cultural projects, recalled their loved ones from exile, and sought counsel from the most radical of their leaders; in fact he gave them every-thing except the one concession they really wanted. And they generally responded with respect, honour, friendship even; everything except the political victory the Governor worked for almost to his dying breath. Sir Charles Bagot, on the other hand, and the Earl of Elgin – diplomats both, and men of culture – gave the Canadiens the respect Metcalfe had shown, and the understanding Sydenham had refused. They received accordingly universal adulation and sincere affection. Indeed in their failures and in their achievements, the four governors showed how important it is that he who represents the Crown should understand and respect the "religion, habits, prepossessions, prejudices" of the people over whom he rules.

The successes and failures of the four governors also point to the im-portance of the ruler's personality. Lord Sydenham and Lord Metcalfe failed. But they had far more in common than their failures. Both sprang from a bourgeois liberal *milieu*, and neither had married. Their horizons were accordingly limited, for the one, to business contacts and trade agree-ments, and for the other, to colonial administration. They had courage, and were not without talent. But they devoted their qualities to long office hours rather than to the more intangible duties of inspiring loyalty. Besides, they were sick. Sydenham was gouty, impatient, and on occasion, for long weeks at a time, bedridden; Metcalfe was dying of cancer. And at no time did either give much evidence of ability in French, or even a desire to conciliate the crowds, who, even in those days, played an important part in deciding the course of politicians.

On the other hand, Sir Charles Bagot and Lord Elgin inspired tremen-dous loyalty. And they too had much in common. They were born aristo-crats, descended from kings and knights whose names shine down through mediaeval mists. By hereditary vocation, almost, they knew how to reign as well as how to rule. Both were humanists of wide culture. Bagot, a perfect man of the world and fluent in French, moved through Lower Canada conversing with *jeux d'esprit*, playfulness, and wit. Elgin, a graduate of Eton and Oxford, enjoyed a reputation for splendid oratory in two languages. Both were happily married to ladies of rank, dignity, and beauty; and both had made it an art to entertain society at a levée and to captivate a crowd in the street. They were helped in their success, of course, by the fact that they eventually conceded to the demands of the Canadiens. But in each instance, they had secured the loyalty of people and politicians before making their concessions. In fact by the attraction of their personalities, they anticipated the definition of the Crown which Her Majesty Queen Elizabeth herself would give some hundred years or so after their rule. "The Crown . . . is a personal and living bond between you and me."

Notes: The Personal and Living Bond

1. *L'Aurore des Canadas,* 2 oct. 1839.
2. *Le Fantasque,* 13 avril, 1840.
3. Private letter, June 15, 1840. Quoted in G.P.Scrope, *Memoir of Lord Sydenham,* London: John Murray, 1844.
4. Archives de l'Archevêché de Québec, Registre des lettres, 19-650.
5. P.A.C., MG 24, A 13 (Hereafter Bagot), vol. 2. Lord Seaton to Sir George Murray, September 6, 1841; Sir George Murray to Bagot, Oct. 7, 1841.
6. *Ibid.,* Parish to Bagot, Sept. 25, 1841.
7. *Ibid.; ibid.,* Westmorland to Bagot, Nov. 7, 1841.
8. AAQ, G-VII, 23. Bagot à Signay, 21 jan., 1841.
9. Bagot, vol. 7. Bagot to Stanley, Jan. 1842.
10. P.A.C., MG 24, A-32. Bagot to Grenville, Mar. 27, 1842.
11. Bagot, vol. 7. Bagot to Stanley, Mar. 26, 1842.
12. P.A.C. Papiers LaFontaine, Cartier à LaFontaine, 18 sept., 1842.
13. *ibid.,* Cherrier à LaFontaine, 1 nov., 1842.
15. Quoted in J.W.Kaye, *The Life and Correspondence of Charles, Lord Metcalfe,* London: 1858, vol. 2, p. 354.
16. *Le Fantasque,* 10 mai., 1845.
17. Toronto Public Library. Baldwin Papers, A 55. LaFontaine to Baldwin, Dec. 2, 1845.
18. C.O. 537-142. Metcalfe to Stanley, Aug. 7, 1843.
19. Archives de Québec, Collection Papineau-Bourassa. D.B. Papineau à sa femme, 27 nov., 1845.
20. Sir A.G.Doughty (ed.), *The Elgin-Grey Papers,* Ottawa: 1937, vol. 1, p. 61. Elgin to Grey, July 27, 1847.
21. *Ibid.,* Elgin to Grey, Sept. 27, 1847.
22. *La Minerve,* 17 jan., 1848.

Le Philanthrope Vattemare, le Rapprochement des "Races" et des Classes au Canada: 1840-1855

Claude Galarneau, Université Laval

De ce côté de l'Atlantique, on a coutume d'identifier la philanthropie et les philanthropes aux seuls Américains. Il en est peu qui ne puissent nommer au moins les Carnegie et les Rockefeller, et le vulgaire assimile le philanthrope au richissime financier qui a laissé des sommes fabuleuses pour le progrès des sciences, des lettres et des arts après avoir fait fortune dans les pétroles ou la banque. Au XVIIIe siècle, l'Europe des Lumières avait connu une autre espèce de philanthropes, moins célèbres par la disposition de leurs biens matériels que par la diffusion de leurs idées et de leurs systèmes de pensée. La première partie du siècle suivant a donné au monde un philanthrope d'une espèce particulière, et presque ignoré de nos jours, sauf de quelques historiens d'Europe et d'Amérique. S'il n'a pas tout à fait réussi dans ses projets grandioses, son passage à Montréal et à Québec a néanmoins suscité chez les Canadiens de 1840 un réveil marqué, et qui n'a pas été lendemains au point de vue culturel.

Fils d'un avocat parisien, Alexandre Vattemare est né à Paris le 7 novembre 1796. Peu de temps après, sa famille se retire dans la campagne normande pour s'éloigner des menaces de la révolution. Le temps des études arrivé, les Vattemare font entrer Alexandre au Séminaire de Lisieux où il commence ses études secondaires. L'élève Vattemare s'y révèle intelligent et doué, mais il exerce des dons de ventriloque au détriment de la discipline, il distrait ses camarades de façon abusive, au point que le directeur du Séminaire demande à sa mère de le retirer. Quelques années après, il s'en va à Paris pour y étudier la médecine à l'hôpital Saint-Louis, sous la direction experte de Jean-Louis Alibert, et montre de nettes aptitudes pour l'exercice de la profession. Malheureusement, il est incapable de faire taire ses instincts de comédien et il est renvoyé encore une fois à cause de ses blagues et de ses créations comiques. Rentré à l'hôpital en 1814 pour aider à soulager les cholériques, il accepte par la suite de reconduire à Berlin 300 militaires allemands qu'il avait soignés à Paris, les divertissant on ne peut mieux par ses facéties incessantes. Les Berlinois goûtent à ce point son talent qu'ils lui conseillent de faire carrière dans la ventriloquie, et un médecin de Brandebourg lui écrit une première pièce intitulée *Madame Thomas*. Le succès est immédiat; "Mr. Alexandre" le ventriloque part en tournées de représentations dans les principales villes de l'Europe centrale et septentrionale pendant cinq ans. En 1820, il rentre dans son pays pour donner quelques spectacles avant d'aller jouer en Angleterre, en Ecosse et en Irlande. Il reviendra sur le continent pour se rendre jusqu'en Russie. M. Alexandre devient célèbre dans toute l'Europe: les Anglais le considèrent comme un nouveau Garrick, les Français comme un protée, car il joue tous les personnages de ses pièces. Des écrivains, tel Walter Scott, lui dédient des poèmes, cependant que des artistes renommés lui dessinent des costumes.

Acteur choyé du public européen pendant quinze ans, Vattemare acquiert une belle fortune qu'il met souvent au service des oeuvres sociales des villes visitées. C'est ainsi qu'il participe à la fondation d'une maison de retraite à Dublin. Mais en plus d'être un comédien généreux, Vattemare est aussi un homme cultivé. Par goût autant que par besoin d'adapter ses comédies aux styles des pays visités, il étudie dans les cabinets, les collections, les bibliothèques, les musées des villes et les galeries des châteaux princiers. Il remarque en passant les lacunes de ces trésors en même temps que les exemplaires nombreux des mêmes livres. C'est alors qu'il lui vient à l'idée de proposer aux possesseurs des collections et aux conservateurs des dépôts d'échanger leurs doubles. Vers 1830, Vattemare est parvenu à obtenir plus de 150 listes de doubles et il en arrive à définir l'utilité et la possibilité des échanges entre collections et bibliothèques, échanges auxquels il participait d'ailleurs depuis 1825. Pendant des années, M. Alexandre joue ses comédies pendant que Vattemare se fait le "missionnaire des échanges," que les souverains, les intellectuels, les hommes politiques et la presse l'accueillent avec bienveillance, aussi longtemps tout au moins que sa société européenne des échanges demeure une affaire privée qu'il soutient de son argent.[1]

Tous les gouvernements de l'Europe répondent avec enthousiasme à son projet d'établissement d'un système général d'échange, "traité pacifique qui ne devait agiter ni les passions ni les intérêts," comme il le dira à Québec.[2] Empereurs, rois, cardinaux, évêques, gouvernements le félicitent. Et les échanges suivent les encouragements entre Moscou, Lisbonne, Madrid,

Copenhague, Rome et Constantinople. Il reste à convaincre les deux grands, l'Angleterre et la France. Vattemare adresse alors une pétition aux Communes anglaises, que présente le Ministre du Commerce, Poulett Thomson, futur gouverneur du Canada. La reine Victoria entérine le projet et offre ses félicitations personnelles à Vattemare.[3]

A Paris, le missionnaire des échanges écrit à la fin de 1835 au Ministre des Affaires Etrangères et au Ministre de l'Instruction Publique pendant que le *Journal général de l'Instruction publique* du 31 décembre fait l'éloge de son système. Le Ministre de l'Instruction Publique lui répond que l'administration et les deux Chambres ont accueilli son projet avec empressement.[4] Et Vattemare affirmera à Québec qu'à la suite de l'appel du ministre "plus de 600,000 volumes provenant des doubles existant dans nos 286 bibliothèques publiques furent envoyés à Paris en un dépôt central, qui fut lui-même tellement encombré en moins de six mois, que le ministre fut obligé d'inviter les bibliothécaires à suspendre leurs envois."[5]

Si les échanges vont bon train et les lettres d'encouragement affluent, l'argent n'arrive pas aussi vite à Vattemare, qui demande aux Chambres françaises en 1839 de voter une loi pour autoriser les échanges entre la France et les autres pays.[6] Il ne semble pas que la loi ait été votée, et c'est alors que des Français – dont La Fayette – et des Américains – dont le général Cass – le pressent d'aller visiter les Etats-Unis.[7] Vattemare n'est pas lent à se décider, convaincu qu'il est des avantages universels de son plan. Il s'embarque donc le 20 septembre 1839 pour un voyage de dix-neuf mois, qui ne devait en compter que trois au départ. Arrivé en novembre à New York, M. Alexandre reprend son rôle de ventriloque en soirée, tandis que Vattemare établit des contacts pendant le jour. Très vite d'ailleurs, M. Alexandre laisse la place à Vattemare et à la diffusion de son système.

Au mois de décembre, alors qu'on discute au Congrès du sort qu'on fera au legs de James Smithson, philanthrope anglais qui a laissé aux Etats-Unis une fortune de 100,000 livres sterling pour la diffusion des connaissances parmi les hommes, Vattemare présente un mémoire pour faire accepter son système international d'échange de livres, de spécimens des sciences naturelles et d'objets d'art. Il prend soin d'expliquer que son projet ne repose sur aucun motif de profit personnel et que, bien au contraire, il n'a en vue que le rapprochement des races et des nations. Le Congrès répond en juin 1840 par la voie du comité de la bibliothèque que le plan de Vattemare est désirable et il autorise le Conservateur à échanger des livres et des documents ainsi qu'à fournir des exemplaires de chaque volume de documents imprimés par les Chambres américaines. Vattemare était d'ailleurs venu à Washington plaider sa cause auprès des membres du Congrès, y déployant un zèle sans limite et utilisant tout le charme de sa personnalité. Sa mission accomplie à Washington, Vattemare entreprend de visiter les

Etats américains auxquels il présente inlassablement son système d'échange. Partout il est reçu avec un enthousiasme extraordinaire. La Louisiane vote une somme de $3000 pour échanger des livres avec les bibliothèques d'Europe et pour établir en Louisiane même un musée et une bibliothèque. Le Maryland et le Maine acceptent d'imprimer cinquante exemplaires de leurs documents législatifs pour les échanger et le Maine vote une somme de $1000 pour les dépenses du système.

Durant son séjour aux Etats-Unis, Vattemare ne se dévoue pas seulement à établir son plan d'échange. Observant que la jeune Amérique a un immense besoin de musées et de bibliothèques pour toutes les classes sociales, il déploie autant d'énergie à susciter la création de bibliothèques locales, faisant particulièrement appel aux jeunes et aux femmes pour la mise sur pied de ces institutions qui seraient ouvertes gratuitement à tous et surtout à la jeunesse pauvre. C'est à Boston qu'en avril 1841, à la fin de son voyage en Amérique, il récoltera son succès le plus éclatant. Il faut dire que Vattemare venait de passer quatre mois à Montréal et à Québec, soit de novembre 1840 à mars 1841, et qu'il avait connu une réussite extraordinaire. Il arrive donc à Boston fort de cette expérience et se met en frais de convaincre les hommes les plus représentatifs et les jeunes Bostoniens de l'importance pour la ville de se donner une bibliothèque. La décision est prise, mais il faudra attendre plusieurs années avant que la bibliothèque ne soit construite, années au cours desquelles Vattemare enverra des livres et écrira des lettres aux Bostoniens. L'édifice est terminé en 1858 et la Boston Public Library est fière de compter parmi ses fondateurs le philanthrope français.[8]

*   *   *

C'est à l'automne 1840 qu'Alexandre Vattemare s'était rendu au Bas-Canada. Etait-ce parce qu'il avait appris que des Français s'y trouvaient encore ou simplement parce que notre pays fait partie de l'Amérique? Quoiqu'il en soit il arrivait à un moment extrêmement pénible de l'histoire des Canadiens français. Pendant cinq ans en effet, nos compatriotes avaient vécu dans un véritable climat d'insurrection et "d'antibritannisme farouche." La Chambre d'Assemblée refusait de voter les crédits pour l'administration de la Province pendant que les 92 résolutions cristallisaient la résistance de la population. Les partisans de Papineau allaient jusqu'à parler d'indépendance. L'exaspération de la Chambre, le déchaînement de la presse et la violence verbale des patriotes avaient abouti aux soulèvements de 1837-1838. L'échec de ces émeutes, la répression féroce effectuée par les troupes anglaises autour de Montréal, les exécutions, les déportations, la haine distillée par la presse de langue anglaise à l'égard des Canadiens français, la suspension de la Constitution de 1791, l'Acte d'Union des deux Canadas, tout cela avait abattu le pays, divisé les deux groupes ethniques, et les

Canadiens français eux-mêmes. Monseigneur de Forbin-Janson, arrivé à Montréal en octobre 1840, avait d'ailleurs commencé à ranimer les Canadiens français par l'éloquence de sa prédication.[9] Et avec la venue de Vattemare au début de novembre suivant, on est fondé à penser que ce sont des Français qui aidèrent les Canadiens français à se ressaisir. La première trace de l'arrivée de Vattemare à Montréal se trouve dans *l'Aurore des Canadas* du 10 novembre, qui annonce le projet du grand philanthrope pour établir un commerce fraternel entre les gouvernements, les sociétés, les institutions littéraires de toutes les nations au moyen d'échange de livres et de produits de toutes espèces. Le coup d'envoi de la presse en faveur de Vattemare est tout de suite marqué au coin du rapprochement entre les hommes: c'est un plan "sublime" que celui de Vattemare, qui veut établir la fraternité entre les nations, commente le journal. Dix jours après, le même journal communique à ses lecteurs que l'infatigable philanthrope est encore en ville, qu'il a fait des progrès considérables auprès des autorités et des institutions, mais qu'il a besoin du concours de la partie éclairée du peuple, étant donné qu'il travaille pour nous et non pour lui-même. Comme Vattemare tiendra sous peu une assemblée pour expliquer au public les buts de sa mission, le journal espère que les gens de toute croyance et de toute couleur politique s'y rendront: "Rencontrons-nous une fois en frères au temple d'Apollon."[10]

Vattemare avait écrit à Mgr Bourget, l'évêque de Montréal, ou l'avait rencontré, pour solliciter son encouragement et lui avait sans doute montré, comme il l'avait fait aux Etats-Unis, quelques-unes des 2000 lettres que les Européens lui avaient écrites, entre autres celles de Mgr de Forbin-Janson et de l'archevêque de Paris en 1836. Toujours est-il que Mgr Bourget lui répond le 23 novembre dans ces termes: "J'ai toujours considéré le genre humain comme ne formant qu'un même corps, qui a pour membre toutes les nations du globe, et pour âme la divine Providence. . . . Toute institution qui tendra à cimenter une union aussi parfaite sera donc à mes yeux une oeuvre éminemment utile. . . ." Mgr Bourget dit à Vattemare toute son admiration pour son plan d'échange et espère qu'il s'assurera des concours empressés. "Ce sont, du moins, les sentiments qui animent à votre égard l'évêque de Montréal et son clergé."[11]

Le concours souhaité commence d'ailleurs à se faire sentir. Denis-Benjamin Viger, "son hôte canadien," a invité l'élite de la société montréalaise à admirer l'*Album cosmopolite*, recueil de reproductions d'autographes que Vattemare avait édité en Europe et dont les profits de la vente alimentaient la caisse de l'Agence européenne des échanges.[12] Joseph-Guillaume Barthe décrit sa rencontre avec Vattemare en termes dithyrambiques: "Je me féliciterai toute ma vie d'avoir vu et entendu d'aussi près l'illustre étranger qui se fait le citoyen de l'Univers en adoptant le monde pour patrie. Son plan me paraît réalisable et est la plus merveilleuse conception du génie inspiré par le plus saint philanthropisme. . . . Ce système a de sublimes et miraculeuses beautés. . . . M. Vattemare s'est sacré d'un sacerdoce universel. . . ."[13] Le 27 novembre, l'*Aurore des Canadas* se dit flatté de voir que les citoyens ont oublié leurs dissensions politiques pour se rencontrer au temple de la science. Le 15 décembre, le journal reproduit les lettres de trois notables de Montréal qui ne ménagent pas leurs encouragements et leur admiration pour le plan Vattemare, lettres publiées par la *Gazette de Montréal*: la première est celle de Mgr Bourget, que l'on connaît déjà, la seconde, de Charles Mondelet et la dernière, de Denis-Benjamin Viger.

L'honorable Poulett Thomson, on le sait, avait présenté le projet Vattemare aux Communes britanniques alors qu'il était Ministre du Commerce. Il eût été étonnant que, devenu gouverneur général du Canada, avec le titre de Lord Sydenham, et dans la conjoncture où se trouvait le pays, le représentant de la Reine lui refusât son patronage. Le gouverneur renouvela son admiration à Vattemare dans sa lettre du 13 décembre. Mais Sydenham, qui autrefois ne voyait dans le plan Vattemare qu'un moyen d'échange des richesses littéraires, lui attribue maintenant une fin plus haute: "un but encore plus noble et plus utile: vous servir du terrain neutre des sciences et des arts pour faire taire les haines de race ou de parti, et unir, par un lien commun, les hommes estimables que des différences politiques ou personnelles ont trop longtemps séparés."[14] Le 19 décembre, Sydenham fait écrire à Vattemare par le secrétaire T.W. Murdock qu'il met à sa disposition "un exemplaire complet des journaux du Conseil législatif et de la Chambre d'Assemblée de cette province, de même que tout autre document public dont il aurait le double," livres qui doivent être donnés aux Chambres françaises. En échange, il espère que la France donnera les documents de son gouvernement. Et Murdock termine sa lettre ainsi: "La commune origine des lois de ce pays et du Bas-Canada ainsi que la similitude du langage existant entre les Français et une grande partie des habitants de cette province, rendront un tel échange intéressant et avantageux."[15] Enfin, les membres du Conseil spécial approuvèrent le projet.[16] De sorte que les autorités civiles et religieuses apportèrent leur concours empressé comme la presse et les chefs de la société montréalaise.[17]

Ce qui encourage Vattemare à poursuive son travail avec une énergie renouvelée. A la mi-décembre, son système d'échange ayant été accepté, il conçoit un projet particulier, semblable à ceux qu'il avait présentés aux villes américaines: c'est la création à Montréal d'un Institut qui réunirait les principales sociétés déjà existantes, telles que la Société d'histoire naturelle, l'Institut des Artisans et la Bibliothèque publique. Ces organismes qui fonctionnent séparément seraient beaucoup plus efficaces en réunissant leurs collections sous un même toit et en se groupant dans un seul Institut.[18] La construction d'un édifice exige cependant une forte somme d'argent qu'il apparaissait sans doute difficile de trouver. Vattemare propose alors à ses supporters de Montréal de demander l'aide financière des pouvoirs publics pour bâtir une grande maison qui logerait en même temps l'Hôtel de Ville, la Bourse et le Bureau des Postes, institutions qui attendent encore une maison digne d'elles, et l'Institut. Le Bureau du Commerce prend l'initiative de présenter une pétition en ce sens au Conseil de ville, assurant que c'est l'intérêt de toute la société qui est en jeu et qu'il y va de l'honneur de la ville que les efforts de Vattemare soient couronnés de succès. "Rien au monde ne relèvera davantage le caractère moral du pays, et rien ne facilitera davantage, l'opération d'un système d'éducation pour toutes les classes de la société, que l'établissement d'un Institut National. . . ."[19] L'édifice compterait un rez-de-chaussée et quatre étages: la salle de conférences au rez-de-chaussée, la Bourse, le Bureau des Postes et la Maison de la Trinité au premier étage, l'Hôtel de Ville et ses services au deuxième, la bibliothèque et la salle des arts au troisième et, au quatrième, le musée.

Comme il y avait nécessairement un certain nombre de personnes qui ne comprenaient pas très bien les plans de Vattemare ou qui se méfiaient de tous ces projets soudainement présentés, un correspondant du *Montreal Herald* avait expliqué très clairement le système d'échange et la création de l'Institut, en soulignant que le public aurait accès libre et gratuit à l'Institut, jouirait de tous ces avantages sans qu'il ne lui en coûte rien et que ce n'est certes pas Vattemare qui profiterait de tout cela. Ce philanthrope étant venu nous tirer de notre assoupissement, le *Herald* demande que chacun travaille dans la mesure de ses moyens au lieu de mettre les bâtons dans les roues.[20] L'éditorialiste de l'*Aurore des Canadas* assure pour sa part que l'on n'a rien à craindre puisque les plus grands hommes ont témoigné leur accord à Vattemare par lettres, comme Lamartine, Lamennais, Lafitte, Washington Irving et le Président des Etats-Unis.[21] La presse prie instamment le public de se rendre à la "Chambre des Nouvelles" pour signer la pétition du Bureau du Commerce, qui est enfin présentée au Conseil de ville le 7 janvier et transmise pour étude à un comité de sept membres, comprenant MM. Ferrie, de Bleury, Guy, Dunscomb, Philipps, Molson et Redpath.[22] Le comité rend un avis favorable au Conseil de ville, qui adopte le projet du Bureau du Commerce le 16 janvier et présente un mémoire au gouverneur général deux jours après pour obtenir les moyens financiers nécessaires à la construction de l'édifice public. Le mémoire, après avoir exposé l'essentiel du plan Vattemare, demande au gouverneur et au Conseil spécial de permettre à la ville de Montréal par une loi d'emprunter la somme de 50,000 livres sterling.[23] Le 22 janvier, Sydenham fait répondre par le secrétaire Murdock qu'il accepte la demande du maire et qu'il présentera un projet de loi au Conseil spécial à cette fin.[24] L'affaire est vite apportée devant le Conseil spécial qui promulgue le 6 février une *Ordonnance pour autoriser et pour mettre la Corporation de la Cité de Montréal en état d'ériger un Edifice Public dans la dite Cité, pour certains objets*.[25] Le préambule de la loi expose le plan de la ville en spécifiant que c'est le projet de M. Alexandre Vattemare et il autorise la ville à emprunter une somme de 50,000 livres, tel que demandé. Plusieurs paragraphes établissent ensuite la situation de l'Institut: les trois sociétés seront placées sous le contrôle des autorités municipales, pourront céder tous leurs biens mobiliers et immobiliers à la ville et se réuniront par acte notarié sous le nom de "l'Institut de Littérature, des Sciences et des Arts, à Montréal." La bibliothèque publique et le musée seront sous l'autorité du dit Institut et ouverts librement à tous et une somme annuelle sera affectée à l'achat de livres et autres objets pour la bibliothèque et le musée.

Pendant ce temps, Vattemare et ses amis font des démarches pour atteindre le plus large public possible. Le 22 janvier, une grande assemblée est tenue à l'hôtel de John Donegani, rue Saint-François-Xavier. L'assistance élit Charles Mondelet comme président et Romuald Cherrier comme secrétaire, et Mondelet explique le plan Vattemare en insistant sur les avantages qu'il présente pour l'éducation populaire et fait un appel pressant à la jeunesse. Vattemare arrive à ce moment et rend compte de l'assemblée qui a eu lieu la veille chez les citoyens anglais de Montréal, qui ont "donné 9 hourras pour les Canadiens d'origine française." Les Canadiens français rendent la politesse aussitôt et l'assemblée propose qu'une souscription soit faite en argent et en livres en faveur de l'Institut, puis vote des remerciements à Vattemare, au Conseil de ville et au gouverneur général. Les jeunes gens proposent enfin qu'une messe solennelle soit chantée pour couronner le tout,[26] ce qui est fait le 28 janvier à l'église paroissiale.

Au cours de ses trois mois à Montréal, Vattemare n'avait pas oublié M. Alexandre. Car l'exercice de son métier de comédien lui fournissait l'occasion d'attirer le public et de se faire connaître. Il commence ses représentations le 21 décembre 1840 au Théâtre Royal, alors qu'il interprète en anglais les *Ruses de Nicolas*, qui lui valent un succès complet devant une salle comble. Il donne son premier spectacle en français le 4 janvier au même théâtre et joue l'*Aubergiste de Calais* ou *Un pour Sept*, pièce qui comprend sept personnages, tous interprétés par le protée Alexandre. Il donne encore quatre représentations, ajoutant le *Diable boiteux* aux deux pièces précédentes.[27] Après sa dernière apparition au Théâtre Royal, l'*Aurore des Canadas*, que a si bien défendu la cause du philanthrope, annonce à ses lecteurs que M. Alexandre est sur le point de s'en aller à Québec avec M. Vattemare, se demandant qui de l'artiste admirable ou du philanthrope sublime on regrettera le plus.[28]

*   *   *

Après le succès remporté à Montréal, il était à prévoir que Québec n'allait pas demeurer en reste. Un journal de cette ville avait pourtant accueilli les démarches de Vattemare avec un brin de scepticisme sinon de moqueries. Il est vrai que celles-ci s'adressaient plus au gouverneur général qu'à Vattemare et qu'elles venaient de Napoléon Aubin, rédacteur-propriétaire du *Fantasque*, journal humoristique. Aubin, suisse-français établi à

Québec depuis 1835, avait épousé la cause des Canadiens français et malmenait avec une verve endiablée le parti anglais. Dans la livraison du 28 décembre, il accuse les journaux de Montréal d'avoir pris prétexte d'une lettre adressée en français par le gouverneur à Vattemare pour se répandre en pures flagorneries, et il termine son article ainsi: "Nous louons certainement son excellence de l'aide qu'elle promet d'accorder à la noble entreprise du philantrope [sic] cosmopolite." Dix jours après, Aubin rapporte que les journaux de Montréal retentissent des éloges de Vattemare et constate avec satisfaction que le gouverneur a déjà donné une collection des lois du Canada à "Mr le zélé philantrope." Et, sur deux pages, Aubin s'amuse follement à décrire les échanges que la France et le Canada pourraient faire comme par exemple un coq gaulois pour un poulet accompagné d'oies et de dindons, le poulet étant Poulett Thomson.[29] Le 29 janvier, le *Canadien* reproduit le reportage que l'*Aurore des Canadas* avait fait de la grande assemblée publique de Montréal. Le lendemain, c'est au tour du *Journal des Etudiants*, que venait de fonder F.X.Garneau,[30] de faire état de l'assemblée et la *Gazette de Québec* en fait autant.

Lorsque Vattemare arrive à Québec, le *Fantasque* le salue d'une façon élogieuse: "Mr. Vattemare, par la seule intervention de son système et l'exposé de ses vues toutes philantropiques, est parvenu à créer chez les deux populations de Montréal une noble émulation vers la science et une unité d'action sur les moyens de la propager. Il a opéré un rapprochement que jusqu'ici nul n'aurait espéré. . . . Le Canada demande véritablement une régénération, les querelles et les jalousies de races ne sont plus de notre siècle. . . ."[31] Aubin ne manque pas d'avertir que le philanthrope a amené avec lui l'inimitable M. Alexandre et souhaite que Québec les accueille aussi bien que Montréal l'a su faire. On voit que l'attitude d'Aubin a nettement changé envers Vattemare, qui s'est d'ailleurs mis au travail sans tarder, fort de l'expérience réussie en trois mois à Montréal. Dès le 8 février, le *Canadien* annonce que Vattemare tente de réunir en un seul Institut la Société Littéraire et Historique, L'Institut des Artisans et la Bibliothèque publique de Québec. Le même jour, *Le Fantasque* consacre quatre pages de son numéro à décrire le système d'échange et le plan de création de l'Institut. Aubin prend soin d'observer que ce système exige la coopération de tous les membres de la société puisqu'il doit servir à la "masse de la population." L'Institut comprendrait une bibliothèque ouverte à tous, un musée d'histoire naturelle, une galerie de tableaux qui servirait en même temps d'école de dessin et de peinture, une salle d'exposition pour les produits des artisans, un amphithéâtre et un cabinet de physique pour l'instruction populaire. On pourrait même facilement instituer à peu de frais, ajoute Aubin, des chaires spéciales de droit et de science médicale pour les élèves qui se consacrent à l'étude exclusive et pratique des hautes professions; puis on pourrait engager les professeurs à donner des cours publics plus superficiels sur les branches convenant à la généralité, telles que la physique et la chimie.

Ce projet exige des moyens financiers importants, en vient à dire Aubin, mais on peut les trouver de deux façons à la fois; d'une part, on emprunterait 50,000 livres sterling à intérêt légal et remboursable en vingt ans, emprunt effectué par la corporation municipale; d'autre part, on ferait une souscription publique établie à une piastre par année par homme de vingt ans. Et Aubin insiste de nouveau pour dire qu'on ne peut s'en remettre aux seuls riches puisque le but "est d'exiter chez toutes les classes un amour pour l'instruction en tout genre et de mettre chacun à portée de la satisfaire. Non! il faut que le temple des sciences doive son origine à l'égalité pour qu'on y trouve l'égalité; il faut que le pauvre, qui a le plus besoin d'instruction, puisse y entrer tête levée . . . il faut que l'humble artisan dise à son fils en le conduisant à l'Institut Vattemare: sois ici chez toi. . . ." L'augmentation des collections se fera enfin par le système d'échange et par les dons des particuliers. Voilà ce que nous avons compris de l'exposé de M. Vattemare, de dire Aubin en terminant, et que le public et la municipalité rivalisent de zèle avec Montréal et les principales villes des Etats-Unis.

Alors que le *Fantasque* met surtout l'accent sur le rapprochement des classes et sur l'éducation populaire, la *Gazette de Québec* insiste sur le rapprochement des races en faisant l'éloge de Vattemare, qui, grâce aux arts et aux sciences, a réussi à rapprocher des partis de Montréal séparés par la haine et les préjugés.[32] Il semble par ailleurs que la tâche de réunir les trois sociétés ne soit pas chose facile. La Société Littéraire et Historique de Québec veut bien quant à elle emboîter le pas à Vattemare, mais elle tient à garder son caractère particulier, d'autant plus qu'elle ne peut disposer de ses biens sans l'intervention de la Législature, puisqu'elle détient une charte de la Chambre d'Assemblée, comme l'explique William Bristow, secrétaire-archiviste de la Société.[33] Comme à Montréal, les autorités religieuses de Québec appuient, bien entendu, le projet dans une lettre à Vattemare publiée dans la *Gazette de Québec* du 9 février. Et au cours de la quinzaine suivante, c'est M. Alexandre qui intervient à la demande des notables de la ville pour divertir la population. Il donne trois représentations au Théâtre Royal et une au Séminaire de Québec pour les élèves de la maison.

Or le temps passe et les journaux s'inquiètent. le *Fantasque* écrit qu' "un sentiment irrésistible de défiance envers les intentions de Mr Vattemare"[34] existe à Québec et que les sociétés sur lesquelles Vattemare comptait hésitent encore. Aubin fait alors une suggestion que les autres vont tout de suite accepter et encourager, c'est l'utilisation du Collège des Jésuites pour loger l'Institut Vattemare – vieille réclamation que celle-là, puisque depuis trois quarts de siècle la population de Québec demande inlassablement l'affectation du Collège à l'éducation, alors qu'il sert de caserne aux troupes anglaises depuis 1759 – la *Gazette de Québec* suggère pour sa part que le public prenne l'affaire en mains étant donné l'inertie des sociétés scientifiques.[35] Le 24 février, une réunion de notables, qu'Aubin qualifie de "spontanée," a lieu au cours de laquelle les participants décident de convoquer une "assemblée générale de jeunes gens de toutes les classes, les classes ouvrières en particulier, favorables à l'avancement de l'éducation."[36] La convocation compte cinquante-six signatures dont quinze sont celles de citoyens de langue anglaise. Parmi les Canadiens de langue française, on relève les noms des peintres A. Plamondon et Théophile Hamel, des journalistes J. Cauchon, F. Eventurelle, Etienne Parent et N. Aubin. Le surlendemain, une assemblée groupant plus de 1500 personnes se tient dans la grande salle de la Chambre d'Assemblée. N. Aubin préside et expose le projet de l'Institut Vattemare pendant que Augustin-Norbert Morin fait la même chose en anglais. Les orateurs insistent sur le retour du Collège des Jésuites à l'éducation et un comité de seize membres est formé pour recueillir des signatures. Les jeunes gens décident qu'une autre assemblée aura lieu le 2 mars, et l'on fait un appel pressant aux femmes.

La population de Québec répond avec enthousiasme et deux à trois mille personnes viennent à l'assemblée, présidée par le maire Caron. Les principales résolutions adoptées demandent que le Conseil de ville prenne les mesures nécessaires à l'application du plan d'échange et de l'Institut Vattemare et que l'Institut ne soit pas seulement un musée mais un centre d'enseignement gratuit pour les classes peu fortunées, hors les heures de travail.[37] Le clou de la soirée fut certes le discours d'Alexandre Vattemare, que les journaux rapportent au texte du 5 au 9 mars, allocution où Vattemare raconte son odyssée d'un quart de siècle en Europe au cours de laquelle il a visité les bibliothèques et les musées, donnant force précisions sur les doubles de collection, faisant état des témoignages écrits reçus de tous les grands d'Europe et d'Amérique et enfin des résultats du système d'échange. C'est le docteur Bardy qui remercie les femmes qui ont répondu à l'invitation et "la jeunesse qui nous avait donné l'élan dans cette noble entreprise." Parmi les autres interventions, il faut signaler celles de A.-N. Morin et de John Neilson qui insistent une fois de plus sur le rapprochement des races par le plan Vattemare et font observer curieusement que si l'Amérique doit tout à l'Europe, le nouveau continent devra peut-être un jour sauver la civilisation européenne d'une conflagration terrible.[38]

Le Conseil de ville n'avait pas été insensible aux appels des citoyens et s'était réuni en séance spéciale le 28 février. Il se déclare heureux que les trois sociétés de Québec mettent leurs collections au service du public dès qu'on aura des locaux disponibles et promet d'apporter son aide.[39] Le 8 mars, le Conseil reçoit le rapport de ses délégués auprès des trois sociétés au sujet du plan Vattemare et le 10, l'étude du rapport est renvoyée à une séance ultérieure, c'est-à-dire aux calendes grecques.[40]

Vattemare quitte Québec le 5 mars pour Boston, remercié chaleureusement par le maire de Québec au nom "de toutes les classes de notre société."[41] Le philanthrope a fait ses adieux aux Canadiens en termes non équivoques. Il dit en substance que ses espoirs ne furent nulle part plus complètement réalisés qu'au Canada: "Je vis chez lui, plus peut-être que partout ailleurs, le feu sacré et la soif des lumières." Après avoir remercié les évêques, le gouverneur général, les Conseils de ville, les sociétés, les membres du Conseil spécial et les citoyens qui ont travaillé avec lui, Vattemare lance un ultime appel aux Canadiens: "Que les habitants de Montréal et de Québec daignent se rappeler toujours les moments que nous passâmes ensemble et qui seront toujours si chers à mon coeur; c'est au nom des engagements qu'ils prirent . . . de s'unir pour travailler ensemble à la régénération intellectuelle de leur patrie, que je les supplie de tenir leurs mutuelle promesses, d'oublier noblement de malheureux préjugés issus de l'ignorance et de l'égoïsme, de confondre leur zèle."[42]

"Le locomotif de la civilisation universelle" parti, comme l'avait appelé Lamartine, il fallait mettre sur pied l'Institut Vattemare. Le 11 mars, un comité général est formé sous la présidence de John Neilson et un sous-comité est désigné pour préparer un plan et rédiger une constitution et des règlements, sous-comité qui comprend neuf membres, dont cinq de langue française: les deux cultes sont représentés par un ministre protestant et un prêtre catholique. Une souscription est faite séance tenante parmi les quatre-vingt-trois membres du comité général pour défrayer les dépenses des réunions à venir.[43] Le comité général comprenait évidemment les plus grands noms de Québec.

Pendant ce temps, Vattemare travaillait à établir son système à Boston, sans oublier toutefois ses amis canadiens. Il écrit à Aubin le 28 avril et le prie de dire que plus il s'éloigne du Canada, plus son estime et son attachement grandissent pour les Canadiens, qu'il considère "avec orgueil comme ses compatriotes." Il demande toutefois à la jeunesse des deux races de ne pas s'en tenir aux applaudissements, car cet enthousiasme tournerait à sa honte si elle n'allait pas plus loin.[44] Vattemare semble avoir pressenti l'inconstance des Québécois puisque le *Fantasque* tance l'inaction du sous-comité le 31 mai et rappelle à la jeunesse le 8 juillet que rien n'a encore été accompli pour donner suite au plan Vattemare. Le 8 septembre, le *Canadien* reproduit un article de la *Gazette de France* qui relate le voyage de Vattemare en Amérique, signalant les assemblées extraordinaires qu'il avait réunies à Montréal et le "zèle des catholiques de l'union américaine en faveur de l'éducation des classes ouvrières." Et l'affaire fut apparemment oubliée.

*　　*　　*

On peut penser que A. Fauteux n'a pas eu tort de juger comme il l'a fait le séjour de Vattemare: "Ce qui est certain," écrit-il, "c'est que jamais peut-être aucun étranger, de passage à Montréal, ne souleva autant d'enthousiasme que ce singulier rêveur. . . . De tout ce bruit, il ne resta rien, rien, pas même le souvenir. Jamais l'on n'aura vu feu de paille s'éteindre avec plus de promptitude et d'aussi complète façon."[45] En ce qui concerne l'enthousiasme soulevé par Vattemare, on ne saurait mieux dire. Quant à considérer son passage comme un feu de paille, c'est à voir. Il est entendu que les mesures pour la création d'un Institut National et les projets acceptés par le Conseil spécial et le gouverneur général pour la construction d'un Hôtel de Ville ont fait long feu et que le projet de Québec a sombré avant même que d'arriver à terme. La fin d'un si beau succès peut en être imputée à l'apathie de la population, comme l'écrira le *Canadien*;[46] l'on peut croire encore que les intérêts personnels ou institutionnels ont favorisé l'échec de Vattemare, les petites sociétés ayant eu peur de perdre leur spécificité, selon le *Morning Chronicle* du 4 mai 1853.

Il y a là quelques éléments d'explication. Mais il faut faire de nouveau appel à la conjoncture politique de la fin de l'hiver 1841 pour rendre compte de cet échec. Le 10 février 1841, Sydenham proclamait le régime de l'Union des Canadas et le 19 février, les élections étaient annoncées. Le Conseil spécial était enterré et les mesures qu'il avait votées s'en allaient avec lui. Les électeurs des faubourgs de Québec se voyaient enlever le droit de vote, les collèges électoraux étaient découpés de façon arbitraire. Bref, les Canadiens se retrouvaient en pleine crise électorale et les luttes politiques reprenaient toute l'attention du public. Si l'échec paraît certain en 1841, il n'a été que momentané. Par son influence, Vattemare a réveillé la population, il a effectivement réussi à rapprocher les groupes antagonistes, mobilisant les autorités politiques, le clergé catholique et protestant, les sociétés littéraires et scientifiques, les notables, les jeunes gens et les femmes. L'enthousiasme avait été si vif que F.-X. Garneau, qui publiait un hebdomadaire depuis le 12 décembre 1840, appela son journal *l'Institut,* alors qu'il l'avait d'abord nommé *Journal des Etudiants,* à partir du 7 mars 1841, comme il s'en explique dans un éditorial de ce numéro. M. Alexandre avait encore diverti les amateurs de théâtre avec des spectacles de qualité, ce qui n'était pas à dédaigner. Vattemare ne repartait pas non plus les mains vides, tant s'en faut, puisqu'il emportait aux Chambres françaises des caisses de livres donnés par Lord Sydenham.

D'autre part, si l'Institut Vattemare n'a pu prendre vie en 1841, l'idée d'un tel organisme a fait son chemin, si bien qu'en 1844, il vient au monde sous le nom d'Institut canadien. Le nom, les buts et l'activité de l'Institut canadien indiquent l'influence directe de Vattemare. Cet Institut veut rassembler les hommes des deux langues, établir des succursales dans les villes de la province avec des bibliothèques publiques et devenir une maison d'enseignement de qualité supérieure, toutes choses que l'Institut canadien a réalisées.[47] Et lorsque Vattemare manifeste l'intention de revenir au Canada lors de son second voyage en Amérique et 1847, la *Minerve* ne

manque pas de lui attribuer la paternité de l'Institut canadien: "M. Vattemare ne verra pas avec une légère satisfaction les progrès que ses idées ont
faits parmi nous, depuis sa dernière visite en Canada. . . . L'Institut canadien, dont M. Vattemare est membre honoraire, a rempli une partie du
vaste plan, dont ce monsieur avait donné l'idée à Montréal en 1839. La
bibliothèque de cet établissement, formée de dons volontaires des citoyens,
renferme déjà près de 1000 volumes, et promet de s'augmenter de jour en
jour."[48] Fauteux n'a pas aperçu cela et ni lui ni personne d'autre ne semble
avoir opéré le rapprochement et saisi le lien entre l'Institut Vattemare et
l'Institut canadien. D'autres phénomènes culturels peuvent être attribués à
l'influence de Vattemare à quelques années de distance, tel que le voyage
de Joseph-Guillaume Barthe, qui va en France en 1853-1855 dans le but
avoué d'affilier l'Institut canadien à l'Institut de France. Signalons enfin
que J. Huston, F.-X. Garneau et G.-B. Faribault sont demeurés en relations épistolaires avec Vattemare.[49]

Le plan d'échange n'est pas davantage demeuré sans résultat. Au
premier don que Sydenham avait fait à Vattemare pour les Chambres françaises en 1841, Faribault en avait ajouté un second en octobre 1846, qui
comprenait 300 volumes de documents imprimés de la Législature et de
la Société Littéraire et Historique de Québec. En retour, la France de
Louis-Philippe remet à Vattemare, qui revient en Amérique en mai 1847,
des collections de livres, de documents, de cartes, de gravures et de
médailles.[50] Le problème se pose alors à Vattemare de savoir à qui il
remettra les livres, puisque selon lui, le grand institut projeté en 1841 n'a
pas été fondé. Le *Canadien* suggère que le dépôt en soit fait à la Saint-Jean-
Baptiste ou à l'Institut canadien.[51] Vattemare avait d'ailleurs l'intention de
venir au Canada en mars 1848, comme il l'avait écrit à Huston le 15
novembre précédent.[52] Il ne semble pas cependant qu'il soit venu à Montréal et j'ignore pour le moment si les collections françaises sont parvenues
au Parlement et à l'Institut canadien.

*   *   *

Après avoir passé un an et demi aux Etats-Unis, le créateur des échanges
culturels internationaux retourne en Europe où il est accuelli avec une
bienveillance accrue par les institutions de haut savoir. Largement subven-
tionné par les Etats américains, Vattemare a connu sans doute ses plus
beaux succès avec les Etats-Unis. Le rapport que Guizot en fit à l'Académie
des Sciences Morales et Politiques en 1855 en donne une bonne idée.[53] A
ce moment, plus de 70,000 volumes américains avaient été envoyés en
France et plus de 100,000 volumes français en Amérique; la seule ville de
Paris possédait une "bibliothèque américaine" de 10,000 volumes, une
collection complète de médailles et monnaies frappées en Amérique du
Nord de 1652 à 1853, une collection de papier-monnaie émis entre 1708 et
1852 ainsi que des cartes, plans, gravures et portraits.

Si les Etats américains ont participé officiellement au système d'échange, ce fut peine perdue en Europe. Aucun gouvernement ne voulut s'engager à établir le système de façon permanente, malgré toutes les tentatives que fit Vattemare pendant plus de trente ans; et ce dernier continua jusqu'à sa mort, survenue en 1864, à soutenir de sa fortune personnelle le Centre européen des échanges. Encore là l'échec ne fut que temporaire puisque les relations culturelles par les échanges reprirent en 1867 avec la signature de la Convention des Princes.

Alexandre Vattemare qui a effectué l'échange de plus de 300,000 volumes en Europe et en Amérique – pour ne parler que des livres – qui a consacré ses dons, sa fortune et sa vie à l'une des plus belles oeuvres humaines qui soit, mérite d'être universellement connu. Son séjour a été aussi bénéfique dans la vie culturelle du Bas-Canada que celui de Mgr de Forbin-Janson dans la vie religieuse et au même moment.

Notes: Le Philanthrope Vattemare

1. Pour la carrière de Vattemare en Europe, voir J.-L.Dargent: *Alexandre Vattemare, 7 novembre 1796-7 avril 1864. Fondateur de l'Agence européene des échanges*, in *Bulletin des bibliothèques de France*, 9e année, no 8, août 1964, 333-339.
2. *Canadien*, Québec, 5 mars 1841.
3. *Ibid.*
4. Bibliothèque de l'Institut de France, fonds Vattemare, *Movement of the Inter-Literary Exchanges*, 1846, 6-9.
5. *Canadien*, 5 mars 1841.
6. Bibliothèque de l'Institut de France, fonds Vattemare, M61F4, (no 15).
7. Elizabeth Richards. *Alexandre Vattemare and his System of International Exchanges*, in *Bulletin of the Medical Library Association*, vol. 32, no 4, Oct. 1944, 413-448.
8. *Id.*, 422-424, 436.
9. Mgr de Forbin-Janson, arrivé à New-York le 18 oct. 1839, avait fait le même voyage que Vattemare jusqu'à la Nouvelle-Orléans, avant d'arriver à Québec le 3 sept. 1840.
10. *Aurore des Canadas*, Montréal, 20 nov. 1840.
11. Archives de l'Archevêché de Montréal, *Registre des lettres du 20 oct. 1839 au 4 mars 1843*, T. II, 249.
12. Cf. Dargent, *Alexandre Vattemare*, 338.
13. *Aurore des Canadas*, 24 nov. 1840.
14. Bibliothèque de l'Institut de France, fonds Vattemare, *Movement of the Inter-Literary Exchanges*, 14.
15. *Ibid.*, 14-15.
16. *Aurore des Canadas*, 18 déc. 1840.
17. Voir également la *Gazette de Montréal* et le *Montreal Herald*.
18. *Aurore des Canadas*, 18 déc. 1840.
19. *Id.*, 29 déc. 1840.
20. *Id.*, 31 déc. 1840; traduit du *Montreal Herald* et signé Un Raisonneur.
21. *Aurore des Canadas*, 31 déc. 1840.
22. *Id.*, 12 jan. 1841.
23. Archives de la Cité de Montréal, 1841, 2, 1ère serie, *Conseil, Rapports et dossiers*.
24. *Ibid.*
25. *Statuts du Canada*, t. 14. *Ordonnances faites et passées par Son Excellence le Gouverneur Général, et le Conseil Spécial pour les affaires de la Province du Bas-Canada*, vol. 6, Québec, John Charlton Fisher et William Kemble, imprimeurs de la rein, 1841, 495-509.
26. *Aurore des Canadas*, 26 jan. 1841.
27. Les 7, 11, 15 et 23 jan.
28. 29 jan. 1841.
29. *Fantasque*, Québec, 7 jan. 1841.
30. Le premier numéro est daté du 12 déc. 1840.
31. *Fantasque*, 4 fév. 1841.
32. *Gazette de Québec*, 9 fév. 1841.
33. *Ibid.*
34. *Fantasque*, 23 fév. 1841.
35. *Gazette de Québec*, 25 fév. 1841.
36. *Fantasque*, 26 fév. 1841.
37. *Gazette de Québec*, 4 mars 1841.
38. *Id.*, 9 mars 1841. Valéry reprendra la même idée un jour: cf. *Regards sur le monde actuel et autres sur le monde actuel et autres essais*, Paris, Gallimard, 1945, 110-111.
39. Archives de la Cité de Québec, *Procès-verbeaux du Conseil d'août 1840 à mai 1842*, 87-88.
40. *Id.*, 92 et 97.
41. *Gazette de Québec*, 9 mars 1841.
42. *Fantasque*, 8 mars 1841.
43. *L'Institut ou Journal de Etudiants*, 13 mars 1841.
44. *Fantasque*, 6 mai 1841.
45. *Les Bibliothèques canadiennes, Etudes historiques*. Extrait de la *Revue Canadienne*, Montréal, Arbour et Dupont, 37 et 42.
46. 3 août 1855.
47. Claude Galarneau. Conférence inédite à l'Association des bibliothécaires de Québec, 11 avril 1962: *Alexandre Vattemare et l'Institut*

Canadien, reprise au Congrès de l'Acfas 1962.

48. *Minerve,* Montréal, 8 juil. 1847.
49. Cf. le *Canadien,* 29 jan. et 1er fév. 1847.
50. *Id.,* 1er fév. 1847.
51. *Id.,* 6 déc. 1847.
52. *Avenir,* Montréal, 27 nov. 1847.
53. Bibliothèque de l'Institut de France, fonds Vattemare, Académie des Sciences Morales et Politiques. Le rapport de Guizot fut commenté dans le *Canadien* du 3 août 1855.

Libéralisme et ultramontanisme au Canada français: affrontement idéologique et doctrinal (1840-1865)

I

Philippe Sylvain, Université Laval

Le dix-neuvième siècle est le siècle du libéralisme. Sous sa forme laïciste, le libéralisme dérive directement de la Révolution française, qui a d'abord reconnu la non-confessionalité de l'Etat, puis laïcisé les services publics et enfin proclamé la séparation de l'Etat et des Eglises. En dépit de l'opposition acharnée de l'Eglise catholique, ces mouvements allaient se répercuter, à des dates et à des degrés différents suivant les pays, dans les nations qui, jusque-là, avaient vécu en un climat de chrétienté. C'est ce que André Latreille exprime par ces lignes d'une rare densité:

Il y a eu, écrit l'éminent historien, *entre 1789 et 1799, une nation, la France, où ils ont en quelque sorte explosé tous à la fois, de sorte qu'en l'espace de cinq ou six années seulement on a passé à un régime de totale laïcisation. . . . A ces trois mouvements . . . , l'Eglise s'est opposée avec une persévérance, avec une sorte d'intransigeance passionnée, dès 1789 et pendant tout le XIXe siècle – le moment le plus dramatique du conflit avec les sociétés "modernes" se situant sous le pontificat de Pie IX, entre 1850 et 1880.*[1]

Cette lutte, qui opposa farouchement l'Eglise aux libéraux européens et sud-américains, ne fut pas moins violente au Canada français. C'est une histoire qui reste à écrire. Pour le moment, je me contenterai d'étudier la période qui va de 1840 à 1865, et qui est marquée, notamment en 1858 et en 1862, par les prises de position d'une vigueur extrême de l'évêque de Montréal, Mgr Ignace Bourget, à l'endroit des libéraux de l'Institut

Canadien, la première fois à propos du libéralisme, la seconde, au sujet d'une question liée étroitement au libéralisme et qui, en Occident, passionnait alors tous les esprits, la question romaine.

* * *

Le 10 mars, le 30 avril et le 31 mai 1858, Mgr Bourget publiait trois lettres pastorales qui sont restées célèbres.[2] L'évêque de Montréal s'en prenait publiquement à l'Institut canadien, aux "livres impies" de sa bibliothèque et aux "mauvais journaux," parmi lesquels se trouvait manifestement visé le *Pays,* organe officiel du parti libéral.

Il est difficile d'imaginer deux familles d'esprit plus dissemblables que celles à laquelle se rattachaient le prélat et les libéraux qui étaient l'objet de ses censures.

L'homme d'Eglise incarnait l'ultramontanisme le plus intransigeant. Il appartenait à cette école baptisée d'un mot employé depuis longtemps dans une querelle qui opposa le gallicanisme au Saint-Siège, et qui fut repris au dix-neuvième siècle pour caractériser les "catholiques tout courts," c'est-à-dire "ceux qui ne voulaient aucun compromis, aucun accord sur les libertés modernes, aucun essai de conciliation entre le libéralisme et l'Eglise."[3] Héritier, non seulement du siège, mais de l'esprit du premier évêque de Montréal, Mgr Jean-Jacques Lartigue dont, au témoignage de son successeur, le "génie pénétrant" avait découvert dans les "bons auteurs" les "saines doctrines" propres à "combattre victorieusement le gallicanisme et le libéralisme,"[4] Mgr Bourget devait s'efforcer, au cours d'un long épiscopat, de prolonger et d'approfondir cette action ultramontaine, afin de faire de sa ville épiscopale, comme il l'écrivait vers 1873, une "petite Rome."[5]

Pour arriver à ce but, il déploya une énergie qui ne se lassa jamais, au point de "sacrifier pour son troupeau," comme il le confessait à son clergé dans la circulaire accompagnant son mandement de démission daté du 8 septembre 1876, "ses veilles, son repos, sa santé, sa réputation, en un mot toute son existence."[6]

Ce n'est pas par hasard que le début de son activité épiscopale coïncide avec la renaissance religieuse qui, en France, sous la monarchie philippienne, avec les Lacordaire, les Gerbet, les Salinis, les Guéranger et les Montalembert, tous anciens disciples de Lamennais, est "à l'origine de toutes les ferveurs et de tous les renouvellements."[7] Louis Veuillot commence à collaborer, en 1840, à l'*Univers,* fondé par l'abbé Migne sept ans auparavant. Sa plume étincelante, qui s'était fait connaître pas ses *Pèlerinages de Suisse* et *Pierre Saintive*, assure d'emblée au journal une vogue et une autorité qui ne feront que grandir. Sainte-Beuve, dont la malveillance aiguisait la perspicacité, écrivait en août 1843: "Toute la littérature catholique a un débit excellent. Pour un littérateur dévot et industriel, c'est une carrière. Tout manuscrit trouve éditeur et acheteur. Ce petit polisson de Veuillot fait des romans catholiques qui s'écoulent."[8]

Les congrégations religieuses d'hommes et de femmes se multiplient à un rythme rapide. Si les Jésuites doivent céder, un moment, devant les passions ameutées contre eux, d'autres ordres illustres, comme celui des Bénédictins à Solesmes avec Dom Guéranger, et comme celui des Dominicains avec Lacordaire, qui reprend avec éclat ses conférences à Notre-Dame, connaissent un renouveau exceptionnel. Des congrégations récentes, comme celles des Oblats de Marie Immaculée et des Clercs de Saint-Viateur, témoignent d'une vitalité qui est le présage d'un avenir fécond.

C'est ainsi que Mgr Bourget pourra, dès son premier voyage en Europe, faire dériver vers son diocèse le surplus de ces activités apostoliques, ainsi que le souhaitait l'*Univers*, en apprenant que "Mgr de Montréal" était "venu en Europe pour y chercher un renfort d'ouvriers évangéliques": "Puisse notre France catholique, si féconde en dévouements, lui en offrir qui soient dignes d'elle et de lui!"[10]

Efficacement épaulé par les Jésuites, les Oblats de Marie Immaculée, les Clercs de Saint-Viateur et les religieux de Sainte-Croix qu'il avait attirés au Canada et auxquels il avait donné une large part dans les missions, le ministère et l'enseignement, et s'étant assuré l'appui d'un journal, les *Mélanges religieux*, réplique canadienne, moins le talent, de l'*Univers*, Mgr Bourget est à même de donner à son diocèse une impulsion décisive, à telle enseigne qu'un prêtre français, qui avait pu observer la réalité canadienne durant les loisirs forcés de son séjour au séminaire de Québec, ne pouvait s'empêcher de comparer, en 1852, "la marche qui caractérise les grandes choses" du diocèse de Montréal "sous l'influence de son évêque," à l'inertie du diocèse de Québec, qui "se laissait vivre et végétait comme une plante sans sève depuis la mort de M. Plessis."[11]

C'est le caractère ultramontain de l'action de Mgr Bourget, qui plaisait au prêtre français qui, d'ailleurs, avait obtenu du pape pour son livre une lettre laudative, précisément parce qu'il se montrait attaché aux doctrines romaines. A tous les plans de la pastorale, l'accent est mis sur une franche adhésion aux impulsions venant de Rome ou de l'ultramontanisme français: préférence accordée par les confesseurs aux directives de la morale liguorienne, grâce aux ouvrages de l'abbé, plus tard cardinal, Thomas Gousset; diffusion du *Catéchisme de persévérance* de l'abbé Jean-Joseph Gaume; désir de voir adopter comme manuels de théologie au séminaire de Montréal des ouvrages de théologiens romains à la place du gallican Bouvier, regrettant "qu'ici comme en France, la Société de Saint-Sulpice qui, sous tant de rapports, est si respectable, ne soit pas à la tête de ce beau mouvement qui s'opère dans le monde entier en faveur des saines doctrines de l'ultramontanisme";[12] introduction de la liturgie romaine, en dépit des réticences de l'archevêque de Québec qui, en adoptant le *Rituel romain*, n'avait "pas eu l'idée d'abroger les règles de discipline et les usages louables qui sont prescrits par l'ancien rituel de Québec";[13] choix de Rome, à la différence encore de Québec qui s'en tient à l'École des

Carmes de Paris, pour le complément de formation des jeunes prêtres d'élite.[14] Même les détails vestimentaires du costume ecclésiastique n'avaient pas laissé indifférent l'évêque de Montréal: en 1858 il imposait à son clergé l'obligation de porter le col romain au lieu du rabat,[15] auquel tenaient les Sulpiciens, en grande partie français. Enfin, à cette injection massive d'ultramontanisme dans tout le corps social, allait s'ajouter un signe tangible et durable du caractère "romain" de Montréal durant cet épiscopat: la cathédrale ayant été rasée par l'incendie de juillet 1852, on la reconstruirait tout simplement sur le modèle de Saint-Pierre de Rome![16]

*   *   *

Ces progrès rapides et spectaculaires de l'ultramontanisme s'expliquent en grande partie, au Canada français comme en France, par l'emprise de Louis Veuillot, qui a fait de son journal une sorte de *Moniteur* du monde catholique. L'encyclique *Inter multiplices* de 1853, qui donnait gain de cause aux intransigeants dans la querelle des classiques païens et chrétiens, a consacré chez le grand journaliste un prestige et une autorité que des évêques comme Mgr Sibour, archevêque de Paris, et Mgr Dupanloup, évêque d'Orléans, trouvent franchement intolérables. Si l'orthodoxie abrupte de Veuillot heurte des hommes d'Eglise, à plus forte raison rebrousse-t-elle les indifférents et les incroyants. Pour les frères Goncourt, Veuillot est "l'aboyeur des idées de M. de Maistre," mais en ajoutant, ce qui marque bien quel cas même les adversaires les plus résolus faisaient du talent incisif du redoutable polémiste, qu'il est "la terreur" de la presse parisienne qui le combat.[17]

C'est surtout quand il séjourne en province que Veuillot mesure l'étendue de son influence dans les milieux conservateurs. En 1858 il villégiature dans les Pyrénées, qu'il arpente à pied, à cheval, en voiture. Il y est souvent reconnu, jusqu'à ce gamin de Bagnères qui, en l'apercevant, se met à courir dans la rue en criant: "Voilà M. Veuillot!" Il a la satisfaction de trouver partout des amis et des admirateurs. "La gloire habite la province," déclare-t-il.[18]

La réputation de Veuillot n'avait pas tardé à franchir l'Atlantique et à s'imposer au Canada français. Dès 1839 on commence à le citer dans un journal canadien.[19] C'était le début d'une influence plus que séculaire.[20] Il n'est pas aventureux d'affirmer que nul écrivain français n'a davantage façonné la mentalité canadienne-française. Des prêtres avec les *Mélanges religieux* à partir de 1840, puis des laïcs comme Joseph Cauchon, "pendant des années l'idole du clergé,"[21] grâce au *Journal de Québec,* fondé en 1842; Ronald McDonald, qui devient, après la retraite d'Etienne Parent, rédacteur en chef du *Canadien* le 7 novembre 1842;[22] et Raphaël Bellemare, qui entre à la *Minerve* en août 1847,[23] sont les premiers thuriféraires de ce culte, qui s'accentuera encore lorsque Henry de Courcy, qui est correspondant de l'*Univers* à New York depuis 1845, écrira simultanément, de

1853 à 1856, dans les journaux canadiens, surtout la *Minerve*,[24] et dans le grand journal ultramontain de Paris, à la vive satisfaction de Mgr Bourget.[25] Enfin, le 2 février 1857, paraît à Québec le premier numéro du *Courrier du Canada*, destiné "à être la fidèle image de l'*Univers* de Paris," et qui a comme rédacteur en chef Joseph-Charles Taché, que ses adversaires libéraux ne tarderont pas à surnommer *Veuillotule*.

En 1858 on peut dire que Veuillot a des disciples non moins enthousiastes au Canada français qu'en France. Des évêques canadiens lui écrivent des lettres admiratives.[27] Des prêtres de Québec lui rendent visite lors de leur passage à Paris: l'historien Jean-Baptiste-Antoine Ferland en compagnie de Henry de Courcy,[28] les abbés André Pelletier et Henry-Raymond Casgrain deux ans plus tard.[29]

*   *   *

Comme Veuillot, par crainte de la propagande subversive et irréligieuse, avait été l'un des principaux artisans, après le coup d'Etat du 2 décembre 1851, du ralliement de la majorité des catholiques au régime autoritaire du Prince-Président, puis du Second Empire, Napoléon III devait jouir au Canada français, dans le milieu catholique et conservateur, d'une popularité sans égale, d'autant plus que son gouvernement se montra, à ses débuts, nettement favorable à l'Eglise: aucun obstacle n'était mis à la réunion des conciles provinciaux; les congrégations religieuses pouvaient se développer; la presse catholique bénéficiait de plus de franchise que toute autre. L'Eglise obtenait ainsi "dans une société opprimée, les libertés les plus étendues dont elle eût joui depuis le Concordat."[30] La guerre de Crimée, Veuillot la salua comme une croisade contre le "schisme gréco-slave."[31]

C'est à la suite des ultramontains français, surtout de Veuillot, que le clergé et les catholiques canadiens-français, sans se rendre compte que la politique de Napoléon III évoluait vers la gauche depuis le refus de l'alliance autrichienne en 1855 et l'admission du Piémont au Congrès de Paris en 1856, continuaient à nourrir un culte fervent pour l'empereur. Mgr A.A. Taché écrivait de Paris à sa mère, le 18 décembre 1856: "Il règne en France un ordre admirable. Le souverain de ce beau pays paraît un homme providentiel."[32] Deux ans plus tard, Mgr Bourget voyait encore dans le gouvernement de Napoléon III rien de moins qu'une "nouvelle alliance avec le Sacerdoce!" "Or," poursuivait l'évêque, "depuis cette réconciliation, voyez comme la France est prospère et heureuse; comme son nom est grand dans le monde entier; comme ses armées sont victorieuses, comme son Souverain est prodigieusement entouré de la protection du ciel; comme son amitié est recherchée et son alliance ambitionnée!"[33]

La ferveur napoléonienne de l'évêque de Montréal rivalisait avec celle des ultramontains français, dont l'intensité atteignait son sommet précisément en cette année 1858, lors du voyage en Bretagne de l'empereur et de l'impératrice, qui allèrent célébrer la fête napoléonienne du 15 août en la basilique de Sainte-Anne d'Auray; l'évêque de Rennes salua Napoléon III, "de tous les monarques français depuis Saint Louis, le plus dévoué à l'Eglise et à son oeuvre de civilisation et de progrès."[34] "Plus d'une fois," écrivait de son côte Louis Veuillot, en lisant les récits du voyage de l'Empereur à travers la Bretagne, "le coeur des catholiques a battu avec celui des Bretons. Ce voyage est aussi un événement religieux; l'influence en sera considérable dans le monde."[35]

Veuillot ne se faisait pas complètement illusion sur Napoléon III.[36] Il voulait seulement le retenir sur la pente où il le voyait glisser. Mais c'était en vain. L'ancien carbonaro, auquel Felice Orsini venait de rappeler son serment dans une lettre célèbre avant d'être exécuté pour avoir attenté à l'existence impériale, se tournait de nouveau vers l'Italie. Et c'était, le 21 juillet 1858, moins d'un mois avant le voyage triomphal en Bretagne, l'entrevue secrète de Plombières avec Cavour, au cours de laquelle l'empereur engageait la France dans la politique qui, d'approche en approche, devait aboutir à l'unification de l'Italie et, par conséquent, à la disparition des Etats pontificaux.

L'unité italienne fut la réalisation la plus éclatante au dix-neuvième siècle du libéralisme politique. Parce que dirigée contre le pouvoir temporel pontifical, cette oeuvre suscita l'opposition acharnée des catholiques. Comme les libéraux canadiens, conséquents avec eux-mêmes, se montraient favorables aux libéraux italiens, qui dépossédaient le pape de ses Etats, le clergé canadien ne pouvait rester indifférent. Certes Mgr Bourget fut leur plus irréductible adversaire.

*   *   *

Les libéraux les plus marquants appartenaient, en 1858, à l'Institut Canadien. Cet Institut avait connu des débuts très modestes. Fondé le 17 décembre 1844 par "quelques commis-marchands, quelques étudiants en droit, jeunes gens à peine connus, pauvres, sans appui, mais à l'âme ardente, au noble coeur, aux convictions profondes,"[37] pour être une sorte d'université populaire où chacun des membres pourrait tout à la fois approfondir ses connaissances, étendre sa culture et améliorer sa langue écrite et parlée, grâce aux avantages d'une bibliothèque commune et de séances hebdomadaires de discussion, l'Institut Canadien ne tarda pas à révéler qu'il était né pour vivre, à la différence de certaines associations qui, établies à la même époque, ne menèrent qu'une existence languissante pour s'éteindre bientôt. Il comptait, en effet, dans ses rangs quelques-uns des jeunes canadiens français les plus doués de leur génération et dont le dynamisme avait "secoué l'apathie proverbiale de ses ancêtres."[38] Ce n'est pas par pure flagornerie qu'Etienne Parent, dans sa conférence *Du travail chez l'homme,* qu'il prononçait devant eux le 23 septembre 1847, leur prédisait que "si jamais notre race joue un rôle distingué dans l'histoire de l'Amérique, votre

Institut aura droit, j'en suis sûr, d'en réclamer, en grande partie, le mérite et la gloire."[39]

Pour élargir leur influence, et parce qu'au Canada comme en France à cette époque "le vrai moyen d'action pour un homme ou pour un parti, c'était la presse,"[40] ces jeunes gens, qui avaient subi fortement l'influence du Lamennais libéral, fondèrent un journal auquel ils donnèrent le titre significatif de l'*Avenir* et dont le premier numéro parut le 16 juillet 1847. Georges Batchelor en fut l'éditeur-gérant jusqu'en novembre, alors que Jean-Baptiste-Eric Dorion le remplaça à la direction du journal.

Quoique la rédaction assurât que l'*Avenir* ne servirait jamais de "réceptable aux petites passions qui trémoussent les individus de petite taille,"[41] le journal ne tarda pas à dériver vers la politique de concert avec l'Institut Canadien.

Jusqu'à la fin de l'année 1847, l'Institut était resté neutre en politique. Aucune division ne se manifestait en son sein. Il avait la confiance du clergé. Le directeur du collège de Saint-Hyacinthe, l'abbé Désaulniers, donnait à sa bibliothèque "cinq magnifiques cartes géographiques françaises."[42] Le sulpicien français Armand de Charbonnel, futur évêque de Toronto, prononçait devant ses membres, le 6 mai 1847, une conférence sur "les caractères de la société chrétienne." A cette occasion, les autorités religieuses du diocèse de Montréal avait mis la cathédrale à la disposition de l'Institut[43]: signe non équivoque de "l'intérêt" que lui portait le clergé et du "désir ardent" qu'il éprouvait "de lui voir acquérir cette haute importance qui le mette à même de procurer sous tous ses rapports le bonheur de la société."[44]

A la fin de l'année 1847, on peut déceler une amorce vers la politique sous l'influence de Louis-Joseph Papineau, rentré d'exil depuis deux ans et qui était, depuis le 8 août 1845, l'un des patrons d'honneur de l'Institut.[45] Choisi pour les représenter au parlement par les comtés de Huntingdon et de Saint-Maurice, Papineau suscite chez les jeunes rédacteurs de l'*Avenir* un "plaisir inexprimable" à la lecture de "certaines parties de son adresse," mais ceux-ci se hâtent d'affirmer qu'ils diffèrent "d'opinion sur le gouvernement responsable d'avec M. Papineau, qui ne veut y voir qu'une déception."

C'était le 24 décembre. Or exactement une semaine plus tard on publie dans le même journal, signée "Anti-Union," la première de deux lettres – la seconde paraîtra dans le numéro du 5 février 1848 – sur "l'Union et la Nationalité."

Il s'esquissait une nette tendance dans la direction de Papineau, que confirmait avec éclat la lettre d' "Anti-Union" du 5 février, dont le style et l'origine, Saint-Hyacinthe, indiquaient à coup sûr que Louis-Antoine Dessaulles en était l'auteur: "S'il y a encore chez nous quelque patriotisme, quelque amour de la nationalité, unissons-nous autour de lui. Il nous mènera encore à la victoire." Ayant retrempé "son patriotisme et l'amour de sa nation au foyer de la France," Papineau était "revenu plus canadien, si la chose était possible, qu'il n'était parti": "Concourons donc avec lui à la destruction de l'union des deux provinces."

Le prestige de l'ancien tribun avait certainement joué dans cette évolution; les liens d'amitié et de parenté aussi, car dans le groupe des collaborateurs les plus brillants de l'*Avenir,* outre Rodolphe Laflamme, Joseph Doutre, Charles Laberge, Joseph Papin, Charles Daoust, il y avait les frères Dorion, Antoine-Aimé, Wilfrid et Jean-Baptiste-Eric, ce dernier surnommé depuis ses jeunes ans "l'Enfant terrible," fils de Pierre-Antoine Dorion et de Geneviève Bureau; or Pierre-Antoine Dorion, marchand à Sainte-Anne-de-la-Pérade,[47] avait été membre de l'Assemblée législative du Bas-Canada, comme Pierre Bureau, père de Geneviève, et tous deux des partisans enthousiastes de Papineau;[48] il y avait aussi dans ce groupe Gustave Papineau, le propre fils de Louis-Joseph; Denis-Emery, son neveu; Louis Labrèche-Viger, fils adoptif de Denis-Benjamin Viger, cousin de Louis-Joseph Papineau; il y avait enfin – *last, but not least!* – Louis-Antoine Dessaulles, qui était non seulement le neveu préféré du tribun, mais son fils spirituel, un "autre lui-même," comme il l'écrivait de Paris, le 11 octobre 1839, à un ami anglais.

Dessaulles était, à l'exception d'Antoine-Aimé Dorion, né le 17 janvier 1818, le plus âgé du groupe, puisqu'il atteignait la trentaine en 1849. Il était aussi le plus cultivé et le plus ferme dans ses convictions libérales. Etant encore collégien, il s'était enthousiasmé pour Lamartine, mais le Lamartine déiste du *Voyage en Orient*, et pour Lamennais, mais le Lamennais libéral des *Paroles d'un croyant*.[49] Il avait rejoint Louis-Joseph Papineau dans son exil parisien. Avec son oncle, admirateur et ami du prêtre révolté contre l'Eglise, il avait pris parti pour l'auteur des *Affaires de Rome,* ainsi qu'en témoigne la longue lettre véhémente qu'il écrivait à son cousin Denis-Emery Papineau, le 29 septembre 1839,[50] tout juste après avoir lu "l'ouvrage de Mr De La Mennais," dans lequel on constatait "par combien d'intrigues, de menées sourdes, de bassesses, on a réussi à obtenir la condamnation du grand écrivain." "C'est là qu'on voit," poursuivait-il, "que ce sont purement et uniquement des considérations politiques qui ont décidé le Pape à la prononcer. C'est l'Autriche qui a condamné Mr De La Mennais, c'est la Russie; ce n'est pas Grégoire XVI." Et Dessaulles, sarcastique, ajoutait: "C'est dans cet ouvrage qu'on voit combien les affaires se font franchement et saintement à Rome."[51]

Liberté de pensée et des cultes, liberté de conscience, libertés civiles et politiques, thèses qu'avait réprouvées l'encyclique *Mirari vos* du 15 août 1832, Dessaulles, à la suite de Lamennais, les faisait siennes en citant et en commentant les passages essentiels des *Affaires de Rome*: "Les raisonnements" de "Mr De La Mennais" lui paraissaient "convaincants."

A vingt ans Louis-Antoine Dessaulles avait donc fait son choix: il serait pour les libertés modernes et contre tous les despotismes. Ce sera le drame de sa vie que de se heurter constamment à l'évêque de Montréal, qui opposera inébranlablement à ses déclarations libérales des arguments tirés de *Mirari vos*, l'une des encycliques "qui a le plus influencé l'histoire contemporaine."[52] Il finira par être vaincu dans la lutte et il viendra mourir, isolé et malheureux, dans ce Paris où, environ un demi-siècle plus tôt, il partait d'un pas allègre dans la vie, muni du viatique menaisien.

De retour au Canada au printemps de 1843,[53] Dessaulles ne pouvait pas ne pas se ranger du côté de Papineau lorsque celui-ci revint à la vie politique Il n'avait aucunement besoin de l'invitation faite aux "jeunes hommes de l'*Avenir*" de ne pas résister "au courant" qui les entraînait vers "l'ère démocratique": "Papineau, quoi qu'on en dise, vous a indiqué la route et vous a mis en main le flambeau qui doit éclairer votre marche."[54]

La doctrine que prônait Papineau sous le titre de "Rappel de l'Union" se rattachait au "Principe de nationalités" ou droit des peuples à disposer d'eux-mêmes. Cette théorie libérale, qu'on appelle aujourd'hui le droit à "l'autodétermination," avait été proclamée par la Constituante en 1790. Dans son exil à Sainte-Hélène, Napoleon l'avrait enrichie de commentaires que des publications avaient révélées au public.[55] Diffusée ensuite par des poètes, des journalistes, des écrivains et des orateurs comme Béranger, Armand Carrel, Lamennais, La Fayette et Lamarque, elle se retrouvait tout entière dans le manifeste du 4 mars 1848 aux puissances étrangères de Lamartine, chef du Gouvernement provisoire, et dans le commentaire éloquent que l'homme d'Etat en fit lui-même à la tribune le 23 mai suivant. C'est sans doute en songeant à Lamartine, à Lamennais, à Béranger et aux autres républicains illustres qu'il avait connus durant son exil sur les bords de la Seine et auxquels la Révolution de Février conférait en ce moment un prestige unique, que Papineau s'écriait lors de l'assemblée du Marché Bonsecours, organisée pour promouvoir la colonisation des Cantons de l'Est: "Paris, avec son concours infini, innombrable, de grands hommes, est le cerveau puissant qui, sans cesse et sans relâche, sécrète, à l'usage de l'humanité, des idées de réforme, de progrès, de liberté et de philanthropie."[56]

A la suite du grand homme, les collaborateurs de l'*Avenir* tournaient leurs yeux vers Paris: "La révolution français doit bouleverser le monde," affirmaient-ils; "il faut que le peuple du Bas-Canada puisse être prêt quand son heure arrivera."[57]

La méthode révolutionnaire l'emportait dans leurs esprits sur la méthode constitutionnelle. Dessaulles surtout, dans le sillage de son oncle, se montrait un adversaire déterminé du gouvernement responsable. Durant tout le mois de mai 1848 il soutint avec fougue que "l'Union" était "sans contredit la plus flagrante injustice, le plus infâme attentat à nos droits naturels et politiques qui pût être commis."[58]

Devant l'effervescence des esprits causée par les proclamations de Papineau et les articles de l'*Avenir*, les amis de l'ordre et du gouvernement n'avaient pas tardé à réagir. A Montréal, L.-O. Létourneux dans la *Revue canadienne*, Hector Langevin, rédacteur depuis un an des *Mélanges religieux*; à Québec, Joseph Cauchon dans son journal, ripostèrent avec vigueur aux adversaires de la politique ministérielle. Il en résulta une lutte acharnée de part et d'autre. C'était la faute à Papineau! Pierre-Joseph-Olivier Chauveau écrivait, en décembre 1848, dans sa correspondence au *Courrier des Etats-Unis*: "En nommant cet ancien tribun des libertés canadiennes, j'ai nommé, pour bien des hommes, qui ne veulent jamais dégager une question de principes de la question d'hommes ou de personnes, j'ai nommé la cause principale de toutes nos difficultés."[59]

Le clergé n'était pas resté neutre dans la lutte, d'autant plus que par la théorie des nationalités la volonté des populations devenait le principe dominateur souverain auquel correspondait l'affirmation du suffrage universel. Un principe révolutionnaire, faisant litière du droit divin, semblait avaliser tous les bouleversements. Les révolutions qui secouaient l'Europe en ce moment en administraient, à ses yeux, une preuve décisive. Les événements inouïs qui venaient de survenir en Italie justifiaient les appréhensions cléricales: ils mettaient en cause l'existence même du pouvoir temporel pontifical que le monde catholique, à peu d'exceptions près, considérait alors comme essentiel à l'exercice de la puissance spirituelle de chef de l'Eglise. Après l'assassinat de son premier ministre Pellegrino Rossi, Pie IX avait quitté secrètement Rome, le 24 novembre 1848, pour se réfugier à Gaète, dans le Royaume de Naples. Le 5 février 1849 l'Assemblée révolutionnaire proclamait la déchéance du pape-roi et votait l'établissement de la république. Les Montagnards de l'Assemblée nationale français s'empressaient d'envoyer une adresse à leurs frères de la Constituante romaine, pour bien marquer l'alliance entre les démocrates des deux pays.[60]

Dès le 18 janvier 1849 Mgr Bourget, par une lettre pastorale, avait ordonné "des prières pour notre Saint Père le Pape Pie IX, obligé de quitter Rome et de se réfugier dans un royaume étranger, par suite des troubles arrivés dans sa capitale, en novembre dernier." Il souhaitait que la "révolution" se détournât de nos rives. Il ne pouvait que déplorer – l'allusion à l'*Avenir* était on ne peut plus claire – "qu'un certain journal français cherch [ât] à répandre des principes révolutionnaires."[61]

L'évêque de Montréal prenait fermement position pour le gouvernement contre les partisans de Papineau et l'*Avenir*:

Qu'avons-Nous à vous recommander pour échapper aux malheurs qui désolent tant de grandes et puissantes nations? Le voici en deux mots: Soyez fidèles à Dieu et respectez toutes les autorités légitimement constituées. Telle est la volonté du Seigneur. N'écoutez pas ceux qui vous adressent des discours séditieux; car ils ne sauraient être vos vrais amis. Ne lisez pas ces livres et ces papiers qui soufflent l'esprit de révolte, car ils sont les véhicules des doctrines empestées qui, semblables au chancre, ont rongé et ruiné les Etats les plus heureux et les plus florissants. Croyez que vous pouvez très certainement conquérir les vraies libertés, celles qui rendent les peuples vraiment heureux, beaucoup mieux par une conduite morale et par une sage soumission aux lois, que par des violences qui nous exposeraient à ces mêmes malheurs que vous avez eu à déplorer et dont vous ne perdez jamais le triste souvenir.[62]

Les jeunes rédacteurs de l'*Avenir* passèrent outre aux objurgations de Mgr Bourget: ils voulaient tirer toutes les conséquences logiques incluses dans le principe libéral des nationalités. Le 14 mars ils se prononçaient avec d'autant moins d'ambiguité contre le maintien du pouvoir temporel pontifical, qu'ils constataient que le clergé, évêque en tête, se rangeait ostensiblement du côté de leurs adversaires politiques: " . . . ceux de nos lecteurs," écrivait leur porte-parole, "qui sentent vivement la beauté et la vérité des principes que nous défendons, comprendront notre insistance, sachant surtout que cette révolution d'Italie est l'occasion d'attaques incessantes contre les principes démocratiques venant de sources d'autant plus à craindre qu'elles sont plus respectables."[63]

On ne pouvait mieux s'y prendre pour cimenter l'alliance du clergé avec le parti de La Fontaine-Baldwin. Par crainte des bouleversements possibles, la religion devenait le rempart de l'ordre politique et social. Un prêtre rattaché à l'évêché de Montréal et intime de Mgr Bourget, l'abbé Adolphe Pinsonnault, qui bientôt s'en prit dans la *Minerve* aux "pygmées" de l'*Avenir*, "toujours disposés à se compter pour des géants,"[64] l'affirmait à Raphaël Bellemare dans la lettre qu'il lui écrivait le 27 mars 1849: "Ne craignez rien, car vous avez l'opinion publique pour vous en ce moment plus que jamais; comptez que la *Minerve*, en soutenant les principes religieux, ralliera l'immense majorité des citoyens et du peuple qui sentent par instinct, comme actuellement en France, que là est le vrai et seul principe d'ordre et de sécurité."[65]

Les jeunes démocrates, devenus la cible de l'abbé Pinsonnault, n'avaient pas été lents à percer ses intentions et le but de sa tactique:

*L'attaque de monsieur Pinsonnault contre l'*Avenir, *écrivait Dessaulles, est loin de n'avoir, comme il le prétend, qu'une portée purement religieuse. Si on rapproche ce fait de beaucoup d'autres, il devient excessivement probable, sinon évident que le clergé fait aujourd'hui des efforts très prononcés pour favoriser, dans le pays, la tentative de réaction contre les idées démocratiques à la tête de laquelle s'est placé le ministère.*[66]

Quelques mois plus tard, les formules n'avaient plus rien d'adouci. C'était une déclaration de lutte à l'outrance: "Un seul mot," écrit le rédacteur au début de septembre dans un éditorial intitulé "Le clergé,"

devra suffire pour mettre les démocrates en garde contre les vues de nos guerroyeurs religieux. C'est qu'ils marchant entre entente complète et intime avec le ministère du jour, que certes on ne soupçonnera pas de vues populaires et progressives. Les hommes qui ont créé le système de l'Union et du gouvernement responsable anglais, étaient bien dignes de s'entendre avec les hommes qui ont maudit leurs compatriotes en 1837 et les ont livrés sans regrets à leurs sanguinaires ennemis.[67]

Le fossé est déjà creusé entre les deux groupes. Il se creusera définitivement lorsque les rédacteurs de l'*Avenir*, de concert avec le *Moniteur canadien* que Jean-Guillaume de Montigny venait de fonder, prônèrent l'annexion aux Etats-Unis. L'absorption du Canada dans la république voisine répugnait invinciblement au clergé, qui se révéla alors, comme l'écrivait Chauveau, "le corps le plus opposé à l'annexion et le plus sincèrement loyal."[68]

Bref, "la lutte entre le libéralisme" et ce qu'un collaborateur de l'*Avenir* appelait "le despotisme moral et religieux," était "devenue inévitable." D'après le même journaliste, "le clergé canadien" voulait "tuer les idées libérales" qui menaient "droit à l'annexion un pays que l'on espérait exploiter encore pendant quelques générations."[69]

L'antagonisme clérical, en exaspérant les démocrates, les poussa aux positions les plus radicales du libéralisme. C'est ainsi qu'ils en arrivèrent à envisager la séparation complète de l'Eglise et de l'Etat. On commença par exiger la suppression de l'obligation légale de la dîme. C'est Dessaulles qui en prit l'initiative dans un article qui soutenait que "les dîmes" avaient "sur les masses" un effet encore "plus immoral que la tenure seigneuriale."[70] Pendant cinq mois à partir de juillet 1849, on réclama "le rappel du système des dîmes." Le *Moniteur canadien* affirma que cet abus cesserait avec l'annexion.[71]

"L'*Avenir* et le *Moniteur* préparent les esprits à la suppression des dîmes," écrivait Mgr Bourget à l'archevêque de Québec à la fin du mois d'octobre de la même année.[72] Les démocrates s'étaient aliéné définitivement le clergé, qui se rangea résolument de côté de leurs adversaires. L'abbé Chiniquy se fit le porte-parole compromettant de ses confrères, à telle enseigne que La Fontaine lui-même en fut agacé; il écrivait le 1er avril 1850 à Amable Berthelot: "Je vois que l'abbé Chiniqui figure dans les assemblées politiques. Ses intentions peuvent être bonnes, mais il n'a pas de jugement. En outre, il devrait se borner à son métier."

La confusion entre le religieux et le politique était consommée. Les évêques, réunis à Montréal, pouvaient bien publier, le 11 mai 1850, une lettre pastorale dans laquelle ils affirmaient, en annonçant la fondation du *True Witness,* qu' "à des journaux impies, ou ennemis de votre foi," ils opposaient "des journaux religieux, non dans des vues politiques, mais uniquement dans l'intérêt du catholicisme si cruellement attaqué de nos jours."[73] Les fidèles n'avaient pas été lents à identifier les "journaux impies" avec l'*Avenir* et le *Moniteur canadien*.

De leur côté, les collaborateurs de ces deux feuilles s'efforçaient de dissiper la moindre ambiguïté touchant leurs sentiments à l'endroit du clergé. Tous les prétextes leur étaient bons. Lors des débats sur le projet qui deviendrait la "Loi Falloux," Victor Hugo avait prononcé, le 15 janvier 1850, dans l'assemblée législative française, un discours violemment anticlérical, que le *Courrier des Etats-Unis* insérait dans son numéro du 16 février. Un mois et demi plus tard, l'*Avenir* le reproduisait à son tour. Les antithèses hugoliennes faisaient merveille dans la polémique que le journal soutenait contre les *Mélanges religieux*, la *Minerve* et le *Journal de Québec*:

Vous êtes, s'était écrié le poète en s'adressant à ses adversaires, les parasites de l'Eglise, vous êtes, non les croyants, mais les sectaires d'une religion que vous ne comprenez pas; vous êtes les metteurs en scène de la sainteté. Ne mêlez pas l'Eglise à vos affaires, à vos combinaisons, à vos stratégies, à vos ambitions. Ne l'appelez votre mère pour en faire votre servante, . . . surtout ne l'identifiez pas avec vous.

Après avoir cité les tirades éloquentes de Hugo, Louis Labrèche-Viger ajoutait, pour en justifier l'insertion dans la feuille montréalaise et mettre les points sur les *i* à l'intention des moins clairvoyants:

Ces paroles pleines de vérité, surtout d'à-propos, que le député français adressait il y a quelques jours au parti clérical de la France, nous pourrions les répéter mot à mot au parti clérico-ministériel qui vient de surgir en Canada de la discussion du pouvoir temporel du Pape *et des* dîmes. *Sans connaître intimement le parti clérical français, nous savons que les paroles de M. Victor Hugo sont vraies, parce que nous en faisons l'application au parti clérical que nous avons sous les yeux et que nous trouvons l'habit juste.*[74]

C'est à la même tactique qu'eut recours Joseph Doutre quelque temps après, en utilisant cette fois-ci un texte épiscopal qui fera le bonheur des libéraux canadiens jusqu'à la veille de la Confédération, et même au-delà, le mandement de l'archevêque de Paris, Mgr Sibour, paru dans l'*Ami de la religion* en septembre 1850 "touchant les écrivains qui traitent des matières ecclésiastiques"; un "avertissement" solennel à l'*Univers* l'accompagnait.[75]

"Le parti de l'*Univers* existe parmi nous," affirmait Joseph Doutre. "Il suit la même marche, il emploie les mêmes moyens, pour arriver au même but."

Après avoir décrit à sa manière l'action en Europe de ce "faux parti religieux", de ce "parti mixte, politico-religieux," "qui persiste à enter son empire spirituel sur le pouvoir temporel des Etats,"[76] Doutre faisait l'application à la politique canadienne de ce qu'il avait constaté outre-Atlantique: "Celui qui, en Canada, a pu observer la conduite d'un parti qui se dit de l'Eglise catholique, celui-là, disons-nous, qui ne verrait pas dans les faits européens que nous avons rapportés un enseignement du plus haut intérêt pour son pays et ses compatriotes, serait ou stupide ou mauvais catholique et un méchant citoyen."

C'est ainsi, poursuivait Doutre, "que l'on voue aux Dieux infernaux ceux qui demandent le changement de rétribution pour les membres du clergé"; "c'est un prêtre qui travaille au confessionnal à rendre l'époux odieux à l'épouse, à jeter la mésintelligence et le désordre dans les familles, parce que l'un des membres d'une famille aura trahi, au jour de la publicité, des idées qui ne cadrent pas avec celles de ce prêtre fanatique." Aussi, concluait Doutre, "les hommes sérieux, après avoir fait la part du ridicule dans toutes ces petites manies, après avoir jeté le mépris sur ceux qui en sont les auteurs et les fauteurs, ne peuvent se défendre d'un sentiment d'animosité contre eux, et plaise à Dieu qu'ils n'en viennent jamais à identifier l'Eglise avec ces parasites de l'Eglise!"[77]

Les démocrates devaient se rendre à l'évidence: le clergé mettait au service de leurs adversaires politiques l'immense influence dont il disposait, tout en réprouvant avec vigueur les thèses libérales. Comme Labrèche-Viger et Joseph Doutre, un collaborateur du *Moniteur canadien* constatait que "le parti clérical" était devenu "une véritable Inquisition politique d'un rigorisme absolu," qui semblait "prendre une part beaucoup plus active dans les affaires temporelles que dans celles d'en haut."[78]

Pour sa part, le clergé était persuadé qu'il devenait urgent de soutenir, dans les élections, les hommes "à bons principes et religieux" comme, par exemple, Jean-Charles Chapais, dans le comté de Kamouraska, contre les démocrates ou "rouges", "cette troupe de gens forcenés réunis pour renverser l'ordre social."[79] En effet, lorsqu'il s'agissait de l'*Avenir*, "la question était pas mal religieuse par ce coin-là." C'est ce que pensait Mgr Turgeon, en écrivant le 1er décembre 1851 à l'abbé Célestin Gauvreau, supérieur du collège de Sainte-Anne-de-la-Pocatière. "Il faut rendre aux rouges le service de les faire dérougir," poursuivait le prélat. "Lorsque la religion est quelque part, il ne faut pas être surpris d'y voir le prêtre." Bien loin donc de dissuader son correspondant de ne pas intervenir dans les élections toutes prochaines, l'exhortait-il à "agir", car c'était son "devoir de prêtre."[80]

Cette ingérence cléricale dans les luttes politiques du comté de Kamouraska constituait une initiative de la plus haute gravité pour le présent et surtout pour l'avenir. "C'était l'étincelle destinée à allumer un incendie, car ce fut là l'origine de la guerre religieuse qui devait bientôt embraser tout le comté, et qui, portée sur d'autres points, finit par s'étendre sur toute la Province."[81]

En outre (et c'était infiniment plus grave encore), l'Eglise canadienne fut petit à petit incitée, sous l'effet de la crainte que lui inspirait le radicalisme de certains libéraux, à "assurer son efficience religieuse en employant la politique," ce qui, "en plus de certains principes de base tels que la suréminence de l'Eglise par rapport à l'Etat, explique l'existence de la théocratie."[82]

Les esprits pondérés parmi les démocrates se rendaient compte que leur groupe, en persistant à soutenir des thèses extrêmes, aboutissaient à une impasse, d'autant plus que des deux côtés de l'Atlantique la "réaction" triomphait. Après le coup d'Etat du 2 décembre 1851, "l'autorité des théories contre-révolutionnaires des disciples catholiques de Maistre était au plus haut."[83] Aussi jugèrent-ils sage de jeter du lest. Le *Pays* succéda à l'*Avenir*, dont le dernier numéro parut le 22 janvier 1852.[84] Une étape cardinale du libéralisme canadien-français prenait fin avec la disparition de la feuille que Jean-Baptiste-Eric Dorion avait soutenue à coups de sacrifices: "l'Enfant terrible" de la paisible paroisse de Sainte-Anne-de-la-Pérade était devenu, grâce à son journal, "l'Enfant terrible" de la politique canadienne.

Mais le libéralisme radical, forcé de s'éclipser pour un moment du domaine de la presse, s'était réfugié à l'Institut canadien.

*   *   *

Le 17 février 1850 un terrible désastre s'était abattu sur l'Institut. Son édifice, sa bibliothèque et l'imprimerie de l'*Avenir* étaient devenus la proie des flammes.[85] Les adversaires n'avaient pas pris la peine de dissimuler la jubilation que leur causait la ruine de l'Institut canadien, ainsi qu'en témoignait un journaliste démocrate:

*A peine le malheur venait-il de fondre sur notre établissement qu'un long cri de joie se faisait entendre dans les rangs des fanatiques religieux et politiques. La fumée de notre atelier portait aux cerveaux de ces hommes des vapeurs d'allégresse, à peine tempérée par le regret que l'incendie n'eût pas dévoré les collaborateurs de l'*Avenir avec le matériel de l'établissement.*[86]

Pour sa part, l'évêque de Montréal ne regrettait certes pas la disparition d'une bibliothèque où, sans doute, voyait-il l'origine de mainte proposition malsonnante qui avait paru dans l'*Avenir* ou le *Moniteur canadien*: "Le feu du ciel," mandait-il à Mgr Turgeon le 9 avril 1850, "a fait justice des livres impies et immoraux de notre Institut canadien. Mais on craint bien que l'enfer ne recompose cette infernale bibliothèque."[87]

Les appréhensions épiscopales n'étaient pas vaines. Les membres les plus actifs de l'Institut Canadien s'étaient déjà mis au travail pour reconstituer leur oeuvre. En avril 1850 on lance un appel au public. Le président, Francis Cassidy, et le secrétaire, N.-G. Bourbonnière, signent une circulaire dans laquelle ils insistent "particulièrement sur l'importance de la recomposition d'une bibliothèque." Un membre de l'Institut, Louis Barillier, s'occuperait d'achats de livres en Europe.[88]

Mais surtout l'Institut connaît, pour ainsi dire, un second départ. Jusque-là il fallait être canadien-français pour en faire partie. En 1850 cette clause fondamentale disparut de la constitution. "L'esprit de l'Institut" fut "altéré profondément," au sentiment d'Hector Fabre qui, dans son journal l'*Ordre*, polémiquait en 1862 contre Dessaulles. Ayant comme mission dès sa fondation d'être "dévoué à la nationalité et aux lettres canadiennes," écrivait Fabre, la "faute" de l'Institut fut bientôt "de n'avoir rien compris, rien senti de national . . . . d'avoir préféré, aux sympathies et au service de notre population, les acclamations des hommes extrêmes et des subsides étrangers."[89]

Cette orientation nouvelle, on voulait l'expliquer dans la suite par l'élection d'un président qui n'était plus un Canadien français: "En 1850," écrivait un partisan de Dessaulles à Fabre, "l'Institut canadien, se trouvant présidé par M. Cassidy, Irlandais de père et de mère, nous avons cru . . . qu'il était temps d'effacer cette flagrante contradiction entre le fait et le droit."[90]

Mais il semble que la vraie raison se trouve dans l'affirmation d'un autre correspondant, celui-ci ami de Fabre: ". . . la *fraternité universelle* qui dilatait alors tous les coeurs fit regarder comme mesquine l'exclusion des autres races, la qualification nationale fut rayée. De ce moment ceux qui assistèrent à l'Institut purent s'apercevoir de la direction que les meneurs désiraient imprimer à la Société."[91]

L'ami de Fabre faisait manifestement allusion aux tenants du principe des nationalités, dont Gonzalve Doutre devait déclarer, quatorze ans plus tard, que "l'Institut canadien le résumait en lui seul."[92]

Prenant à partie "les séparatistes nationaux," Doutre soutenait que ce n'est ni le sang, ni la langue, ni la religion qui sont les éléments fondamentaux de la nationalité, mais l'intérêt bien compris. "C'est une ambition infâme à mes yeux, poursuivait-il, que de chercher à former, nous Canadiens français catholiques, une nationalité à part au détriment des protestants, des juifs, etc., qui auront de leur côté les mêmes droits de former une nationalité distincte,"[93] car "une nation, c'est la réunion de tous les habitants d'un même pays."[94]

La conséquence était évidente: ". . . en Canada, il est impossible d'espérer que la nationalité soit entièrement composée des catholiques d'un côté et des protestants de l'autre."[95]

L'Institut Canadien, microcosme de la nationalité canadienne, devait donc comprendre désormais des anglophones à côté des francophones, des protestants et des catholiques: la conférence que Gonzalve Doutre prononçait à sa tribune le 1er décembre 1864, en s'inspirant de la conception latine du principe des nationalités, expliquait rétrospectivement l'orientation de l'Institut depuis 1850.

Comptant déjà des anglophones dans ses rangs, l'Institut Canadien s'agrégea des protestants de marque avec Narcisse Cyr et Théodore Lafleur. Tous deux étaient des Canadiens français qui avaient renoncé à la foi de leurs pères à l'Institut protestant suisse de Grande-Ligne; après avoir fait des études théologiques à Genève, ils étaient revenus au Canada, Cyr en 1848, Lafleur deux ans plus tard, dans le dessein d' "évangéliser" leurs compatriotes;[96] et peu après leur retour, ils entraient à l'Institut Canadien.

Le prosélytisme intense auquel se livra Narcisse Cyr dans le *Semeur canadien*, qu'il fonda en 1851 et auquel s'abonna officiellement l'Institut, n'était pas de nature à plaire aux libéraux modérés qui avaient réussi à substituer, dans la presse, le *Pays* à l'*Avenir*. Mais à l'Institut les esprits avancés l'emportèrent. On se donnait comme président en mai 1852 un radical d'entre les radicaux dans la personne du "citoyen" Pierre Blanchet; de même une tentative, en décembre de la même année, d'exclure de la salle de lecture le journal de Cyr aboutit à un échec.

De guerre lasse, les modérés voués à l'impuissance par les radicaux, avaient dû se résoudre à constituer comme une sorte d'association rivale, l'Institut national, qu'ils placèrent sous le patronage de Mgr Bourget.[97]

Cette sécession ne perturba en rien la marche ascendante de l'Institut, si l'on en juge par le détachement olympien avec lequel Joseph Doutre, dans le "huitième rapport annuel" publié en décembre 1852, signalait que neuf membres dans le cours de l'année avaient quitté l'Institut canadien, dont deux "pour entrer dans une nouvelle société fondée le printemps dernier."[98]

Après avoir obtenu, en juin 1853, la personnalité civile, l'association se porte acquéreur, au début de l'année suivante, d'un vaste édifice rue Notre-Dame. Un journaliste ami peut alors écrire: "L'Institut canadien est maintenant bâti sur le roc."[99]

Il continue à recevoir du renfort. Il y avait, par exemple, l'admission en 1853 de deux exilés politiques français, dont les convictions républicaines vont accentuer encore le radicalisme du groupe. L'orientation bonapartiste prise par le *Courrier des Etats-Unis* avait forcé Henri-Emile Chevalier à quitter la rédaction du journal new-yorkais et à émigrer à Montréal en mars 1853.[100] Chevalier est bientôt à même d'exercer une influence prépondérante dans son nouveau milieu, car en octobre 1854 on lui confie un cours sur l'histoire et la littérature françaises,[101] et le mois suivant on le nomme bibliothécaire.[102] Et un de ses amis, Félix Vogeli, vétérinaire de profession et collaborateur au *Courrier de Saint-Hyacinthe* (qu'un compatriote, P.-J. Guitté, vient de fonder), ne tardera pas à se faire remarquer par ses interventions énergiques contre tout contrôle de la bibliothèque.

Une activité intense anime l'Institut. Durant l'année 1854 quarante-sept séances ont lieu, et on admet 165 nouveaux candidats, ce qui porte le groupe au nombre de 600 membres.[103] Mais surtout cette activité se traduit sur le plan politique par l'élection au parlement d'onze membres, que des adversaires s'efforcent de ridiculiser dans un pamphlet, *La pléiade rouge*, que Courcy commente avec verve dans l'*Univers*. Le succès a des effets capiteux. L'un des collègues des nouveaux élus, Joseph-Guillaume Barthe, ignorant sereinement le ridicule, s'entremet à Paris, où il réside alors, pour faire affilier l'Institut Canadien à rien de moins que l'Institut de France![104]

Pas un personnage de marque de passage à Montréal qui ne soit reçu officiellement par l'Institut, surtout s'il a la chance d'être connu pour ses tendances antiréactionnaires et ses sympathies républicaines. En octobre 1853 Marc Caussidière, ancien préfet de police sous le Gouvernement provisoire, que l'insurrection de juin avait relégué en exil à Londres, est l'objet d'une chaleureuse réception, que suit un banquet "en l'honneur de l'illustre proscrit."[105]

Au printemps de 1854, c'est Madame Manoël de Grandfort qui, retournant en France d'une tournée infructueuse de conférences en Louisiane, où elle avait bravé le préjugé voulant que seules les actrices se produisent en public, s'arrête à Montréal et fait à la tribune de l'Institut trois exposés applaudis sur l'influence et l'avenir de la femme.[106] L'ouvrage qu'elle publie à Paris l'année suivante sous le titre *L'autre monde*, témoigne de l'attachement de l'auteur aux Canadiens, qui avaient reçu l'auteur avec enthousiasme, à la différence des créoles, qui s'y voyaient injuriés: ils avaient boudé ses conférences![107]

Au mois de septembre 1854, par l'entremise d'Emile Chevalier, l'Institut a le privilège de recevoir Paul Arpin, ex-rédacteur en chef du *Courrier des Etats-Unis*. Le républicain intransigeant, l'adversaire irréductible de Napoléon III que le bonapartiste Eugène Masseras a supplanté à la rédaction du *Courrier*, y prouvait "qu'avec toutes ses défectuosités, le républicanisme américain était infiniment supérieur aux constitutions anodines des princes les plus populaires du continent européen."[108]

Deux ans plus tard, l'Institut se met en frais pour faire un accueil exceptionnel à Jean-Baptiste Desplace, qui voyage alors en Amérique en vue de recueillir des abonnements au *Cours familier de littérature*, que Lamartine commence à publier. Le meilleur conférencier du groupe est mis à contribution. "Inspiré par la grandeur de son sujet," au témoignage de son ami Emile Chevalier, Louis-Antoine Dessaulles "se surpasse,"[109] mais il insiste tellement, de concert avec ses amis libéraux, pour faire de Lamartine un grand poète chrétien, que des protestations ne tardent pas à paraître, d'abord dans la presse conservatrice locale, puis dans l'*Univers* de Paris.[110]

*   *   *

Cette levée de boucliers contre lui ne surprit certes pas Dessaulles: il en était coutumier, car il était certainement le polémiste le mieux armé et, par conséquent, le plus craint des adversaires de l'Institut canadien.

Il suivait avec attention le progrès de ultramontanisme depuis son entrée dans la vie publique.[111] Il se heurtait à lui dans l'intimité de sa propre famille. Dessaulles, en effet, était le cousin de l'abbé Alexis-Frédéric Trudeau, vicaire général du diocèse de Montréal, et par son mariage, en février 1850, avec sa cousine Zéphirine Thomson,[112] était devenu le beau-frère de soeur l'Ange Gardien, qui appartenait à la congrégation de la Providence, fondée par Mgr Bourget. C'est elle qui sera chargé par sa communauté de prendre soin des dernières années de l'évêque de Montréal.[113]

On a vu que Dessaulles était revenu menaisien libéral de son séjour en Europe. Collaborateur de l'*Avenir*, il avait pris parti contre le système des dîmes et contre le clergé dans des articles signés "Campagnard." Il n'avait qu'à ouvrir les ouvrages du prêtre révolté, surtout les *Discussions critiques et pensées diverses sur la religion et la philosophie* publiées en 1841, où Lamennais "s'abaisse, à la façon des plus médiocres adversaires de l'Eglise, jusqu'à ramasser contre elle ces fautes, ces désordres, ces scandales, dont aucune société, où il entre un élément humain, ne saurait se préserver complètement,"[114] pour y trouver formulés "les meilleurs arguments de l'anticléricalisme."[115] C'est sans doute en songeant particulièrement aux diatribes de Dessaulles que les évêques canadiens, en publiant leur lettre pastorale collective du 11 mai 1850, se plaignaient de ces démocrates qui "ramassent dans leurs journaux les ordures de tous les siècles et de tous les pays, pour les jeter à la face de leur clergé, comme s'il était responsable des fautes de tous les clergés du monde, depuis Judas jusqu'à nous."[116]

Dessaulles devait bientôt ajouter à sa panoplie, outre l'histoire euro-péenne de l'Eglise, des traits empruntés à l'Eglise locale, qu'à partir de 1852 il recueille minutieusement dans un carnet,[117] afin de prouver un jour que "plus un prêtre est exagéré ou brutal dans son langage contre ceux dont il se fait l'adversaire politique, plus il est probable, je devrais presque dire *certain*, qu'il a quelque chose de grave à se faire pardonner."[118]

De l'*Avenir* Dessaulles porte son activité à l'Institut Canadien, où il devient rapidement le conférencier le plus en vue, le plus intransigeant aussi sur la question du libéralisme, multipliant les sarcasmes à l'endroit de ses adversaires politiques, les partisans du gouvernement responsable, auxquels, selon lui, "M. Victor Hugo dirait dans son poétique et admirable langage: Vous êtes les parasites du libéralisme! Vous êtes la maladie de la liberté!"[119]

Cette intransigeance, il la manifeste à propos du principe des nationali-tés dont il s'est fait, après son oncle, l'avocat le plus déterminé. Au prin-temps de 1850, dans ses conférences sur l'annexion aux Etats-Unis, il exalte "le dogme sacré de la souveraineté du peuple" auquel la hiérarchie a, d'après lui, "déclaré une guerre à mort,"[120] parce qu'au Canada "le clergé et le peuple en sont encore aux notions politiques du dix-septième siècle."[121] L'opposition cléricale à l'annexion, il l'attribue à "la soif de suprématie temporelle de ce parti qui, avec un rabat pour égide, jette un cri de colère et de détresse à chaque conquête nouvelle de la civilisation moderne."[122]

Mais la "réaction" par excellence, Dessaulles la voit incarnée par Pie IX qui, après la chute de la république mazzinienne, revient en avril 1850 de son exil de Gaëte pour reprendre possession de son trône à l'ombre des baïonnettes françaises:

En Europe, Messieurs, s'écrie-t-il en s'adressant à ses auditeurs de l'Institut canadien, et en Europe seulement, je vois trois hommes, soutenus par quelques centaines de privilégiés, tendre leurs bras en avant pour faire rétrograder les civilisations. . . . Ces trois hommes, vous les connaissez comme moi. C'est Sa Majesté l'empereur d'Autriche, l'infâme bourreau de la Hongrie et de l'Italie! C'est Sa Majesté le czar de toutes les Russies, l'infâme bourreau de la Hongrie, de la Pologne et de la Circassie! C'est enfin leur ami et allié, le roi de Rome, le chef visible du catholicisme. Voilà, Messieurs, les seuls représentants importants du despotisme dans le monde civilisé![123]

Si de l'ordre politique, il passe à l'ordre social, Dessaulles discerne chez les clercs, qui ont la direction de l'enseignement dans les collèges, une attitude étrangère, sinon hostile, au monde et aux activités laïques: "On fait à des enfants qui ne sont pas destinés à la prêtrise, une vie de petit séminaire; on les façonne à de minutieuses règles, à des exigences multipliées, je dirais presque au joug monastique."[124]

C'est surtout à propos de l'opposition au progrès et à la liberté tels qu'il les entend que Dessaulles vitupère le clergé. En 1854, un prêtre irlandais ayant osé traiter l'affaire de "Galilée et l'Inquisition" dans le sens ultramontain,[125] il en prit la contrepartie avec vigueur pour montrer qu' "avec les ignorants ou les fanatiques, on n'a jamais raison impunément."[126] Il est facile de deviner qu'à travers l'Inquisition dont Galilée avait été la victime, le conférencier en vise une autre, qui s'efforce "de blâmer tout changement, de repousser toute amélioration, d'enrayer tout progrès, d'anéantir toute découverte, de comprimer toute intelligence, de tuer toute liberté, de détruire toute indépendance d'esprit, de prohiber toute manifestation de raison et de génie, de proscrire toute expression libre de la pensée humaine."[127]

Ces propos étaient tenus devant les membres de l'Institut Canadien le 14 mars 1856. Ils ne détonnaient pas dans l'ambiance générale du groupe. Mais ils suscitaient une vive émotion chez les adversaires, tant par la personnalité du conférencier et son influence politique (car il se faisait élire cette année-là au Conseil législatif pour le comté de Rougemont) que par la coïncidence de ses propos avec l'activité fébrile de ses amis. Car à l'Institut canadien on ne s'en tenait plus au plan purement spéculatif. Après le succès électoral de 1854, on voulut passer à l'action. Tandis que Charles Daoust, élu député de Beauharnois, réclamait dans le *Pays*, dont il était le rédacteur en chef, la séparation de l'Eglise et de l'Etat, Joseph Papin se faisait au parlement l'interprète de ses collègues libéraux pour faire aboutir dans les faits une conséquence particulièrement importante de cette séparation, la neutralité scolaire. Or cette question avait été discutée à l'Institut Canadien dans une "convention sur l'éducation" animée par un comité dont les membres les plus en vue étaient Pierre Blanchet et Narcisse Cyr! "Il ne peut y avoir de religion d'Etat," s'écriait Papin au parlement, en résumant la thèse de ses amis, "et s'il en est ainsi, l'Etat ne peut en aucune façon donner de l'argent pour l'enseignement d'aucune foi religieuse."

C'était atteindre l'Eglise canadienne au point sensible: Mgr de Charbonnel et les catholiques haut-canadiens luttaient alors avec acharnement pour l'existence légale des "écoles séparées." George-Etienne Cartier était donc sûr de s'attacher indéfectiblement les catholiques et de les retenir efficacement dans les rangs du parti libéral-conservateur en faisant voter des lois qui garantissaient aux deux races principales du pays la liberté d'organiser ses écoles selon sa foi, sa langue et ses besoins particuliers.[128]

C'est ainsi que l'Institut Canadien était devenu un épouvantail pour les conservateurs. Les thèses libérales qu'on soutenait à sa tribune, le prosélytisme protestant de Cyr et de Lafleur, l'opposition des députés libéraux à l'école confessionnelle et leur alliance récente avec George Brown, considéré comme l'ennemi-né des Canadiens français, tout contribuait à le faire redouter du clergé et des catholiques. Un membre de l'Institut Canadien, mais qui se rattachait au parti libéral-conservateur, le Français légitimiste Alfred Rambau, se demandait en juillet 1855 dans son journal ce que les "rouges" avaient fait de l'Institut Canadien:

L'institut, créé d'abord pour être un centre de réunion, où chacun irait puiser les lumières de l'instruction, où le jeune homme apprendrait à penser et à raisonner, à parler et à écrire, où il trouverait constamment un choix de livres instructifs dans toutes les branches, et surtout d'une moralité irréprochable, et une collection complète de journaux de tous les pays; cet institut, l'espoir des jeunes Canadiens, qu'est-il devenu entre leurs mains? A force d'intrigues, en y introduisant tous leurs affiliés, ils sont parvenus à en avoir le contrôle presque exclusif, et ils ont changé la tribune de cet établissement national . . . en chaire de discorde, de rébellion et d'irréligion. C'est là que les Doutre, les Blanchet et les Cyr vont vomir sur la jeunesse canadienne leurs doctrines anti-sociales, anti-religieuses et révolutionnaires. C'est à l'institut que M. Doutre a donné sa mensongère interprétation du bill seigneurial. C'est à l'institut que le citoyen Blanchet a demandé les écoles mixtes. Enfin, c'est à l'institut que se traitent maintenant toutes les questions du rougisme le plus outré.[129]

*   *   *

Le clergé ne pouvait pas voir sans inquiétude s'accentuer l'emprise de l'Institut Canadien à tous les plans de la vie canadienne-française: politique, social et religieux. Mgr Bourget surtout déplorait d'autant plus l'influence grandissante, dans sa ville épiscopale, d'un foyer d'idées qu'il jugeait subversif, que l'Institut national, placé sous son patronage, ne faisait que traîner une vie languissante. Aussi crut-il bon, dès 1854, de faire une première mise en garde. Lors du second concile provincial tenu à Québec en juin 1854, il usa de son influence auprès des autres évêques pour qu'un règlement disciplinaire indiquât aux prêtres et aux fidèles l'attitude à prendre au sujet des "instituts littéraires." Le texte, très explicite, visait manifestement l'Institut canadien: "Lorsqu'il est constant qu'il y a dans un institut littéraire des livres contre la foi ou les moeurs; qu'il s'y donne des lectures contraires à la religion; qu'il s'y lit des journaux immoraux ou irréligieux, on ne peut admettre aux sacrements ceux qui en font partie, à moins qu'il n'y ait sujet d'espérer que, vu la fermeté des bons principes, ils pourront continuer à les réformer."[130]

Cette clause finale laissait une échappatoire à l'élément le plus pondéré de l'Institut Canadien qui prit, au printemps de 1855, l'initiative d'une réforme portant sur la bibliothèque et sur l'exclusion de certains journaux de la salle de lecture; mais cette tentative échoua par le vote contraire de la majorité.[131]

L'évêque de Montréal se trouvait alors en Europe. Il avait assisté, le 8 décembre 1854, à la proclamation solennelle de l'Immaculée Conception par la bulle *Ineffabilis Deus*, qui ne mentionnait pas la nécessité de l'adhésion de l'épiscopat, mais faisait reposer toute la valeur de la définition sur la sentence pontificale, ce qui impliquait l'infaillibilité du pape. C'est pourquoi des gallicans virent dans la proclamation de ce dogme le prétexte à "une vague nouvelle d'ultramontanisme."[132]

Ce que Mgr Bourget constatait outre-Atlantique était bien de nature à renforcer, s'il se pouvait, ses convictions ultramontaines comme à l'ancrer dans ses préventions contre le libéralisme.

Si à Rome il assistait à l'exaltation de la personne du pape, si en France le Second Empire lui semblait, comme à tous les ultramontains, avoir contracté une alliance durable avec l'Eglise, ailleurs, dans des pays considérés jusqu'alors comme franchement catholiques, il voyait les forces libérales s'employer à la combattre.

En Italie même, dans un Etat resté aussi longtemps clérical que le Piémont, les libéraux poursuivaient leur oeuvre laïcisatrice, ayant à leur tête Rattazzi et Cavour. Après les lois Siccardi de 1850 c'était, le 22 mai 1855, le vote de la fameuse "loi des couvents," qui supprimait une partie des chapitres collégiaux et tous les ordres religieux excepté ceux qui s'adonnaient au soin des malades ou à l'enseignement, en attribuant le produit de leurs biens sécularisés à l'entretien du clergé paroissial.[133]

En Belgique, les libéraux étaient sur le point de s'engager dans la voie du "sectarisme" avec le ministère Frère-Orban. L'époque de l' "unionisme," qui avait marqué les premières années de l'indépendance, était révolue. A partir de 1857, la laïcisation devait se poursuivre plus coordonnée, plus véhémente.[134]

Aussi Mgr Bourget, lorsqu'il fut de retour dans sa ville épiscopale, en juillet 1856, se vit-il affronté de nouveau à ces libéraux dont les principes et l'oeuvre lui avaient paru si détestables en Europe. Son intransigeance ultramontaine se heurtait à l'intransigeance radicale, car "les libéraux radicaux sont aussi intolérants que les ultramontains": "Si ces deux fractions de l'opinion s'opposent, ce n'est pas tant parce que leurs principes religieux ou areligieux sont contradictoires, mais parce qu'elles veulent l'une et l'autre imposer leur idéologie à la cité."[135]

*   *   *

Pour les ultramontains de l'école de Veuillot, l'idéal politique était "l'Etat officiellement catholique et soustrait à la pression de l'opinion publique."[136] Selon un excellent témoin, l'abbé Henri Maret, doyen de la faculté de théologie de la Sorbonne, dans le mémoire qu'il adressait, le 4 décembre 1857, au ministre des cultes, les ultramontains, qu'il appelait "le parti ultra-catholique," aspiraient à restaurer la théocratie directe ou indirecte, d'après laquelle le souverain pontife "possède de droit divin une véritable juridiction politique dans le monde entier, juridiction qui le rend arbitre des grandes questions sociales et même politiques."[137]

La condamnation des libertés politiques modernes allait de pair, chez les ultramontains, avec celle de la science, dont les méthodes d'investigation et de critique leur semblaient nécessairement liées au naturalisme et au rationalisme. A leurs yeux, "tout ce qu'inspirait la méthode critique était suspect"; ils flairaient "partout le naturalisme et l'hétérodoxie."[138]

Enfin les "ultra-catholiques" mettaient l'accent sur l'aspect autoritaire de l'Eglise. Ils recevaient un appui efficace du Saint-Siège, qui voulait "refaire de l'Eglise catholique une Eglise fortement centralisée comme au XIIIe siècle."[139] Pour l'abbé Maret, il existait à Rome "la tradition d'une dictature universelle," qui servait d'appui au parti ultramontain et étendait progressivement la pratique des interventions de la Curie dans l'administration des diocèses.[140]

Ainsi, dans tous les domaines, politique, scientifique et religieux, les catholiques intransigeants se plaçaient au centre du principe autoritaire. Cette position leur paraissait seule capable de sauver le christianisme de "l'esprit moderne," de "la société moderne," de ce qu'il y avait "d'antichrétien au fond de tous les systèmes actuels," comme l'écrivait Dom Guéranger en 1858.[141] Il ne pouvait être question pour eux d'alliance ou de compromis. La vérité avait des droits inaliénables que l'autorité avait mission de faire respecter. Chercher des accommodements avec un siècle foncièrement antichrétien était illusoire. D'où il suivait, pour Dom Guéranger, que "toute la force de l'Eglise, tout son avenir aujourd'hui est dans le développement et l'application du principe surnaturel."[141]

"On ne saurait nier le mérite de cette affirmation," écrit Xavier de Montclos, dont je m'inspire dans cette analyse de l'esprit ultramontain. Mais comme le fait remarquer le même historien, par l'ensemble de leur doctrine, les intransigeants n'évitaient pas le *surnaturalisme*. Lacordaire le voyait bien, qui considérait l'école de l'*Univers* "comme du jansénisme travesti absorbant le naturel dans le surnaturel: 1° en *politique*, l'Etat dans l'Eglise; 2° en *philosophie*, la raison dans l'autorité; 3° en *littérature*, les classiques profanes dans les classiques chrétiens, etc."[142]

Lacordaire aurait pu ajouter que la pensée intransigeante de Veuillot était dans la ligne du Lamennais première manière, de l'auteur de l'*Essai sur l'indifférence* dont la doctrine, le traditionalisme, tendait à une revendication absolue des droits de la religion, parce qu'elle faisait du surnaturel la condition même de toute vie intellectuelle.[143] C'est à cause de cet aspect de la pensée menaisienne que Veuillot et ses collaborateurs devaient toujours garder une réelle sympathie pour le grand précurseur, malgré sa rupture avec l'Eglise.[144]

L'ultramontain Mgr Bourget se rattachait donc, comme tous les partisans de Veuillot, au Lamennais première manière. Il est pour le moins piquant de constater que le conflit qui l'opposa aux libéraux canadiens illustrait, à sa facon, les deux versants opposés de la pensée menaisienne, le versant intransigeant d'une part, de l'autre le versant radical, dont s'inspiraient nos libéraux, surtout Dessaulles, qui avait connu à Paris le prêtre revolté contre Rome et à qui un bon témoin, son concitoyen l'abbé Joseph-Sabin Raymond, devait reprocher un jour de s'être fait au Canada "son admirateur et le propagateur de ses idées.[145]

Notes: Libéralisme et ultramontanisme: I

ABRÉVIATIONS:

AAQ   *Archives de l'archevêché de Québec.*

ACAM   *Archives de la chancellerie de l'archevêché de Montréal.*

APC   *Archives publiques, Ottawa.*

APQ   *Archives de la Province de Québec, Musée provincial, Québec.*

ASQ   *Archives du séminaire de Québec.*

MDM   *Mandements . . . diocèse de Montréal.*

RHAF   *Revue d'histoire de l'Amérique française.*

RLB   *Registre des lettres de Mgr. Bourget,* ACAM.

Je remercie tous ceux qui m'ont permis de consulter les archives dont ils ont la garde, mais je veux mentionner ici d'une façon toute particulière M. l'abbé François Beaudin, archiviste de la chancellerie de l'archevêché de Montréal, qui à mis à ma disposition, avec une bonne grâce dont je lui suis infiniment reconnaissant, le riche dossier de documents inédits concernant l'Institut canadien.

1. André Latreille, "L'Eglise catholique et la laïcité," dans l'ouvrage, écrit en collaboration, *La laïcité* (Centre de sciences politiques de l'Institut juridique de Nice, Paris, 1960), 61-62.

2. *Mandements, lettres pastorales, circulaires et autres documents publiés dans le diocèse de Montréal depuis son érection* (13 vol., Montréal, 1887-1926), III, 356-411, et VI, 24-38.

3. A.Simon, *L'hypothèse libérale en Belgique* (Wetteren, 1956), 17.

4. Mandement de Mgr Bourget proclamant Edouard-Charles Fabre évêque de Gratianapolis et coadjuteur de Montréal, MDM, VI, 360.

5. Texte manuscrit inédit qui commence par ces lignes: "Il y aurait un Mémoire à faire ou plutôt pour montrer par des écrits et par des faits que l'administration du diocèse de Montréal a toujours, dès le principe, été dirigée d'après les saines doctrines de l'ultramontanisme, afin d'en extirper le gal-

licanisme." ACAM 901.045 - 872.1.

6. MDM, VII, 344.

7. Charles-H. Pouthas dans l'ouvrage, écrit en collaboration, *Histoire de la France pour tous les Français* (2 vol., Paris, 1950), II, 256-257.

8. Sainte-Beuve, *Correspondance générale* recueillie, classée et annotée par Jean Bonnerot (12 vol. parus, Paris, 1935-1962), Va, 230.

9. Voir l'étude, fondée sur des dépouillements d'archives, de Charles-H. Pouthas, "Le clergé sous la Monarchie constitutionnelle (1814-1848)," *Revue d'histoire de l'Eglise de France,* 29 (1943), 19-53.

10. *Univers,* 23 juin 1841.

11. Brasseur de Bourbourg, *Histoire du Canada, de son Eglise et de ses missions, depuis la découverte de l'Amérique jusqu'à nous* (2 vol., Paris, 1852), II, 236-237. — Sur ce prêtre français et les péripéties de son séjour à Québec, voir mon ouvrage sur *La vie et l'oeuvre de Henry de Courcy* (Québec, 1955), 189-224.

12. Lettre de Mgr Bourget au cardinal Barnabo, 25 sept. 1858, RLB, X, 340.

13. Circulaire de Mgr Turgeon à son clergé, 8 déc. 1853, dans *Mandements, lettres pastorales et circulaires des évêques de Québec* (17 vol., Québec, 1887-1955), IV, 128-129.

14. L'un des trois étudiants ecclésiastiques de Québec aux Carmes en 1856, l'abbé Louis Beaudet, ne peut s'empêcher de faire remarquer au supérieur du séminaire de Québec, l'abbé Casault, qu'il existe entre les jeunes prêtres de Montréal qu'il voit passer par Paris avant de se rendre à Rome, et ceux de Québec une "grande différence." Le séjour de ces prêtres montréalais à Rome, écrit Beaudet à Casault, le 16 jan. 1856, servira à "secouer tout ce qui sent le gallicanisme et à puiser dans sa source la plus pure toutes les

traditions de l'ultramontanisme."
Cité par Monique Laurent, *La
correspondance de l'abbé Louis
Beaudet, 1853-1858.* Thèse dacty-
lographiée d'histoire, mémoire de
licence ès lettres (histoire), Laval,
1965, 26.

15. MDM, III, 378. — Le col romain fut
adoptée à Québec en 1875 seulement.

16. Léon Pouliot, "Monseigneur Bourget et la reconstruction de la cathédrale de Montréal," RHAF 17 (mars
1964), 488.

17. Jules et Edmond de Goncourt,
*Journal, mémoires de la vie litté-
raire.* Texte intégral établi et an-
noté par Robert Ricatte (4 vol.,
Paris, 1959), I, 163.

18. René Laurentin, *Lourdes. Documents authentiques* (6 vol. parus,
Paris, 1958-1965), III, 40.

19. *Canadien,* 27 déc. 1839.

20. M. Gérard Filion écrivait dans Le
Devoir du 1er février 1960: "Pour
les jeunes gens que nous étions il y
a trente ans, le grand journaliste
catholique était encore Louis
Veuillot, et on jugeait nos polé-
mistes canadiens non pas en fonction de ce qu'ils écrivaient mais de
ce qu'aurait écrit Louis Veuillot s'il
eût été à leur place."

21. Henri-Raymond Casgrain, *Souve-
nances canadiennes* (Exemplaire
dactylographié, ASQ), III, 54.

22. Wilfrid Lebon, *Histoire du collège
de Sainte-Anne-de-la-Pocatière* (2
vol., Québec, 1948-1949), I, 52.

23. Marie-Claire Daveluy, "Un Canadien éminent: Raphaël Bellemare,"
RHAF 12 (déc. 1958), 335.

24. Il y a aux APC, dans les *Papiers
Bellemare* (M.G.29, E3), 25 lettres ou billets datés du 2 février
1854 au 28 avril 1856, de Henry
de Courcy à Bellemare au sujet de
sa collaboration à la *Minerve.*

25. Voir dans mon *Henry de Courcy,*
p. 216, n. 121, l'extrait d'une lettre
datée du 12 sept. 1854, de Mgr
Bourget à Courcy.

26. Casgrain, *op. cit.,* III, 52.

27. Le Fonds Veuillot du Département
des manuscrits de la Bibliothèque
nationale de Paris (*Nouvelles
acquisitions françaises,* Lettres

adressées à Louis Veuillot, 24,225-
24,233) contient trois lettres écrites
respectivement par Mgr Adolphe
Pinsonnault, évêque de London,
lettre datée du 29 août 1856,
de Mgr Jean-Charles Prince,
évêque de Saint-Hyacinthe, datée
du 3 sept. 1856, et de Mgr Walsh,
archevêque d'Halifax, datée du
26 sept. 1856: ces trois lettres à
propos de l'*Univers jugé par lui-
même,* pamphlet dirigé contre
Veuillot.

28. L'abbé Ferland rencontra Louis
Veuillot à un dîner chez Alfred de
Courcy, le 26 mai 1856. *Journal de
voyage* inédit de l'abbé Ferland,
19-20. AAQ.

29. Casgrain, *op. cit.,* II, 146-149.

30. Jean Maurain, *La politique ecclésiastique du Second Empire, de
1852 à 1869* (Paris, 1930), 80.

31. Cité par Louis Girard, "Révolution ou conservatisme en Europe
(1856). Une polémique de la presse parisienne après la guerre de
Crimée," *Mélanges Pierre Renouvin. Etudes d'histoire des relations
internationales* (Paris, 1966), 126.

32. Dom Paul Benoît, *Vie de Monseigneur Taché, archevêque de
Saint-Boniface* (2 vol., Montréal,
1904), I, 344.

33. MDM, III, 399.

34. Cité par George Weill, *Histoire de
l'idée laïque en France* (Paris,
1925), 124.

35. *Univers,* 24 août 1858.

36. Voir L. Girard, *op. cit.,* 126-127.

37. Denis-Emery Papineau, président
de l'Institut canadien, dans le
"Douzième rapport annuel," *Patrie,*
19 déc. 1856.

38. J. Huston, "De la position et des
besoins de la jeunesse canadienne-
française," *Avenir,* 21 août 1847.

39. *Avenir,* 2 oct. 1847.

40. Georges Weill, *Histoire du catholicisme libéral en France, 1828-
1908* (Paris, 1909), 66.

41. *Avenir,* 16 juil. 1847.

42. *Ibid.,* 28 juil. 1847.

43. Lettre de remerciements, datée du
12 mai 1847, de L. Labrèche-Viger,
secrétaire de l'Institut canadien, au
chanoine J.-O.Paré, secrétaire de
l'évêché. ACAM 901.135-847.1.

44. Réponse du chanoine Paré, Montréal, 15 mai 1847, à Labrèche-Viger.
45. Certificat d'admission dans la collection Papineau-Bourassa, APQ.
46. *Avenir*, 5 fév. 1848.
47. Il est piquant de remarquer que, à Sainte-Anne-de-la-Pérade également, dans une maison voisine de celle des Dorion, naquit celui qui serait, avec Mgr Bourget, l'adversaire le plus déterminé des libéraux, Mgr Laflèche!
48. Détail tiré de la notice nécrologique d'Antoine-Aimé Dorion par Wilfrid Laurier, dans La *Patrie*, 4 oct. 1890.
49. L.-A.Dessaulles, *L'Index* (s.l.n.d.), 55.
50. *Collection Gagnon*, Bibliothèque municipale de Montréal.
51. Sur les influences subies par Grégoire XVI dans l'affaire Lamennais, voir Jean-René Derré, *Metternich et Lamennais d'après les documents conservés aux Archives de Vienne* (Paris, 1963). M. Derré prouve par des pièces décisives que "les principes de la Sainte-Alliance inspiraient manifestement le comportement politique" de Grégoire XVI et de la Curie (76).
52. A.Simon, *L'hypothèse libérale*, 12.
53. *Journal* d'Amédée Papineau (Exemplaire dactylographié, APQ), V, 104-105.
54. *Avenir*, 19 fév. 1848.
55. Las Cases publia le *Mémorial de Sainte-Hélène* en 1823 et Antommarchi, ses *Mémoires* en 1825.
56. *Avenir*, 19 avr. 1848.
57. *Ibid.*, 15 avr. 1848.
58. *Ibid.*, 3 mai 1848.
59. *Courrier des Etats-Unis*, 28 déc. 1848.
60. Pierre de La Gorce, *Histoire de la Seconde République française* (2 vol., Paris, 1919), II, 75.
61. MDM, II, 20.
62. *Ibid.*, 31.
63. *Avenir*, 14 mars 1849.
64. *Minerve*, 23 avr. 1849.
65. APC, *Papiers Bellemare*.
66. *Avenir*, 2 mai 1849.
67. *Ibid.*, 11 sept. 1849.
68. *Courrier des Etats-Unis*, 2 août 1849.
69. *Avenir*, 20 sept. 1849.
70. *Ibid.*, 25 juil. 1849.
71. *Moniteur canadien*, 16 nov. 1849.
72. RLB, V, 332-335.
73. MDM, VIII, 83.
74. *Avenir*, 30 mars 1850.
75. *Ami de la religion*, 149 (3 sept. 1850), 533-549.
76. *Avenir*, 28 sept. 1850.
77. *Ibid.*, 6 nov. 1850.
78. *Moniteur canadien*, 24 mai 1850.
79. Manifeste électoral de J.-C. Chapais, dans le *Journal de Québec*, 4 jan. 1851.
80. Lettre reproduite intégralement par Julienne Barnard, *Mémoires Chapais* (3 vol. parus, Montréal, 1961-1964), II, 70.
81. P.-B.Casgrain, *Letellier de Saint-Just et son temps* (Québec, 1885), 83.
82. A.Simon, à propos de l'ouvrage de G. Jacquemyns, *Langrand-Dumonceau, promoteur d'une puissance financière catholique*, dans la *Revue d'histoire ecclésiastique*, 59 (1964), 609.
83. Louis Girard, "Histoire et constitution, 1851-1858," *Bulletin de la Société d'histoire moderne*, 62 (1963), 6.
84. *Journal* d'Amédée Papineau, VII, 136. — *L'Avenir* devait reparaître sporadiquement jusqu'en novembre (*Pays*, 29 nov. 1852).
85. *Journal* d'A.Papineau, VII, 50.
86. *Avenir*, 30 mars 1850.
87. RLB, VI, 52.
88. J.-B.-E. Dorion, *L'Institut Canadien en 1852* (Montréal, 1852), 52.
89. *Ordre*, 24 jan. et 12 fév. 1862.
90. *Ibid.*, 26 fév. 1862.
91. *Ibid.*, 17 mars 1862.
92. Gonzalve Doutre, *Le principe des nationalités*. Lecture publique faite devant l'Institut Canadien de Montréal le 1er déc. (Montréal, 1864), 67.
93. *Ibid.*, 54.
94. *Ibid.*, 44.
95. *Ibid.*, 53.
96. Théodore Lafleur, *A Semi-centennial Historical Sketch of the Grande Ligne Mission Read at the Jubilee Gathering* (Montréal, 1885), 20.
97. Léon Pouliot, "L'Institut Canadien

de Montréal et l'Institut National," RHAF 14 (mars 1961), 481-486.

98. *Pays*, 23 déc. 1852.
99. *Moniteur canadien*, 16 fév. 1854.
100. *Courrier des Etats-Unis*, 12 mars 1853.
101. *Pays*, 10 oct. 1854.
102. *Ibid.*, 3 nov. 1854.
103. J.-L.Lafontaine, *L'Institut Canadien en 1855* (Montréal, 1855), 89.
104. Jean Bruchési, "L'Institut Canadien de Québec," *Cahier des Dix*, n° 12, 1947, 101-107.
105. *Pays*, 4 oct. 1853.
106. "Rapport annuel" du président, *Pays*, 22 déc. 1854.
107. Edward Larocque Tinker, *Les écrits de langue française en Louisiane au dix-neuvième siècle* (Paris, 1932), 100.
108. *Pays*, 23 sept. 1854.
109. *Patrie*, 1er déc. 1856.
110. Sur cette affaire, voir mon étude "Lamartine et les catholiques de France et du Canada," RHAF 4 (déc. 1950), 375-397.
111. L.-A.Dessaulles, *Réponse honnête à une circulaire assez peu chrétienne. Suite à la grande guerre ecclésiastique* (Montréal, 1873), 7.
112. *Journal* d'A.Papineau, VII, 43.
113. F.-L.Béique, *Quatre-vingts ans de souvenirs* (Montréal, 1939), 190.
114. Charles Boutard, *Lamennais, sa vie et ses doctrines* (3 vol., Paris, 1908-1913), III, 136-137.
115. G. Weill, *Histoire du catholicisme libéral en France*, 51.
116. MDM, VIII, 68.
117. APC, M. G. 24, B 59. Ainsi décrit: "Notebook in which he entered notes as to clerical activities in politics and similar matters, 1852-1874. Arranged alphabetically, 57 p."
118. L.-A.Dessaulles, *La grande guerre ecclésiastique. La comédie infernale et les noces d'or. La suprématie ecclésiastique sur l'ordre temporel* (Montréal, 1873), 43.
119. L.-A.Dessaulles, *Six lectures sur l'annexion du Canada aux Etats-Unis* (Montréal, 1851), 35.
120. *Ibid.*, 15.
121. *Ibid.*, 48.
122. *Ibid.*, 17.
123. *Ibid.*, 16.
124. *Ibid.*, 189.

125. *True Witness*, May 12, 1854.
126. L.-A.Dessaulles, *Galilée, ses travaux scientifiques et sa condamnation*. Lecture publique faite devant l'Institut Canadien de Montréal, le 14 mars 1856 (Montréal, 1856), 9.
127. *Ibid.*, 14-15.
128. Louis-Philippe Audet, *Histoire du Conseil de l'Instruction publique* (Montréal, 1965), 31-32.
129. *Patrie*, 10 juil. 1855.
130. MDM, II, 466.
131. Hector Fabre, dans *l'Ordre*, 24 jan. 1862.
132. Opinion de l'abbé Bernier, citée par Jean-Rémy Palanque, *Catholiques libéraux et gallicans en France face au concile du Vatican, 1867-1870* (Aix-en-Provence, 1962), 18.
133. Arturo Carlo Jemolo, *L'Eglise et l'Etat en Italie, du Risorgimento à nos jours* (trad. Madeleine et Robert Juffé, Paris, 1960), 25-27.
134. A.Simon, *Le cardinal Sterckx et son temps* (2 vol., Wetteren, 1950), I, 169.
135. A.Simon, "Considérations sur le libéralisme," *Risorgimento*, 4 (mai 1961), 23.
136. Roger Aubert, *Le pontificat de Pie IX* (Histoire de l'Eglise, Fliche et Martin, 21, 2e édition, Paris, 1963), 228.
137. Abbé G. Bazin, *Vie de Mgr Maret, évêque de Sura, archevêque de Lépante, son temps et ses oeuvres* (3 vol., Paris, 1891), II, 27.
138. Alfred Baudrillart, *Le renouvellement intellectuel du clergé de France au XIXe siècle. Les hommes. Les institutions* (Paris, 1903), 38.
139. R. Aubert, *op. cit.*, 276.
140. Bazin, *op. cit.*, 29.
141. Dom Prosper Guéranger, *Essais sur le naturalisme contemporain. I. M. le prince de Broglie historien de l'Eglise* (Paris, 1858), XIII.
142. Cité par Xavier de Montclos, *Lavigerie, le Saint-Siège et l'Eglise, 1846-1878* (Paris, 1965), 90.
143. *Ibid.*, 86.
144. G.Weill, *Histoire du catholicisme libéral*, 51.
145. *Minerve*, 15 mars 1867.

Imperial Sentiment in the Province of Canada during the Crimean War 1854-1856

A. W. Rasporich, University of Calgary

The effect of the Crimean War upon the development of loyalist and imperialist sentiment in the Canadas has hitherto remained an undefined relationship in Canadian historiography.

There are two probable reasons for the relative obscurity of this issue in the formulation of mid-nineteenth century Canadian political opinion. The first is that there was no official military contribution on the part of Canada. This want of direct action by what has generally been regarded as a pragmatic Canadian society at mid-century, has led to the tenuous *sequitur* that Canadians may not have cared about the fate of British troops in the Crimea.

The second reason probably lies in the generally held whig presumptions on this period.[1] The Union period has to a great extent been viewed as one in which the pioneer society of the Canadas was exercising an increasing control over political, economic, and administrative processes. The advance from responsible government towards self-governing Dominion status in the two decades from 1849-1867 has tended to set up a similar equation of whiggish advance in the political thought of this period. The monies and fervent rhetoric which were summoned to the support of a Great Britain battling the "dark" forces of Imperial Russia do indicate, however, that the loyalist sentiments of English Canada (and to a lesser extent of French Canada), were becoming more, rather than less intense, as the ties of Empire were being cast aside.

The key dates for the sublimation of Canadian atttachments from the pragmatic to the ideal are 1846 and 1849. The first marks the withdrawal of the British Home Government from the sphere of colonial preference and protection in the economic and military affairs of the colonies. The second marks, even more dramatically, the political maturation of the Province of Canada into a self-governing colony. Lord Durham had been in part right when he predicted in his *Report* that responsible government would be made the link of an enduring and advantageous connection of sentiment and interest to the Mother Country. Although interest waned in the commercial revolution which transformed the economy of Canada within ten years of the repeal of the Corn Laws, sentiment for the monarchy, for British political tradition, and for the Empire increased. One need only examine the zealous rhetoric poured out in petitions of loyalty to the Governor-General and the Queen in the annexation crisis of 1849-50 to observe that the bonds of Empire had by no means disappeared from the hearts and minds of Canadians.[2] The transformation of former political and commercial ties into new bonds of kinship, loyalty and tradition was now well under way. Whereas British politicians in this period rarely used the term "Empire,"[3] Canadian colonials, particularly in Canada West, competed with each other in their flowery affirmation of loyalty to Queen and to Empire.[4]

The impulse towards a romanticization or idealization of the Imperial connection continued throughout the early eighteen fifties in central Canadian newspapers of both Reform and Tory leanings. Upon every occasion which demanded it, and even on others that did not, there was a strong response to the call of Empire. Perhaps the strongest reaction to the problems of the Mother Country came from Montreal Tories who had to dispel the suspicion of treason which hung over them like a pall since their involvement in the annexationist activities of 1849-50. Montreal's *Gazette,* mouthpiece of the English-speaking Tory merchants of that city, managed to outdo even the most rabid Tory journals of Canada West in imperialist eloquence. Most English Canadian newspapers were at one in their sentimental effusions over the Queen's Birthday on the twenty-fourth of May, or over the death of the Duke of Wellington late in the year 1852.[5] The *Gazette* went further than most, however, in approving future British expansion into the Caribbean islands in the Bay of Honduras. In his use of flowery anglo-saxon racial mythology, the editor-publisher, Thomas Fenney, strongly resembled stylists of late nineteenth-century imperialist harangues.[6]

Apart from a few *rougeistes*, the French-Canadian response towards the diminishing role of the Imperial government was self-consciously loyal in the early eighteen fifties. It was, after all, the faithful British subjects of Canada East like LaFontaine, Taché, Cartier, and Cauchon who had routed the forces of republicanism and annexation in 1850.[7] From this date until the outbreak of the Crimean conflict, there was a similar but less extreme development of loyalism in French Canada. Ludger Duvernay, the editor of *La Minerve* and a close friend of George-Etienne Cartier, wrote glowingly in late 1850 of the pomp and ceremony of Canadian parliamentary ritual and sang the praises of Queen Victoria.[8] Similarly, Joseph Cauchon, the astute politician, office-seeker and editor of the *Journal de Québec*, took great pains to prove to the "Loyalist" editor of the *Toronto Patriot* that the French Canadians had proven their loyalty in 1775, and 1812, whereas the Tories had turned traitor in 1849.[9] It is small wonder then that the English Tories were so sensitive about their loyalism after 1850!

What must be noted about French-Canadian response to the Mother Country in this period is that loyalty to the person of the monarch and her representative the Governor-General, and attachment to the imperial connection for utilitarian reasons such as defence, were the practical limits of French-Canadian sentiment for Empire. There was little enthusiasm for the military glories of English civilization, glories symbolized in the Duke-of-Wellington cult that blossomed briefly in English Canada in late 1852. Nor was there support for the concept of an expanding British territorial Empire – not, at least, such as existed in the high Tory press of Montreal and Toronto. There was then a direct parallel in the attitude to Empire held by French-Canadian politicians to the attitudes of their contemporaries like Lord John Russell in England. The sooner that the British retreated from her imperial control of colonial government and administration the better.[10] The French-Canadian conservative also disliked the term "Empire" as much as English politicians like Grey or Russell.[11] It was only when challenged openly to prove their loyalty, as in the annexation crisis of 1849-50, or more subtly in the Crimean War or the Indian Mutiny that the *bleus* responded to the call of Empire.

The outbreak of war between England and Russia in 1854 posed some interesting and rather delicate problems for Canadians. Would Canada be expected to contribute men or money if the war began to go badly for the Allies? If ideological support were given to the allied cause, what position would be taken on the alliance with Napoleon III? For admirers of the Napoleonic régime in French Canada there was the problem of priority in their sentimental attachment to Napoleon III and to Queen Victoria. For others who viewed that regime as internally a despotism and externally a rampant imperialism, there was some question as to the extent one should acknowledge the alliance between England and France. Another interesting and even disquieting relationship was the one existing between Canada and the United States. Would the Americans, through real or feigned sympathy for Russia, take the opportunity as they had in the War of 1812 to wring either diplomatic or economic concessions out of Great Britain? The problem did become more than a hypothetical one, for early in 1856 a diplomatic incident between England and the United States was created by the dismissal of the British Minister, Mr. Crampton, as envoy to the United States. This crisis touched Canadians very closely since there was virtually no British military establishment left to protect British North America should the Americans decide once again to play the jackal in their foreign policy.

The nature of the Canadian military response was very limited. There were a few Canadians and Nova Scotians who enlisted in the British army like Alexander Dunn, the son of the ex-Receiver-General of Upper Canada, or Frederick H.D.Veith of Nova Scotia.[12] Both of these men were, however, residing in Great Britain at the outbreak of war and can hardly be said to have been caught up in a wave of popular enlistments in Canada. Similarly the Nova Scotian hero of the defence of Kars, General Fenwick Williams, can scarcely be considered a part of an enlistment programme during the war in the Maritimes. The major Canadian military contribution was a passive one, since the date 1855 marks the formation of a Canadian volunteer militia which would be uniformed, armed, and required to carry out a prescribed course of training. This force was then to be a semi-professional corps which would supplement the old "sedentary militia,"[13] and replace the void created by the withdrawal of most of the British regulars to the Crimea.

Despite the failure to provide a regular regiment, such as the one formed four years later for the quelling of the Indian Mutiny, there were proposals made for the raising of such a unit for the Crimean campaign. Sir Allan MacNab, the rabid anglophile Premier of Canada, suggested that such a regular regiment could be raised in Canada with the inducement of land grants as a reward for service.[14] The proposal to send such a regiment overseas angered especially the *rouges* of Lower Canada, and the Clear Grits of the Upper Province. Even MacNab's Tory colleagues in Canada West were so afraid of the possibility of an attack from the United States after Canada had bled itself dry of soldiers, that MacNab had to back down. This was neither the end nor the beginning of such proposals, which had in fact been in evidence before MacNab's espousal of a contribution to the British army.[15] The Quebec *Morning Chronicle*, mouthpiece of the English mercantile element in that city, was the most insistent in its support of active military aid. Late in 1855, the editor, St. Michel, still proposed the dispatch of a force to Europe:

. . . *We lately published an article in the* London Morning Post *in which it was announced that it is intended to raise a Foreign Legion which will bear the name of "the Royal British North American Regiment" and consist of 2800 men. We are now enabled to state on good authority that this intelligence is substantially correct and that a force composed of two battalions, one to be raised in each section of the Province will be immediately organized. Sir Allan MacNab, when in London, had repeated interviews with Lord Palmerston, and it has been agreed that the regiment will be essentially native Canadian in its character, both as regards officers and men, irrespective of origin.*[16]

That such verbal commitments were even made attests to the interest of many English Canadians in the cause of the Mother Country. The ease with which the 100th Royal Canadian Regiment of Foot was raised within three months in 1858 does offer positive testimony to the growth of strong imperial sentiment in English Canada during the Crimean War.

The second means of indicating a positive commitment to the imperial cause was that of monetary donation to the Patriotic Fund. The fund was originally set up in England as a reaction to the losses suffered in the Battle of the Alma in September of 1854. The intention of the founders of the Royal Commission of the Patriotic Fund was to provide some financial support to the widows and orphans of the soldiers killed in this or a future engagement. There was little, if any, popular opinion expressed through the press before the motion was suddenly brought forward in the Legislative Assembly by Francis Hincks on November 6, 1854. To judge from the strong support for the fund which followed, it appears that Hincks was certainly in advance of the popular feeling about such an emotional issue. In his motion he apologized for having surprised the House without giving prior notice, and proceeded to explain his action by emphasizing that, "Upon this occasion the ministry should lead rather than follow the people in manifesting a proper spirit of sympathy in the war."[17]

The reactions to Hincks' motion were especially candid since the House had obviously been taken by surprise. The general reaction to Hincks' speech appeared to be favourable since he and others who struck the chords of loyalty for the embattled Mother Country received a resounding, "Hear! Hear!" A.T. Galt, who responded to Hincks' panegyric on the English struggle for civilisation against barbarism, did so in a manner to conciliate the French-speaking group within the House and his own constituency of Sherbrooke. Galt appealed to the French Canadians by stressing the allied efforts of England and France. He hoped that the fund would admit of no distinction between "those who have fallen for liberty's cause, whichever of the nations they belonged to [Hear, Hear], but that the funds which might be appropriated should go to the Patriotic Fund open in England and France."[18] A number of English-Canadian speakers like Robinson, Young, Gamble, and Larwill echoed Hincks' sentiments and were duly accorded approval by the House.

The French-Canadian members then made clear their position on the Fund. A.A. Dorion of Montreal, a *rouge*, yielded to the sense of the House, but did not openly express any approbation of the cause engaged in by England or France. His justification for a grant by the Legislature was couched in gallic terms of honour, and the sympathy "which he believed was generally felt for the brave soldiers of both nations now struggling and dying for the cause of freedom."[19] In taking this position, Dorion was seconded by

Joseph Cauchon who merely registered his approval and sat down. That the House's mood was strongly favourable to the fund and that it would have viewed any opposition as heartless and perhaps disloyal, were things indicated in the failure of the *rouge*, Joseph Papin, to voice even the token opposition that he and a few other *rouges* expressed a few days later on the extended discussion of the bill. Papin curtly refrained from comment and also sat down.

It is significant that there was no vocal opposition from the radical French-Canadian bloc, since some of the same men expressed in the editorials of *L'Avenir* their distaste for the imperialistic wars of Europe. The only strong opposition during the first reading of the motion came rather from one whose loyalty could never be called into question, – W.H. Merritt. A loyal public servant of Canada since the eighteen twenties and thirties, Merritt had little to fear in denouncing the morality of England's participation in the war, since he had always been on the side of right in questions of loyalty in 1837 as a Tory, and in 1849 as a Reformer. He denounced both the Turks and the Russians as tyrannical nations from time immemorial, and therefore could see little beneficial result from such a war on the part of either England or France. Merritt also disagreed with the fundamental premises that the Allies fought for the liberties of the world, since in fighting for Turkey, they were not fighting for the more important liberties of Hungary, Poland or Italy. The issues as he saw them were not at all the same as those of 1848.

On the seventeenth of November, Sir Allan MacNab, the gallant knight of Dundurn, introduced a motion for the support of widows and orphans in the sum of £20,000, and the House remained in Committee to discuss the motion. Opposition was much more in evidence on this issue since a specific sum had finally been suggested. Merritt gained supporters from those members who were niggard about the lavish expenditure of public monies, and those advocates of self-help who opposed any form of state relief.[20] The French-Canadian dissidents Papin, Marchildon, and Bruneau finally found their voices but uttered less than nominal opposition to the grant. Perhaps the reason for their reservation was the acerbity of those who stood for the imperial connection. Hincks labelled the opposition to the motion as miserly, despite its moderate and reasoned tone. Those who were unprepared to spend five cents a head for the whole population upon something so valuable as the liberty of Europe were deficient not only in generosity but in political ideals. Solicitor-General Ross, feeling confident that the great majority of the French Canadians in the party were behind Morin, Chabot, Turcotte, and Cauchon, made the small group of dissenters from Canada East writhe in their seats with a similar use of sarcasm:

He [Ross] *felt disappointed that any other Frenchman should oppose it, when they considered what England had done for Quebec on the occasion of that disastrous fire which had been alluded to. The sum then re-*

ceived by Quebec from all quarters amounted to upwards of £160,000 and from Liverpool and Manchester alone there came as much as this Province was now asked to contribute.[21]

George Brown then attempted with some success to soothe wounded sensibilities with a positive appeal to the imperial connection. The resolution was then immediately adopted and reported to the House. Since no member dared be branded as disloyal by asking for a division, the resolution passed unanimously.

The Legislative Council offered no opposition to the Lower House's determination. The two speakers most eloquent in its favour were the two *bleus,* E.P. Taché and Narcisse Belleau. Taché's speech was a curious mixture of appeals, because he played not only upon the nobler sources of imperial sentiment such as loyalty, honour, and generosity, but also upon the commercial motive. He began by denouncing the commercial motive for the grant, and then proceeded to relate in great detail the virtues of the contribution as excellent advertising in both France and England. The nadir of Taché's declamation was reached when he cannily pointed out that, "The grant of this £20,000, say the commercial men, just on the eve of the great universal exhibition in Paris, will call attention to Canada, especially as half of the sum is to be presented to the widows and orphans of French soldiers."[22] The contribution to the Patriotic Fund was voted on without any dissent in the Council, and was forwarded by Lord Elgin to the Home Government with a fervent address of loyalty to the Queen appended to it.[23]

The popular reactions to the Patriotic Fund can be gauged by the reports in the press on contributions by national societies, religious denominations, and by individuals. The most prominent area of support in Canada West, both in terms of its publicity and the success of its canvass, was that of Toronto and its hinterland. The press in Toronto, led by Brown of the *Globe* and Beaty of the Toronto *Leader and Patriot,* both reported and actively promoted public meetings for the Fund.[24] Even the ex-rebel William Lyon Mackenzie, who was inclined to be rather reticent about a war in a continent dominated by reaction after 1848, indirectly endorsed the movement by reporting the progress of the fund.[25] It was however Brown, the Grit and mid-Victorian liberal, who was inclined to be the most strident in his support for the Fund. He immediately endorsed Hincks' proposal of November 6 in the *Globe* of the eighth of November. By references to the want of feeling that might have existed in Toronto as compared to New York he attempted to shame his readers into acts of greater generosity:

We have no active part to play in the contest, and the more reason is there for us taking a share in succoring those by whose loss we and all other subjects of the Empire are benefitted. We do not venture to point out how the first movement should be made. If there is liberality in our community corresponding to the interest which they have displayed in the present war, then we are sure that it will find some means of showing itself, and that Canadian contributions to the 'Patriotic Fund' will be commensurate with the standing and position of the Provinces as the first colony of Great Britain. We perceive that the British residents of New York and others have already opened their subscription list for the same purpose. Even the names published in the Albion [English newspaper in New York] *we find that the presidents of national societies commenced the work by contributions of £100 each. Shall we be behind our loyal countrymen in the United States? Most assuredly we should not. Who will be the first to move?*[26]

Brown's position on the fund was qualified by his usual reservations of voluntaryism, since he no doubt viewed the Fund as a sort of religious crusade. He was most annoyed by the insistence of the worthies of the corporation of Toronto that there should be a £1000 subscription to the Fund from the city. There was no doubt some element of ethnic jealousy involved since Brown was very active in the promotion of donations from the St. Andrew's Society, and he made it known that the St. George's Society was the sinister power behind the motion for a flat subscription from the Corporation of Toronto.[27] A fierce Scottish pride in attachment to Empire forced Brown into a massive inconsistency, since he had not uttered a word of voluntaryist protest against the £20,000 provincial contribution. He did however make good his boast that more would be collected under the voluntary scheme, since he proudly announced in March of 1855 that over £1000 was subscribed for and collected in Toronto by the St. Andrew's Society. His optimistic estimate was that over £2500 would be collected from all sources in the Toronto area, – more than double what would have been collected under the original plan.[28] This total in no way matched one grandiose estimate that some £50,000 could be easily collected from all sources in Toronto, if everyone would yield but a day's income to the Fund.[29] It did nevertheless represent a donation of a similar, and probably higher proportion per capita than the provincial donation.[30]

In Montreal the Patriotic Fund was promoted very actively by Francis Hincks' newspaper, the *Pilot*. Immediately after the introduction of Hincks' motion for support of widows and orphans, his editor, Rollo Campbell, endorsed the public contribution and urged private generosity in aid of the Fund. His appeal was frankly imperialistic and even racial: "We know of nothing so likely to touch the heart of the Mother Country as this mark of sympathy and interest from her powerful and prosperous child. May the branches of the Anglo-Saxon family, in all parts of the world, ever be ready to reciprocate generous and kindly offers to each other."[31]

A fund-raising concert in Montreal soon followed in the early New Year. The use of the concert to raise money was of course radically different from Toronto's sober meetings for the organization of a canvass.[32] The loyal British of Toronto needed no ulterior motive such as entertainment to manifest their largess; but the English and French of Montreal apparently did. The mettle of Upper Canadian loyalists was no doubt stiffer, since imperialist oratory by the likes of Robert Baldwin and John Hillyard Cameron sufficed to rally the faithful to the cause. On the other hand, the loyal British subjects of Montreal required a little self-indulgence in orchestral numbers and patriotic song either as an impulse to greater giving or as a palliation of an injured purse. Regardless of the motive, the Montreal affair at City Hall was a refreshing mixture of brief but impassioned eloquence by the Mayor, classical music, waltzes and quadrilles by the orchestra, and patriotic songs for the allied troops by all who were present. The content of the patriotic song serves as an excellent gauge of those attending:

Then rise ye men of Canada, a song of triumph high,
For France and England's victories beneath an Eastern sky
Their dauntless valor, as of yore, shone bright and lustrous still
What banners waved triumphantly, o'er Alma's fatal hill
As melts the snow before the sun, so Russia's boasted might,
And other fields shall show, ere long how French and English fight
Hurrah! Ye sons of Canada, for that brave and gallant band,
Who brothers are, and children of, the same old fatherland
Fear not the din of war, not battle's fierce alarms,
The red cross flag, and tri-color, defy the world in arms![33]

Prominent citizens of the city like Cusack P. Roney, A.M. Ross, and L.V.Sicotte started the subscriptions to the fund with contributions varying from £10 to £25. Five days later the Mayor announced that £350 had been realized from subscriptions, and admissions to the concert. He also announced that subscriptions from Lord Bury, Lady Head, and the Hon. John Young, totalling £45, had just arrived that very day.[34]

By April of 1855 the total contributions to the Montreal Fund from concert proceeds, from subscriptions by the national societies and various congregations, and from individuals was a respectable £2091. Since the fund was then closed in April by Thomas Evans, the Secretary of the local committee of the Fund, it is likely that unnoticed donations from the national societies trickled in over the summer.[35] The greater percentage of the Montreal contribution, apart from admissions to the concert, was made up of English-Canadian contributions. Even though the St. Jean-Baptiste society buildings were decorated with Union Jacks and French tri-colors for the concert in January, there is no record in the *Pilot* or *La Minerve* of a fund-gathering campaign by that society as there were of the contributions by the St. George's Society and the St. Andrew's Society. French-Canadian contributions in Montreal, as in Quebec city, appeared to come from only a few prominent politicians like L.V. Sicotte and G.E. Cartier who had a strong commitment to bridging the gap which separated the two cultures.

The Fund did not appear to do as well in Quebec City as in either Montreal or Toronto, if accounts in the press in Quebec City[36] can be credited. This phenomenon is not really attributable to the lack of an English-speaking element in Quebec since the non-French population of Quebec in 1851 was 43%, compared to 54% in Montreal. It may perhaps be accounted for in part by the presence of the Provincial Government in Quebec for most of the war; for the government had of course just made a blanket contribution for the Province of £20,000, and residents of Quebec may well have felt that this was in great part their contribution.[37] Another reason may be that the prominent provincial politicians like Hincks, Cauchon, Morin, and Taché dominated so exclusively the proceedings of the fund meeting in Quebec City in late January of 1855.[38] Although the city's commercial and political élite was present, it was completely overshadowed; and the élite may have felt less enterprising than it might have been, left to its own devices. When the meeting closed and subscriptions were opened, some £560 was subscribed within the space of a half an hour. Many of the names which appeared on the subscription list were members of the Provincial Legislature or Executive so that the figure was less impressive as a municipal contribution than it seemed at first sight.[39] The percentage of gallic to anglo-saxon names among the remaining subscribers was approximately fifteen to twenty per cent. This figure in no way approaches the 60% figure for the French-speaking population of Quebec; so that it appears once again that French-Canadian sentiment for Empire or for the allied cause in the Crimea was not strong if measured on the scale of pounds and pence contributed to the Patriotic Fund. The unanimity which was apparent in the vote for the £20,000 contribution by the Provincial Legislature, was not then matched by a similar zeal for private contributions among the French-Canadian population of Quebec and Montreal. The relatively strong response of the English Canadians in Toronto, and even the outlying districts of Canada West,[40] would appear to indicate that the Members of Provincial Parliament who represented these areas were in closer communion with the feeling of their constituents.

The third means available to colonials, apart from contributions of men or money was the expression of ideological approbation of Great Britain's struggle in Europe. The effusion of loyal sentiment was, as indicated previously, a necessary part of the Patriotic Fund meetings and concerts; but it was also demonstrated in the form of public addresses to the Queen, public meetings and illuminations for the celebration of victories, days of humiliation and prayer for the success of Allied arms, and comment in the Provincial Legislature and press. All of these means were used very effectively by those imperially-minded elements in the population of Canada West. The patterns already observed in the regional responses of Canada to the Patriotic Fund tended to be reinforced in the emotion generated over the British cause in the Crimea.

Public petitions to the Queen were the most direct means available to the loyal citizens of the Province of Canada. These petitions to the Governor-General and Queen were largely the product of the bursting imperial pride of the citizens of Canada West. Particularly prominent communities in this section of the Province were the major towns in the Niagara peninsula, Toronto, and the hard core Loyalist country of Lennox and Addington. Governor Edmund Head would have included a few other towns in the first rank from his triumphal tour of Canada West in October of 1855. Up until the time of his dispatch of late October, describing his tour in the West, he had visited Kingston, London, Hamilton, Cobourg, Brantford, Woodstock, Dundas and Paris. There is little doubt left in Head's dispatch to his superiors that he considered these towns in the western portion of the Province far warmer to the cause of Her Majesty's arms than those in the eastern section:

At all the above places without exception, I have been received with every mark of attention and respect as the Queen's Representative. At the same time, although I was accompanied by two, or three members of my executive council, there are not manifestations of feeling of a party or political character of any kind. But what struck me more than anything was the universal expression of loyalty and rejoicing in connection with the fall of Sebastopol and the progress of the Allied arms in the East. One might almost suppose the sympathy of the Canadian people with the cause of England to be shown more eagerly on account of the adverse feeling which is said to prevail in the United States.

I believe that every address presented to me since I left Lower Canada – no matter from what body, – whether the corporation of a City – a mechanics institute or a literary association–has contained some expressions of hope or congratulation with reference to the War. Almost every decoration of a street or room exhibited the word "Sebastopol" or some such emblem such as a bear claimed by France and England. The toasts and speeches at all public entertainments conveyed the same impression of loyal pride at the success of British arms.

The illumination at Montreal and Quebec gave evidence of similar feelings but these facts have not met my eye since I entered Upper Canada, and, such as they are, I report them to you, Sir, because they will, I am sure, be a source of pleasure to Her Majesty and Her Majesty's Advisers.[41]

An analysis of the contents of the loyal addresses to the Queen from the citizens of Canada West reveals a pattern of romantic and imperial parlance. It was inevitable that the phrase "Your Majesty" and "Your Majesty's brave soldiers" would be the most prominent in any such humble address to the Crown. The most prominent argument used, however, was that concerning the despotic encroachment of Russia upon the liberties of Europe. This line of reasoning invariably led to the conclusion that Great Britain was therefore justified in the eyes of God and humanity in upholding the rights of "Independent nations and Constitutional Government," and of "Justice, Liberty, and Civilization."[42] It is significant that only one address of seven mentioned a most logical argument favoured in the English press at this time, – that England was preserving the balance of power in Eastern Europe.[43] *Realpolitik* was generally looked upon as the property of despots and not of freedom-loving Englishmen. Once the war was given a sense of righteous justification it naturally followed that God should be on the side of right in the form of "Divine Providence," "Almighty God," "The God of Armies," or "The Supreme Ruler of Armies and Nations." Another common premise which underlaid at least half of the addresses was that there existed common ties of race and blood to the mother country. This appeal to racial lineage was expressed by the petitioners from St. Catharines in the closest possible terms. The issue of the war to them was most vital since "it influences us as members of the same body, in whose veins the same blood circulates."[44] The Lincoln militia were careful to point out the difference between "sons of Britain who have adopted Canada" and "the descendants of those faithful subjects styled 'the Unity of the Empire Loyalists'." There was no doubt left in this petition that the latter were a superior breed of loyal Briton.[45]

A general feature of many of these addresses was the aspiration of the humble petitioners to transcend the great space which separated Canadians from the scene of conflict. The result was a grandiloquent romanticization of the imperial connection. The words "heart," "sentiment," "feelings" and "sympathy" recurred constantly in conjunction with other adjectives to express distance from the scenes of horror and strife. Torontonians felt particularly deprived of the bloody carnage in the Crimea; – "In this prosperous and contented portion of your widespread Dominions, we are far removed from the battlefields on which our fellow subjects have so nobly fought and bled; but our hearts are with them in the conflict."[46] Yet another group of petitioners from Hamilton used the ties of Empire and personal loyalty to the Queen as an anodyne to ease the pain of remoteness; – "Though far distant from the scene where Your Majesty's brave and noble soldiers have won . . . for their country fresh Laurels, we beg to assure Your Majesty that we, in common with all Your Majesty's dutiful and loyal subjects in this part of the Empire feel the liveliest interest in the great contest in which Your Majesty is engaged."[47] Loyalty to Queen and global Empire did serve then as conceptual comforts of the petitioners' romantic yearnings for the glories and the defeats of Alma, Balaklava, and Sebastopol.

Although the English Canadian addresses of Canada East were substantially the same as those of Canada West,[48] French-Canadian memorials to the Governor-General and the Queen on the issue of the Crimean campaign were neither as numerous nor as fervent in their espousal of the British cause. Where they were as warm in their occasional addresses was in their profession of personal loyalty to the Sovereign and the Governor-

General and in their support of the war as a combined effort of the allied nations of England and France against Russia. There appeared also to be an internal difference in the petitioning of Lord Elgin and Edmund Head as Governors-General. Elgin appeared to be more popular personally (because of his association with responsible government and the party of Lafontaine) than was Head, who replaced him in late 1854. The latter really made himself offensive to the French-Canadian press when he made his tactless remarks concerning the comparative backwardness of French Canada while on his tour of Canada West late in 1855.

Lord Elgin and the Queen were the object of a few patriotic addresses by the French inhabitants of Canada East on the return of the Governor-General from his visit to England in the summer of 1854. Affirmations of the warmth and interest of the French citizens of Quebec City, were made in a motion put forward by Jean Bruneau, a member of the Provincial Legislature. He was careful to stress that the war effort was a joint product of the alliance between Great Britain and France, "the two great nations of Europe with whose previous history and ultimate destiny Canada must always feel a deep interest."[49] The mayor of Montreal, Wolfred Nelson, similarly welcomed Elgin as he passed through that city in June of 1854. Nelson's speech to the Governor-General was, however, more concerned with Elgin's heroic stand on self-government than on the Crimean War which only received token sympathy.[50] Much warmer was the joint address to the Queen which was drawn up a week later by the prominent English and French citizens of Montreal. The address of this meeting, which was presided over by Wm. Badgeley and M. Deslisle, stressed the joint efforts of *"les nations anglaises et françaises dans la lutte à laquelle ils ont été forcés de prendre part contre les aggressions d'une puissance despotique, ambitieuse, et intolérante."*[51] The commentary made upon the proceedings of this meeting by the editors of *La Minerve* revealed even more fully the insular attitudes of French Canada upon the war. They maintained that the main purpose of the meeting was to indicate to the United States that there was no hope of annexing Canada, since there were no republican sentiments held by French Canadians. Another useful purpose of the meeting was to apprise France and Europe of *"les sympathies que notre ancienne colonie conservé encore pour la France."*[52] The weight of French-Canadian supplications to their British rulers thus rested upon different foundations. There was little of the pungent rhetoric of British imperialism or the militant support of Her Majesty's arms. The most enthusiastic aspect of their addresses was often a recognition of the co-operation of French and English troops in the Crimea, or of the sentimental attachments to the ancient *mère patrie*. Whereas the English Canadian damned his isolation from the epicentre of conflict, the French Canadian accepted his insularity more gracefully, and used the patriotic address as a means of fostering better relations with his English-Canadian brethren. Whereas the English-Canadian addresses-militant demanded a "just and honourable peace," the French-Canadian memorials simply yearned for the establishment of stability and prosperity that the return of peace would bring. Their addresses ended with a characteristic plea for the return of either "a solid and permanent peace" or a "general and advantageous peace."[53]

Another means which was available to religious Canadians was that noted Anglo-Saxon custom of war, the day of humiliation and prayer. These days of prayer for the success of national armies had been called in the Canadas and the Maritimes as early as the seventeen nineties, and subsequently in the War of 1812.[54] The first to take action in this direction in May of 1854 was the Protestant population of Montreal, composed of Anglicans, Presbyterians, and Congregationalists.[55] The day chosen by these denominations was Wednesday, May 2, to coincide with the day appointed by the Queen in England for fast and humiliation. There was an attempted obstruction by Judge Mondelet to an adjournment of the bilingual bench of the Superior Court to celebrate the fast day on the grounds that all the powers involved in the war were a pack of "bloody murderers."[56] Perhaps because of this intemperate outburst and the non-participation of the Catholic clergy in the day of humiliation, it was decided by the prominent citizens of Montreal to stage a demonstration of loyalty in the wake of the day of prayer to allow French Canadian Catholics to demonstrate their interest in the war.

This meeting was attended by at least three or four prominent French Canadian citizens of the city. Apart from a strongly loyal speech by William Badgeley, it was the combination of George-Etienne Cartier and C.S. Cherrier which provided the bulk of comment on the Crimean campaign. Cherrier concentrated on the anti-despotic nature of the Allied cause and the necessity of preserving the balance of power against the barbarian hordes of the North. Cartier preferred instead to carry over the spirit of the day of humiliation by his emphasis on the sacred cause of the Allies. He derided the Orthodox Church which demanded first loyalty to the Czar rather than to Christ, and promised that such barbaric and degraded Christianity would never triumph over Catholicism and Anglicanism.[57] If these professions of faith were not enough to relieve the animus created by Mondelet's intemperate outburst, the address of loyalty to the Queen which passed unanimously must surely have vindicated French-Canadian allegiance.

The Fast Day which was observed in Montreal in April of 1855 created much less controversy. The necessity for heroics by the French-Canadian political leaders of Montreal was obviated by the participation of the Roman Catholic Church in the day of fast and prayer. Not only the Catholic Churches, but the Free Church, all wings of the Presbyterian Church, and the Jewish synagogues conducted religious services on the appointed day. Sermons and addresses appropriate to the occasion were delivered and collections for the Patriotic Fund were made at the highly competitive Churches of England and Scotland. The editorial comment in Hincks' *Pilot* on the necessity of such fast days was itself a model of the archetypal sermon of self-abasement. The essential moral flaw really lay with the nation itself and war was but a visitation of Divine Providence upon a sinful people. The reader was then urged to "Wash you, and make you clean . . . cease to do evil, and learn to do well." With moral rectitude established in society, the victory of the side of good over evil would not be far behind.[58] The reaction of Brown Chamberlin's Tory *Gazette* was much more militant. The homily that was offered to the readers for the Fast Day was a bellicose harangue against the peace party in England which had advocated disarmament. The period of prolonged peace which had existed in Europe since the Napoleonic wars had also destroyed the moral fibre of all European nations. A good and just war would soon re-establish virtue and nobility of deed in the British Empire:

We have not trouble at arriving at the fact that long peace does tend to national selfishness, cupidity, and abatement of the military spirit. Commerce, however great a civilizer it may be, is intensely selfish in its nature and so intense does this sometimes become that it tempts men to do things that cannot be squared with the rules of morals. . . . War leads to dreadful suffering, but we have seen it ably argued, that heroic virtue arises out of suffering, and that the generous and noble affections often acquire extraordinary force amid scenes of unutterable wo[sic], that the human heart is purified by suffering, and that in that ordeal the sins and selfishness of nations are washed out. There is something that also appeals to some of our best national feelings in the heroism of defensive war. We cannot think of the deeds of heroism of British soldiers at Alma, Balaklava, and Inkerman without a thrill of enthusiasm; and the display of such heroism with the national sympathy it has called forth, is no sign of national decay.[59]

The citizens of Toronto generally assumed the more militant posture of the Montreal *Gazette*. George Brown left no doubt that the Wesleyan Day of Humiliation on May 2, 1854 was recruitment of God for service on the side of right; — "The clergy were willing with something of promptitude which in war summons our soldiers and sailors forth to perilous service to hasten to the altar on their behalf, and join in committing the issues of the national struggle to the God of Battles."[60] Similarly, Bishop Strachan did not seek self-purgation in his plea for a day of public prayer, but "that they may unite with their Religious Brethren at home in their devotions and charities, and so feel themselves in all respects an acknowledged portion of the British nation."[61] Divine approbation rather than reprobation were then assumed by Kirkmen and Anglicans in Toronto. Like their Tory brethren in Montreal they perverted the original sense of a day of humiliation into one of supplication for divine aid and even into self-congratulation that the aid of divine providence had already been won.

A third form of publicly demonstrating interest in the progress of Allied arms was that of public illumination. An illumination in effect meant that the city or town would be lit up in a glorious binge of candlepower provided by the local gasworks. Transparencies, portraits, and illustrations would then be provided at the largest hall in town to depict the victory and the heroic deeds of the allied troops. Religious services and torch-light processions usually accompanied such festivities. The event which created the greatest popular reaction was the fall of Sebastopol in late summer of 1855. All three major cities in Canada were eventually illuminated to celebrate the victory; but the loyal English of Montreal could not restrain a spontaneous display of emotion upon receipt of the news of victory:

The moment the news of the fall of Sebastopol reached this city; it spread like wildfire, and on every countenance might be seen the greatest delight. Persons were running hither and thither to tell the glorious news to their friends. Flags were immediately hung out from Dolly's Hill, and Clarke's, Mr. Jones of Tattersall's, and several other places. The Pilot *office at once hoisted the Union Jack and Tri-color on their mast above the office. On the reception of the news at the High School, it was read to the boys, who, breaking through all restraints made the roof ring with their cheers and were granted a holiday. The ships in the harbor were decked out with their colors flying. The* Britannia *hoisted a bear's skin below the Union Jack. In the evening, considering the short time between the receipt of the news and nightfall, the illumination was very general. . . .* [62]

This natural display of enthusiasm did not approach the brilliance of the illumination and demonstrations held a week later in the major cities and towns. In Montreal, the great majority of the buildings and shops were owned by Scots or Englishmen, but there were a few French-Canadian shopowners who decorated their shops. Even the radical *Institut Canadien* was adorned with portraits of the principals, and with the Union Jack and Tri-color. What is more important, the whole of the Montreal celebrations and illumination appeared as a tribute to the co-operation of both victorious nations and their rulers.[63] The Quebec demonstrations of October 8, were initiated in a spirit of competition with those of Montreal. The *Morning Chronicle* urged its readers, "Let us not be behind hand in our degree, but emulate the zeal of the sister city."[64] The resultant celebration in Quebec City was then as gaudy as the one in Montreal, and even more self-consciously bicultural. There was a splendid service held at the French Cathedral, and a traditional *Te Deum* sung with great enthusiasm and earnestness. The congregation then separated to the vibrant strains of "God Save the Queen," "La Marseillaise," and "Mourir pour la Patrie." According to St. Michel, the editor of the *Chronicle*, it was a united gesture of all political parties for the principles of "constitutional freedom, loyalty to their Sovereign, and detestation of tyrannical aggression."[65] The self-congratulation with which the press described the amicable festivities in

Montreal and Quebec is testimony not so much to the enthusiasm generated for the Empire, but to the greater understanding promoted by the Allied cause to better race-relations in Canada. Loyalty to Queen and Empire really served as handmaiden to this nativist purpose.

Toronto celebrations of the fall of the fortress at Sebastopol were similar in size and intensity to those of Montreal and Quebec. As was usual, the Toronto demonstrations were much stronger in their long and loud professions of loyalty to Empire and Queen. The public meeting at which the mayors and other dignitaries of local and provincial politics spoke was really the focal point of the festivities in Toronto. The High Tories of provincial stature, Chief Justice Robinson and John Hilyard Cameron, spoke in glowing tones of the valour of Her Majesty's armies. It was only Robinson who even attempted to transcend the bias of the celebration as one of the British Empire. He made a strong attempt to relate the Allied victory to a future amelioration of French-English relations in Canada:

The people of a great portion of Canada are of French origin. We cannot but suppose — for we only have to place ourselves in their situation to be convinced of it, — that they retain a great deal of sincere and deep-rooted affection for the country they have left. Hitherto it has been out of their power to rejoice in the successes of that country, without evincing a feeling of something like disloyalty towards the country to which they owe their allegiance. But on the present occasion they may rejoice as heartily as we in the success of the Allies, and we can join them in celebration, with as cordial good will as they can do.[66]

It is significant to note that Robinson was not interrupted by cheers from his audience on this occasion. Rather, the applause came for bombast on the storming of the fortress, for the Empire, Her Majesty, and Her Majesty's soldiers and sailors. Although such a speech would have won automatic applause from the mixed cultures of Quebec and Montreal, it could only be appreciated by a few provincial politicians of Canada West who were lively to the problems of the Union.[67]

The illuminations held in Toronto in connection with the Queen's Birthday in both 1854 and 1855 were as well organized demonstrations of loyalty as those connected with the fall of Sebastopol.[68] In fact, if the number of activities was any gauge to sentiment, loyalty to the Queen ran ahead of the fortunes of her armies in the Crimea. The loyal citizenry of Hamilton and Niagara were sent for by special excursion boats and by the Northern Railroad early in the morning of the twenty-fourth. After a hectic morning's preparation, there was a procession of the City Fathers, and a number of bands such as the Royal Canadian Rifles Band and the bag-pipers. After the inevitable Toronto public meeting, which was dominated by both Tory and Reform luminaries like Henry Sherwood and Robert Baldwin, a fervent address of loyalty was sent to the Queen. Then began the evening entertainment, which centred around a fire-works display, a brilliant illumination, and a torchlight procession through the city. George Brown's beatific comment in the *Globe* the next day on these vulgar displays of public spirit was: "We are not of those who think that such celebrations are lost time: an impression is made by them on the minds of the masses hardly to be attained in any other way."[69] There was then little essential difference in Canada West between a Grit like Brown, a moderate Reformer like Baldwin, or a High Tory like Henry Sherwood on the issue of loyalty to the Queen and Empire.

The partisan press of Canada West was similarly united on the basic issue of the necessity and justice of the war against despotic Russia. That the rabid Tory journal, the *Hamilton Gazette*, the moderate-Tory Toronto *Weekly Leader and Patriot*, and the liberal *Globe* should denounce the enemy in harshest terms because of their strong attachment to Empire was almost predictable.[70] Some of the arguments advanced by the editors of these newspapers were: that England upheld the cause of freedom, liberty, and civilization against the autocratic Czar; that she protected the rights of true Christianity against despotic Orthodoxy both in the Near East and in all of Europe; and that she upheld a traditional balance of power which had been in effect since Greek and Roman times in favour of civilization against northern barbarism. The more radical or democratic press, as represented by William Lyon Mackenzie's *Weekly Gazette* or the Clear Grit journal, *The North American* were similarly agreed on the justice of England's cause. Mackenzie left little doubt that he was as appalled as the Tories and the moderate Reformers by the Russian attempt to subvert the liberties of Europe during and after the revolutions of 1848. The Czar's ambition was no less daring than that of Napoleon I, and the Russian masses no wiser than the revolutionary French who followed Napoleon.[71] William McDougall, the editor of the *North American*, similarly harboured an early distrust for the expansion of autocratic Russia, for the Czar was not "so frugal of human life as to have his plans thwarted for the sake of humanity." He also agreed with the commonly held view that the Russian system of government was nothing but an oriental despotism supported by a backward mass of Slavonic barbarians. There was no question that England and France had to arrest this aggression against Turkey, or Cossack rule would extend from the Mediterranean to the English Channel.[72] Napoleon Bonaparte's prophecy concerning the Russian conquest of continental Europe would then be fulfilled.

This fundamental agreement by the press of the upper province on the despotic character of Nicholas II was counteracted by a general confusion about the alliance with France, and about the character of the Emperor, Napoleon III. This bewilderment appeared to stem from an uncertainty about the domestic and foreign aims of Napoleon, and from a realization that, good or evil, Napoleon was an ally and merited ideological support. George Brown was an early admirer of the stable regime which Louis

Napoleon had erected from the ruin of revolution,[73] but had come to mistrust the increasing despotism of the Emperor. However strongly he felt about the means that Napoleon had used to gain power, he still felt that Russian despotism was a far greater evil incapable of redemption. Napoleon could, on the other hand, salvage his reputation if he persisted in the struggle for the liberties of Europe in the Crimea.[74] William Lyon Mackenzie appeared to go through a similar process of gradual disenchantment with the second French Republic as it changed into the second Empire; but like Brown, he turned a blind eye to the illogicality of an alliance with one despotic power to defeat another. Mackenzie only indirectly allowed his hostility to show near the end of the war by reprinting a speech by a member of the peace party in England against the disgraceful alliance with Napoleon.[75] H.B. Bull, the Tory editor of the Hamilton *Gazette*, had an even more difficult time justifying an alliance with Napoleon since he openly despised both the inability of the French to govern themselves and the despotic ambitions of Napoleon III.[76] He fully ignored the contradictions of his position until the Queen's visit to France in the summer of 1855. The inconsistency was glossed over by Bull's quick insistence that the alliance between France and England was one between two freedom-loving peoples. The only journal which advanced from a negative attitude to an openly sympathetic one was the London *Free Press*. The key to its conversion was the birth of a son to Napoleon III early in 1856. There was then the possibility that the Napoleonic regime could free itself from despotism by establishing a hereditary monarchy of notably efficient Bonapartes![77] Although Napoleon appeared then to have his critics in Canada West prior to the war, these criticisms went largely unexpressed during a war effort which required his services.

The ominous presence of an expansionist Republic to the South when the defences of the colony were at minimal strength created divided opinions in the provincial press of Canada West. These divisions became most acute when war threatened between the Mother Country and the United States early in 1856. The traditional anti-American posture of the Tory press was easy enough to understand. A hostile attitude was immediately assumed towards American annexationist impulses and maintained throughout the war.[78] This Tory determination to resist a possible American invasion became increasingly firm in 1856 when there was a deterioration in the diplomatic relations between Great Britain and the United States.[79]

The position of Brown of the *Globe* on this question, as on others during the war, was typically Tory. He strongly denounced the American press throughout the first half of the Crimean War for their pro-Russian sympathies. The United States as the great bastion of liberty in the West was, by her alliance with the Russians, stabbing England in the back as she fought for the liberties of Europe and the world.[80] Brown also used these opportunities to point out that Brother Jonathan's treatment of his

Negro brethren hardly qualified Americans for consideration as a liberty-loving nation. The United States was then second only to Russia as a leading exponent of serfdom throughout the world.[81] When relations became strained between the two nations in late 1855, Brown showed that he was a Loyalist clad in a garb of liberalism. He promised that Canada would never become a part of that degraded Republic:

If people tried to take Canada, they would find an abundance of strong arms and strong hearts on the shores to meet them. No, no, Canada can or will hold her own, if need be, better in 1855 or 1875 than she did in 1812. She maintained the integrity of the British Empire then when her whole population consisted of but a few hundred thousands, and repelled the entire force of the United States consisting of as many millions, and if the melancholy necessity should ever arise, she would do so again.[82]

That Brown's position as a liberal was anomalous in its trenchant anti-Americanism implies that there were other groups which were less hostile to the United States during the war. The liberal press of London in Canada West, perhaps because of the vulnerability of that section of the province to invasion or because of its commercial connections with the United States, was most pacific in its pronouncements on the crisis of 1856. Josiah Blackburn, editor of the moderate-Reform *Free Press*, appealed to the commercial interests which held the two nations together to prevent a war which would be a sin against humanity. Although Blackburn despised American sympathies for the Czar, and claimed that Britain could and would defend right in the East and West, he still felt such a conflict would fly in the face of "blood, friendship, commerce, and civilization."[83] The London *Weekly Atlas*, a liberal journal of the same city,[84] was similarly horrified at the prospects of war between the two most enlightened and civilized Anglo-Saxon nations on earth. That the voracious despots of Europe should shed the blood of their miserable serfs was expected, but that the two great 'reasoning' nations of the earth should spill the blood of noble Anglo-Saxon subjects, was beyond belief.[85]

The concern that was shown by the pacific elements in London was to some extent based upon the disruption of commercial connections with their American neighbours. This localized apprehension for material prosperity was matched by the concern of other newspapers in the province over the general effect of the Crimean War on the trade of Canada West. Although the commercial motive was not nearly so prominent in the party press of Canada West as it was in the English mercantile journals of Canada East, there was a lively interest expressed in both the *Globe* and the Ottawa *Citizen* on the possible profits to be realized through the Crimean War. In late January of 1854, George Brown announced the general preparations for war, and in bold type above it, "ENORMOUS RISE IN BREAD-STUFFS! BREAD RIOTS IN ENGLAND!" He was also quite lively in his editorial comments to the significance of the rise in the prices of breadstuffs in Great Britain. He naturally blamed the Czar's ambition for this by his closing off the Baltic and Black Seas, but did not fail to note to his readers that it seemed probable that present levels would be maintained until exertions in the Americas would fill the demand for breadstuffs.[86] R. Bell, the editor of the Ottawa *Citizen*, also noted the increase in demand in timber which would result from the War; – "One would think that if the ports of the Baltic were to be closed against English ships that at least those gentlemen who wage war upon the red pine forests of the upper Ottawa will feel the effects rather advantageously."[87] In direct contrast to these calculations of war profits, the high Tory newspapers of Canada West made no mention of the sordid commercial motive since their commitment to Empire was more purely ideological in character.

The English press of Quebec and Montreal saw the war by much the same lights as their brethren in the upper section of the province. The war was assumed to be a just struggle for the freedom of Europe against the ambitious designs of the autocratic Czar.[88] The problem of the French alliance was not nearly the problem it was in Upper Canada since the electorates of the two cities were almost evenly divided between both races.[89] Even Napoleon III was found to be much less objectionable in his position as despotic ruler of France. The *Pilot* went so far as to claim that as long as Napoleon "continues to wield the destinies of that noble empire, so long will the cordial alliance of England, and France continue, and so long will the entire world feel the blessings which result from that alliance, to civilization and humanity."[90]

Concerning the relationship of the United States to Canada during the war, the *Gazette* of Montreal was as hostile to America's expansionism and her *soi-disant* freedoms as were the Tory papers of Toronto and Hamilton. Brown Chamberlin, the Tory editor of the *Gazette*, saw a similar pattern of American neutral claims being pressed forward, as they were prior to the War of 1812. His countercharge against so-called British violation of American neutral rights was that the Americans were holding British sailors in Charleston prisons. One could, after all, expect little more of an immoral republic steeped in crime, corruption, and slavery.[91] The liberal and commercial *Pilot* was less hostile to the Americans, no doubt because of the close commercial links which now existed between Montreal and New England. The same commercial and racial arguments which were advanced by the liberal press of London in Canada West, were repeated by Hincks' *Pilot*.[92] His hopes of commercial gain from the war were quite evident in the high expectations he nurtured for the increased wheat and timber trade. Shrewd observation soon showed that British insurance rates on her shipping would be driven up by the war and that much produce of the Western country would go to American neutral-shipping ports. The acute disappointment expressed over that probability does not detract from the essentially commercial outlook which the *Pilot* held of the war.[93]

The French-Canadian press was less alive to the fortunes of Her Majesty's armies in the Crimea. The war news, derived from common dispatches arriving in the mail clippers and from Parisian sources like *L'Univers* and *Le Moniteur*, was reported quite faithfully in *La Minerve* and *Le Journal de Québec*. Editorial comment in these conservative journals was neither so prolific nor prolix as that of the English press in both sections of the province. The two themes which did emerge from the editorial opinion of these two journals were the anti-despotic character of the struggle against Russia, and the heroic stature of Napoleon III and the French people. Loud professions of imperial sentiment and militant support of Her Majesty's forces were rarely made except in conjunction with the passage of the provincial contributions to the Patriotic Fund or with local celebrations of the fall of Sebastopol.[94]

The negative aspects of the Tsarist autocracy were lampooned in the conservative press. Through the use of such French diatribes against the despotic character of Imperial Russia as L. Dussieux's *Force et Faiblesse de la Russie*, Duvernay of *La Minerve* drew a caricature of the autocratic political structure, labyrinthine bureaucracy, and harsh criminal code of Russia.[95] On other occasions *La Minerve* delivered a blistering attack upon the Orthodox Church and its attempted persecution of Catholicism. Echoing the Parisian pundit of ultramontanism, Louis Veuillot, the editor noted that France was now the true protector of the Church at Rome as in the days of Charlemagne. The true sentiments of the Catholic hierarchy in Rome were that Russia should be buried in her attempt to proselytize in the near East. If the other major Catholic power, Austria, remained aloof from its responsibilities as a defender of Catholicism, there should be no complaint if another Christian power like England defended the rights of Christianity.[96]

It is interesting to note that *La Minerve* was forced to rely to a great extent on the pronouncements of Veuillot, and the *mandements* of the Bishop of Paris in lieu of strong leadership on the question of the war from the Bishop of Montreal. Montreal's ultramontanist Bishop, Ignace Bourget, appeared not to take a strong public stand on the Crimean War. His *mandements* and circular letters from 1854-56 were largely occupied with clarification of the dogma of the Immaculate Conception, the promotion of the temperance society of Montreal, and the establishment of absolute loyalty to papal sovereignty in an ultramontane Roman Church.[97] Since he found no difficulty in strongly endorsing Her Majesty's attempt to quell the Indian Mutiny in 1858, and had upheld in some measure the cause of loyalism in 1849-50, questionable allegiance to the Queen and Empire was probably not the motive for his reticence. More likely is the possibility that the attempt of the Papacy to break away from its dependence on Napoleonic power and influence since 1850 was fully supported by Bourget. Public support for Napoleon III in the Crimean campaign likely would have created a confusion in his firm policy of allegiance to the Papacy in Rome. In Quebec, Bishop Turgeon, and his successor, Mgr. Baillargeon obviously found no such obstacles to a strong promotion of the Allied cause, for they published periodically circular letters to the clergy appealing for heavenly benediction upon the armies of England and France, and for a quick return to peace.[98] Baillargeon, as noted previously, sang a *Te Deum* on the occasion of the fall of Sebastopol, and another at the conclusion of the War.[99] Bishop Signay of Quebec had been warmer in 1849-50 to the cause of loyalty and less scrupulous about the professions of secular allegiance than was Bourget. His successor Turgeon and Baillargeon maintained this tradition in the Crimean War.[100]

Juxtaposed against the mephistophelian darkness of autocratic Russia in the French-Canadian mind, was the glorious Empire of Napoleon III. Although there was periodic reference to the alliance of France and England against Russian barbarism,[101] the positive thrust of French newspaper opinion was in the direction of a Napoleonic cult. Joseph Cauchon had long been an admirer of the Second Republic of Louis Napoleon, and the subsequent Empire. It was the political stability and economic prosperity created by a popular Napoleonic régime which appealed to Cauchon.[102] The Crimean campaign was seen as an excellent outlet for the genius of Napoleon III, because it could now be given a chance to manifest itself externally. The position of Ludger Duvernay's *Minerve* was, on the other hand, initially hostile to the empire in early 1853, since he did not regard the Empire as pacific as was implied in Napoleon's slogan, "L'Empire, c'est la paix." He thought it would have been more appropriate if it had read, "L'Empire, c'est la guerre inévitable."[103] With the advent of war *La Minerve* warmed to Napoleon and reprinted in great detail the plans of his marriage to Eugénie de Montigo, the dispatches of Napoleon to the Czar, and the addresses of the Emperor to the French people.[104] By the end of the war the Duvernay brothers sang the praises of the Empire as loudly as the official press in France. They now believed that the Empire really did stand for order, prosperity, peace and honour.[105] That a cult of Napoleon had indeed been born can be seen from the reversal of the liberal-nationalist, *Le Pays* from a position of outright hostility to Louis Napoleon for his interference in the Roman revolution of 1849 to one of adulation of the stable and prosperous Napoleonic Empire.[106]

The only major newspaper which seems to have been able to remain immune to the pressures of Napoleon-worship during the war was the radical organ of liberal-republicanism, *L'Avenir*. The distrust with which J.B.E. Dorion had viewed Louis Napoleon's second republic, blossomed into a virulent hatred by the end of the Crimean campaign.[107] The reasons for this hostility were not only the co-operation of the two powers in an imperialistic war in the East, but more important, their co-operation in the expulsion of the republican exiles like Victor Hugo from the Channel

Islands. By 1856 Europe was viewed with disgust by Dorion because it was once more in the clutches of monarchical reaction. The Continent was little more than an armed camp in which the French and British Empires held the most prominent barricades.[108] Dorion was quite frankly unable to work up any enthusiasm for England's role as one of the last refuges of civilization, and openly condemned those like E.P. Taché who gloried in their status as loyal British subjects during the Crimean campaign.[109] Nor could he summon any sympathy for England as she innocently awaited a stab in the back by the Americans in early 1856. The British were, after all, in the Crimea for entirely selfish reasons of partitioning Turkey and boosting iron and steel war-production for the benefit of the English aristocracy. Dorion therefore had little compunction in dismissing the holy war in the Near East as but another example of nineteenth-century English imperialism.[110]

The private opinions of Louis-Joseph Papineau on the Crimean war are of some importance in amplifying the reactions of liberal-republicans in French Canada. Like the *rouges* of *L'Avenir* Papineau was concerned with the spread of despotism in Europe prior to the war. His fears applied as well to Napoleonic despotism as to Cossack Orthodoxy in the East. The scourge of Europe was no longer the barbarian horde of Attila, but the crusading Orthodoxy of Russia which would swallow up impious Latins in its progress westward.[111] After the outbreak of hostilities, Papineau felt no compulsion to rally to the British standard. He rather took the opportunity to vent his spleen on those who supported the British constitution, the Union, and the *status quo*.[112] After an initial panic over the horrible prospects of war, Papineau decided that the war would not, after all, undermine civilization, and that contact with the West might even help civilize the Russians.[113] Although he felt that the Russians should be stopped if possible, he maintained that the Turks were morally no better:

L'Ambition du Czar est redoubtable, il doit être puni, si possible. Mais les Turcs sont moins susceptibles de se polir au contact de l'Europe, que les Russes. L'on ne peut avoir des sympathies pour les premiers, l'on a peur de ceux-ci, voilà tout. Je ne sais si Lord Elgin va nous demander de nous faire Mahometans. Les dames s'y opposeront; au reste cette bagatelle n'intéresse plus guères les hommes de notre âge, hélas.[114]

Papineau's apathy over either England's or France's fate in the war was sustained throughout the war. Even the prospect of a war with the United States was viewed in the same light as by the *rouges*. He even appeared to take delight in the prospect of a land war which the British could never win.[115] Neither Papineau nor the *rouges* then differed on the basic issue, that the despotic wars of a morally degraded Europe were of secondary importance. What really mattered was that the principles of democracy and republicanism be allowed to develop in the western hemisphere.[116] Their posture thus resembles to a striking degree that taken by the Jeffersonian Republicans to Europe during the Napoleonic Wars from 1803-14.

Within the Provincial Legislature the war provoked little direct comment other than that passed upon the contribution to the Patriotic Fund and the Militia Bill of 1855. Periodic addresses of loyalty to Her Majesty were passed by the Legislature at the commencement of the conflict, and at infrequent intervals during the progress of the war.[117] There is little doubt that the rhetoric employed in the addresses was calculated to bind French and English Canadians together since they were "the inhabitants of a country peopled mainly by the descendants of those two powerful Empires."[118] The zenith of racial harmony was reached at the close of the war with the birth of an heir to Napoleon III. The stabilization and legitimization of the Empire by the birth of the heir-apparent, the Prince of Algeria, won the special approval of the Tory monarchists and the *bleu* admirers of Napoleon. Although the French-Canadian conservatives left the justification of the Napoleonic Empire to their English brethren in Canada East, all but the *rouges* and a few Clear Grits voted for an adjournment in honour of the French Prince. The French members then proceeded to drown out the voiciferous opposition of William Lyon Mackenzie with a rapping of desks and the singing of French songs. This outburst of sentiment for the French Empire was all too brief to justify speculations concerning the development of unified opinion in favour of Napeoleon III in the Provincial Legislature. The glorification of the Napoleonic Empire which found expression in the French-Canadian conservative press found no vocal exponent in Her Majesty's Legislature. All that the Napoleonophile, Joseph Cauchon, could say in the Assembly was that, good or bad, Napoleon was the representative of his people and should be respected accordingly.[119] For the French Canadian to speak of the alliance of two great empires struggling for the noble cause of civilization was therefore acceptable, but to elevate Napoleon III to the same status as Queen Victoria was not. An open address of congratulation on the birth of the Prince of Algeria was therefore not even countenanced by the House.

The Canadian response in all of its several forms to Great Britain's involvement in the Crimean War was much greater among English Canadians in both sections of the Province. The imperial war effort for these colonials was the focus of a great deal of romantic zeal. The almost universal approbation which was expressed for the plight of the Mother Country by Loyalists and immigrant Britons of all political factions was not indicative of public opinion within Great Britain herself. In the Home Government there were deep divisions within the Aberdeen Ministry over the necessity of war and the degree to which it should be prosecuted. Prominent politicians like William Gladstone, Sir James Graham, and Sidney Herbert, in conjunction with the peace groups outside of Parliament, prevented the development of a militant ideological unanimity such as existed in Canada.[120] The war-hawk mentality pervaded the English colonial mind except for a few radicals like Mackenzie who were most reluctant to express their pacifism, lest they be labelled disloyal. The warmest advocates in fact, of a more vigorous prosecution of the war by the Aberdeen and Palmerston ministries were liberals like Brown and Hincks.[121] Colonial Britons were then both qualitatively and quantitatively more aggressive in their imperialism than their superiors in the Mother Country who were not only in retreat from Empire but were severely divided on the justice and necessity of the Crimean War. The intense imperial sentiment voiced in Canada during the war in fact predated the development of a similar imperial sentiment in Great Britain by Dilke, Adderley, and Froude by a decade to a decade and a half.

The French Canadians on the other hand were less unanimous in their support of British arms. Great pains were generally taken to prove their loyalty to the Governor-General and to the Queen throughout the war, lest anyone suspect a lack of warmth to the cause of Her Majesty's arms. Where attachment to the British Empire and the British troops in the Crimea did find expression it was often in relation to the Napoleonic Empire and the French armies. Such divided sympathy between Queen Victoria and Napoleon III was quite acceptable when declared within the relatively safe confines of the French language press, but quite obviously clashed with the unilateral devotion of English imperialists in public meetings and in the Legislature. Confronted by these obstacles to a duality of imperial and racial allegiances during a war which might have offered ample opportunity for the widest expression, French Canadians remained inwardly-oriented. The predisposition of their political ideas and actions still lay in the directions of Canadian self-government and the development of French-Canadian nationality. The bulk of their romantic or sentimental energies were expended in the idealization of the internal growth and expansion of their own culture. External professions of loyalty to Queen and Empire were but a means to secure the realization of greater internal ideals; whereas English Canadians saw in them the means of identification to an ideal Empire which was the real embodiment of the Divine. The greatness of the French Canadian contribution during the war lay in the general support they lent to schemes devised by English Canadians to manifest their deeply felt attachment to the Empire. The great question of the Crimean campaign for Canada was seen quite clearly by George-Etienne Cartier as he delivered a speech on the survival of French Canadian nationality at the Côte-de-Neiges cemetery late in October, 1855: – *"Les principales races qui habitent le Canada descendent des deux grandes nations européennes réunies aujourd'hui sous les mêmes drapeaux pour empêcher une nationalité affaiblie de succomber sous le loi du plus fort. Comment pourraient-elles s'empêcher de vivre en harmonie sur cette terre qui est leur propriété commune?"*[122]

Notes: Imperial Sentiment

1. A notable exception is Professor J.M.S. Careless' pioneering article on the conservative nature of liberal newspapers of the mid-Victorian period, "Mid-Victorian Liberalism in Central Canadian Newspapers, 1850-67," *Canadian Historical Review*, XXXI, (Sept. 1950), 221-236.
2. See *Addresses and Petitions to the Governor-General, 1849-56*, Record Gp. 5, B 3, vols. 13-15, *P. A. C.*
3. Richard Koebner and H.D. Schmidt, *Imperialism, The Story and Significance of a Political World 1840-1960*, Cambridge, at the University Press, 1964, chaps. II, III, 27-81.
4. See Petition of the Inhabitants of Perth, May, 1849, *Addresses and Petitions*, vol. 13, *P. A. C.*
5. See Montreal *Pilot*, Oct. 4, 1852; *British Colonist*, Oct. 5, 1852; Hamilton *Gazette*, May 17, 24, 1852; Nov. 1, 18, 1852; May 29, 1854.
6. Montreal *Gazette*, Aug. 28, 1852; See also *British Colonist*, "Our Anglo-Saxon Empire," Nov. 20, 1849.
7. See J. Monet, "The Last Cannon Shot – A Study of French Canadian Nationalism, 1837-50," Unpublished Doctoral Dissertation, University of Toronto, 1964, 505-707.
8. *La Minerve* Sept. 9, 1850.
9. *Le Journal de Québec*, March 22, 1851.
10. See for example *La Minerve*, Jan. 31, 1850.
11. Koebner and Schmidt, *Imperialism*, 27-49.
12. F.H.D.Veith, *Recollections of the Crimean Campaign and the Expedition to Kinburn*, Montreal, J.Lovell and Sons, 1907; A.A.M. Lower, *Canadians in the Making*, Longmans Green, Toronto, 1958, 220.
13. C.P.Stacey, *Canada and the British Army, 1846-71, A Study in the Practice of Responsible Government*, University of Toronto Press, 1963, 93-5.
14. *Globe*, May 23, 1855.
15. See *Globe*, Apr. 6, 1854; Feb. 2, May 26, 1855; Quebec *Morning Chronicle*, Dec. 1, Dec. 21, 1854; Toronto *Leader*, Jan. 12, Jan. 17, 1855.
16. Quebec *Morning Chronicle* reported in *Globe*, Sept. 24, 1854.
17. *Mirror of Parliament*, Nov. 6, 1854, 74.
18. *Ibid.*, 75.
19. *Ibid.*
20. *Mirror of Parliament*, Nov. 17, 1854. Capt. Rhodes and Mr. McKerlie were of these two schools.
21. *Ibid.*
22. *Mirror of Parliament*, Nov. 20, 1854.
23. Elgin to Grey, Nov. 20, 1854, CO 42/602, #585.
24. See *Weekly Leader and Patriot*, Feb. 7, 1855, Sept. 12, 1855.
25. *Mackenzie's Weekly Gazette*, Jan. 12, 1855.
26. *Globe*, Nov. 8, 1854. See also Nov. 16, Dec. 16, Dec. 23, 1854; Feb. 23, Mar. 25, 1855.
27. *Globe*, Jan. 24, Feb. 7, 1855.
28. *Globe*, Mar. 7, 1855. Brown's estimate appears quite accurate since the York and Peel collections closed at £1445 in September of 1855. This added to the St. Andrew's private donation of £1000 would come very near to the predicted total.
29. *Globe*, Feb. 2, 1855.
30. The provincial donation breaks down to 1/50 of a pound per person, and the York and Peel donation to 1/30 of a pound per person.
31. Montreal *Pilot*, Nov. 8, 1854.
32. See *Globe*, Feb. 16, May 26, 1855.
33. *Pilot*, Jan. 12, 1855.
34. *Pilot*, Jan. 17, 1855.
35. *Pilot*, Apr. 23, 1855.
36. See Quebec *Morning Chronicle*,

Dec. 6, 1854, and Jan. 25, 1855; *Journal de Québec*, Jan. 23, 1855.

37. See the speech of J. Bell Forsyth for an acknowledgement of this motive. Quebec *Morning Chronicle*, Jan. 25, 1855.

38. Quebec *Morning Chronicle*, Jan. 25, 1855.

39. Some of the most prominent legislators and executive officers were C.Alleyn, J.Cauchon, F.Hincks, A.N.Morin, E.P.Taché, and J.B. Forsyth.

40. The *Globe* of Feb. 3, 1855, reported contributions of £500 from Elgin county, £537 from Kingston, £250 from Dundas county, and £250 from Northumberland and Durham counties.

41. Head to Molesworth, Clifton House, Niagara Falls, C. W., Oct. 22, 1855, *C. O.* 42/599.

42. St. Catharines Petition in Head to Russell, June 3, 1855, *C. O. 42/*598; Hamilton Address in Head to Molesworth, Oct. 29, 1855, *C. O. 42/*599; Woodstock Address in Head to Molesworth, Oct. 20, 1855, *C. O. 42/*599.

43. St. Catharines, Head to Russell, June 3, 1855, *C. O. 42/*598.

44. *Ibid.*

45. Head to Labouchere, May 31, 1856, *C. O. 42/*604.

46. Toronto address in Head to Grey, Nov. 8, 1855; *C. O. 42/*599. See also *Globe* Oct. 28, 1854.

47. Head to Molesworth, Oct. 29, 1855, *C. O. 42/*599.

48. See Quebec *Morning Chronicle*, Apr. 23, 1855; Montreal *Pilot*, June 1, 1854.

49. Reported in the Montreal *Pilot*, May 22, 1854.

50. *La Minerve*, June 13, 1854.

51. *Ibid.*

52. *Ibid.*

53. Quebec *Morning Chronicle*, Oct. 9, 1855; Montreal *Pilot*, May 22, 1854.

54. See S. F. Wise, "Sermon Literature and Canadian Intellectual History," *United Church Archives Bulletin*, no. 18, 1965, 3-19.

55. *La Minerve*, Apr. 29, 1854.

56. *Ibid.*

57. *La Minerve*, May 6, 1854.

58. Montreal *Pilot*, Apr. 17, 1855.

59. Montreal *Gazette*, Apr. 18, 1855.

60. *Globe*, May 1, 1854.

61. J.Strachan to the Secretary of Canada West, June 3-6, 1854, *Provincial Secretary's Correspondence, Canada West, P. A. C.* See also City of Toronto Memorial for a day of humiliation and prayer, Apr. 24, 1854; Memorial of Presbyterian Church and Church of Scotland to Secretary of Canada West, Quebec, June 2, 1854, *Provincial Secretary's Correspondence, Canada West, P. A. C.*

62. Montreal *Pilot*, Sept. 28, 1855.

63. *Ibid.*, Oct. 5, 1855. See also Montreal *Gazette*, Oct. 9, 1855.

64. Quebec, *Morning Chronicle*, Oct. 8, 1855.

65. *Ibid.*, Oct. 9, 1855.

66. *Globe*, Oct. 6, 1855; Toronto *Weekly Leader and Patriot,* Oct. 10, 1855.

67. For other Sebastopol illuminations in Canada West see *Globe*, Oct. 11, 1855 for the illumination in Cobourg; Hamilton *Gazette*, Oct. 11, 15, 1855.

68. *Globe*, May 25, 26, 1855.

69. *Globe*, May 25, 1855.

70. See Hamilton *Gazette*, Dec. 12, 1853; Toronto *Leader* Dec. 5, 1855; *Globe*, Jan. 30, Mar. 30, Mar. 9, Oct. 4, Oct. 20, 1854; Jan. 30, 1855.

71. Mackenzie's *Weekly Gazette*, Apr. 21, 1854. See also Ottawa *Citizen*, Apr. 8, 1854; *Anglo-American Magazine,* Toronto, 1856, v, 18-26.

72. *North American*, Sept. 27, Nov. 17, Nov. 22, 1853; Feb. 23, 1854.

73. *Globe*, June 29, Dec. 14, 1852.

74. *Globe*, Apr. 6, 30, 1855.

75. *Mackenzie's Gazette*, Dec. 14, 25, 1855.

76. Hamilton *Gazette*, Apr. 2, May 6, 1852; Apr. 9, 1855.

77. London *Free Press*, Jan. 15, 1852; Apr. 5, 1856.

78. Hamilton *Gazette*, July 22, 1852; Aug. 31, 1854; Mar. 1, June 4, 1855.

79. See Head to Labouchere, May 31, 1856, *C. O. 42/604*, Lincoln Militia Petition to the Governor-General.
80. *Globe*, Dec. 20, 1854; June 14, 1855. See also Ottawa *Citizen*, Jan. 20, 1855.
81. *Globe*, Jan. 18, 1855; Oct. 8, 1855.
82. *Globe*, Dec. 6, 1855.
83. London *Free Press*, Feb. 27, 1856. See also Feb. 14, 1856.
84. For verification as a liberal journal see Marcus Gunn to the editor of London *Atlas*, Apr. 17, 1856, London; Marcus Gunn Papers, *P. A. C.*
85. See editorials "Must We Fight?" and "Anti-Bellum" contained in "One M.P.P. to the Sec. of State," recorded June 28, 1856, *C. O. 42/608*. There were some notable anomalies on this problem in British-American relations. The radical W.L.Mackenzie was most hostile to American expansion during the war. (*Gazette*, Dec. 15, 1854, May 23, 1856.) The conservative Toronto *Leader*, on the other hand was quite pacific towards the Americans. (*Leader*, Oct. 31, 1855.)
86. *Globe*, Jan. 30, 1854.
87. Ottawa *Citizen*, Mar. 18, 1854.
88. Montreal *Gazette*, Apr. 18, 1855; Quebec *Morning Chronicle*, Apr. 23, 1855, July 13, 1854; *Pilot*, Oct. 25, 1855, June 28, 1854.
89. Montreal *Gazette*, Oct. 9, 1855; Montreal *Pilot*, Sept. 3, 1853; July 17, 1854.
90. Montreal *Pilot*, July 17, 1854.
91. Montreal *Gazette*, May 16, Aug. 9, 1855, Jan. 24, 1856; Quebec *Morning Chronicle*, Oct. 6, 1855.
92. Montreal *Pilot*, Oct. 12, 26, 1855; July 15, 1856.
93. *Pilot*, Apr. 18, 1854. See also Quebec *Morning Chronicle*, July 13, 1854.
94. *Journal de Québec*, Nov. 21, 1854; *La Minerve*, Nov. 11, 1854.
95. *La Minerve*, Dec. 27, 1854.
96. *Ibid.*, Apr. 6, 1854. See also *Ibid.*, Nov. 16, Mar. 7, Apr. 29, 1854; *Journal de Québec*, Dec. 23, 1854.
97. Ignace Bourget, *Mandements, Let-tres Pastorales, Circulaires et Autres Documents* (Montreal, Chapleau Frères, 1869) III, 121-38, 142-4, 181-2, 223-34.
98. H.Têtu, C.O.Gagnon, *Mandements, Lettres Pastorales et Circulaires des Evêques de Québec*, Québec, A.Côté, 1889-90, IV, 157-60, 217; V, 277-8.
99. *Ibid.*, V, 278.
100. *Ibid.*, III, pt. 3, 537-542; I. Bourget, *Mandements*, II, 66-8. For further discussion see Leon Pouliot, "Au Lendemain de l'émerite de 1849, Une Lettre de Mgr. Bourget à Mgr. Tourgeon, May 2, 1849," *Revue de l'Amérique Française*, IX, 1955-6, 117-19.
101. *La Minerve*, May 2, 1854; *Journal de Québec*, Apr. 29, 1854.
102. *Journal de Québec*, Feb. 10, 1853.
103. *La Minerve*, Jan. 18, 1853.
104. *Ibid.*, Mar. 8, 1853; Mar. 11, 1854; Apr. 25, 1854; Oct. 14, 1854.
105. *Ibid.*, Sept. 23, 1856; Feb. 17, Aug. 11, 1857.
106. See *La Minerve*, Nov. 11, 1854; *Le Pays* Mar. 29, June 5, 1856.
107. *L'Avenir*, July 19, 1849; Jan. 11, Feb. 15, July 8, 1856.
108. *Ibid.*, July 8, 1856.
109. *Ibid.*, Jan 4, 1856.
110. *Ibid.*, Jan. 18, Feb. 8, 1856.
111. Papineau to E.B.O'Callaghan, Jan. 25, 1852, *O'Callaghan Papers, P. A. C.*
112. Papineau to R. Christie, Jan. 20, 1854, *A. P. Q., Papineau-Bourassa Collection 573.*
113. Papineau to E.Corning, Feb. 24, 1854, *Papineau Collection, P. A. C.* Papineau to R.Christie, May 16, 1854, *A. P. Q., Papineau-Bourassa Collection 545.*
114. Papineau to Christie, May 16, 1854, *A. P. Q., Papineau-Bourassa Collection, 545.*
115. Papineau to his wife, Nov. 11, 1855, *A. P. Q., Papineau-Bourassa Collection, 106.*
116. Papineau to E.Corning, Feb. 24, 1854, *Papineau Collection, P. A. C.* Vol. 1.
117. Elgin to Newcastle, June 15, 1854, *C. O. 42/594*; Elgin to Grey, Jan.

22, 1855, *C. O. 42/602*; *Mirror of Parliament*, Jan. 1855, 181.

118. Elgin to Newcastle, June 15, 1854, *C. O. 42/594*.

119. *Mirror of Parliament*, Apr. 2, 1856, 89.

120. See for example articles on "War and Peace" in *Bentley's Miscellany*, XXXVI, 1854, 217; "Peace and Patriotism," *Blackwoods*, LXXVII, 1855, 97.

121. See Koebner and Schmidt, *Imperialism*, 81-106.

122. J.C.Tassé, *Discours de G.E. Cartier*, Montreal, Seneca et Fils, 1893, 65-66.

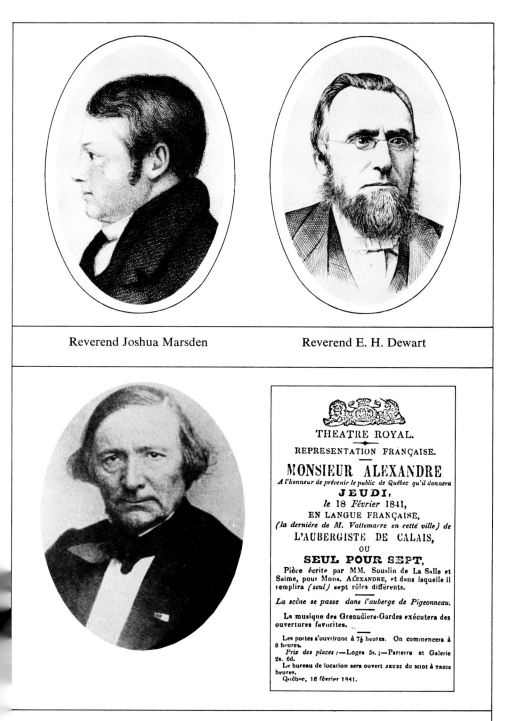

Reverend Joshua Marsden

Reverend E. H. Dewart

Alexandre Vattemare

Une annonce dans *La Gazette de Québec*,
jeudi, le 18 février, 1841

Louis Veuillot

Mgr Ignace Bourget

Prince Roland Bonaparte

Louis-Antoine Dessaulles

Railway accident at Beloeil, 1864

The Old Victoria Tubular Bridge, opened in the year 1860

E. Churchill & Sons' ship "Marlborough," 1383 tons reg.
Built at Churchill's shipyard, Hantsport, 1863

Steamer *Quebec* at dock in Montreal Harbour
c. 1870-1872

" 'Gavazzi Riot' at Montreal" – Perhaps the height
of Protestant-Catholic animosity

Illumination of Montreal to celebrate the Fall of Sebastopol

The Honourable
Henry Sherwood

The Honourable
J. W. Johnston D.C.L.

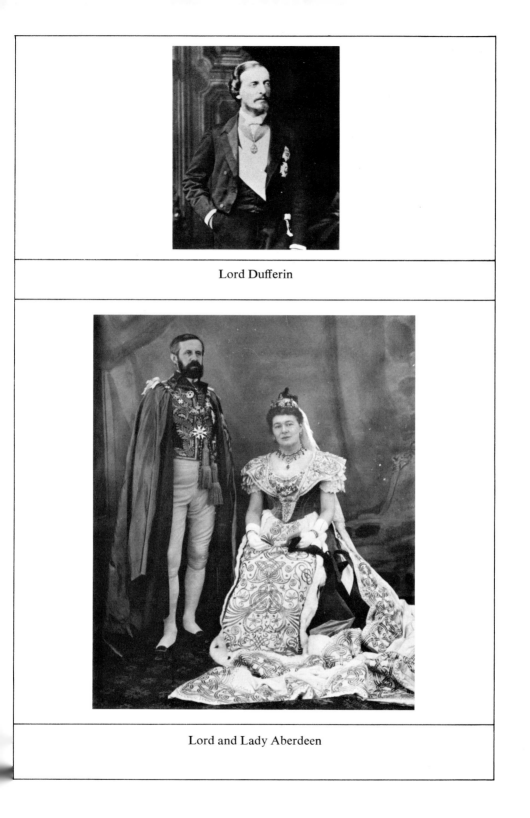

Lord Dufferin

Lord and Lady Aberdeen

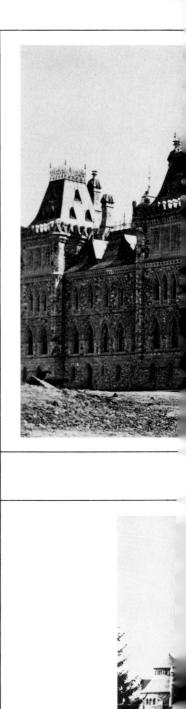

ABOVE: Thomas Fuller, chief designer
of the Parliament Buildings, Ottawa
BELOW: Frederick W. Cumberland who designed
and built University College, Toronto.
Drawing of the proposed
University College before the building
was commenced.

ABOVE: The Parliament Buildings (Centre Block), Ottawa, c. 1869
BELOW: East view of University College in the 1860's

La Basilique, Quebec

Cathédrale Marie-Reine du Monde,
"St. James Cathedral," Montreal

Baronde Gauldrée Boilleau, consul général de France à Québec, 1859-1864

Abel-Frédéric Gautier, consul général
de France à Québec, 1864-1872

Metlakatla, British Columbia

Church and Indian Band, Metlakatla

The Inauguration of Dufferin Terrace, Quebec

"Muffining"

The Dufferins at the Curling rink at Rideau Hall

At the foot of the Toboggan Slide

Rideau Hall in the Lorne period. Ballroom 1873 at left,
original Rideau Hall 1838 at centre,
Tent Room 1876 at right

Lord Lorne

Lord Monck   Lord Grey

The Idea of Progress in the Province of Canada: A study in the History of Ideas

Laurence S. Fallis, Jr., University of West Florida

The purpose of this essay is fourfold: first, to document the existence in the Province of Canada in the middle decades of the nineteenth century (1840-1870) of a structure of ideas, opinions, beliefs and expectations which it is convenient to label the "idea of progress"; second, to indicate who did and who did not participate in this particular belief system; third, to suggest why a given class or social group either accepted or rejected the idea of progress; and fourth, to assess the practical impact of the acceptance of the idea of progress upon Canadian life and thought. Since this study can best be regarded as a scholarly reconnaissance in force into the vast *terra incognita* of nineteenth century Canadian thought – and not a definitive pronouncement – the reader is warned at the onset that the conclusions are highly tentative.

I

In the fall of 1854, the Legislative Assembly of the Province of Canada turned from the partisan warfare which had occupied the attention of the parliamentarians during the summer to more peaceful endeavours. The Board of Trade of the City of London had as a gesture of inter-imperial solidarity, invited the Province of Canada to contribute to the display being prepared by the British Empire for submission to the great exhibition and trade fair to be held in Paris in 1855. Thus it was that the Legislative Assembly petitioned the Governor General, the Earl of Elgin, to appoint a committee to supervise the preparation of the Canadian entries. His Excellency graciously responded to the supplications of her Majesty Queen Victoria's most loyal Canadian subjects by appointing a committee composed of the leading politicians of the Province.

One of the first decisions of the committee was to hold a competition to obtain "a short and concise work on Canada, having for its object to make the foreigner acquainted with the Country."[1] The winning entry, which bore the revealing motto "*labor omnia vincit*," was submitted by a British emigrant to Canada, J. Sheridan Hogan. Hogan's purpose in writing his essay was to point out the tremendous changes that had taken place in Canada since his arrival in the 1820's. Population had increased dramatically. The land that was once a wilderness had yielded its harvest of wheat and timber to the labour of the pioneer. Where once savages launched their fragile birch canoes upon the turbulent waters of Lake Ontario, cities and towns had arisen as if by magic. On all sides was the evidence of that prosperity and abundance which bespoke the honest toil of the Canadian people. The experience of Europe was a compound of conquest, misery and despair. The experience of the New World was grounded in the reality of improvement. The law of the Old World was decay; the law of the New World was progress.[2] Hogan was not a philosopher nor was he conscious that he was giving voice to one of the great ideas of Western civilization. None the less, Hogan's little essay provides us with a window opening onto the public mind of the Province of Canada in the middle decades of the nineteenth century, and as such, provides a convenient starting point from which to begin an exploration of the idea of progress.

Mid-Victorian Canadians were convinced that they were living in what was time and again referred to as an "age of Improvement."[3] As one enthusiastic essayist put it:

THANK HEAVEN! we live in the nineteenth century, in the era of unparalleled improvement in science, in art, in literature, morals and religion. Never before did such glorious days as these dawn upon the human race; never were such vistas of fore-shadowed splendour opened up to the view of the contemplative philosopher, as in this enlightened age, when the human mind has burst the fetters of ages, purified from the gross defilement, which overshadowed as with a pall, former ages that have disappeared, and are now almost forgotten. How shall we contrast the darkness of former ages with the meridian splendour of modern times. . . ."[4]

This contrast between the past and the present was pointed out by Sir Richard Henry Bonnycastle who noticed that the Canadians now imagined themselves as about "to become ranked among the [great] nations of the world. . . ."[5] And why not? As early as 1847 the *Canada Farmer* could announce to its readers that "civilization has spread, like a resistless tide, over the face of the country. . . ."[6] Just one year later Canadians were warned by Robert Sullivan that "no country, no community, can with safety be stationary. To improve with the improving, to advance with the advancing, to keep pace with the foremost, or to sink into contempt and poverty, or what is worse, into slavery and dependence, seems to be the fate of nations."[7] As if in response, the *Canadian Gem and Family Visitor* reassured its readers that "Canada is destined to become one of the finest countries upon the face of the globe."[8]

The 1850's saw no lessening of the enthusiasm for progress. There was an awareness that the progress of the nation was the result of "Canadian energy, Canadian ambition, Canadian self-reliance, skill and enterprise . . . ."[9] It was possible to turn the Province into a veritable "Garden of Eden"[10] but only if Canadians put their shoulders to the wheel of progress. To outsiders it was already clear that Canada had made such rapid strides that it was becoming difficult to give an adequate account of the country. As the great Nova Scotia jurist Thomas Chandler Haliburton once confessed to a Scottish audience, Canada was;

A country so vast, that it is difficult to convey an adequate idea of its size; so fertile, that nothing short of official returns will exonerate a description of it from the charge of exaggeration; so prosperous, as not merely to rival, but to surpass all other countries on the face of the earth; so healthy in climate, so beautiful in scenery, so abundantly supplied with magnificent lakes and rivers, so full of commercial resources, and so rich in minerals, that I am overpowered with the magnitude of the task I have imposed upon myself, in attempting to convey even a faint idea of it.[11]

Canadians, however, were not so reticent about the glories of the nation in which "everything has by degrees . . . year after year advanced, so that we seem living in a new world,"[12] nor were they slow to point out that "the first half of the nineteenth century has changed the destiny of the human race; and in no place has its effects been more visibly portrayed than in our Province."[13]

The decade of the 1860's represents in many ways the high water mark of the doctrine of progress in the Province of Canada. It was in this decade that Egerton Ryerson announced that upon Canada a Divine munificence had "lavished all the needful elements of national greatness."[14] It was in the 1860's that Thomas D'Arcy McGee could remark that "the law of our youth is growth, the law of our growth is progress."[15] It was during this decade that Canadians began to see the history of their country in terms of the progressive expansion of wealth and civilization. Finally, it was in the 1860's that there was published perhaps the single most important elaboration of the idea of progress to appear in the Province of Canada: Henry Youle Hind's *Eighty Years Progress of British North America:*

Showing the Wonderful Development of its Natural Resources, by the Unbounded Energy and Enterprise of its Inhabitants: Giving, in a Historical Form, the Vast Improvements Made in Agriculture, Commerce, and Trade, Modes of Travel and Transportation, Mining, and Educational Interests, Etc., Etc. for the Past Eighty Years. . . . Hind began by asserting what was for the contemporary reader a commonplace, that from the time of the Greeks to the middle of the eighteenth century the world had made little progress. "It has remained for the present age," Hind continued, "to witness a rapid succession of important inventions and improvements, by means of which the power of man over nature has been incalculably increased and resulting in an unparalleled progress of the human race." Nowhere had this progress been more spectacular than in North America, where the rise to power of the United States had been the subject of universal comment. What was not noticed, Hind argued, was the equally rapid growth of the British colonies in North America. They had, Hind wrote:

In eighty years increased tenfold, not only in population but in wealth; they have attained to a point of power that more than equals that of the united colonies when they were separated from the Mother Country. They have, by means of canals, made their great rivers and remote inland seas accessible to the shipping of Europe; they have constructed a system of railroads far surpassing those of some European powers; they have established an educational system which is behind none in the old or new world; they have developed vast agricultural and inexhaustible mineral resources; they have done enough, in short, to indicate a magnificent future – enough to point to a progress which shall place the provinces, within the days of many now living, on a level with Great Britain herself, in population, in wealth, and in power.[16]

Hind rehearses here the chief themes which one can follow to the vast contemporary literature of progress. Progress was the result of the interaction of human energy and the magnificent potentialities of the New World. As the result of the application of reason to the solution of the complex problems of development there had occurred in the British territories in North America a continuous growth in the social patrimony; there had been a successive increase in the assets handed down from one generation to the next. History was indeed purposeful and that purpose was the establishment in North America of a free society based on an abundance of resources and opportunities for social and economic advancement. Canada had the necessary resources to carry out a program of economic growth. Her social institutions, her educational system, her attention to religion and morality would insure her against an over-emphasis upon purely material development. The past was but a prologue to the glories of the future, and the day would arrive when Canada and the other British colonies in North America – bound together in a confederation – would take their place among the great nations of the world. Such was the burden of

Hind's message. It was a far from ignoble dream, this vision of a great civilization in the north. And without such dreams to sustain them, Canadians would have found the transition from colony to nation – the theme which has pre-occupied historians of the period – an even more painful experience.

II

How did the idea of progress – a doctrine European in origin and philosophic in content – find its way into the interior of North America? To this question three answers may be given. First, the idea of progress arose out of the historical experience of the Canadian people and was a reflection of the character of life in North America. Second, Canadian society in the nineteenth century was profoundly influenced by the large scale movement of men and ideas from the British Isles to Canada. These immigrants, many of whom obtained positions of influence and importance in the colony, brought with them as part of their intellectual baggage the idea of progress, an idea which found its richest articulation in Victorian England. Third, Canadians had at hand the experience of the United States from which to draw up practical programs to promote the improvement and progress of the Province. It would not be a profitable exercise to attempt to separate these several influences and to say of a given doctrine of program that it was American or British or Canadian in origin. Ideas have paid scant attention to the national frontiers dividing the nations of the North Atlantic Triangle, and mid-Victorian Canadians, eclectic and pragmatic as they were, took whatever suited their needs from the source most readily at hand.

That the movement of Canadian history was progressive was the central discovery without which it would be impossible to imagine the emergence of the idea of progress in the Province of Canada. At bottom the idea of progress was a philosophy of history. It served as both an explanation and a justification for social and economic change. The idea of progress by making change appear to be natural, if not inevitable, made change acceptable. As such, the idea of progress was the chief ideological ingredient in the emergence in North America of the idea of the open society. Mark Schorer has written that "myths are the instruments by which we continually struggle to make our experience intelligible to ourselves."[17] This was precisely the social function of the idea of progress.

The dissemination of the doctrine of progress was largely the work of the British immigrant élite which dominated mid-Victorian society. As J.M.S. Careless has pointed out, "Canada, perhaps, never before or since [had] been so British."[18] British immigrants were heavily represented in such critical areas as journalism, the universities, the law, and politics. Their opportunity to mould public opinion was great. And an analysis of the literature of progress reveals that indeed the chief exponents of the gospel of improvement were immigrant editors, college professors, lawyers and politicians. The motivation of this group is not difficult to understand. As immigrants, they had turned their backs on the Old World and had entrusted their lives and fortunes to the fate of the New World. The immigrants therefore were faced with two tasks. First, they had to convince themselves and their fellow countrymen that the future of Canada would be a glorious one and second, they had to devise programs and plans which would assure the transformation of their dreams into reality. The solution of the immigrant élite to the first problem was to embrace with enthusiasm the doctrine of progress; the solution to the second problem was to give leadership and direction to the general drive for economic, social and cultural improvement which permeated Canadian society.

A third source of the idea of progress was the United States. As A.A. Ekirch and Albert Weinberg have demonstrated, the doctrine of progress flourished in America as vigorously as it did in Britain and the British colonies.[19] The rhetoric of Manifest Destiny and the program for the exploitation of America's natural resources found their counterpart, albeit in somewhat diminished splendor, in the Province of Canada. It was an age of improvement: it was an era of progress. Britain and America showed the way. Canadians, unwilling to be left behind hastened to do all that was necessary to join the great movement of humanity toward the ever more brilliant future.

III

Canada did not exist in isolation from the rest of the world. Central to an understanding of the development of the ethic of progress in the Province of Canada is a knowledge of the role played by the United States and Great Britain in the affairs of British North America in the middle decades of the nineteenth century. Progress depended upon peace and security. To achieve these objectives it was necessary for Canada to avoid conflict with her neighbor to the south – the American Republic – and at the same time to hold fast to the Mother Country in order to secure the protection of British sea power in the event of war with the United States. To avoid conflict with the United States was no easy matter. Boundary disputes, the desire of certain elements in America to annex Canada, the Fenian invasion, and a host of serious economic problems insured the existence of tension in the Canadian-American relationship. The aim of every responsible Canadian statesman was to prevent the escalation of these problems into a general war in North America. Everything that British America could do to promote good relations with the United States would in the long run pay good dividends. The survival of Canada as a separate political entity in North America depended upon the benevolent neutrality if not the friendship of the great Republic. So long as Americans thought of Canada – when they thought about it at all – as a backward and unprogressive British colony, lanquishing under the moribund rule of the British Crown, Canada was safe. The great danger was that Americans would discover that Canada was something worth taking; that a military adventure might be worth the risk of a war with Britain. Canadians, therefore, seldom complained of American ignorance about the Province and its resources. Canadian modesty in this regard was the better part of wisdom. Those who live by the banks of a river wherein sleeps a crocodile, tread softly.[20]

Just as Canada wished to avoid unnecessary conflict with America, so to, in her relations with Great Britain there was a desire to avoid doing something which might endanger the British connection. It was to Britain that Canada turned for protection, for capital, for population, and for ideas. The connnection with the Mother Country was in many ways incompatible with the political and economic independence achieved during the long struggle for responsible government. Yet, in practical terms, it was vital. British sea power provided the necessary counter-weight to American military supremacy; British capital made possible, the development of Canada's resources; Britain provided the bulk of the immigrants so necessary to the growth of the population of Canada; Britain was the source of Canada's intellectual class. Canada needed Britain and no amount of political rhetoric could obscure this fact of life.[21]

But the Mother Country in the years before Confederation was in the midst of one of those periodic retreats from the burdens of empire which from time to time the British allowed themselves. Little Englandism – as this particular deviation from the true course of imperial development has been labeled – meant that there was little interest in the fate of Britain's colonial possessions and indeed in some quarters a desire to see the overseas empire disappear. Few people were interested in Canada outside the small circle of colonial officials, diplomats and bankers whose work brought them into contact with the affairs of the Province. *The Times* (London) gave voice to the sentiments of many Britons when in a leader in the summer of 1854 it declared: "We seldom hear anything about it [i.e. British America] unless it be something unpleasant. . . . As it is, we only hear of these Provinces as we do of Mount Etna, that is, when there is an eruption."[22] It has been said that nothing was guaranteed to empty the British House of Commons more rapidly than a colonial topic on the order paper. While Canada needed Britain, the evidence indicates that Britain really did not need Canada and, indeed, possession of Canada might be a liability in the eventuality of a war with America. Under these conditions – an indifferent Britain and a potentially hostile America – Canada had to make her own way. Not really free, yet not really in bondage – this was an experience which could only have been frustrating but an experience which reveals in bold relief the heart of the Canadian dilemma.[23]

IV

It is important to recall at this point that not all Canadians shared in the hopeful view of the future of Canada elaborated by the proponents of the doctrine of progress. Indeed certain groups within Canadian society viewed the drive for improvement with suspicion. Unquestionably, the existence of a large French-speaking agrarian population in the colony hindered the spread of the idea of progress. We still know far too little about French Canada in the pre-Confederation period to be able to speak with much confidence about attitudes and opinions entertained by the citizens of Canada East (Quebec) on the leading questions of the day. The usual picture of French society – drawn largely from the accounts of travellers – is that of a backward and unprogressive race, rooted in tradition and opposed to change.[24] Everything we know about French Canada suggests a general lack of enthusiasm for growth as an end in itself. On the other hand, the French-Canadian commercial, agricultural and political élite made important contributions in the Province to the debate over the implications of the idea of progress. The French Canadian was caught between his desire to protect his race against the encroachments of Anglo-Saxon society, and his desire to build up the country which was the common home of the two great founding races of Canada. This internal conflict within French Canada was not resolved during the middle decades of the nineteenth century, and it has not been solved even today.

Opposition to the doctrine of progress on philosophic grounds does not appear to have been very extensive. There is an almost total absence of a literature of pessimism in the Province of Canada. Potential opposition to the doctrine on the part of Ultra-Tories or Conservatives was undercut by a number of factors. In the first place, progress was respectable. Its slogans were on the lips of the leading statesmen, businessmen and publicists of the Province. Politicians of all persuasion could agree that progress, like virtue, was a good thing and ought to be encouraged. The governor general, a man whose pronouncements carried great weight in the Province, rarely let an opportunity pass to express the vice-regal approval of the many deeds undertaken by Canadians in the name of progress. A second factor was the absence in Canada to those forces which gave rise to doctrines of pessimism in Europe and in the Mother Country; the fear of violent social and political change, the spectre of over-population and the existence of an aristocracy.[25] Canadians rejected, first in 1776 and again in 1837, violence as a technique of social change. The potentialities of the

North American continent were a standing rebuke to the gloomy predictions of Malthus. Finally, an aristocracy as it was known in the Old World never existed in either the United States or Canada. Hence there was no coherent set of values in active competition with the doctrine of progress. Therefore the factors working to produce the triumph of the idea of progress in Canada were assured of success because they were virtually unopposed.

V

John Baillie has written that "it is truer of the votaries of progress than of the adherents of any of the great religions that they believe without knowing either quite what they believe or quite why they believe it."[26] It was for this reason that the central doctrines of the idea of progress were never defined nor were the implications of the idea of progress ever clearly elaborated. Hence the connection between the general concept of progress and the programs which were the natural result of a belief in progress is difficult to trace. This problem is not peculiar to the study of the idea of progress but is in fact the central methodological difficulty confronting the student of intellectual history. The clearly defined path from premise to conclusion, the precise causal pattern linking ideas with action, and the definitive pronouncements traditionally associated with historical inquiry are conspicuous by their absence.[27] The historian can only gather together the contemporary periodicals and newspapers, the manuscripts and the guide books, the grade school primers and the collections of sermons, and from these materials extract the recurring images, metaphors, clichés and platitudes which constitute the rhetoric of the idea of progress.

Nowhere was the rhetoric of progress more efficaciously employed than in the area of morality. Here it is possible to watch that process of reification whereby an abstraction like "progress" is hypostatized. The progress of manners and morals is of course hard to measure. The source for such an analysis are fragmentary; the interpretation of the documents difficult. Yet it is necessary to attempt an assessment of the progress of morality in the Province of Canada because Canadians regarded moral progress as important as, if not more important than, progress in the realm of material and economic development. The fact that recent historians of Western morality have raised serious doubts about the concept of moral progress should not blind us to the fact that there are certain objective and concrete ways in which we can gauge the progress of manners and morals.[28] The first test is to see whether or not a given society manifests a concern for moral values; that is to say, whether or not there is any indication that a given society realizes the relationship between its ethical system and its general cultural development. A second test is to assess the level of concern for the welfare of humanity. Here we are looking for evidences of a humanitarian spirit, for an awareness of and a desire to alleviate human suffering and human misery and for indications of a highly developed social conscience. Finally, a third test consists of assessing the impact of religion and religious values upon a given peoples. All the available evidence indicates that in the Province of Canada the results of such tests would yield the conclusion that morality and moral progress was a reality, not just an illusion.

"Having shewn [sic] the rapid advance of Canada in population, in wealth, and in all the various arts which can minister to man's material enjoyments," wrote J.S.Hogan in 1855, "it seems right to consider whether equal advances have been made in the moral condition and the general tone of society."[29] And in a similar vein, James George pointed out in his lecture *What is Civilization? . . .* that civilization "consists in the conscience and intellect of a people thoroughly cultivated, and the intellect in all cases acting under the direction of an enlightened conscience."[30] A concern for the progress of morality is a central theme of the literature of progress and so pervasive was the belief in the intimate connection between morality and progress that few authors took the trouble to elaborate upon the obvious. The contemporary literature is, rather, directed toward the correction of specific abuses in Canadian society. Hence the best way to understand the moral and religious climate of the Province of Canada is to gather together a variety of seemingly unrelated topics – religion, temperance, personal morals and the rise of humanitarianism – the study of which will allow us to draw some meaningful conclusions about the moral life of mid-Victorian Canada.

VI

"Canada," Colonel Bonnycastle informed his readers in 1846, "is a fine place for drunkards; it is their paradise. . . . "[31] Whisky was cheap and available in quantities sufficient to satisfy the most demanding of thirsts.[32] As early as the 1830's, intemperance had become a major social problem. In both Upper and Lower Canada temperance societies were established to "refine and elevate the state of society" through the suppression of intoxicating beverages.[33] After the Union of the Provinces in 1841, the Legislative Assembly of the United Canadas found itself faced with an annual flood of petitions demanding total or partial prohibition.[34] The demand for reform came from both sections of the Province, and in the grand work of ridding the world of "the awful curse of intemperance" Protestants and Roman Catholics were united in a common cause.[35] The arguments advanced by the advocates of temperance were often quite ingenious. The burden of the temperance argument however was clear. The social and economic progress of the Province of Canada depended on the suppression of the liquor trade.

"Your Petitioners," a temperance group informed the Legislative Assembly in 1852, "regard intemperance as a great moral, and social evil, destructive of health, virtue and happiness, and producing only disease, lunacy and crime, entailing heavy burdens on society, and erecting a fatal barrier in the path of individual and national progress."[36] According to a committee of the Legislative Assembly, "intemperance leads to crime, to insanity, to pauperism. One-half of the crime annually committed, two-thirds of the cases of insanity, three-fourths of the pauperism are ascribable to intemperance."[37] The meaning of these statistics was obvious. Intemperance was exacting a drain upon the human and financial resources of the Province that Canada could ill afford. Every drunkard represented one less productive member of society, one less shoulder applied to the wheel of progress. It was the broad-axe, not the gin bottle, which advanced the cause of civilization. Vigorous use of the former insured peace, prosperity and plenty. But diligent cultivation of the latter would only lead to ruin and decay. The appeal of the temperance men was based on a shrewd assessment of the economic and social costs of wide-spread intoxication. Drink and patriotism were incompatible. Progress depended upon sobriety.

VII

No finer example of moral progress can be found than the great crusade launched in the nineteenth century against the institution of chattel slavery. In this noble cause, Canadians took an active role. Slavery was abolished in Upper Canada in 1793, forty years prior to its abolition in Great Britain. Canada, moreover, early became the terminus of the so-called underground railway, an escape route designed to aid runaway slaves in their bid for freedom. After the passage of stringent fugitive slave legislation in the United States in 1850, the volume of traffic on the underground railway into Canada increased substantially. It has been estimated that between 25,000 to 30,000 Negroes found refuge in Canada West, settling primarily in the townships along the shores of Lake Erie. Finally, an Anti-Slavery Society of Canada was established in 1851. This group was closely associated with both the Presbyterian and Methodist churches, and enjoyed the support of George Brown who thundered in the highly influential Toronto *Globe* against the inequities of the "peculiar institution."[38]

Still other examples of Canadian participation in the great humanitarian movements of the nineteenth century can be seen in Canadian support of the movement to improve conditions in the jails and in insane asylums; to reform the criminal law and to establish organizations dedicated to the abolition of war.[39] One final example, reflecting a general movement in the British Empire to protect the interests of the aborigines, was the development of a rational and humane Indian policy. Following the guidelines laid down by the British, the Canadian government adopted a policy toward the Indians which was in marked contrast to the policies governing relations between the Indian and the White Man in the United States. Instead of simply dislodging the Indians from their lands, the government recognized the Indians' title to and interest in the soil and proceeded on the assumption that this interest could only be extinguished by free agreement between the tribes and the Crown. Hence in exchange for their lands the Indians obtained reserves – often in highly desirable agricultural regions – cash payments, annuities, educational and religious facilities and the opportunity to become through assimilation members of the superior culture. "We consider that it may be fairly assumed to be established that there is no inherent defect in the organization of the Indians," wrote the Indian Commissioner in 1858, "which disqualifies them from being reclaimed from their savage state."[40] That this process involved the destruction of the Indian's traditional social order did not seem to bother contemporaries half as much as it does later day critics.[41] To make of the heathen savage a Christian agriculturalist was a far from ignoble basis upon which to predicate a social policy.

VIII

"The most important subject that can suggest itself, in considering the state of a Christian nation, is its religion, and the influence it exercises on the people. On this foundation, as on a rock, is ever built the permanent advancement of a country, – its reputation and its happiness."[42] If statistics are any indication of the state of religion, the Province of Canada must surely be counted among the nations of the elect. According to the census of 1851, there were 1,747 places of worship in Canada West and 660 places of worship in Canada East. To this total must be added the private homes, barns and stores used by itinerant preachers. Church membership embraced the vast majority of the population. Roughly one-half of the population was Roman Catholic, one-seventh were members of the Church of England, one-eighth were Methodists, one-tenth were Presbyterians, and the remainder of the population belonged to a variety of Protestant sects such as the Baptists, the Lutheran Church, Unitarians and Congregationalists.[43] There were few Jews or other non-Christians.[44]

The contributions of organized religion to the progress of Canada were numerous. In the area of education the Roman Catholic Church supported a vast educational establishment in Canada East as well as providing for the maintenance of such institutions of higher learning as Laval, St. Michael's and Regiopolis. Protestants, while generally in favour of a system of public primary and secondary education, opted for denominationalism in higher education. Such colleges as Queen's (Church of Scotland), Victoria (Wesleyan Methodist), McMaster (Baptist), Knox (Presbyterian) and Trinity (Church of England) attest to the importance attached by the major Protestant groups to education.[45] Closely associated with education was the interest on the part of both Protestants and Roman Catholics in missionary work. The goal of the missionary was to prepare his savage charges – Indian and Eskimo – for the benefits of Christian civilization, and hence, progress (the two, i.e. progress and Christianity being identical). Roman Catholics, Methodists and Presbyterians bore the brunt of the missionary labour.[46] Finally, we have already noted the support lent by the major religious groups in the Province to stamp out the vice of intemperance.

But of far greater importance was the little noted contribution of religion to social stability. Progress presupposed a stable political and social order. Canadians, living as they did in what can best be characterized as a marginal environment, could little afford the dangerous social and political experimentation which was the hallmark of the Great Republic to the south. Canada's resources were too slender, the cost of failure too great to allow for radical social innovation or for rapid political transformation. Hence the whole tone of life in the Province of Canada in the period I have been examining was, in contrast to the tone of life in the United States, profoundly conservative. This led to the erroneous assumption on the part of Americans and others that the Canadians were a backward, unprogressive peoples. Nothing, as we have seen, could be more farther from the truth. But there is no question at all that the several churches of Canada played an important role in the formation of Canada's conservative ideology and social structure. From the Gaspé to Sandwich, from pulpits Roman Catholic and Protestant, from the *Christian Guardian* (Methodist) to the *True Witness* (Roman Catholic) the message was the same. Order, stability, industry and sobriety were the watchwords. Progress was a gift bestowed by the Almighty only upon a people worthy of His munificence. Canadians assumed that progress was as much a function of grace as it was of human industry. And of course they were right. *Si quaeris monumentum, circumspice*.[47]

Notes: The Idea of Progress in Canada

1. Executive Committee for the Paris Exhibition 1855, *Report* (Toronto, 1856), 14.
2. J. Sheridan Hogan, *Canada: An Essay* (Montreal, 1855), 10-11.
3. *Canadian Agricultural Journal*, I (1844), 40.
4. *Literary Garland*, II (1840), 401.
5. *Canada and the Canadians in 1846* (London, 1846), II, 274.
6. *Canada Farmer*, I (1847), 1.
7. *On the Connection Between the Agriculture and Manufactures of Canada* (Hamilton, 1848), 4-5.
8. *Canadian Gem and Family Visitor*, II, (1849), 74.
9. *Journal of Education for Upper Canada*, III (1850), 40.
10. Samuel Strickland, *Twenty-seven Years in Canada West* (London, 1853), I, 65.
11. *An Address on the Present Condition ... of British North America* ... (Montreal, 1857), 23-24.
12. *Canadian Sons of Temperance and Literary Gem*, I (1851), 173.
13. *Journal and Transactions of the Board of Agriculture for Upper Canada*, II (1858), 171.
14. *The New Canadian Dominion ...* (Toronto, 1867), 7.
15. *Speeches and Addresses ...* (London, 1865), 173.
16. (Toronto, 1867), 3-4.
17. Mark Schorer, "The Necessity of Myth," in Henry Murray, ed., *Myth and Mythmaking* (New York, 1960), 355.
18. J.M.S.Careless, "Mid-Victorian Liberalism in Central Canadian Newspapers, 1850-67," *Canadian Historical Review*, XXXI (1950), 234.
19. A.A.Ekirch, *The Idea of Progress in America, 1815-1860* (New York, 1951), 72-165; Albert Weinberg, *Manifest Destiny: A Study of National Expansionism in American History* (Baltimore, 1935), 118.
20. The literature of Canadian-American relations is extensive. For a sample see: Donald Warner, *The Idea of Continental Union* (Lexington, 1960); W.L.Morton, "British North America and a Continent in Dissolution, 1861-71," *History*, XLVII (1962), 139-156; D. G.Creighton, "The United States and Canadian Confederation," *C.H.R.*, XXXIX (1958), 209-222; David Hill, "Some Aspects of the Rise of Canadian Nationalism, 1858-1865," unpublished Ph.D. dissertation, University of Southern California (1955); C.P.Stacey, "Fenianism and the Rise of National Feeling in Canada," *C.H.R.*, XII (1931), 238-261. For some examples of American ignorance about Canadian affairs see: *Anglo-American Magazine*, IV (1854), 31-32; *News of the Week* (Toronto), 5 July, 1860.
21. Province of Canada, *Sessional Papers* (1860), #38.
22. Cited in *News of the Week* (Toronto), August 5, 1854.
23. For a sample of the contemporary British view of Canada see: "British America," *Blackwood's Edinburgh Magazine*, II (1843), 447-454; "Canada," *British Quarterly Review*, XXXIII (1861), 374-391; "Canada," *Fraser's Magazine for Town and Country*, XLVII (1853), 183-190; "Canada and Her Frontier," *Journal of Popular Literature*, 3rd ser., XIX (1863), 62-72; "On the Commercial Progress of the Colonies and Dependencies of the United Kingdom," *Journal of the Statistical Society of London*, XXVII (1865), 34-49; "Shall We Retain Our Colonies?," *Edinburgh Review*, XCII (1851), 475-498.
24. Gerald M. Craig, ed., *Early Travellers in the Canadas 1791-1867* (Toronto, 1955), xvi; Province of Canada, Legislative Assembly, *Journals* (1850), Appendix T.T.
25. K. F. Helleinger, "An Essay on the Rise of Historical Pessimism in the

Nineteenth Century," *Canadian Journal of Economics and Political Science*, VIII (1942), 514-536.

26. *The Belief in Progress* (New York, 1950), 88.

27. Arthur O. Lovejoy, "Reflections on the History of Ideas," *Journal of the History of Ideas*, I (1940) 3-23; F.L.Baumer, "Intellectual History and its Problems," *Journal of Modern History*, XXI (1949), 191-203; John Higham, "American Intellectual History; A Critical Appraisal," *American Quarterly*, XIII (1961), 219-233.

28. Crane Brinton, *A History of Western Morals* (New York, 1959), 413-444.

29. J. Sheridan Hogan, *Canada: An Essay* (Montreal, 1855), 69.

30. (Kingston, Canada West, 1859), 13.

31. Richard Henry Bonnycastle, *Canada in 1846* (London, 1846), I, 154.

32. Edwin C. Guillet, *Pioneer Inns and Taverns* (Toronto, 5 vols., 1954-1962).

33. Ontario Archives, French Papers, Temperance Societies 1849-1957; M.A.Garland, "Pioneer Drinking Habits and the Rise of the Temperance Agitation in Upper Canada prior to 1840," *Papers and Records of the Ontario Historical Society*, XXVII (1931), 341-364; Edwin C. Guillet, *Early Life in Upper Canada* (Toronto, 1933), 289-299.

34. Province of Canada, Legislative Assembly, *General Index to the Journals of the Legislative Assembly of Canada* . . . (Ottawa, 1867), 442-450.

35. Société de Tempérance (Montréal), *Annals de la Tempérance* (Montreal, 1854); Toronto Public Library, Broadside Collection," Association Catholique de Tempérance Totale du Diocess de Montréal (1842)"; R.D.Wadsworth, *The Temperance Manual* . . . (Montreal, 1847).

36. Ontario Archives, French Papers, "Draft Petition of the Sons of Tem-

perance of Canada West to the Legislative Assembly, 1852"; Province of Canada, Legislative Assembly, *Journals* (1856), Appendix #62; *ibid.*, (1860), Appendix #3.

37. Province of Canada, Legislative Assembly, *Journals* (1849), Appendix Z.Z.Z.

38. Fred Landon, *Western Ontario and the American Frontier* (Toronto, 1941), 204-215; Kenneth Stampp, *The Peculiar Institution: Slavery in the Ante-Bellum South* (New York, 1963), 118, 122; Dwight L. Dumond, *Antislavery: The Crusade for Freedom in America* (Ann Arbor, 1961), 339-342.

39. Province of Canada, Legislative Assembly, *Journals* (1850), Appendix Y.Y.Y.; Province of Canada, *Sessional Papers* (1863), #24.

40. Province of Canada, Legislative Assembly, *Journals* (1858), Appendix #21.

41. Diamond Jenness, *The Indians of Canada* (Ottawa, 1960), 249-264.

42. J. Sheridan Hogan, *Canada: An Essay* (Montreal, 1855), 74.

43. *Ibid.*, 75. According to Kenneth Scott Latourette, *Christianity in a Revolutionary Age* (New York, 1961), III, 248-249, as late as 1911 more than 95% of the population of Canada were said to possess a church connection as against 43.5% in the United States.

44. Louis Rosenberg, "Two Centuries of Jewish Life in Canada," *Canadian Jewish Population Studies* (Montreal, 1961).

45. John S. Moir, *Church and State in Canada West* (Toronto, 1959), 83-85, 116-118.

46. "Claims of the Home and Colonial Missions," *Eclectic Review* (1840), LXXII, 446-455; E.C.Woodley, *The Bible in Canada. The Story of the British and Foreign Bible Society in Canada* (Toronto, 1953).

47. In this regard see important paper by S.F.Wise in *United Church Archives Bulletin*, XVIII 1965), 3-18 on "Sermon Literature and Canadian Intellectual History."

The Idea of Confederation: 1754-1858

L. F. S. Upton, *University of British Columbia*

The Canadian experience has rarely been presented as history for the thinking man. Traditionally, emphasis has been put on the achievements of pragmatic politicians, solid businessmen and well-adjusted immigrants. The story of Confederation has been fitted into this unexciting and extremely practical mould, so that it often appears that our present form of government was devised overnight by one or two politicians. John A. Macdonald and George Brown, we might be excused for believing, went to Charlottetown in 1864 and placed their daring innovation before an astonished group of lesser men quite unprepared to cope with such intellectual giants. Canadians have never credited themselves with the kind of debate that graced the United States Constitution of 1789 in the Federalist and Anti-Federalist Papers. They have thus deprived Confederation of that respectability which only time and mature deliberation can bestow on the institutions of mankind.

There was in fact a considerable body of literature that prepared the way for change in British North America. As Governor General Sir Edmund Head rather wearily observed of union in 1856, "there are few persons to whose minds this scheme has not presented itself in some shape or other . . . ."[1] As P.S. Hamilton, a Haligonian lawyer, put it with considerably more enthusiasm, union in some form "had been highly recommended by nearly every author of respectable reputation . . . extensively discussed by the provincial press, and by the people at their firesides."[2] By the 1860's,

British Americans were, if anything, too familiar with the idea of federation, union, confederation – they were no more precise in their terminology than were the framers of the British North America Act. This familiarity is hardly surprising, for the idea was as old as the British Empire in America, and was the basis for the division of the continent between the United States and the Dominion of Canada.

This essay will trace the development of the idea of a union, under the Crown, of all Britain's North American colonies. Union was first advocated in 1754 as a system of defence against the French and Indians. After the majority of Britain's American possessions established a union outside the Empire, the idea was transferred to the colonies that eventually formed the Dominion of Canada. Advocates of a greater union had a variety of plans in view. Before 1840 the most frequently heard were the proponents of a union of Upper and Lower Canada. Others envisaged union as a step towards integration in a British imperial world community with representatives sitting at Westminster and sharing in the construction of imperial policy. There were those who looked for a union of the Maritime provinces as Nova Scotia reclaimed her own. An idea that foreshadowed confederation was frequently brought out as one of a number of alternatives for the future, without much conviction in its intrinsic merits. Such plans as these are variants of the main theme, mere accidents in the continuity of aspiration which is the subject of this essay.

The arguments for a British North American union showed certain consistencies. The first was fear of an outside power: before the American Revolution this was either France or Britain; afterwards, it was the United States. The need for defence against the territorial ambitions of Americans was rehearsed time and time again; so was the wisdom of creating a counterbalance to their growing strength. This preoccupation with the long shadow cast by the neighbouring republic cannot be overemphasized, for in those dark recesses flourished democracy, disloyalty and rebellion. It was many years before the idea of union became even tenuously linked to the virtues of bringing government closer to the people. Most of those who thought of confederation considered the French Canadians as a special "problem" that could be "solved" by a union that would neutralise them in a majority of Englishmen. This accounts in part for the noticeable lack of enthusiasm amongst French Canadians for union, although, once they had experienced the English close at hand after 1840, they began to think of striking a bargain that would leave them in undisputed control of their own province. Another perennial concern was the need to dignify colonial status by consolidation into a larger group that would allow the development of talents cramped and confined in so many tiny societies. Increasingly, European nationalist enthusiasms were reflected in the search for a nationality that could only be found in one British America. From nationalism to imperialism was a short step, and although there were one or two earlier mentions of it, expansion did not appear as an important motive until the 1850's and the limitless horizons opened by the railway. Last but not least came the almost indecent subject, independence. Most advocates of union felt obliged to rebut any connection between the two; only a few considered union as a training ground for a yet very distant separation from Great Britain. This renunciation of independence posed a difficult question: since all the truly great matters of state would still be under the control of an imperial government, what would a union of British North America do?

The Albany Congress of 1754 is the logical starting point for an inquiry into the idea of confederation, although some interest in colonial union can be discerned at an even earlier date. The plan advanced at the Albany Congress was not only important in itself, but in the extent to which it caught the imagination of numerous colonial Americans who held to it from that time on. Some of these moved north after the American Revolution; men such as William Smith of New York and young Jonathan Sewell of Massachusetts built plans for the future of their adopted country on the solid foundations laid at Albany. John Beverley Robinson, descendant of a Virginia family living in Upper Canada, was very anxious to prove that the ideas presented at Albany were the work of the impeccably loyal Thomas Hutchinson, Governor of Massachusetts, and not of the rebel Benjamin Franklin.[3] It was necessary to avoid such contamination because Albany remained a source of inspiration to many Loyalists as the great might-have-been that could have averted revolution. In their new homes on the continent they had a second chance to reform the American empire.

The British colonials assembled at Albany sought a defence against the Indians and their French allies. The necessary co-ordination of effort, it was felt, would come only if one super-government were established in America for this limited purpose. There would be a president general appointed by the Crown and a grand council of delegates elected by the several colonial assemblies, empowered to conclude treaties with the Indians, regulate trade and land purchases from the Indians, and provide for the overall defence of mainland America. To this end the new authority could raise taxes in the various colonies for the payment of soldiers, the building of forts, and the equipping of vessels.[4] The plan came to nothing; it ran afoul of provincial rights even before the London government had a chance to strike it down. But many men continued to believe that a form of American government, interposed between London and the individual colonies, would be the ideal solution for the imperial crises that racked the continent in the 1760's and 70's. On the eve of the revolution, in 1774, Joseph Galloway of Pennsylvania presented the Continental Congress with a plan for such a government in very much the same words as those used at Albany twenty years before. While each colony would preserve its present constitution, a president general and elected grand council would have the power to regulate matters of general concern respecting "Great Britain and the colonies, or any of them, the colonies in general, or more than one colony . . . . " Since Galloway was mainly concerned with the constitutional crisis over taxation that preceded the American Revolution, he stipulated that this grand council should control the granting of aids to the Crown in wartime.[5]

Galloway's plan was debated and shelved, and most of Britain's American colonies went on to create a confederate government without benefit of membership in the Empire. Yet the idea of a union under the Crown was not discredited. The future was much discussed at British army headquarters in New York city in the closing days of the war. Sir Guy Carleton was then Commander-in-Chief, and was a receptive audience to any plan that would make use of the considerable talents with which he considered himself endowed. A major (soon to be colonel) of the Royal Engineers, Robert Morse, was sent by Carleton to survey the area for new Loyalist settlement on the mainland side of the Bay of Fundy. When his report was delivered in 1784 it concluded with an appeal for a united government stretching from Nova Scotia to Quebec, with Cape Breton Isle as the site of the capital. "An able man," wrote the colonel, should preside over the union of "all that remains to Great Britain upon the continent of America." The excellence of the British constitution, contrasted with the anarchy of the United States, would draw immigrants from the republic and make British America a formidable rival to the young United States.[6]

A more detailed survey of the future was drawn up by Jonathan Sewell, former judge of vice-admiralty in Massachusetts, who found himself an exile in Bristol after the war. He considered that one general government for the whole of British North America was necessary to prevent a repetition of the ills that had led to the American revolution. Provincial assemblies should be retained, he conceded, but steps should be taken to curb the democratic element in them, and to reduce the power of the town meeting that had produced so much chaos in Massachusetts. The lord lieutenant or governor general of British America should carry out his duties with the advice of a council but not of an assembly. Together, the governor general and council could bring before themselves any or all of the provincial governors for information, reprimand or suspension. In an emergency they could tell provincial governors how to act, and would in any event have a superintending power over all laws made by any of the provincial assemblies. Central authority would be further strengthened by having control of defence. In this way Jonathan Sewell hoped to erect an authority within America sufficiently strong to keep the colonies loyal to Britain.[7] His ideas clearly descended from the Albany Congress plan of 1754.

Five years later, a more knowledgeable plan for creating a confederation in British America was sent to the Imperial Government in an official dispatch from the Governor of Quebec, Guy Carleton, now Lord Dorchester. The plan was the work of William Smith, once Chief Justice of

New York and now of Quebec, a Loyalist whose father had been one of the delegates at the Albany Congress. Smith himself had long been an advocate of some form of union under the Crown similar to that proposed by Joseph Galloway. He too hoped to establish a strong authority on this side of the Atlantic that would at the same time make Britain's colonies more independent of her detailed control and ensure their continuing loyalty to her. In words with what was to become a familiar ring, he advocated the establishment of a central power "to make laws for the peace, welfare, and good government of all or any" of the British North American colonies. Smith looked forward to the expansion of these colonies for, as he pointed out, most of North America was still unclaimed, and the land from Hudson Bay to the Gulf of Mexico would eventually belong to the greater power on the continent. The British position would be inestimably strengthened by the creation of a federal authority headed by a governor general, an appointed legislative council, and a general assembly elected by the majority of each of the provincial assemblies. Bills presented to this body would require approval by a simple majority of the legislative council and a double majority in the assembly where it would be necessary to have a straightforward majority of all votes and also affirmative votes from a majority of the provinces. The governor general would not intervene directly in provincial governments unless he were actually physically present, but at the same time all provincial legislation would be forwarded to him for his approval.[8]

Chief Justice Smith's plan was dismissed as unrealistic by the British government, which had already decided on partitioning Quebec and creating more, rather than fewer, authorities in America. Yet it was Smith who embedded the idea of a union into Canadian thought. His own son, William Smith, who became a councillor of Lower Canada, corresponded with the Duke of Kent on the possibilities of some form of union.[9] The Duke had lived in Quebec from 1791 to 1794 and was regarded by members of its governing class as a powerful voice at court. Another correspondent was Smith's son-in-law, Jonathan Sewell, son of the Judge Sewell whose ideas have already been noted.[10] Sewell was fully aware of his American heritage and of the part both his father and father-in-law had played in trying to create a better future for the colonies through union. He produced his own plan in 1807 and referred it to the Duke of Kent for patronage.

Sewell was much concerned with the power of the French Canadians in the assembly. He argued the need for a united system of defence for Upper and Lower Canada, New Brunswick, Nova Scotia, and Prince Edward Island, a task which would be made easier by lessening the influence of "the democratic branches of the colonial assemblies." He did not propose to dispense with these assemblies, merely to leave them with power *"only* to enact laws for the welfare and good government of the provinces, severally and in matters which are purely of local interest." A united provincial parliament should be established with the governor general and an upper and lower house. In the upper house would sit members selected in equal numbers from the legislative councils of each province. In the lower house there would be a delegation of five from each provincial assembly. Since these men were few in number, Sewell argued, they would be easier to control and gratify in terms of reward from the government. This authority would have the power to enact laws for the "welfare and good government of the united British provinces, in all matters of general interest." Sewell specified some of the matters of general interest: religion; commerce and inland navigation; defence; and the raising of taxes for these purposes. He foresaw the real possibility of a conflict of interests between provinces and the united government, and where either felt that their sphere of competence had been infringed upon, they should, by a joint resolution of all three branches of their legislature, submit the matter to the decision of both Houses of the British Parliament or of his Majesty in Privy Council. Sewell apparently intended his union government to be the dominant voice in British America, for the governor general was to have the appointment of all officers in each and every province of the union.[11] Sewell lived to be Chief Justice of Lower Canada and to present his ideas to Lord Durham in 1838.

John Beverley Robinson was the son of a Loyalist who had made his home in Upper Canada. Even before he was old enough to vote, he was appointed Solicitor-General, and rose rapidly to the dignity of Chief Justice of Upper Canada. In 1823 he published his thoughts on uniting all British America in a pamphlet, together with the earlier proposals of Sewell. The occasion was the Union Bill of 1822 which had been introduced in the British House of Commons to reunite Upper and Lower Canada. This bill had been largely inspired by the desire to create an English majority in a united assembly. There was another possibility. From Nova Scotia to Upper Canada, Robinson stated, the colonists were united in their loyalty and in their preference for monarchical over republican institutions. There was no inclination to join the United States, for such absorption would only leave the colonies "remote sections of a territory already too extended." But the Americans, always hostile to Great Britain, remained a distinct threat, and union was the best defence against it. Since the colonies could never protect their commerce unaided, there was no need to fear that union would lead them towards independence from Britain. "One grand confederacy" should be established under the title of the United Provinces of British North America, or, alternatively, made into a kingdom under a viceroy. If a confederacy, then the governor general would meet with a legislative council and assembly drawn from across the continent. The council would put the provinces on a parity, with three members chosen by each legislature. The assembly would ensure representation by population, and total fifty-four members if Newfoundland were included; assemblymen would be chosen either by the provincial assemblies "or by the people." French Canadians would have no reason to complain of an arrangement that put them on an equal footing with other British subjects. The powers of the confederacy would embrace trade and militia regulation, the preservation of "public tranquility," and the supervision of religious matters. The general assembly ought also to act as a tribunal for the impeachment of public officials. Each provincial government was to remain in control "of all such matters as are purely local and affect only *its own* good government." Robinson saw that it would be difficult to prevent conflicts in jurisdiction between the general and provincial governments, and his suggested tax arrangements indicate that the smaller units would retain the upper hand. The "joint Parliament," he wrote, would use as revenue only what was left over after the provinces had met their own expenses out of the duties collected within their own borders.[12]

The embarrasing fact that Robert Gourlay devised and circulated a scheme for Canadian confederation from an English lunatic asylum has never been glossed over. On the contrary it has frequently received passing mention to indicate the truly lamentable results of *thinking* about Canada. As might be expected, the plan was somewhat muddled. All the provinces from Newfoundland to Upper Canada were to be confederated with a capital at Quebec city. Each colony would remain "as free within itself as any of the United States" and each would send two non-voting members to the Imperial Parliament. Union would necessarily include free trade with the United States, and, gradually, control of defence. The system should be reviewed from time to time, and, so Gourlay apparently hoped, move toward a stronger union wherein all provincial laws were replaced by a uniform code interpreted by a supreme court. Gourlay's most imporant contribution to the idea of Confederation was, however, his emphasis on a new use for a union: economic advancement through the building of "Grand Commercial Canals . . . maintained by tolls" under the authority of the central government. This was an object of truly "national" scope and far more specific than the generalised hopes and fears that had spurred earlier planners.[13]

Move now from the House of Correction, Cold Bath Fields, 1825, to the floor of the House of Commons, April, 1837. The debate concerned Canadian affairs, and the Assembly of Lower Canada was under strong attack for bringing government to a standstill in that province. The Assembly's agent, James Roebuck, member for Bath, made a vigorous defence. Englishmen should realise, he argued, that all North Americans absorbed influences emanating from the United States, and the result was "an American mode of thinking and feeling" as distinctive as the European one. One basic assumption of this "mode" was that a confederate union made good sense: Great Britain should turn the idea against its inventor by creating her own northern federal republic to check and control the United States. Roebuck proposed the calling of a general assembly at

Montreal with five delegates from the legislatures of each of Upper and Lower Canada, New Brunswick, Nova Scotia, and Prince Edward Island. Roebuck was concerned with very immediate interests, for his general assembly was to be a tribunal for the impeachment of officials and judges, the very men he blamed for the impasse in the province. His speech devoted much more time to the judicial than to the legislative aspects, although these latter, he conceded, would require great skill in definition. Since the central law making body would represent governments, not people, its scope should be limited to "general communication, whether by rivers, canals, roads, or railroads, and, perhaps the post-office."[14] Gourlay's emphasis on canals thus got respectable endorsation, and central control of communications was basic to every federal design from then on.

Confederation had at least one supporter in the Maritimes at this period. Richard John Uniacke was the Attorney-General of Nova Scotia and founder of a powerful political family. He had first turned his thoughts to the future in 1806, during the Napoleonic Wars. He then envisaged two unions, one of the Canadas, and one of the Maritimes. He wanted to ensure that English influence would preponderate over French in the upper provinces, and that, united, Britain's colonies would successfully rival the growth of the United States. Twenty years later Uniacke had a much longer and better reasoned document ready for British governmental approval. It was no longer the power of France that had to be feared, but rather the threat of the "restless and ambitious Government" next door to the colonies. It was Britain's duty to show the world "that good government can be formed without violent revolutions," and to provide sufficient scope for the talent stored up in her American empire. A United Provinces of British North America should be formed to govern through one assembly, the "Grand Council of the Confederacy," with power to provide for the common defence; "to preserve the public peace throughout the whole territory"; to promote commercial intercourse, public works and institutions "beneficial to the Union"; and to tax for these purposes. The constitution would also provide for the addition of new territory as the country expanded, the first mention of such ambitions since Chief Justice Smith's wistful daydreamings of 1790. Within this confederacy the individual provinces would retain their own governments with powers over "the Religion, Laws, Tenures of Lands, Institutions, and Administration of Justice" as at present. They could tax for local purposes, but levy no duties on trade. Realizing that such powers could leave a no-man's land of disputed jurisdiction, Uniacke spent several months in London daily awaiting discussions on his proposals.[15] Rumours of his mission reached back to America, to be picked up by such papers as William Lyon Mackenzie's *Colonial Advocate*. The Colonial Office files opened and engulfed the plan. It was to be no spur to action, merely a memento of discussions at the genteel tables of Halifax.

By the time Lord Durham began his investigations in British North

America, the idea of union was well known. Sober men from the ruling castes of three provinces had advanced their own plans, and so had such an anti-establishment man as Robert Gourlay. Even William Lyon Mackenzie claimed to have circulated hundreds of copies of his own plan for a "Cabotia."[16] Union of the whole of British North America was naturally considered as one way through an inscrutable future following the rebellions of 1837. A Select Committee of the Legislative Council of Upper Canada ruminated over a possible confederacy (including even Newfoundland) in which "each colony might retain its own Legislature, for purposes purely local in their object."[17] The idea was very much alive as Lord Durham conferred with the influential men of the colonies.

Lord Durham gave the possibility of a true confederation very serious thought. In a draft paper he prepared and sent to Lieutenant Governor Harvey of New Brunswick for comment, Durham postulated a union of Upper and Lower Canada, with Nova Scotia, New Brunswick, Prince Edward Island and Newfoundland joining at their option. The new government would be headed by a governor general and an executive council, both crown appointed, and each provincial assembly would send five members to a general assembly with an additional member, elected by popular vote, for each 50,000 or 100,000 residents. Such a representation, partially weighted according to numbers, would have to be kept up-to-date by a decennial census. So much for the general level; at the provincial level Durham also saw the need for alteration. The provincial governors would continue to be appointed as before, by the Crown, but the governor would choose the members of the executive council. The elective assembly would be the strongest partner in provincial government, for its legislation could not be blocked, only amended, by the council, and the assembly's exclusive control over revenue would be explicitly recognized.

The object of the general government, wrote Durham, should be to "control and regulate all such matters as may be common to all, or to some two or more" of the provinces. This would be done by transferring certain powers from the provincial to the general level of government. Durham was very insistent that the provincial legislatures were "to possess all powers not expressly conferred upon the general government," and that each provincial government was "to be supreme in its own limits." The power of the governor general was "in no degree to clash with or override" the provincial governor's authority. Durham listed the areas of responsibility for his general government, subject to the prerogatives of the Crown: communications, currency, customs, post office, commerce, banking and bankruptcy beyond one province, external relations both commercial and political, boundary disputes both interprovincial and international, land grants, vice-admiralty jurisdiction, and the raising of taxes for these purposes. In addition, the general assembly was to have the right to try impeachments of officials from all levels of governments. A necessary part of this new structure would be a "Supreme Court" to hear appeals from all inferior courts and to determine interprovincial disputes, jurisdictional clashes and offences against matters under the exclusive control of the general government. This draft was the most detailed and reasoned consideration of the idea to that time, and shows how the increasing complexity of nineteenth century life was beginning to load increasing duties on to a central government. Durham had faced the problem of authority in a confederation, and he had left the residue of power with the provinces.[18]

Further study of British North America's problems brought some changes in Durham's outlook. In his Report, he presented federation as the best possible solution for the colonies' problems, but one that would have to await the development of more common interests, such as a railway from Quebec to Halifax. A legislative union, he wrote, would "at once decisively settle the question of races," pacifying the French by giving them control of their own province, and neutralising their power for mischief by safeguarding British interests through the general government. Further, a union would counterbalance the growing power of the United States and provide scope for the expansion of a colonial talent. Durham now thought that the tendency of any federation would be towards a complete legislative union, leaving the provincial assemblies "with merely municipal powers," and control over the distribution of funds for local projects only. He did not specifically mention where residual power would lie in such a federation, but the implication was clearly that the general government should have the upper hand. This was a reversal of his earlier position. The first necessity, however, was to unite Upper and Lower Canada.[19]

The fact that Lord Durham had mentioned the idea of confederation in his Report gave the topic a degree of publicity and respectability it had never before enjoyed. When Britain began to sever the bonds of empire by her free trade policies of 1846, other changes were to be expected. Rumours circulated of an impending move towards a wider union. Commenting on one of these reports in its issue of September 8, 1847, *Le Canadien* noted: "*Les Canadiens français envisagent la question de la fédération des provinces anglaises avec une certaine crainte, il est vrai; mais cette crainte est mélangée d'un sentiment très-vivace d'ésperance dans l'avenir.*" Anything would be better than the situation created by the union of the two Canadas in 1840, anything, that is, other than a legislative union of all British North America. *Le Canadien* considered that all the colonies would prefer a federation with a congress to regulate matters of general interest, while leaving each control of its own affairs. In view of the fact that Britain was currently relaxing the economic ties of empire there was no reason to expect her opposition to such a political arrangements. French Canadians *"anticipent donc avec confiance dans une fédération, une plus grande liberté d'action, une plus grande sécurité pour leurs intérêts locaux que sous l'action directe d'un gouvernement éloigné qui ignore leurs besoins et leurs voeux.*" Apparently one part of Durham's Report would be acceptable: the Canadiens would be happy to have control of their own province. But the tone of the comments shows that local government was going to be something far more important than the humdrum activities of municipal corporations whose powers would gradually erode to a general government.

Britain's *laissez-faire* policy also provoked a number of English Canadians into thinking about their future. Disgusted by the mother country's apparent abandonment of her colonies, a group of merchants and their sympathizers formed the British American League in 1849. This group has been generally discredited, for an excess of emotion drove some of its members to call for annexation to the United States. Yet this League also considered the possibility of a British union from the Atlantic to the Great Lakes and, possibly, stretching beyond to include the Hudson's Bay Company lands as well. The League also made the first attempt to organize pro-confederation sentiment on a multi-provincial basis. The matter was discussed at a Kingston meeting in July, 1849. Present, but not saying much beyond cautioning against haste, was the young John A. Macdonald. Union was upheld as a way of restoring (not preserving) the Anglo-Saxon ascendancy, of opening a wider field for business and political talent, of counterbalancing the power of the United States. The meeting also heard strong denunciations of the idea and assertions that the Canadas would in fact grow closer to their republican neighbours.

In November, the League's second convention, held at Toronto, adopted a plan calling for a federal union of the Canadas with New Brunswick, Nova Scotia, Prince Edward Island and Newfoundland. There was to be a viceroy or governor general at the head; a legislative council appointed by the Crown or elected by the provincial legislatures, with members sitting for six years and retiring by thirds as in the American Senate; and an assembly chosen by the provincial legislatures or by popular vote. Obviously a little more clarity was required here! A deputation of members from the federal legislature was to have seats in the House of Commons in London. The powers of the new government were to cover taxation, public debts, river and lake navigation, internal improvements in general, the post office and militia. A supreme court would also be a necessary innovation. Provincial governments would be left as they were to transact local business. A League committee was set up to negotiate with the supporters of the idea in the Maritimes. The only nibble of interest came from Saint John, and the meeting held there showed little enthusiasm and considerable fear lest provincial rights be lost to a new central government. The last activity of the League came when a meeting of May, 1850, called on its members to petition for the establishment of a general convention of delegates to act with the other colonies towards forming a federal consititution. Thereupon the League expired.[20]

The British American League contributed to a pall of disillusionment over the whole topic of confederation. The Colonial Secretary of the time, Earl Grey, had originally held high hopes of the idea. He had accompanied his father-in-law, Lord Durham, in 1838, and been infected with some of the enthusiasms of the Report. Grey directed the attention of the new Governor General, Lord Elgin, to the prospects for a general union. Elgin thought a federal government would have nothing to do but create trouble, for there was no foreign policy to conduct, no army or navy to control. Grey reluctantly agreed, but insisted that "all that can be done is to throw out the general idea & to endeavour by degrees to lead men's minds in that direction," i.e. towards a union.[21] When a member of the Canadian Assembly, H.J. Boulton, introduced resolutions favouring a wider union in 1851, Elgin tersely described them as "pure bunkum."[22] Another critic, who for once found himself on the same side as government house, was William Lyon Mackenzie. Returned from his exile in the United States, Mackenzie now saw federal union as necessarily "a clumsy machine overloaded with patronage." What need was there, he asked, for such a complexity of government in British America?[23] Elgin agreed.

One man who refused to be discouraged was Henry Sherwood, assemblyman, who published a series of letters in *The British Colonist* in 1850 setting forth a "Federative Union of the British North American Provinces." His concern with the idea went back to 1838, when he had chaired the Upper Canadian Assembly's committee on the state of the province. Sherwood now spent little time over explaining the benefits that would follow from a union, for, presumably, these were well enough known to be self-evident. Instead, he explored the method of organizing a federation in greater detail than any had yet attempted. The result is a most valuable contribution to the literature of confederation.[24]

Sherwood prepared a draft act for the Imperial Parliament creating new constitutions for the provinces and for a central government in British North America. The union legislature would consist of a viceroy and two elective houses. The upper house would be the legislative council, or senate, with fifteen members from each province chosen by the provincial governments and holding office for six years, retiring by thirds. The assembly would allow for representation by population, with one seat for every 12,000 people, or 177 members for a start. Changes in representation would follow a decennial census. Provincial government would become much more democratic under their new constitutions: the governor would be popularly elected every two years, although if none of the candidates got two thirds of the vote the viceroy could intervene and choose one amongst them. The upper house of each province would have thirty-six members sitting for six years apiece, but retiring by thirds; the assembly would have a three year term. Although the governor had no power to dissolve the legislature, the provincial electors were thus assured of frequent trips to the polls.

The powers of the federative government, as Sherwood depicted them, extended broadly to all matters concerning the interests of more than one province, and the provinces would be "limited to the adoption of laws for their local and domestic governments respectively." When it came to spelling out the constitutional methods of defining this distinction, Sherwood was far less clear cut: the federation had power "extending to all matters of common concern . . . except such as are hereinafter excepted." The powers of the federal government were prefaced by a list of fifteen areas reserved to the Crown; then came seventeen things the federal government could not do (for example, establish slavery); finally, what the parliament of British North America would do was presented under specific heads: control customs, the post office and militia, regulate trade, borrow money, legislate for bankruptcies, naturalization, uniform weights and measures, copyright and patent laws, and hold jurisdiction over its own specially created federal district. Where amendments could be made to this constitution, the procedure would be by a joint resolution of both federal houses to the Imperial Government.[25]

Sherwood presented no such close definition of provincial powers, for each legislature could "make laws for the peace, welfare and good government of such Province for all purposes not inconsistent with this Act." Provincial legislators would only be able to amend the act as it affected themselves by joint action with the federal houses, and this implied a degree of subordination, as did the viceroy's reserve power to choose the provincial governor. But the provincial parliament, Sherwood emphasized, could legislate "as fully as the Parliament of British North America" did in its sphere. Such phrasing invited disputes, and a supreme court would be needed to determine boundaries between federal and provincial jurisdiction. This court, however, would consist of the chief justices of each province, and the tone of its findings might well be imagined.[26]

In publishing a detailed study of the form of a future confederation, Sherwood had taken a big step toward establishing the scope of the problem. He had drawn inspiration largely from American practice, adapted some earlier Canadian ideas, and above all, assumed the continued colonial status of the provinces.

Sir Edmund Head was one of the few colonial governors who might be termed an intellectual. As Lieutenant-Governor of New Brunswick, he was pursuing the same idea in private that Sherwood was expounding in public. A former Oxford don, Head entered colonial administration at the urging of Earl Grey. Head found the idea of a British American federation quite a stimulating one. In 1850 (or 1851 – it is impossible to tell from the obsurity of his handwriting) he set his ideas down for the benefit of the Colonial Secretary. Head noted that it was impossible, "for any man of common intelligence and education" (true professorial style), to doubt that the existing state of affairs in British America was anything more than provisional. The colonies there faced a future where they would either become independent or join the United States. Independence as single units was out of the question, and it was Britain's duty to foster common interests that would prepare the colonies for independence as a unit; otherwise, instead of balancing the power of the United States, they would fall, one by one, into the neighbouring republic. At the same time, union should be in such a form as to insulate Britain from the troublesome French of Canada East, who had the tendency to adapt the Irish motto "England's weakness is Ireland's opportunity" for their own ends. Everything that concerned imperial matters could best be handled by a federal government where the French power for mischief was effectively nullified by an overall English majority.

To set things moving, Head suggested that four or five basic propositions should be put to the existing local legislatures. Four delegates from each should meet with royal commissioners to draft a bill for passage by the British parliament. This law would be in the nature of a charter defining spheres of jurisdiction that would thenceforth be amendable to judicial, not political, interpretation. A federal government with its capital at Quebec city could usefully bring the colonies together "for certain purposes" of common concern: the supervision of customs duties, commercial regulations, the post office, currency, "and perhaps the great leading lines of railroad and canal." All other matters, "the details of schools, byroads, and the ordinary administration of justice" should be left to the local legislatures, who would hold "the residue of all powers neither reserved by the mother country nor handed over to the federal government." This constitution would be amendable by a majority of the provinces joining with the federal government in a recommendation to the British Government. It would be very important to frame a judicial tribunal that would "be the living interpreter of the constitutional tie," and Head considered this topic at great length. The Judicial Committee of the Privy Council would be unsatisfactory, he thought, as it sat in London, and it would be necessary to have a high court in Quebec city, of three to five judges chosen by the British Government, to decide in cases of disputed jurisdiction.[27]

Sir Edmund's ideas are of more than antiquarian interest because he went on from New Brunswick to be Governor-General of Canada in 1855 and was there as the whole topic of union began to feature in the realm of practical politics. Further, Head was, after Durham, the most intelligent of all those who collected their thoughts on confederation, and he was not under the same pressure as Lord Durham had been. Head could talk of independence as the eventual destiny of the British colonies with a calmness that no English colonial could have permitted himself, and thus fitted confederation into his scheme of things as a preparation to that end. Drawing extensively from the troubles of the United States, and these were most acute in the 1850s, he was able to assess the strengths and weaknesses of an existing confederation, and apply them to the future of British America.

Sir Edmund Head was not the only one in the Maritimes concerned with the future of British North America as a whole. In February, 1854, the Nova Scotian Assembly considered a resolution favouring "the union or confederation of the British North American provinces." J.W. Johnston delivered an unhurried speech for the occasion.[28] Reciting the simple adage that in union is strength, he noted the geographical unity of the British colonies: "The Gulf of St. Lawrence brings us all together." Railways now had the potential to overcome all physical obstacles to unity and to bring about the realization of a dream as old as the English presence in America. Johnston had been reading the American historian Bancroft, and gave an account of the Confederation of New England in 1643, of William Penn's plans in 1697, and of the Albany Congress of 1754. He cited the Duke of Kent's letter to Sewell as quoted in the Durham Report, as well as the Report itself, and lingered approvingly over the recent efforts of the British American League. The example of the United States, Johnston continued, showed that confederation was possible, and British Americans had the necessary strength for the task. Their interests once harmonized by union, they would have a wider scope for their talents and a chance to escape from the anomalous position of being colonists in America. It was possible for a colony to enjoy a wide degree of independence and still be loyal to the Empire; let no one fear that independence itself was in his mind. But, rather than a confederation, Johnston proposed a legislative union as recommended in the Durham Report. Local interests would be safeguarded by municipal councils, and the existing provincial government would become redundant. He did not elaborate on this sweeping proposal, but he had said enough to ensure the defeat of the resolution.

Nevertheless, this speech remained a source of inspiration to Nova Scotian unionists for several years. The text was printed in 1865 as a contribution to the debate then going on as to whether Nova Scotia should accept or reject the proposals of the Quebec Conference. The man who at that time gained Johnston's approval for the publication was a Haligonian lawyer, P.S. Hamilton, secretary of the Union League. It was Hamilton who, in 1855, had begun to round out the arguments and fill in the details lacking in Johnston's assembly speech. In his *Observations upon a Union of the Colonies*, the second of three pamphlets on the topic, Hamilton drew heavily from the common stock of confederation ideas and added some of his own. Union would satisfy a "craving after nationality" and establish British Americans as men of distinct identity in the world. It would give hope: "To the British American, as such, the past is a blank. A consummation of the Provincial Union would be to him an assurance that the future would not present the same dreary void." All lived next door to one of the world's two most rapidly expanding nations, the ultra-democratic United States. (The other was ultra-monarchical Russia.) Despite distance, despite disunion, despite the giant neighbour, the British colonies had prospered, and Hamilton produced several sets of tables to show that the colonial growth rate was much greater than the Americans': how much greater would their prospects be if all Britons stood together. United, they could look forward to the day when a hundred million people would live in their land.[29]

There were only two ways in which the British American colonies could be drawn closer together. The first method, the one most frequently canvassed, was that of federation. This naturally came to mind because of the experience of the United States with this form of government. But, argued Hamilton, there were many objections to a federal union for British America. One of the basic duties of a federal government was the conduct of foreign policy, and if you subtracted this, and its attendant obligations, from the powers of the United States, what had you left? Control of the post office, supervision of patent and copyright laws, and no more. Since British America would continue as a colony, what would its federal government have to do? Were it to be trusted with defence, and were it given the territories of the Hudson's Bay Company, then it might amount to something. Even so, there would still be the difficulty of balancing federal powers off against provincial. "Which is to be the rule; and which the exception; upon points of authority, which shall be the principal; and which the subordinate?" If the federal government were all-powerful, it would destroy the provincial government; if it were not supreme, it would become "an object of contempt" and the result would be a mutually exhausting struggle between provincial and federal authorities. Some had thought of establishing a supreme court as an arbiter, but this would be a great innovation in the British political context, where parliament was the highest court. Such a new judicial body would only complicate matters by becoming a fourth power over a British American colonial confederation.[30]

After such a pessimistic survey of the evils of a federal union, Hamilton turned to his alternative with surprising optimism. A legislative union bringing all the provinces together "bodily and with powers unimpaired," would be acceptable to all, for it would produce no greater change than a mere transfer of the seat of government to one central location. Local interests would be protected by dividing the whole country into some 140 municipal corporations, each of which would have "the entire arrangement of its exclusively local affairs." Thus the only serious objection to a union – the loss of local rights – would be met. For good measure, Hamilton did consider and dismiss two lesser points of possible criticism. Since one great object of the union was "a complete breaking down of all local prejudices, and a fusion of races, throughout the provinces," it was ridiculous to argue the difference between French and English as a reason for not uniting; and, for that matter, the union of Upper and Lower Canada had proved to be a complete success. The second minor objection was that of distance, now easily brushed aside in the railway age.[31]

Hamilton had introduced a new dimension to the literature of confederation by stating the case for a legislative union, but his examination of the inherent and potential weaknesses of confederation was a much more closely reasoned piece of work. He gives the impression of having thought long and hard on the negative side of the question, while allowing a shallow optimism to carry him along when he approached his own pet projet. No Canadian at this time would have characterised his political arrangements as completely successful, nor would any have so lightly dismissed the French Canadian's desire to retain his distinctiveness. To a large extent, Hamilton's optimism lay in his failure to appreciate the nature of Canadian politics, and Halifax was not the best vantage point for such an understanding. But Hamilton had faith in his arguments and republished his pamphlets at Montreal in 1864, after the Quebec Convention, hoping to influence the various provincial legislatures that would be considering the Seventy-two Resolutions. His mark appears on much of the ammunition expended during the Canadian debates, for none worthy of the name were ever held in his own province.

The last work to be surveyed in this essay is by far the most comprehensive. In July and August, 1857, Joseph-Charles Taché, a physician with a considerable reputation as an intellectual, who had represented Canada at the Universal Exhibition in Paris, published a series of articles in his newly-established *Courrier du Canada*. His object was to familiarize his readers with the whole of British North America, from Newfoundland to Vancouver Island. An article was devoted to each province and territory, its climate, terrain, people, produce and political institutions. Statistical essays compared the relative positions of the areas and their general political and social history. Taché then analysed the political systems of the United States and Great Britain, and discussed how far they were relevant to British America's problems. From these observations he went on to consider the possibilities of some form of union, and concluded with a plan of his own drafting. The whole was brought together and published in 1858 at Quebec as *Des Provinces de l'Amérique du Nord et d'une Union Fédérale*.

Taché avoided dismissing the English Canadians with that scant regard many of them had shown towards the French, but he was quite properly much concerned with the interests of his own people. This is his greatest contribution to the idea of confederation, for he demonstrates the assumptions held by its French-Canadian supporters. His argument ran along familiar lines to a large extent. The political situation in the Canadas was so impossible that something had to be done: *"on parle beaucoup, on décrète beaucoup, mais on ne gouverne pas."* Necessary economic advances, such as the building of an intercolonial railway, were held up by the prevalent disunity, and there was, of course the American threat: "*Il ne pourrait rien arriver de plus malheureux pour le Canada et les canadiens que d'aller . . . mêler leur intérêts a ceux de la république voisine. . . . les français iraient s'annexer à un peuple qui assassine les nationalités. . . .*" Great Britain, as evidenced by her economic policy, had accepted the fact that the colonies would one day be independent, and all she was now interested in retaining was control of the external relations of the empire, a responsibility Canadians could not want for themselves. All these considerations made change in the present situation of British America both desirable and possible.[32]

What direction should change take? Certainly not towards a political union, for "*il faudrait la réunion d'éléments homogènes qui n'existent pas ici.*" But if this were not possible, "*il n'y a rien de plus forte après l'unité que l'union.*" A confederation was desirable with a new government at the general level alongside the provincial governments. A clear distinction would have to be made between things of the material and those of the moral order. All matters of a general nature in the first category could be safely entrusted to a federal government, if those in the latter were controlled by the provinces. "*C'est aux gouvernements separés des provinces, c'est aux nationalités que nous laissons le soin de ces choses* [de l'ordre moral] *supérieures en importance aux plus grands progrès. . . .*" The powers of the federal government would be delegated to it by the various provinces: the regulation of commerce, the control of money, weights and measures, the tariff, large scale public works, the post office and militia, and the conduct of criminal justice above the summary level. "*Tout le reste, ayant trait aux lois civiles, à l'éducation, à la charité publique, à l'établissement des terres publiques, à l'agriculture, à la police urbaine et rurale, à la voierie, enfin à tout ce qui a rapport à la vie de famille, si on peut s'exprimer ainsi, de chaque province, resterait sous le contrôle exclusif des gouvernements respectifs de chacun d'elle, comme de droit inhérent. . . .*"[33]

The governments necessary to create a confederation would have to be given written constitutions. These would have to be based on certain stated general principles: freedom of the person in religion, education, opinion, petition, assembly, equality before the law, the inviolability of property; political freedom in the right to universal suffrage and the admissibility of all to public office. The federal government would consist of a governor named by the metropolitan authority and acting on the advice of responsible ministers. A senate, equally representative of each province, would be elected by the people or by the several provincial legislatures. The assembly would be elected directly by the people, its membership proportioned according to population. At the provincial level there would be a division of power somewhat along American lines, with an elective president and a cabinet of his own choosing as the executive. The president, however, would not be able to interfere with law-making, the sole concern of the two elected provincial houses. Federal government officials stationed in the various provinces would be chosen from lists provided by the local governments, who thereby retained patronage. Provinces thus constituted would be able to act as states almost independent of the British Empire. There would be no contact between them and the mother country, for the sole link would be the governor at the federal level. When independence did come, the provinces would have no changes to make in their political structures.[34]

Hoping that all men would accept the logic of a clear-cut distinction, Taché was not worried about providing machinery for solving jurisdictional disputes. He did however consider one problem that had not been touched on before: language. The official language in a province should be that of the majority of its inhabitants, French in Lower Canada, English in the others. The same principle would also hold true in the federal sphere, but since a third of the people spoke French "*il faudrait exiger partout le droit de faire usage de cette langue et le droit aux traduction des documents d'une nature publique, tout en acceptant, partout ailleurs que dans le Bas-Canada, la langue anglaise, comme langue officielle sans exclusion de la langue française, comme moyen de communiquer avec les fonctionaires et comme organe des délibérations parlementaires.*"[35]

In July, 1858, Alexander Galt, member for Sherbrooke, brought three resolutions before the Canadian Assembly: divide Canada into two or three provinces and unite them federally; create a local government in the Northwest with a view to its eventual admission into the new union; explore the possibility of a union of all British North America. Members displayed little interest in the grandiose scheme of a young man; they had heard it all before. Theirs was not the indifference of hostility but of over-familiarity. By then there was such an accumulation of writings on the idea of confederation that no literate person could be ignorant of the topic. This time, however, a complexity of pressures built up that would not let the issue alone. Confederation, so long a solution in search of a problem, had at last found its place and time in history.

The various proposals can now be brought together to provide a picture of confederation as seen in 1858, and to establish a consensus of opinion on the subject – always remembering that the legislative unionists provided the necessary dissent within permissible limits.

Five colonies were to be joined together: Upper and Lower Canada (no one thought the union of the two Canadas worth preserving), Nova Scotia, New Brunswick, Prince Edward Island. All assumed that British North America would remain a dependent colony, at least in the foreseeable future. It followed that the authority for remodelling its government would not be the people, but the Queen in the Imperial Parliament: the initiative for the change could come from the various colonial legislatures. The continuing tie with the Empire would be further acknowledged in the royal appointment of a governor-general, as before, on the advice of the Imperial Government. There was no expression of discontent with the British forms: the whole political framework in which the colonists worked would be retained; responsible government, with its incorporation of English practices and precedents, was not susceptible of improvement.

The new federal government would preserve the bicameral legislature through a senate and assembly. There was some doubt whether the senate should be elected by popular vote or by provincial legislatures, but there was never any suggestion that its members be federal appointees. The senate was to be the forum where provinces large and small would act as equals. Any disequilibrium would be corrected by the assembly, representative of people by head count. Less had been said about the provincial governments, for it was generally assumed that they would retain their familiar legislatures with some democratizing experiments as, for example, the election of the governor.

The scope of federal and provincial powers had attained a fair degree of clarity through the years. The federal government would control matters of general concern, the provinces those of local interest. The provinces were thought of as the core institutions, those that would hand over certain of their powers for use by a central government. No one had argued for a union government that would be all-powerful, turning certain responsibilities back to the provinces; those who spoke for legislative union assumed there would be no provincial governments at all. If there were going to be two levels of government, it was apparent that clashes over jurisdiction would result and that a supreme court would be necessary. This court would have to sit in British America and be composed of residents, for its function would necessarily involve matters of legal-political significance that could not be left to a distant judiciary in London. Since there would be differences within the new structure, it would also be necessary to provide for the amendment of the founding law through petition to the Imperial Government by the federal and provincial legislatures acting in concert.

Thus stood an idea on the brink of its translation into practical politics. For a hundred years the union of British America had had its advocates in times of crisis. Before the American Revolution it was a remedy for French and Indian hostility or for the encroachments of parliament. Immediately after that war it was presented as a guarantee that the same mistakes would not recur to drive the remaining portions of America out of the Empire. Thenceforth it became a remedy for assorted ills that proved to be less than fatal: irresponsible officials, troublesome French, aggressive Americans, unmanageable assemblies. But the purely defensive nature of the idea was gradually replaced by a positive aspect. The demands of the increasingly complex life of the nineteenth century, with its enormously expensive technology, necessitated organisation on as large a scale as possible. For British America this required a level of government above that of the provinces, one that could bring about a single trading area with a co-ordinated policy of public works, and a large enough revenue base either to finance these undertakings of itself or to raise the necessary money on its credit. By the mid-1850's there was common agreement that this would be the prime function of a federal government. The intellectual foundations had been laid for the first fifty years of Confederation, dominated by the prolonged railway construction boom backed by the creation of a nationally protected industry.

One hundred years of thought went into the British North America Act. What of the next hundred years? The act froze the development of ideas about confederation. It directed attention to the detailed working of a political arrangement and to the conflicting interpretation of constitutional lawyers over what had been intended in 1867. With eyes turned to the past, it became very difficult for the federal government to gain powers to face the future. As changing patterns of industry and different social values focussed attention on new undertakings in the twentieth century, the federal government was trapped by an idea that had stopped short.

The Development of an Idea

1754 BENJAMIN FRANKLIN; The Albany Plan of Union, Leonard W. Labaree *et al.* eds., *The Papers of Benjamin Franklin*, New Haven, 1963, v, 387–392.

1774 JOSEPH GALLOWAY; Plan of Union, Julian P. Boyd, *Anglo-American Union*, Philadelphia, 1941, 112–114.

1784 ROBERT MORSE; "Report on Nova Scotia", Douglas Brymner, ed., *Public Archives Report, 1884*, Ottawa, 1885, xxvii–iv.

1785 JONATHAN SEWELL SR.; Plan of Union, Boyd, *Union*, 157-172; identified as Sewell's work in W.H. Nelson, "The Last Hopes of the American Loyalists," *Canadian Historical Review*, XXXII, 1951, 22–42.

1790 WILLIAM SMITH; Plan of Union, Adam Shortt and Arthur G. Doughty, eds., *Documents Relating to the Constitutional History of Canada, 1759–1791*, 2nd ed., Ottawa, 1918, 1018–1020.

1807 JONATHAN SEWELL; *Plan for a General Legislative Union of the British Provinces in North America*, London, (1823).

1823 JOHN BEVERLEY ROBINSON; *ibid.*

1825 ROBERT GOURLAY; Letter to the "Commons of Upper Canada", December 24, 1825, MG II, Q 343 pt. 1, Public Archives of Canada.

1826 RICHARD JOHN UNIACKE; R.G. Trotter, ed., "An Early Proposal for the Federation of British North America", *Canadian Historical Review*, VI, 1925, 142–154.

1837 JAMES A. ROEBUCK; Speech in House of Commons, April 14, 1837, in *Hansard's Parliamentary Debates*, 3rd series, XXXVII, London, 1837, 1209–1234.

1838 LORD DURHAM; Confidential Paper for Lieutenant Governor Harvey, MG 24, A 17, vol. 5, Harvey Papers, Public Archives of Canada.

1839 LORD DURHAM; *Report on the Affairs of British North America*, C.P. Lucas ed., Oxford, 1912, II, 304-323.

1850 BRITISH AMERICAN LEAGUE; C.D. Allin, "The Genesis of the Confederation of Canada," *Annual Report* of the American Historical Association, 1911, I, 41–48.

1850 HENRY SHERWOOD; *Federative Union of the British North American Provinces*, Toronto, 1851.

1850/1 SIR EDMUND HEAD; Chester Martin, "Sir Edmund Head's First Project of Federation, 1851," Canadian Historical Association, *Annual Report*, 1928, 14–26.

1854 J. W. JOHNSTON; *Speech delivered by the Hon. J.W. Johnston . . . 10th February, 1854*, Halifax, 1865.

1855 P. S. HAMILTON; *Observations upon a Union of the Colonies*, Halifax, 1855, reprinted Montreal, 1864.

1857 J. C. TACHE; *Des Provinces de l'Amerique du Nord et d'une Union Fédérale*, Quebec, 1858.

Notes: The Idea of Confederation

1. Quoted in D.G.G.Kerr, *Sir Edmund Head: A Scholarly Governor*, Toronto, 1954, 164.
2. P.S.Hamilton, *Observations upon a Union of the Colonies*, Halifax, 1855, 3.
3. C.W.Robinson, *Life of Sir John Beverley Robinson*, London, 1904, 165.
4. Leonard W. Labaree *et al.*, eds., *The Papers of Benjamin Franklin*, New Haven, 1963, v, 387-392.
5. Julian P. Boyd, *Anglo-American Union*, Philadelphia, 1941, 112-114.
6. "Report on Nova Scotia" in Douglas Brymner, et., *Public Archives Report*, 1884, Ottawa, 1885, XXVII-LIV.
7. Boyd, *Anglo-American Union*, 157-172; identified as Sewell's work in W.H.Nelson, "The Last Hopes of the American Loyalists," *Canadian Historical Review*, XXII, 1951, 22-42.
8. Adam Shortt and Arthur G. Doughty, eds., *Documents Relating to the Constitutional History of Canada, 1759-1791*, 2nd ed., Ottawa, 1918, 1018-1020.
9. The Duke of Kent to William Smith, December 29, 1815, Smith Papers, New York Public Library.
10. The Duke of Kent to Jonathan Sewell, November 30, 1814, in Lord Durham, *Report on the Affairs of British North America*, C.P. Lucas, ed., Oxford, 1912, 11, 321.
11. *Plan for a General Legislative Union of the British Provinces in North America*, London, 1823.
12. *Ibid.*
13. Robert Gourlay to the Commons of Upper Canada, December 24, 1825, M.G. 11, Q 343, pt. 1, Public Archives of Canada.
14. *Hansard's Parliamentary Debates*, 3rd series, XXXVII, London, 1837, 1209-1234.
15. R.G.Trotter, ed., "An Early Proposal for the Federation of British North America," *Canadian Historical Review*, VI, 1925, 142-154.
16. Colonial Advocate, Dec. 14, 1826.
17. *Report from the Select Committee of the Legislative Council of Upper Canada on the State of the Province*, Toronto 1838, 72-73.
18. Confidential paper for Lieutenant Governor Harvey, M.G. 24, A 17, vol. 5, Harvey Papers, Public Archives of Canada. It would appear that Durham leaned heavily on Roebuck's ideas at this stage of his mission, R.G.Trotter, "Durham and the Idea of a Federal Union of British North America," Canadian Historical Association *Report*, 1925, 55-64.
19. C.P.Lucas, (ed.) Durham Report, 11, 304-323.
20. C.D.Allin, "The Genesis of the Confederation of Canada," American Historical Association, *Annual Report*, 1911, 1, 241-248.
21. A.G.Doughty, (ed.) The *Elgin-Grey Papers*, 4 vols., Ottawa, 1937, 37.
22. *Ibid.*, 890.
23. *Ibid.*, 890.
24. Henry Sherwood, *Federative Union of the British North American Provinces*, Toronto 1851.
25. *Ibid.*, 9, 13-15.
26. *Ibid.*, 17-20.
27. Chester Martin, "Sir Edmund Head's First Project of Federation, 1851," Canadian Historical Association, *Report*, 1928, 14-26.
28. J.W.Johnston, *Speech delivered by Hon. J.W.Johnston . . . 10th February, 1854*, Halifax, 1865.
29. Hamilton, *Observations*, 9, 13, 18-25.
30. *Ibid.*, 30-35.
31. *Ibid.*, 51-54.
32. J.C.Taché, *Des Provinces de l'Amérique du Nord et d'une Union Fédérale*, Quebec, 1858, 100, 117, 144.
33. *Ibid.*, 139, 149, 151, 148
34. *Ibid.*, 241-243, 155-156.
35. *Ibid.*, 188.

The Canadian National Style

Alan Gowans, University of Victoria

If I were to begin this essay by saying that Canada is fortunate in possessing a good many buildings of great historical and artistic significance, few readers would believe me, and many may read no further; no conviction is more firmly fixed in the Canadian mind than that expressed in William Colgate's observation in *Canadian Art*: "Very few of our buildings . . . can by any stretch of the imagination be considered good architecture, or even architecture at all." Yet once examine this attitude critically, and it will soon be seen as hard to refute only because it begs the question. If you begin by assuming that "architecture" means Great Buildings, and that Great Buildings are things like major medieval cathedrals and well-preserved Greek temples and imposing royal palaces, then of course Canada has no "architecture." But then by that standard no other countries have much "architecture" either. What proportion of the total buildings of England or France or Germany consists of large medieval cathedrals, Greek temples, or imposing royal palaces? If we really hold that only buildings of this calibre are worth studying, architectural history becomes one of the most restricted fields in all scholarship.

Or again, you might argue that Canadian architecture is not worth studying because it is "unoriginal," derived from models elsewhere. How much is not, anywhere? Logically, if you disdain Canadian architecture because it is derived from English or French prototypes, you ought likewise to disdain English or French architecture that is derived from Italian Renaissance or classical Roman prototypes – which in effect means all of it of any pretensions from the late seventeenth to the mid-nineteenth century, and most of it thereafter. You ought to disdain Gothic architecture because it is derived from Romanesque, and Romanesque because it is derived from Byzantine and Early Christian, and so on, back to the caves. Or conversely, if you defend study of classically-inspired architecture in England or France on grounds that it went beyond simple copying, and represents a creative variant adapted to distinctly different cultural and geographic conditions, you should defend Canadian architecture on the same grounds, for it departed from its models in the same way.

The plain fact is that any architecture is worth studying if it springs from a distinctive historical experience, if it is a characteristic of a particular culture, and if it has excellence judged on its own terms. And by these standards – the only valid ones – Canada has plenty of good architecture, well worth study, unrecognized only because of an irrational inverted snobbery. This snobbery costs Canada dear. It helps acerbate racial problems – for while it is bad enough for English Canadians to deride their own culture, the derision for French-Canadian culture which follows naturally from their attitude is far worse. It cripples Canadian art-historical studies: for to discourage study of Canadian art history (as at least one Canadian university I know more or less officially does) in favour of "more important" study of European materials means to deprive students of all natural opportunity to do primary research in documents and archives. And it inhibits healthy growth in contemporary art; for the student who has been taught that only European art history is important will naturally come to assume that only European artists are important now – why should the present be different from the past? and if it is, at what conceivable point do we decide that the change of status has occurred?

Very well (you may say); granted all this ingenious argument, what Canadian architectural monuments can you specifically name as being something more than simply "cultural expressions?" Are there any that have positive merits, that can stand comparison with monuments of the same period in America or Britain or France? I think there are – far more than commonly supposed. For purposes of this paper I will cite only two, University College in Toronto and the Parliament Buildings complex in Ottawa. Though neither has been preserved entirely as originally built in the 1850's[2] (very few buildings of any age *have* been so preserved anywhere), these two would rank among the most important buildings of their decade anywhere in the world: and for Canada they have the special significance of representing a National Style. They and their counterparts and descendants all over the country for the next thirty years form a body of architecture which in many ways is perhaps the greatest single witness to the character of the new nation created in 1867.

To say that the importance of buildings like these has not been generally appreciated is to say the very least, of course. They suffer the disadvantage not only of being Canadian buildings, but of being Victorian – and only within the last twenty years or so, and then only among a relatively few people, has "Victorian" come to mean a kind of architecture worth study and appreciation, not simply a term of abuse. To understand the proper significance of these buildings, then, something should first be said about that distinctive attitude towards architecture which came to maturity in the early years of the nineteenth century, which remained dominant through so many vicissitudes until well into the twentieth century, and which for want of a better word we characterize as "Victorian"; and specifically we need to understand how the idea of a National Style was one of its most characteristic creations and manifestations.

Central to the Victorian attitude was the concept of architecture as having "meaning." It was the counterpart of a vogue for anecdotal moralizing pictures that began to transform the concept of painting at the same time; and both movements had a common origin – in the social upheaval which from the middle of the eighteenth century on brought a new mercantile industrializing class to power at the expense of the old landed hereditary aristocracy. Along with power, this new class – the bourgeoisie – inherited the old aristocracy's functions of artistic patronage; but the bourgeoisie's ideas as to the proper nature and function of art were quite different. Raised on the "popular arts" of the eighteenth century, the new patrons had learned to expect "reality" and explicit content from their artists rather than formal values, and they naturally proceeded to reward those artists who satisfied such tastes, at the expense of champions of the older goals of traditional beauty and idealization. The overall result was a change not simply in taste or outward forms, but a fundamentally new way of looking at and judging art altogether, a new conception of what art is and what painters do in and for society.

In painting, the first characteristic manifestation of this new concept was the Victorian academic picture: then, two or three generations later, came a wholesale shift from Beauty or Reality as the goal of painting, and this in turn inexorably led to complete subjectivity, abstraction, and non-objectivity.[3] A comparable change transformed the theoretical basis of architecture, though of course the tangible and outward aspect of building forms could never change so dramatically as pictures. The new ruling class expressed its taste for anecdotage in a demand for buildings decked out in ornament drawn from other historical epochs that gave it "meaning," and their taste for "realism" in a passion for studying the architecture of the past not for its general principles of proportion or fitness, but as a well-catalogued source from which to draw "correct" forms at will. And in this attitude, rather than in the use of any particular forms (for obviously this attitude justified using any and every form that seemed appropriate), is the essence of what we call Victorian architecture.[4]

Contrary to what is often supposed, the novelty of Victorian architecture did not lie in eclecticism – for all architecture, and indeed all art, must to a greater or lesser extent draw on what has gone before. Neither was it in the use of applied rather than organic ornament; that too is characteristic of all historical styles, to a greater or lesser degree. It was–the point is worth emphasis – in the idea of using borrowed forms for purposes of specific extrinsic symbolism, in valuing and employing forms not necessarily for any aesthetic pleasure or functional appropriateness (though that might be involved), but primarily for the ideas associated with them: Roman for strength or republican virtue; Greek for liberty; Gothic for the traditional Christian past; and so on. One of the ideas most eminently expressible in this way was that of the Nation, for the same social upheaval that produced a new concept of art also produced a new concept of the Nation, and it too came to maturity in the early years of the nineteenth century.

Hitherto, what had been called a nation or a state had been less a territorial or ethnic unit than a complex of loyalties to place and class; now it became a personified Idea resting on a linguistic or racial base. History-writing ceased to be a matter of chronicling; it became a species of biography, describing the Nation's birth, its growth, its adventures, its hopes and fears and destiny. And now that the Nation had personal character, with recognizable attributes, those official buildings in which the Nation's laws were made and its destiny determined needed to have some appropriately distinctive dress – that is to say, forms from the past which could be related to what was conceived as the Nation's character had to be borrowed to ornament it. So came into being the various "National Styles."

The first national style to appear was in the new United States of America – appropriately enough, since the United States was the first specimen of the new kind of Nation. It was very largely the achievement of Thomas Jefferson, author of the Declaration of Independence, versatile statesman, third President, and from his youth an enthusiastic architect of much more than amateur competence. He promulgated it first in the State Capitol of Virginia at Richmond, which he designed in 1785 on the model of the Maison Carrée in Nîmes, not – and this is the significant thing – because he considered the Maison Carrée to be the most beautiful building he had ever seen (in fact, his personal taste ran to Adamesque and Louis Seize forms) nor yet because it was the most functional model for his purpose (it was in fact almost the most unfunctional model he could have chosen), but primarily for symbolic associations. To Jefferson's mind this (as he supposed) republican Roman temple embodied the principles of republican simplicity, virtue, and strength on which he wanted to see the new American republic based; indeed, he went further and maintained that in many functional respects the new American republic was a reincarnation of the republic of ancient Rome, and as its legitimate successor was entitled to expropriate Roman architecture for its own. Jefferson later embodied these same principles in his own house, Monticello at Charlottesville, remodelling it at considerable sacrifice of utility and convenience to approximate the form of the Pantheon in Rome, and still later in the campus of the University of Virginia (1825), where rows of various kinds of temple houses converged on a central Pantheon, symbolizing the unity of all the new States in adherence to a common republican ideal, and providing an architectural setting where the minds of the young patricians of Virginia would be suitably formed and fixed on the old Roman principles of duty and morality, *gravitas, firmitas, pietas.*[5]

Jefferson's immediate inspiration was undoubtedly the neo-classical movement associated with (among others) the painter Jacques-Louis David, with which he had become acquainted on his diplomatic mission to France immediately after the Revolution.[6] At this time it seemed to him that the objectives of the American and French Revolutions were so fundamentally the same that Roman forms equally well symbolized the aspirations and premises of both, and with only slight concession to events, he clung to this conviction for the rest of his life. But by the 1820's few Americans still agreed with him. The rise of Napoleon Bonaparte, and the transformation of the new French Republic into an Empire bent on ruling all Europe and who knew how much besides, inevitably affected the kind of associations read into Roman forms; gradually they came to seem less and less symbolic of republican freedom, more and more of imperialist despotism; and as this happened, Roman was steadily superseded as the American national style by Greek. When Baltimore erected a column to honour George Washington in 1815, Roman Doric was unhesitatingly chosen for it; but by the 1830's, when the architect of the Baltimore monument (Robert Mills) was chosen to design another to honour Washington in the nation's capital, he just as unhesitatingly chose Greek as the symbol of Liberty. Yet Roman remained strongly enough sanctioned by tradition and early association to be the chosen style for the vast enlargement of the Capitol in Washington undertaken in the 1850's, and for its grandiose new dome completed in 1863 (modelled, interestingly enough, on St. Isaac's Cathedral in Leningrad). In the late nineteenth and twentieth centuries Roman was revived again as a national style, most dramatically for the World's Columbian Exposition in Chicago of 1893 (a blown-up and slicker version of Jefferson's University of Virginia campus, designed by Richard Morris Hunt and McKim, Mead, and White), and to this second revival belong the Jefferson and Lincoln memorials on the Mall in Washington, all sorts of Roman-bath railroad stations, and innumerable post-offices, county court-houses, and the like; and there can be no real doubt that the extraordinary tenacity of the Colonial Revival through the 1950's and 1960's, and the general "colonial madness" evidenced by the crowds at

Colonial Willamsburg, Ford's museum at Dearborn, and elsewhere, is ultimately rooted in a feeling that somehow classical forms, even in "colonial dress," are representative of American roots and ideals.

Very much the same thing happened, though sooner, to the Roman forms which became the French National Style in the Revolutionary and Napoleonic periods. After the collapse of the Napoleonic Empire, the arches and eagles and Roman temples which he had made symbolic of his regime were discredited; but the romantic reaction that set in during the 1820's (of which Delacroix's paintings are perhaps most representative) did not succeed in establishing Gothic or any other romantic style in place of Roman. Instead, by the 1840's it was plain that the official French style would remain a classical variant – Renaissance Italianate in that decade, turning into the Second Empire revival of Louis Quatorze architecture in the course of the 1850's, the rebuilt Hôtel de Ville in Paris and the "New Louvre" being admirable examples.

It took longer for a National Style to develop in Britain than in America or France, and as might be expected, the process was much influenced by what happened there. As early as the 1760's Robert Adam had proposed in his dedication to George III of *The Ruins of the Palace of Diocletian at Spalato* that such Imperial Roman architecture might well be legitimately emulated in Britain to symbolize and celebrate the fact that Britain now had an Empire as large or larger than Rome's; but with both her great enemies in the succeeding period claiming Roman for themselves, serious acceptance of Roman as a British National Style proved out of the question. Classical architecture in Britain from the 1780's on became increasingly oriented towards taste and aesthetics (Edinburgh, in the Napoleonic Wars monument on Calton Hill, as well as the Scottish National Gallery and Academy buildings, offers particularly good examples of the process). And already in those years at the end of the eighteenth and the beginning of the nineteenth century there was a clear trend towards considering Gothic as a British National Style. It was manifested especially in James Wyatt's restoration of British cathedrals to "cleanse" them of any classical additions (Hereford, Salisbury, Durham e.g.) and his adding to ancestral mansions new or remodelled rooms in Gothic, like the Ancestors' Gallery at Wilton. On this rather haphazard foundation a whole structure of dogma was reared in the next generation by the movement for a Gothic Revival in architecture dramatically led by Augustus Welby North Pugin. Pugin is often characterized as a Catholic fanatic; he may have been that, certainly, but it was not primarily because he supposed Gothic to be a Catholic style that he wanted to revive it throughout Britain. Rather it was that he supposed the Gothic Age to be the one in which Britain was most truly British, and to revive this (as he considered it) moribund spirit of Britishness in the nineteenth century he demanded a revival both of the religion of that age and of its architecture. The great monument to the triumph of these ideas was the new Houses of Parliament begun after the fire of 1832 which destroyed Westminster Old Palace. Westminster New Palace in its traditional Gothic dress began to rise over the same years that the Reform Bill of 1832 was transforming Britain from the old pattern of a state based on hereditary obligations and loyalty to the new kind of personified Nation supported by and demanding romantic popular support, and was the great symbol of that process. This Gothic national style was consolidated in the 1840's, the decade when the Scott Monument was erected overlooking Princes Gardens in Edinburgh, and Anglican churches in Gothic became almost mandatory.

In 1858 Ottawa was selected permanent capital of the Province of Canada, and in 1859 a national competition held for a House of Parliament and flanking departmental buildings to be located there. Though several different styles were included among the entries, there was never any real argument – for all intents and purposes it was taken for granted that since Gothic had become Britain's National Style, Gothic would be Canada's also, and that was how the style of the winning designs was described, both for the House of Parliament by Thomas Fuller (with Chillion Jones as his partner) and for the departmental buildings by Frederick Waburton Stent (his partner being Augustus Laver).

In the event, however, the Gothic of Canada's Parliament Building turned out to be quite different from the Gothic of Westminster New Palace. Not that it was any more or any less archaeologically accurate; in fact neither building represented any real revival of the actual principles of Gothic architecture, for until very late in the century, the Victorian architectural mind valued past styles far less for what they were than for what they said, so that accuracy was not important in either case. But where the London buildings essentially constituted an eighteenth century palace, classically low in line, symmetrical, orderly, balanced, dressed up in an out coating of Gothic pinnacles, buttresses, and tracery, the Ottawa Parliament was housed in quite a different type of building. Verticality was emphasized not only in its decorative lines, but in its compositional massing, and since it was a city-block long, this produced impressively monumental effect. Furthermore, its ornamental detail was drawn from a variety of sources – all medieval, to be sure, but widely disparate in time and place. The end result was an immensely picturesque pile, irregular, visually dramatic, eye-catching in its texture and variegated outline. Superficially the two government seats resembled each other; in fact, their differences were fundamental. Westminster New Palace represented one of the great monuments of the first or Early Victorian phase of nineteenth century architecture; the Ottawa Parliament Buildings were an equally great monument to the second, or High Victorian phase. Indeed, since High Victorian architecture was just coming to maturity during the 1850's in both England

and America, the Ottawa parliament buildings represented not only one of its greatest examples but also one of its earliest.

Exactly how they came to be so advanced has never been properly investigated. It is unlikely that the architect in charge, Thomas Fuller, was responsible. Neither his preceding work, like the Town Hall at Bradford-on-Avon near his native Bath, which he designed in 1854, nor the Cathedral at Antigua, which he designed a year or so later, showed any remarkable skill, nor did his later work at the State Capitol in Albany, or as Chief Architect of the Dominion. The same could be said of Stent, Jones, and Laver; for all of them the Parliament Buildings were far and away the most impressive, avant-garde, and successful works with which they were ever associated. There is a strong possibility that the real inspiration for the work was Frederick William Cumberland of Toronto, who had come out from England in 1847, and who designed and built University College in 1856. His work was consistently distinguished thereafter. University College was quite as impressive as the Parliament Buildings; indeed, the resemblance between them is close enough to suggest that one was at least in part a model for the other, and certainly in these two buildings Canada had for their time two of the most up-to-date and important buildings in the world. It has been noted on occasion that the model for University College was the University Museum in Oxford, built by Deane and Woodward on the inspiration of John Ruskin. If so, that is odd, for in fact University College was begun several years before the Oxford Museum. It may be that Cumberland had in some manner become acquainted with the preliminary thinking or plans for the Oxford Museum before he left England; he had been a classmate of John Ruskin's at Oxford. Or it may be that the relationship between the two buildings was the other way round, unthinkable though that may be to the colonial Canadian mind. In any case, a paper like this is no place to go into such problems; the important point to realize here is that with its Parliament Buildings the new nation of Canada began its existence not only with an architectural work of major importance, but with its own distinctive National Style as well.

The High Victorian style of the Parliament Buildings became Canada's National Style much as Canada became a nation – more or less by accident. Yet for this very reason, the one was perfectly suited to express the other. Unlike the Early Victorian Greek or Roman or Gothic Revivals, High Victorian represented more a general way of building than a particular set of forms; there was no one neat package of ideas associated with it. It brought to mind an image of no one historical epoch in particular, but pastness in general, an effect deliberately heightened by its gingerbread ironwork along rooflines and its variegated parade of asymmetrical towers and pinnacles and shifting roof-angles, which made buildings appear to fade into a space as indefinite as the times from which their diverse forms were drawn. In the same way, the new Dominion had been built on no one dominant emotion, philosophy, or historical event; though Canada was a nation with a long past, it looked back to no one period or people in particular for inspiration or roots. High Victorian architecture was by definition a mixture of many diverse and originally incompatible elements, each remaining recognizable, but also recognizably changed in its new setting. In the same way, English, French, and American elements among the new nation's people all remained recognizable and conscious of their origins to a degree not paralleled in the United States, but they were also collectively different from their relatives who had stayed at home. High Victorian Gothic differed from medieval Gothic, and High Victorian Baroque from the Baroque of Rome or Versailles, just as English Canadians differed from Englishmen, French Canadians from Frenchmen.

Only a style with the mixed forms, and broadly general associations of High Victorian could function as a national style for a country like Canada. Early Victorian architecture involved a "battle of the styles" which inevitably became a racial issue in Canada: the Gothic Revival came to Montreal, for example, as a symbol of Catholicism in the parish church of Notre Dame; then the Anglicans appropriated Gothic, and the Catholics turned to Italianate for St. Jacques Cathedral, with inalienably Roman associations. Classical Revival architecture offered a similar battleground for "British classical" versus "American classical" ideologies. But the nature of High Victorian architecture precluded any such controversies. True, the Second Empire style with its heavy preponderance of classical elements had a certain association with France, and the Ruskinian Gothic, with its equally heavy preponderance of medieval detail, had a comparable association with Britain; but in neither case could there be anything like the particularity of Early Victorian classical or Gothic Revivals. Though Second Empire High Victorian was modelled on Louis Quatorze's precedent, it was obvious that it in turn depended on Italian prototypes, and in the style as actually developed, all sorts of elements from all sorts of sources could be and were thrown into the pot, leaving little exclusively French about it. The same was true of Ruskinian Gothic. In contrast to the Pugin's kind of Gothic Revival, promoted on grounds that it was peculiarly and characteristically English, the appeal of Ruskin's High Victorian Gothic was to broad aesthetic and moral sensibilities; so far from being drawn from any one period, the vivid colour, textural contrasts, and variety of form on which its effect depended were achieved by drawing from all sorts of sources – and even when Venetian Gothic dominated, that source was itself a tissue of borrowings from Byzantine, Lombard, and French inspiration. So High Victorian could be adopted freely by anyone, anywhere – and it was. The city halls of Quebec and Winnipeg and Victoria, court-houses and fire stations and operas all over the country, all could show a broad stylistic unity. High Victorian could be and was adapted to all types of buildings – to churches and houses, banks and schools and offices. It equally well could be and was adapted to regional vernacular building traditions, so that you can find High Victorian versions of the traditional Quebec City town house and of the great Québecois parish church tradition, of the traditional Scottish-cum-New-England house-types of Nova Scotia, of the distinctive farmhouses of Ontario and the classical cottage-types developed in British Columbia. In this sense, too, High Victorian was truly a National Style.

Finally, in distinction to the preceding Early Victorian revival styles, High Victorian was a spontaneous response to cultural needs and psychological conditions, rather than any product of abstract intellectual theorizing. This meant that it could grow and develop naturally, and so it did. It would require a book to describe in detail how perfectly High Victorian architecture expressed the cultural climate of the 1860's and 1870's, and how naturally there grew out of it the great arts-and-crafts tradition of North American architecture, of which Richardsonian Romanesque was the best representative; I have in fact devoted a large section of one book to this theme, and will not repeat it here except to note that in the course of the 1880's Ruskinian and Second Empire High Victorian was logically and smoothly superseded by the organic arts-and-crafts manner not only in monumental buildings like the old City Hall in Toronto or the Parliament Buildings in Victoria, but also in innumerable excellent smaller houses and churches all over the country, so that by the 1890's Canada could show as fine a display of High Victorian architecture of all kinds as could be seen anywhere in the world.

Nor is there time here to explain in detail how and why intellectual and aesthetic fashions changed from 1900 on, how High Victorian was displaced by the slick academic archaeology of the Late Victorian "revivals of the revivals," and then the whole Victorian concept of architecture rejected out of hand by the "moderns," so that "Victorian architecture" came to be an indiscriminate synonym for "bad architecture"; that too I have dealt with elsewhere.[7] It will be enough to make two points only. First, that fortunately now people here and there are beginning to appreciate Victorian architecture again – not, of course, that there is (Heaven forbid) any movement to have a "Victorian revival," but that we are beginning to see Victorian architecture no longer as a horrible example to be shown young architects as a demonstration of how not to build, but as a historical manifestation like any other major epoch in architectural history, to be studied as history and to be judged by its own standards; and second, that one result of this has been a re-evaluation of the function of architectural ornament and the idea of visual pleasure and excitement in architecture generally.

In contemporary architecture of the 1960's three trends are discernible. The first is a survival of International Style functionalism – of that rigid doctrinaire insistence on absolute honesty of structural expression of new technological materials, which results in steel-and-glass cages, picture-windows and open corners whether wanted and needed or not, and so on.

The second is the "brute style" associated (not altogether fairly, perhaps) with Kahn and Rudolph – buildings that contrive by massive and over-whelming sculptural forms to dominate those using them, in which "function follows form." And third there is a new emphasis on the use of screens, textured surfaces, and other devices that will give buildings character and provide visual pleasure; this trend has developed at the same time and pace as the developing appreciation of Victorian architecture generally, and especially of High Victorian, and I think that there is a clear relationship, conscious or not. It is no accident that this third trend is becoming stronger all the time in Canadian architecture of the 1960's, for I think that in this country there is a natural feel for it. For recognized consciously or not, High Victorian was a truly National Style for Canada, and the feeling for it remains deep and instinctive, in the indefinable but very real way such feelings do. In the years from 1860 to 1890 Canada achieved a unified architectural expression that was a perfectly fitting expression of the unexpected but none the less very great success of the Confederation of 1867, and if I were to venture a prediction, I would say that the Centennial of Confederation may very well come to be seen in retrospect as the time when a second National Style – albeit in the appropriate forms and context of mid-twentieth-century art – first became evident.

Notes: The Canadian National Style

1. *Canadian Art,* Toronto, 1943, 245-6.

2. Except for some remodelling of its interior after a fire in the 1890's, University College stands reasonably intact. The Parliament Buildings complex has fared worse, having lost its main block by fire in 1916 (rebuilt a few years later in the slicker, more erudite Late Victorian manner), but the East and West blocks remain on the exterior in almost pristine condition and on the interior also are not too badly altered; the Parliamentary Library is quite intact, and for all the buildings good photographs provide evidence of what has gone.

3. This is the central argument of my book, *The Restless Art – A Study of Painters and Painting in Society 1750-1950,* Philadelphia, 1966.

4. There is a longer discussion of this point in the introduction to Section III of my *Images of American Living,* Philadelphia, 1964.

5. Cf. the detailed discussion in *Images of American Living, loc. cit.,* "Jefferson."

6. The development of the idea of symbolic and didactic art in the eighteenth century is admirably traced by James A. Leith, *Art and Propaganda in France,* University of Toronto Press, 1962.

7. A detailed study of the relationship between High and Late Victorian architecture will be found in the section on Late Victorian in *Images.* I have developed the history of the Arts & Crafts movement in North America in *Rural Myth and Urban Fact in the American Heritage,* Wemyss Foundation publication, Wilmington, Delaware, 1965. Yet to be analyzed is the precise relationship between the collapse of the Victorian concept of art and loss of popular devotion to the romantic concept of the Nation. Plainly, they fell together, just as they had risen together; plainly, too, the primary agent was the Great War, which pushed the demands of the Nation for blind unconditional support altogether too far. And once the central romantic image of the era collapsed, faith in all the others collapsed too.

Libéralisme et ultramontanisme au Canada français: affrontement idéologique et doctrinal (1858-1865)

II

Philippe Sylvain, Université Laval

Les considérations qui précèdent sur l'ultramontanisme permettent de distinguer ce qui, au plan des principes, séparait Mgr Bourget des libéraux canadiens: tout un monde! Le monde issu de la Révolution française. Pour les intransigeants de l'école de Veuillot, la Révolution était, en effet, le *mal*, le *mal absolu*. "Oubliant ou méconnaissant les leçons de l'histoire," écrivait l'abbé Maret au ministre des cultes, le 26 décembre 1857, au sujet de Veuillot, "il ne sépare pas les erreurs et les crimes de la Révolution des vérités qu'elle a mises en lumière, des améliorations civiles, politiques, sociales, qu'elle a introduites; il méconnaît la nécessité, la légitimité, la grandeur de ses résultats généraux, dans lesquels se retrouvent l'action et l'influence de la raison et du christianisme, de la philosophie et de l'Evangile." Pour Maret, "le système théocratique," qui était "le fond de toutes les pensées d'école" de Veuillot, expliquait "des opinions aussi excessives, aussi téméraires, aussi dangereuses" à l'endroit de la société moderne issue de 89.[1]

Sur le plan politique, l'évêque de Montréal était également aux antipodes des libéraux. Ecrivant, le 3 octobre 1860, à son protégé George Edward Clerk, rédacteur en chef du *True Witness,* Mgr Bourget ne cachait pas les sympathies qu'il éprouvait pour les "principes" du journaliste conservateur:

En parcourant vos colonnes avec tant soit peu d'attention, l'on est bientôt convaincu que vous êtes un véritable conservateur, travaillant de toutes vos forces à unir fortement cette colonie à la Mère-Patrie; et pour réussir dans cette entreprise, vous faites, avec votre logique irrésistible, mouvoir puissamment le principe religieux, qui est en effet la seule base solide de la société civile et politique.[2]

Convictions ultramontaines et sympathies conservatrices se conjuguaient étroitement dans les trois lettres pastorales que Mgr Bourget publiait le 10 mars, le 30 avril et le 31 mai 1858, en suivant un plan très concerté. Dans la première, l'évêque décrivait les effets néfastes de la Révolution, qu'il attribuait à la diffusion des mauvais livres; par la deuxième il indiquait les moyens de prévenir la propagande révolutionnaire au Canada par l'application des règles de l'Index; et la troisième stigmatisait ceux qu'il considérait comme les fourriers, dans notre pays, da la "révolution," les libéraux de l'Institut canadien.

Dans le plus pur esprit ultramontain, la Révolution, aux yeux du prélat, n'avait accumulé que des "désastres," qui pourraient bien se reproduire au Canada, si "le mauvais esprit qui avait fait couler" en Europe "tant de larmes," traversait "un jour les mers pour couvrir notre chère patrie de décombres et de ruines": "Que deviendra alors l'heureux peuple du Canada si, endoctriné par des hommes sans principes, il n'a plus où mettre sa confiance?"[3]

Reprenant la thèse que la célèbre publiciste ultramontain Mgr Gaume développait alors dans les tomes successifs de son ample ouvrage sur *La Révolution*,[4] il soutenait que "les moyens employés pour tromper les peuples et égarer les nations furent les mauvais livres, les publications mensongères et les discours irréligieux"; il ne pouvait se dissimuler "que les plans d'attaques contre la religion étaient ici absolument les mêmes que ceux employés ailleurs avec tant de succès."[5]

L'homme d'Eglise en arrivait ensuite à des applications pratiques: si vous faites partie d'un institut littéraire, ne permettez pas "qu'il s'y introduise des livres contraires à la foi et aux moeurs"; si, effectivement, il y en a, "vous devez en conscience faire tous vos efforts pour les faire disparaître en usant, par exemple, de toute votre influence et en vous unissant à tous ceux qui tiendraient comme vous aux bons principes, pour que ces mauvais livres soient jetés au feu"; si cela vous était impossible, "il ne vous resterait plus d'autre parti à prendre que de vous retirer, en protestant énergiquement et publiquement que vous ne faites plus partie d'une pareille institution."[6]

C'était une prise de position visant directement l'Institut canadien, que l'évêque assimilait à "une chaire de pestilence" pour tout le pays.[7]

Mis en cause par la plus haute autorité du diocèse, les membres de l'Institut se réunirent le 13 avril suivant. Quelques années plus tard, Hector Fabre indiquait le double but que ses amis et lui se proposaient dans cette séance extraordinaire: "C'était d'abord de retrancher de la bibliothèque un certain nombre de livres immoraux et irréligieux, en mettant à cette oeuvre de réforme le plus large libéralisme compatible avec les intérêts moraux de la population et la sécurité publique. C'était ensuite de replacer la société sur ses bases nationales, de lui rendre en un mot sa constitution originelle."[8]

Mais le groupe de Fabre ne constituait qu'une minorité, qui fut incapable d'imposer ses vues, sur les deux points, à la majorité. Dans la discussion sur les "mauvais livres," la majorité adopta, comme on devait s'y attendre, l'attitude conforme au libéralisme qu'elle professait: elle refusait à qui que ce fût le droit de surveillance et de prohibition en matière de livres et de lectures. Pour le libéral, en effet, "chacun a le pouvoir de choisir à son gré ses aliments intellectuels; les cas d'empoisonnement qui peuvent en résulter ne sont que des inconvénients accidentels, amplement compensés par un bien supérieur à tout: la liberté."[9]

Cette thèse, Félix Vogeli la soutint avec force; pour lui, "une bibliothèque était une collection des oeuvres de l'esprit humain: on n'avait pas plus le droit d'exclure un ouvrage mauvais que le naturaliste n'avait le droit de rejeter de son casier une plante sous le prétexte qu'elle était vénéneuse."[10]

De son côté, Pierre Blanchet proposa des résolutions qui furent adoptées à plusieurs voix de majorité: la bibliothèque de l'Institut était *exclusivement* composée de livres moraux, scientifiques, philosophiques, historiques, propres à nourrir le coeur et à développer l'intelligence"; elle "n'avait jamais contenu de livres d'une nature obscène ou immorale, et les différents comités permanents ou spéciaux, ainsi que les bibliothécaires, n'avaient pu, après de longs et consciencieux travaux de quatorze ans, trouver dans la bibliothèque *un seul livre* obscène ou immoral."

Les libéraux qui approuvaient ces résolutions savaient fort bien que la bibliothèque de l'Institut canadien renfermait plusieurs oeuvres inscrites au catalogue de l'Index. Dessaulles l'avouait dans une lettre qu'il écrivait, le 3 juin 1884, à son ami Paul Théodore-Vibert: "On avait Voltaire (moins *La Pucelle* qui a été retranchée de suite), Rousseau, l'Encyclopédie, puis les légistes gallicans, les économistes et nombre d'auteurs sérieux du siècle actuel, mais pas orthodoxes comme Michelet, Martin." En éliminant les ouvrages à l'Index, "il aurait fallu perdre 300 ou 400 volumes, ce que l'association ne voulait pas admettre."[11]

Mais surtout, comme Dessaulles l'affirmait dans la même lettre, le groupe radical dont il était le porte-parole de plus en vue, "ne voulait pas du contrôle ecclésiastique." En citant les résolutions que Pierre Blanchet avait fait voter dans la séance du 13 avril 1858, pour prouver que "jamais société n'avait menti avec plus de cynisme et d'audace," Hector Fabre corroborait à l'avance l'assertion de son adversaire: " . . . ces résolutions mensongères étaient acclamée par des cris sauvages, parmi lesquels on distinguait le cri: *A bas les prêtres!*"[12]

Les partisans de la thèse modérée de Fabre ne tenaient pas plus que les radicaux à être sous la coupe du clergé, comme Mgr Bourget lui-même dut s'en rendre compte,[13] mais ils constataient que trop de leurs collègues n'avaient pas la maturité et la culture nécessaires pour aborder sans discernement certains ouvrages qui figuraient sur les rayons de la bibliothèque de leur association. Ils croyaient "que si la société a le droit de régler la vente du poison, l'Institut devait avoir le droit de défendre à ses membres de s'empoisonner." C'est ce qu'écrivait à Fabre un des sécessionnistes de 1858, en ajoutant: "Voltaire et Rousseau peuvent être lus sans danger par des hommes mûrs et instruits, mais je ne connais que des fous pour les mettre entre les mains d'hommes presque sans instruction comme la grande majorité des membres de l'Institut."[14]

Faute de pouvoir s'entendre, on se sépara. Le 22 avril 1858, quelque cent trente-cinq membres remettaient par lettre leur démission au président de l'Institut canadien:

La parole de Sa Grandeur Mgr de Montréal, écrivait le rédacteur de la Minerve, *a porté de nobles fruits. De courageux jeunes gens, des hommes dans la force de l'âge, ceux-là mêmes qui ont assisté à la naissance de l'Institut canadien, ceux-là mêmes qui l'ont élevé de leurs deniers et de leurs talents, n'ont pas un instant hésité à s'en séparer, après avoir vainement tenté d'en chasser les mauvais livres.*[15]

* * *

Dès le 30 avril, soit une semaine seulement après le départ des sécessionnistes, Mgr Bourget publiait une deuxième lettre pastorale dans laquelle il s'en prenait nommément à l'Institut canadien. Approuvant le geste des membres qui avaient donné leur démission pour ne pas "contribuer", écrivaient-ils dans leur lettre du 22 avril, "au maintien d'une association" qu'ils considéraient "comme dangereuse pour la jeunesse et pour le pays sous le rapport religieux, moral et national," l'évêque ajoutait que "la bibliothèque de l'Institut était mauvaise et très mauvaise."[16]

Il formulait ensuite les règles de l'Index. Ainsi il passait outre aux timidités de Mgr Baillargon, administrateur du diocèse de Québec. En effet, Mgr Bourget avait soumis un projet de "règles pratiques adoptées par l'archevêque et les évêques de la Province ecclésiastique de Québec, soussignés, dans une réunion tenue à l'Archevêché, le 28 août 1856"; l'article 7 de ce projet était ainsi libellé: "Que les règles de l'Index et autres décrets pontificaux sont en vigueur dans cette Province, quand ils ont été publiés à Rome dans les formes voulues par le droit."[17] Or Mgr Baillargeon lui avait répondu, le 26 septembre suivant, à ce propos: "A mon avis il ne serait pas opportun d'adopter cette règle et il serait très dangereux de la publier."[18]

L'intrépide ultramontain qu'était l'évêque de Montréal n'avait que faire de la circonspection apeurée de son supérieur hiérarchique. Aux grands maux les grands remèdes, devait-il penser. Cette promulgation officielle des règles de l'Index était une mise en demeure d'avoir à se soumettre, sinon "il s'ensuivrait qu'aucun catholique ne pourrait plus appartenir à cet Institut; que personne ne pourrait plus lire les livres de sa bibliothèque et qu'aucun ne pourrait à l'avenir assister à ses séances ni aller écouter ses lectures."[19]

Les libéraux se rendirent compte que la lutte se circonscrivait entre eux et l'évêque de Montréal. Ils virent même dans l'attitude épiscopale à l'endroit de l'Institut canadien "le parti pris de le détruire si on le pouvait," comme l'écrivait Dessaulles en mars 1862.[20] Du moins avait-elle provoqué, indirectement, la fondation, le 10 mai 1858, de l'Institut canadien-français par les sécessionnistes du 22 avril précédent, qui se proposaient ouvertement ce but. Inauguré le 16 décembre suivant dans l'immeuble de la Société d'histoire naturelle, rue Saint-Jacques, à l'endroit précis où quatorze ans auparavant, à un jour près, l'Institut canadien avait été fondé, il prit tout de suite, au témoignage de l'ultramontain Cyrille Boucher, "une tournure vraiment nationale," qui lui faisait répéter, après Victor Hugo: "Ceci tuera cela."[21]

C'était aller un peu vite! Quoi qu'il en soit, les libéraux se virent bientôt l'objet d'une dernière censure épiscopale dans une troisième lettre pastorale publiée le 31 mai 1858; c'était une condamnation sans appel des principes non seulement de leur Institut, mais du parti politique auquel ils se rattachaient et du journal qui était l'interprète officiel de leurs convictions, le *Pays*.

*   *   *

Désireux de conférer à sa réprobation du libéralisme canadien-français la plus grande autorité et le plus d'efficacité possible, Mgr Bourget emprunta ses arguments[22] à la célèbre encyclique de Grégoire XVI du 15 août 1832, *Mirari vos*, qui condamnait le libéralisme sous deux de ses formes, l'une révolutionnaire, qui tendait à abattre les rois, l'autre intellectuelle qui, par le moyen des libertés modernes, exprimait une tendance naturaliste. Dans le texte pontifical, la séparation entre l'Eglise et l'Etat paraissait comme le rejet de la mission surnaturelle de l'Eglise dans la société civile.[23]

Grégoire XVI avait résolu dans le sens traditionaliste et autoritaire le grand problème auquel le monde catholique se trouvait confronté depuis le début du siècle: l'attitude à prendre à l'égard du monde issu de la révolution intellectuelle et politique du dix-huitième siècle et particulièrement du régime des libertés civiles et religieuses proclamé dans la *Déclaration des droits de l'homme et du citoyen*.

Utilisant le texte grégorien, déjà très abrupt, Mgr Bourget en accentua encore la vigueur, en lui donnant une interprétation maximaliste, dont les formules tranchantes et absolues ne peuvent qu'étonner profondément aujourd'hui. En effet, pour reprendre la remarque de l'historien belge Mgr Aloïs Simon, à propos de Grégoire XVI, "nos conceptions contemporaines sur la liberté de pensée et la recherche désintéressée de la vérité, nos habitudes de tolérance nous placent . . . aux antipodes de ces attitudes intellectuelles autoritaires et, par là même, souvent passionnées."[24]

Les thèses que les libéraux canadiens avaient proclamées depuis que Papineau avait eu recours au principe révolutionnaire des nationalités dans le "Rappel de l'Union," étaient réprouvées avec force par l'évêque de Montréal.

L'encyclique *Mirari vos* avait blâmé sévèrement l'exaltation de la souveraineté du peuple; Mgr Bourget, guidé par l'ouvrage de Gaume, choisit l'exemple de la Révolution française et de l'Empire napoléonien pour en attribuer les "horribles commotions" à "la liberté d'opinions que l'on cherchait à faire régner à la place du principe de l'obéissance, que la Religion enseigne à ses enfants, envers tous les gouvernements"; aussi devait-on se "préserver de cet épouvantable malheur, en repoussant avec horreur ce mauvais principe" que l'on travaillait "à répandre par tous les moyens possibles, et surtout par la voie des mauvais journaux."[25]

Mirari vos avait répudié la séparation de l'Eglise et de l'Etat à l'encontre de la doctrine menaisienne; or Dessaulles, disciple de Lamennais, avait préconisé cette séparation en soulevant, comme nous l'avons vu, la question des dîmes. Cette thèse, les libéraux canadiens n'avaient cessé de l'exposer par la plume et par la parole. Ainsi le rédacteur en chef du *Pays*, Charles Daoust, beau-frère de Joseph Doutre, dont l'élection en 1854 comme député du comté de Beauharnois avait été "l'un des plus beaux triomphes de la démocratie",[26] s'était écrié, le 8 février 1858, lors d'un banquet offert par des amis politiques:

Depuis que je m'occupe des affaires publiques, j'ai toujours été d'opinion que l'Eglise et l'Etat devraient avoir une existence séparée, vivre chacun de leur propre vie et non s'identifier dans une action commune. Cette opinion, je la crois plus que jamais fondée, et nous ne serons sûrs de voir régner la paix, l'harmonie, la prospérité de cette province du Canada que lorsque ce principe aura reçu sa pleine consécration.[27]

Après avoir cité ce "langage impie," mais sans en indiquer l'auteur ni la provenance, Mgr Bourget ajoutait:

. . . vous reconnaissez, N.T.C.F., les partisans de la liberté effrénée, dont vient de nous parler le Père commun. Lui, qui écrit sous les divines inspirations du St-Esprit, il signale comme favorable et salutaire la concorde de l'Empire avec le sacerdoce. Eux, sous d'autres inspirations sans doute, ils ne craignent, pas de dire que la paix, l'harmonie, la prospérité ne pourront régner ici que lorsque la Religion et le Gouvernement seront entièrement séparés.[28]

Voulant faire "comme toucher du doigt la fausseté et l'absurdité de ce principe que la Religion est un obstacle *à la paix, à l'harmonie et à la prospérité des gouvernements*," le prélat avait recours à un exemple contemporain, mais qui ne tarda pas à se révéler ruineux pour son avancé, comme il dut le constater dès l'année suivante: "la "nouvelle alliance" du Second Empire avec le "Sacerdoce": ". . . l'expérience est là, ajoutait-il témérairement, pour attester que les enseignements de l'Eglise sont vrais; et par une conséquence nécessaire, que ceux du libéralisme sont faux et trompeurs."[29]

La condamnation des thèses libérales postulait celle du parti politique qui s'en réclamait et tout d'abord du journal qui les véhiculait. Après avoir distingué parmi les "mauvais journaux" le "journal irréligieux," le "journal immoral," le "journal hérétique" qui n'étaient autres sans doute que le *Montreal Witness* de John Dougall mais surtout le *Semeur canadien* de Narcisse Cyr, Mgr Bourget en arrivait au journal anticlérical, qu'il qualifiait d' "impie," car "chaque prêtre étant le représentant de Jésus-Christ" et "l'autorité dont il est revêtu, étant celle de Jésus-Christ lui-même, ce serait attaquer cette divine autorité que de vouloir faire perdre au Clergé son influence."[30]

Manifestement sous la plume du prélat le "journal impie" était une variété du "journal libéral," puisque les libéraux s'étaient toujours énergiquement opposés à l'activité cléricale dans le domaine politique; d'ailleurs l'évêque de Montréal en apportait immédiatement lui-même la confirmation: "Le *Journal libéral*," écrivait-il, "est celui qui prétend, entr'autres choses, être *libre* dans ses opinions religieuses et politiques; qui voudrait que l'Eglise fût séparée de l'Etat; et qui enfin refuse de reconnaître le droit que la Religion a de se mêler de la politique, quand les intérêts de la foi et des moeurs y sont intéressés."[31]

Pour démontrer "qu'il n'est permis à personne d'être *libre dans ses opinions religieuses et politiques*," l'homme d'Eglise, à la suite de Grégoire XVI qui, dans *Mirari vos*, avait affirmé "que le jugement sur la saine doctrine, dont les peuples doivent être instruits, et le gouvernment de toute l'Eglise, appartiennent au Pontife Romain," partait du principe que Jésus-Christ avait "donné à son Eglise le pouvoir d'enseigner à tous les peuples la *saine doctrine*," c'est-à-dire

cette doctrine pure qui leur apprenne à se gouverner, comme le doivent faire des peuples vraiment chrétiens. Car c'est là évidemment un point de haute et importante morale. Or, tout point de morale est sous le domaine de l'Eglise, et tient essentiellement à son enseignement. Car sa divine mission est d'enseigner aux Souverains à gouverner avec sagesse, et aux sujets à obéir avec joie.[32]

C'est ainsi que la pensée de l'évêque de Montréal débouchait directement sur la thérocratie, dans laquelle l'abbé Maret voyait le résumé de la doctrine sociale et politique de l'ultramontanisme. En effet, comme l'écrivait, six mois plus tôt, le doyen de la faculté de théologie de la Sorbonne, selon les ultramontains "le Souverain Pontife, outre son autorité spirituelle, sacrée pour tous les catholiques, possède de *droit divin* une véritable juridiction politique dans le monde entier, juridiction qui le rend arbitre des grandes questions sociales et même politiques; et sous certains rapports, les rois et les chefs des nations ne sont que ses vicaires." De ce principe théocratique découlait des "privilèges sociaux et politiques pour le clergé de chaque nation," et "l'intolérance civile" était "élevée au rang des dogmes religieux."[33]

L'intransigeance ultramontaine de l'évêque de Montréal n'avait d'égale que l'intransigeance libérale de Dessaulles et de son groupe. Nous les verrons se heurter de nouveau en 1862 au sujet de la question romaine. Pour le moment, les condamnations doctrinales du prélat constituaient un appoint politique d'une extrême importance pour le parti conservateur. Dans ses *Souvenirs politiques*, Charles Langelier, remontant à cette époque et rappelant "les dénonciations si violentes" dont les premiers libéraux avaient été l'objet de la part du clergé, se demandait comment leur parti avait pu "survivre à une guerre pareille."[34]

*   *   *

Mais si de la scène canadienne ils levaient les yeux pour embrasser l'horizon international, les libéraux avaient des motifs de se réjouir. En effet, l'une de leurs thèses les plus chères recevait, dans la décennie suivante, la sanction des faits. La formation du royaume italien est la première grande réalisation concrète du principe des nationalités. A partir de 1859, l'Autriche est peu à peu refoulée hors de la péninsule, des principautés et un royaume, celui de Naples, disparaissent, l'Etat pontifical se désagrège et le royaume d'Italie se parachève sous le couvert du nouveau droit qui s'impose triomphal, celui des peuples à disposer d'eux-mêmes.

Les libéraux canadiens eussent été infidèles à eux-mêmes s'ils n'avaient pas partagé l'allégresse des libéraux du monde entier à l'endroit des principaux artisans de l'unification italienne, un Cavour, un Victor-Emmanuel, un Garibaldi.

En revanche, c'est dans la détresse que les catholiques vécurent ces années dramatiques. A leurs yeux, le mouvement de l'unité italienne n'était autre qu'une tentative concertée des forces hostiles à l'Eglise pour réduire celle-ci à l'impuissance.[35] En France surtout, les catholiques firent bloc derrière le pape. "On ne saurait exagérer l'incidence de la question romaine sur la vie du catholicisme français à cette époque."[36] A peu d'exceptions près, les catholiques ne comprirent pas le sens des aspirations du peuple italien et la volonté de ses élites à obtenir l'indépendance nationale,[37] à la différence des libéraux.

Parmi ces derniers, il faut signaler le propre cousin de Napoléon III, le prince Napoléon qui, dès le début de la guerre d'Italie, pouvait témoigner de son "ardeur" et de son "dévouement" pour "la cause de l'émancipation et de la liberté italiennes," comme il l'écrivait à Cavour le 27 mai 1859.[38]

Son mariage avec la fille de Victor-Emmanuel, la princesse Clotilde de Savoie, le 30 janvier précédent, l'avait lié définitivement à la politique unificatrice du roi du Piémont et de son ministre.

Le prince Napoléon disposait d'un journal. En 1859, sous son patronage, Adolphe Guéroult avait fondé l'*Opinion nationale*, qui devint l'organe des bonapartistes de gauche et qui, avec le *Siècle*, le *Constitutionnel* et la *Presse*, fut l'interprète des libéraux italianissimes. Nul plus que Guéroult n'a insisté avec davantage de sympathie et de compréhension sur l'idée de la souveraineté nationale; nul n'a montré avec plus de continuité que l'idée de la fédération des peuples italiens, au nom de laquelle Napoléon III avait pris les armes en 1859, était maintenant dépassée et qu'il fallait résolument admettre le principe unitaire.[39]

En plus de la sympathie dont ils témoignaient à l'endroit de la cause italienne, les journaux libéraux et anticléricaux étaient partout, en France, en Angleterre, en Allemagne comme au Piémont, de beaucoup supérieurs aux journaux catholiques comme nombre, tirage et même importance des nouvelles.[40] Ils tenaient leurs renseignements de trois agences qui s'étaient associées le 18 juillet 1859, quatre jours après Villafranca, pour se répartir le travail de la "chasse aux nouvelles" à travers l'Europe: Havas, Reuter et Wolff, respectivement pour la France, l'Angleterre et l'Allemagne.[41] Les nouvelles européennes parvenaient au Canada par l'intermédiaire des journaux anglais qu'alimentait l'agence Reuter, grâce à un câble télégraphique qui reliait Londres à Paris depuis 1851. Comme la première liaison électrique entre l'Europe et l'Amérique ne réussit pleinement que près de huit ans après l'échec de septembre 1858,[42] les journalistes canadiens devaient attendre l'arrivée des vaisseaux venant d'Angleterre pour satisfaire la curiosité impatiente de leurs lecteurs.

*   *   *

Au Canada français comme en France, la presse se divisa suivant ses tendances idéologiques au sujet de l'Italie. La presse ultramontaine était représentée à Québec par le *Courrier du Canada*, dont Joseph-Charles Taché assumait la rédaction depuis la fondation du journal et qui céda sa place de rédacteur, le 31 octobre 1859,[43] au Français légitimiste Auguste-Eugène Aubry, professeur de droit romain, depuis janvier 1857, à l'université Laval;[44] à Montréal, c'était l'*Ordre*, journal fondé en novembre 1858 par Cyrille Boucher et Joseph Royal, anciens élèves du collège Sainte-Marie et dont le guide le plus écouté, après leur ancien professeur, le jésuite français Larcher, était le chanoine Venant Pilon, rattaché à l'évêché de Montréal et fervent admirateur de Louis Veuillot.[45]

Le principal organe de la presse libérale était évidemment le *Pays*, dont le rédacteur en chef était toujours Charles Daoust, assisté d'Emile Chevalier. Daoust devait d'ailleurs se retirer en juin 1859[46] et Chevalier restait seul chargé de la rédaction du journal jusqu'au mois de novembre suivant, alors qu'il repartait pour la France en même temps que son ami Félix Vogeli et un collaborateur français de la *Minerve*, Félix de La Ponterie, pour jouir de l'amnistie accordée aux exilés politiques par Napoléon III le 16 août précédent.[47]

Les premières escarmouches entre ultramontains et libéraux canadiens se produisirent au début de la guerre d'Italie: les ultramontains, à la suite de Veuillot, continuaient à se montrer favorables à l'Autriche, puissance conservatrice catholique; c'est ainsi que le *Pays* jeta à la figure de Cyrille Boucher l'épithète qu'il jugeait infamante d'*autrichien*.[48] Par contre, les libéraux exaltaient Garibaldi, au grand déplaisir de Taché, qui devait admettre que le héros avait "toutes les cajoleries du télégraphe et d'une certaine presse,"[49] mais qui ne persistait pas moins à croire que le célèbre général était "le type du conspirateur et du flibustier," dont "la révolution et le désordre" s'étaient fait "un drapeau."[50]

C'est après les victoires de Magenta, de Solferino et les préliminaires de paix de Villafranca que les dissidences s'accentuèrent. Tandis que le *Courrier du Canada* et l'*Ordre*, de concert avec l'*Univers*, applaudissaient bruyamment à la paix qui devait sauvegarder le pouvoir temporel du pape, le *Pays* était d'avis que l'armistice frustrait les espérances des libéraux italiens, et annonçait la démission de Cavour. Le rédacteur du journal libéral, Emile Chevalier, se réjouissait de l'annexion prochaine de la Toscane au Piémont et souhaitait que le même sort échût aux Romagnes, qui faisaient encore partie de l'Etat pontifical.[51]

Chevalier était Français; Joseph Royal constatait donc "avec plaisir" que "dans toute la presse canadienne," il n'y avait que le *Pays* qui se faisait "la copie des voeux révolutionnaires de la presse mazzinienne de l'Europe, parce que sa rédaction était étrangère."[52]

Pour les ultramontains, "la question italienne était surtout une question catholique, qui se posait entre le Pape et l'Eglise d'une part, et l'Erreur et la Révolution, sous une forme ou sous une autre,"[53] comme l'écrivait le veuillotiste Taché; sourcilleux à l'extrême, les journalistes de l'*Ordre* reprochaient au catholique libéral La Ponterie, qui était sur le point de quitter la rédaction de la *Minerve* pour retourner en France, d'apprécier les événements italiens "au point de vue révolutionnaire": eux-mêmes n'avaient pas cru devoir se former leur propre opinion sur une question d'une telle importance: "Ils n'avaient fait que suivre l'*Univers*, qui leur avait paru la meilleure autorité à suivre en ces graves matières."[54]

* * *

Le 22 décembre 1859, date de la parution des pages intitulées *Le Pape et le Congrès*, marqua en France "la séparation entre l'Empereur et le parti catholique."[55] La brochure, anonyme mais en réalité écrite sous l'inspiration de Napoléon III par le sénateur-publiciste Arthur de La Guéronnière, était destinée à faire accepter à l'opinion française que le pape perdît les

Romagnes. Elle eut un résultat opposé. Elle fut interprétée comme la condamnation du pouvoir temporel. La thèse papale, d'après laquelle le sort de l'Etat pontifical tout entier se jouait dans la question des Romagnes, en fut renforcée.[56]

Les ultramontains partageaient naturellement ce point de vue. L'*Univers*, qui avait publié l'encyclique *Nullus certi* du 19 janvier 1860 rejetant la proposition de Napoléon III, fut supprimé dix jours plus tard. La consternation s'empara des veuillotistes canadiens. Aubry écrivait dans son journal à l'annonce de cette fatale nouvelle: "Il est tombé, ce noble et vigoureux champion de la cause catholique! Il est tombé, mais glorieux et invaincu! Il est tombé, indignement sacrifié à la révolution!"[57] "L'*Univers* de Paris est supprimé", s'indignait de son côté Joseph Royal. "La France et la cause catholique perdent leur plus courageux, leur plus dévoué et leur plus puissant défenseur."[58] Mgr Bourget, qui était bien revenu de ses illusions à l'endroit de la "nouvelle alliance" de l'Eglise et du Second Empire, faisait part aux fidèles de son désarroi: "Ce qu'il y a de plus admirable," écrivait-il dans sa pastorale du 19 mars 1860, "c'est que la presse qui se montre si dévouée au Saint-Siège et qui est l'expression vraie et sincère du bon coeur français, est laissée à la merci des plus grands ennemis de la Papauté, qui se trouvent avoir le pouvoir en main et qui en abusent pour supprimer les bons journaux."[59]

Les événements suivaient inexorablement leur cours. L'Italie centrale vota son annexion au Piémont et le 24 mars fut signé le traité franco-sarde portant que le Savoie et Nice seraient réunies à la France. Dès le 26 mars Pie IX lançait une bulle d'excommunication contre les spoliateurs des Etats pontificaux.[60]

L'unité italienne était en marche; cette première phase, qui consistait en annexions par référendums, était pour l'opinion mondiale la confirmation éclatante de l'introduction dans le droit public européen du principe jugé encore révolutionnaire du droit des peuples à disposer d'eux-mêmes. "Tous les efforts de Napoléon III vont désormais tendre à "sauver la face," à faire croire aux catholiques français et aux souverains de l'Europe continentale qu'il fait tous ses efforts pour empêcher cette unité de se réaliser. Mais il est probable que, désormais, au fond de lui-même, il souhaite la solution unitaire."[61]

*   *   *

Il était réservé aux catholiques du monde entier d'autres émotions. Le 5 mai 1860 Garibaldi s'embarquait à Quarto près de Gênes avec ses *Mille*. On connaît l'épopée qui marqua la conquête de la Sicile et de Naples par le célèbre condottiere. Victor-Emmanuel, pour arrêter Garibaldi et l'empêcher d'exploiter ses victoires en faveur de l'anarchie, décida de traverser avec ses troupes ce qui restait des Etats pontificaux, vainquit à Castelfidardo, le 18 septembre 1860, la petite armée pontificale commandée par

Lamoricière, et Ancône dut capituler le 29 septembre. "C'est auprès des évêques que Castelfidardo produisit le plus d'effet. Le gouvernement perdit alors la confiance de beaucoup de prélats qui lui étaient restés fidèles même après l'annexion des Romagnes au Piémont."[62]

Dans le discours du trône, le 4 février 1861, Napoléon III expliqua pourquoi il avait appliqué "le principe de non-intervention" lors de l'invasion du territoire pontifical par l'armée piémontaise. La discussion de l'adresse s'ouvrit au Sénat le 28 février. Elle porta tout entière sur l'Italie. L'événement marquant fut le grand discours prononcé, le 1er mars, par le prince Napoléon. La question romaine, d'après lui, ne comportait que deux solutions: ou bien une intervention armée de la France pour rétablir l'ancien régime en Italie, ou bien l'unité italienne avec Rome pour capitale, le pouvoir temporel du pape étant restreint aux quartiers de la rive droite du Tibre. Il dénonça violemment la politique rétrograde du Vatican. Il attaqua les traités de 1815 et défendit la cause du progrès, de la démocratie et de la liberté: "Nous ne sommes pas," s'écria-t-il, "les représentants de la réaction, mais de la société moderne."[63]

Cavour écrivait au prince Napoléon deux semaines plus tard: "V. A. a rendu à l'Italie un bien grand service. Tout le monde lui en reste reconnaissant, mais personne mieux que moi ne peut en apprécier l'étendue. Le discours de V. A. est pour le pouvoir temporel du Pape ce que Solferino a été pour la domination autrichienne." Il lui prédisait même la gloire à ce sujet: "La destruction du pouvoir temporel sera un des faits les plus glorieux et les plus féconds dans l'histoire de l'humanité, auquel le nom de V. A. demeurera à jamais attaché."[64]

Les événements se précipitaient. Le cardinal Antonelli, secrétaire d'Etat, puis Pie IX, dans son allocution consistoriale du 18 mars 1861, déclarèrent que le Saint-Siège ne pouvait renoncer à ses droits sur aucune partie de son territoire. Le Chambre des députés italiens répondit, le 27 mars suivant, en proclamant Rome capitale du nouveau royaume; elle déclarait d'ailleurs que l'indépendance du pape serait respectée.

Pendant neuf ans les trois parties intéressées restèrent sur leurs positions: le gouvernement italien réclamant Rome comme capitale; le Saint-Siège refusant de renoncer à ses provinces perdues; le gouvernement impérial persistant à vouloir réconcilier l'Italie et le Saint-Siège, et exigeant jusque-là le maintien de ce qui subsistait des Etats pontificaux.

Le prince Napoléon croyait que la question romaine allait bientôt se résoudre, dans le sens de ses aspirations, bien entendu. Il l'écrivait à George Sand le 17 mars 1861: ". . . je n'aime pas la parole sans l'action comme conséquence; aussi j'espère que l'affaire de Rome ne pourra tarder à se régler."[65]

Mais il dut déchanter, surtout lorsque mourut trois mois plus tard, le 6 juin, le principal artisan de l'unification italienne, le comte de Cavour, dont le décès inopiné lui fut un rude coup, comme à tous les libéraux, si bien que dans la presse libérale on ne retrouvera pareille émotion qu'à l'assassinat du président Lincoln. "L'éloge est sans restriction, la douleur est sans mesure."[67]

* * *

Le passage à Montréal et à Québec, en septembre 1861, du cousin de Napoléon III raviva les ferveurs libérales et, par réaction, déchaîna les colères ultramontaines.

J'ai raconté en détail ailleurs "La visite du Prince Napoléon au Canada."[68] Dans les notes rapides que le voyageur impérial confiait à son carnet et que l'on ne publia qu'en 1933,[69] une remarque affleure sans cesse: l'hostilité du clergé canadien à son endroit.

A son arrivée à Montréal, il est remué par un accueil empreint d' "une vive sympathie et des sentiments" qui lui "font battre le coeur," mais il ne tarde pas à se rendre compte que "le clergé catholique est très influent et très violent." Aussi lorsque l'Institut canadien lui remet, le 13 septembre, une adresse le félicitant d'avoir "si éloquemment développé les vues libérales du gouvernement de la France sur les plus grandes questions de la politique européenne," se propose-t-il d'encourager cette "utile institution," "la plus éclairée du pays et indépendante du clergé."

A Québec, pour lui présenter leurs hommages, le gouverneur général Sir Edmund Head, le procureur général George-Etienne Cartier, le maire de la ville prennent la tête d'un défilé qui comprend "la moitié de la ville," comme il l'écrit avec satisfaction dans son carnet: "C'est une véritable procession attestant une bien grande sympathie pour la France, d'autant plus que la réception que la population me fait a lieu malgré le clergé, qui a dit beaucoup de mal de moi et a voulu empêcher toute manifestation."

En revanche, si les autorités cléricales de la toute récente université Laval ne pouvaient pas décemment ignorer la présence du prince à Québec, l'accueil qu'on lui ménagea fut d'une froideur toute protocolaire: "Encore une institution en enfance," nota-t-il. "Les cours sont faibles et plus sur le papier qu'en réalité. Les bâtiments sont beaux. C'est tout à fait dirigé par le clergé. Les prêtres, l'évêque (qui remplace l'archevêque en enfance), le recteur, le vicaire général et les professeurs me reçoivent avec gêne et un embarras facile à voir."

Bref, "tout dans ce pays" lui paraissait "différent" et, à son avis, "mieux qu'aux Etats-Unis, sauf l'influence du clergé catholique": "Il est impossible de voir plus de bien-être que dans ces habitations de paysans canadiens, propreté remarquable, accent normand."

Cet anticléricalisme décidé n'empêcha pas le prince Napoléon de reconnaître que "le clergé a le mérite de conserver ses traditions et la langue française au Canada." C'est ce qu'il écrivait après avoir visité l'église des Ursulines, où il avait remarqué "quelques tableaux assez bons, un Philippe de Champaigne": "Ces quelques échantillons d'art, qui me manquent si complètement depuis que je suis en Amérique, me font un bien vif plaisir et me reposent l'esprit. Je passe avec délices une bonne heure dans ce milieu un peu plus élevé et artistique de l'église."

$$* \qquad * \qquad *$$

"Grande hostilité du clergé contre moi": tel était le constat d'ensemble que l'illustre voyageur consignait sur son carnet en prenant le chemin du retour via New York pour rembarquer sur son navire particulier, le *Jérôme-Napoléon.*

C'est parce qu'il était la vivante incarnation du libéralisme qui était en train de dépouiller le pape de ses Etats que le prince Napoléon s'était attiré l'animadversion des ultramontains des deux mondes. N'était-il pas encore le cousin de Napoléon III, qui avait déclenché, par son intervention militaire en Italie aux côtés du Piémont, l' "activité" des "éléments les plus hideux de la démocratie italienne," et dont la politique cauteleuse avait permis la réalisation des "desseins pervers de la révolution," comme s'exprimait George-Etienne Cartier lors d'une manifestation des catholiques de Québec, le 4 mars 1860, tenue pour protester contre les "spoliations piémontaises"?[70]

Le chef du parti conservateur bas-canadien se faisait ainsi l'interprète applaudi des ultramontains, dont la colère ne connaissait plus de bornes depuis que le gouvernement impérial de la France avait laissé percer ses sympathies italiennes par la publication de la brochure *Le Pape et le Congrès.*

La conquête épique du royaume des Deux-Siciles par Garibaldi avait encore accentué l'antagonisme libéral-ultramontain.

Durant l'été 1860, l'Europe n'avait connu qu'une passion: Garibaldi. E. de Forcade écrivait dans la *Revue des Deux Mondes* du 1er septembre: "Si par aventure l'Europe entière avait en ce moment à faire autour d'un nom une manifestation collective de suffrage universel, le nom qui sortirait triomphant des urnes du suffrage universel européen serait, qui oserait en douter? celui de Giuseppe Garibaldi."[71]

Le *Pays,* dont le rédacteur en chef depuis le départ d'Emile Chevalier était Médéric Lanctôt, se faisait naturellement l'écho de l'enthousiasme garibaldien de l'Europe, à l'indignation de Cyrille Boucher. "Les événements qui se passent aujourd'hui en Europe," écrivait-il dans l'*Ordre* en juillet 1860, "ne sont rien autre chose qu'une lutte entre le bien et le mal, entre le principe divin de l'autorité et le principe diabolique de la révolution."[72]

"Il ne faut pas se faire illusion," mandait de son côté Mgr Bourget à son clergé, le 26 novembre suivant, "l'esprit révolutionnaire fait ici, comme ailleurs, ses invasions, et il s'en trouve quelques-uns parmi nous qui condamnent le Pape et approuvent Garibaldi."[73]

La défaite de l'armée pontificale à Castelfidardo atterra les ultra-montains. "Le Piémont, avec une audace sans nom," écrivait Boucher, "a envahi les Etats pontificaux contre tous les droits divins et humains."[74] Pour Aubry, "le roi Victor-Emmanuel mettait le comble à son usurpation sacrilège,"[75] mais le rédacteur légitimiste du *Courrier du Canada* persistait à croire que "l'unité italienne," n'ayant "jamais existé," n'existera jamais."[76]

Au moment où les catholiques de Montréal, de Québec et de Trois-Rivières joignaient leur détresse priante à celle de leurs coreligionnaires du monde entier dans des services funèbres célébrés pour commémorer le sacrifice suprême des pontificaux tombés à Castelfidardo, les soldats piémontais étaient déjà entrés à Naples, et les 21 et 22 octobre les anciens sujets de François II votaient à une énorme majorité la réunion au Piémont du royaume des Deux-Siciles. Les 4 et 5 novembre les Marches et l'Ombrie en faisaient autant, à telle enseigne que l'unité de l'Italie sous le sceptre de Victor-Emmanuel était virtuellement réalisée, car dès cette époque il apparaissait nettement que Rome et la Vénétie ne pourraient pas demeurer longtemps en dehors des limites du nouveau royaume.

*   *   *

Rome surtout était le point de mire de toutes les espérances et de toutes les appréhensions. Les libéraux, d'une part, souhaitaient ardemment que le vote du 27 mars 1861 de la Chambre italienne se réalisât le plus tôt possible; de l'autre, les catholiques, dans leur ensemble, ne pouvaient concevoir la papauté privée d'un large appui territorial, car pour eux, comme on l'a vu, puissance spirituelle pontificale et pouvoir temporel étaient intimement liés: attenter à l'un, c'était s'en prendre sacrilègement à l'autre. Bien peu possédaient la clairvoyance de l'abbé, devenu Mgr Maret, qui écrivait alors dans ses notes personnelles: "La question romaine, quoiqu'elle enveloppe celle des droits temporels du souverain pontificat qui doivent être sauvegardés dans les limites du juste et du possible, la question romaine, sans perdre son caractère ecclésiastique, est . . . aussi une question politique, une question européenne, une question laïque, une question libre."[77]

Désireuse de convaincre l'opinion mondiale que Rome gagnerait à devenir la capitale du royaume italien, la presse libérale s'en prit au système administratif des Etats romains, que lord Clarendon, au Congrès de Paris, avait dénoncé comme étant "le pire qui fût jamais." Pour sa part, Maret approuvait Napoléon III d'insister auprès de Pie IX pour qu'il réformât son gouvernement temporel, car, écrivait-il, "les reproches faits à celui-ci, même en faisant la part de l'exagération et de l'injustice, me portent le rouge au front."[78]

Par contre, les journalistes ultramontains soutenaient que le gouvernement de Pie IX était "paternel," et faisaient grand état des conclusions du long rapport que l'ambassadeur de France à Rome avait rédigé, peut-être à la demande du cardinal Antonelli, pour prouver que, depuis le retour de Gaète, le gouvernement pontifical "avait marché résolument dans la voie des réformes et des améliorations, qu'il avait réalisé de considérables progrès."

Tout cela était en partie exact. Seulement, comme l'écrit le chanoine Aubert, "le véritable problème n'était pas là": "le problème, surtout depuis 1848, était devenu politique, dominé qu'il était par la double aspiration que rappellerait un jour l'inscription du monument de Victor-Emmanuel à la place de Venise: *Patriae Unitati, Civium Libertati.*" "Ce fut le drame de l'Italie et du Saint-Siège au XIXe siècle," ajoute Aubert, "que cette double aspiration, qui nous semble si légitime aujourd'hui, apparût alors aux yeux de Pie IX et de ses principaux conseillers, par suite des circonstances, comme incompatible avec les exigences d'indépendance spirituelle du gouvernement suprême de l'Eglise."[79]

*   *   *

C'est par la critique du système administratif pontifical que Louis-Antoine Dessaulles, devenu depuis le 1er mars 1861 le rédacteur en chef du *Pays*,[80] avait affirmé derechef sa solidarité avec les libéraux européens, en particulier avec le prince Napoléon, dont le discours du 1er mars, le jour même de son entrée en fonction comme rédacteur du *Pays*, l'avait rempli d'enthousiasme. C'est probablement Dessaulles qui avait pris l'initiative de l'adresse par laquelle l'Institut canadien, dont "les sympathies" étaient "acquises aux grandes causes," félicitait à son passage à Montréal le "prince qui, dans ses travaux législatifs," avait "si éloquemment développé les vues libérales du gouvernement de la France sur les plus grandes questions de la politique européenne."[81]

Pour cette raison, Dessaulles avait déploré plus que tout autre l' "attitude hostile inspirée par l'esprit de parti" à l'endroit de l'illustre visiteur, qui venait de gratifier la bibliothèque de l'Institut canadien d'ouvrages dont il s'employait à décrire, dans le *Pays* du 19 décembre 1861, la perfection artistique de l'impression et la richesse des reliures: "Ç'a été un préjugé injustifiable," poursuivait Dessaulles, "un acte d'impolitesse nationale bien regrettable que l'abstention de la population canadienne vis-à-vis d'un homme qui sait encourager ainsi le goût de la science et des études." Selon lui, le prince Napoléon n'avait pas "insulté le Pape" dans son discours du 1er mars: "Son discours au Sénat était sans doute la condamnation du système administratif des Etats romains, et il n'allait pas au-delà, et encore était-il très modéré dans l'expression. *Mais on ne l'avait pas lu,* et sur la foi d'autrui, on le disait aussi impie qu'*une production de Voltaire.*" "Quand donc," concluait Dessaulles, "cessera-t-on de refuser à autrui le droit de penser par soi-même dans tout ce qui n'affecte ni le dogme ni la morale?"[82]

Pour sa part il ne se privait pas de penser par lui-même, et ses articles sur l'administration pontificale témoignaient d'une liberté d'appréciation qui tenait sa vigueur d'une précision documentaire dont on ne retrouvait pas l'équivalent dans les autres feuilles canadiennes. Dessaulles, en effet, s'appuyait sur la presse libérale européenne, de beaucoup supérieure au point de vue technique à la presse catholique, comme on l'a vu, mais surtout il puisait ses renseignements dans l'*Annuaire des Deux Mondes*,[83] sorte d'annexe de la *Revue des Deux Mondes*, que François Buloz avait fondé en septembre 1851 pour être, comme il l'écrivait dans la préface du premier volume, "une grande enquête toujours ouverte sur les intérêts contemporains, et où viendraient se refléter chaque année les luttes, les efforts, les progrès ou les pertes des peuples qui se disputent la prépondérance politique et commerciale."[84]

A Mgr Bourget, qui lui avait reproché de recueillir ses renseignements dans le *Siècle* et les journaux anticléricaux du Piémont, Dessaulles affirmait, dans la lettre qu'il lui adressait le 7 mars 1862, que l'*Annuaire des Deux Mondes* était la source essentielle de ses informations:

C'est le seul ouvrage suivi où l'on puisse se procurer l'ensemble et les détails de l'histoire contemporaine, et je ne puis en vérité m'expliquer comment il se fait qu'aucun de mes adversaires n'ait eu l'idée que je ne pouvais réellement puiser que là. Rien ne démontre plus clairement la déplorable ignorance où l'on est, dans ce pays, sur tout ce qui touche à la question romaine. Voilà le seul livre où on puisse en avoir l'historique et personne ne le connaît![85]

C'est ainsi qu'au point de vue documentaire la partie n'était pas égale entre Dessaulles et l'évêque de Montréal qui, dans les sept lettres qu'il adressait au *Pays* en février 1862, ne tenait ses informations sur l'Etat pontifical que des feuilles ultramontaines de l'Europe et même de Montréal et de Québec, comme l'*Ordre* et le *Courrier du Canada*.

De plus, totalement dominé par son dévoument au souverain pontife, Mgr Bourget ne soupçonna jamais la nature et la complexité des problèmes politiques soulevés par l'unification de l'Italie. Son attitude rejoignait celle de tous les ultramontains, qu'ils fussent d'Europe ou d'Amérique, chez qui on décèle invariablement une extraordinaire méconnaissance du sentiment national italien.

*   *   *

Le 24 février 1862 le secrétaire de l'évêché de Montréal, le chanoine J.-O. Paré, écrivait aux directeurs du *Pays*: "J'ai l'honneur d'être chargé par Mgr l'Evêque de Montréal de vous adresser les lettres ci-jointes et de vous prier de les faire publier dans les prochains numéros du journal *Le Pays*."[86]

Deux jours plus tard Mgr Bourget lui-même, dans une circulaire à son clergé, mentionnait l'envoi de ces lettres, puis ajoutait: "Si ces Messieurs refusent de les publier, et surtout s'ils ne font point changer la marche de leur journal, elles seront imprimées par les feuilles catholiques de cette ville."[87]

Le 6 mars suivant le chanoine Paré donnait un supplément d'information à l'éditeur du *Pays*: "En vous priant de publier dans vos colonnes les sept lettres ci-jointes que Monseigneur de Montréal a cru adresser à Messieurs les Directeurs du journal *Le Pays*, je crois devoir vous faire observer que ces lettres, n'étant que des avis charitables que Sa Grandeur a cru devoir donner à ces Messieurs, il ne conviendrait pas d'engager à ce sujet une discussion parfaitement inutile."[88]

Les lettres épiscopales[89] développaient les arguments déjà utilisés dans le "Premier supplément au Mandement du 31 mai 1860 concernant les Journaux qui ont attaqué la bulle de Sa Sainteté Pie IX excommuniant les envahisseurs des Etats pontificaux, et autres."[90] Elles se suivaient à deux jours d'intervalle à partir du 12 février 1862.

"Je crois, Messieurs," écrivait Mgr Bourget dans sa première lettre, "que vous êtes tous catholiques, mais je suis forcé de vous dire que votre journal ne l'est pas," parce que le *Pays* se montrait favorable aux annexions qui aboutissaient à l'unification de la péninsule sous l'autorité de Victor-Emmanuel:

L'Evangile fait aux peuples chrétiens un devoir strict d'obéir à leurs gouvernements et de rendre à César ce qui appartient à César. Le Pays les affranchit de ce devoir, et il ne cesse de faire l'éloge de ceux qui secouent le joug de l'obéissance, en se révoltant à main armée. . . . Le Pays se fait un grand mérite d'exalter, de vanter et d'encourager des impies, des sacrilèges, des excommuniés, des hommes enfin qui sont les ennemis acharnés de l'Eglise et de son Pontife.

L'un des griefs les plus véhéments de l'évêque de Montréal à l'endroit de la feuille libérale était d'exalter le roi du Piémont et de reproduire les discours d'un homme "qui s'est emparé, il ne saurait l'ignorer, par fraude et corruption d'une partie des Etats Pontificaux," comme de faire de Garibaldi "le champion d'une cause sacrée," qui personnifiait "si bien la révolution italienne dans ses aspirations les plus élevées." "C'est ainsi," affirmait Mgr Bourget, "que *Le Pays* infiltre l'esprit révolutionnaire, que l'Ecriture sainte condamne."

Selon le prélat, le rédacteur du *Pays* tromp[ait] ses lecteurs en leur représentant la révolution italienne sous de si belles couleurs:

Que s'ensuivrait-il donc s'il réussissait à séduire ses concitoyens et à leur faire opérer une semblable révolution en Canada? Nous verrions se renouveler ici ce qui se passe maintenant dans ces malheureux pays. Nous aurions notre Garibaldi, notre Cavour, notre Ricasoli, notre Brofferio, notre Crispi, et bien d'autres qui, en se disputant le pouvoir ou en culbutant les gouvernements éphémères qui ne s'accommoderaient pas à leurs passions et à leurs intérêts, mettraient tout à feu et à sang.

Ayant stigmatisé les artisans de la "révolution" italienne, Mgr Bourget se tournait ensuite vers les augustes victimes de cette révolution et invoquait l'autorité pontificale pour étayer son argumentation: *"Le Pays* ayant porté devant notre public de graves accusations contre le Pape et son gouvernement temporel, il devient nécessaire de faire entendre la voix de cet illustre accusé."

Malheureusement les documents pontificaux que citait l'évêque de Montréal, n'avaient pas, au point de vue politique et historique, le caractère décisif et péremptoire qu'il voulait bien leur conférer. En effet, comme le fait remarquer le chanoine Aubert, il faut regretter dans l'opposition de Pie IX au Risorgimento sa tendance

à identifier les malheurs de l'Eglise avec les progrès des formes de gouvernements inspirés des principes libéraux, sans se rendre compte du danger qu'il y avait à présenter avec une telle insistance des réalités politiques qui s'avéraient dans le sens de l'histoire comme l'incarnation nécessaire des idées anti-chrétiennes et comme associées inévitablement au triomphe d'une philosophie hostile à l'Eglise.[91]

A la suite du pape, qui entretenait des 'illusions" sur les forces réelles dont l'impulsion irrésistible avait conduit, en quelques mois, le petit royaume piémontais au royaume unifié d'Italie,[92] Mgr Bourget affirmait que ne n'était pas "le peuple" qui avait "fait la *révolution* italienne, mais les Scribes et les Pharisiens du christianisme, c'est-à-dire certaines gens lettrées qui ont trompé le peuple et qui l'ont porté à demander que la Papauté fût détrônée, comme les Scribes et les Pharisienes de la Synagogue poussèrent le peuple juif à demander que le Sauveur fût crucifié."

Le prélat se croyait donc en droit de conclure ainsi sa troisième lettre:

Les écrits du Pays . . . *ne respirent que mépris, insulte et outrage. Car il se fait un plaisir malin de blâmer l'entourage du Pape, c'est-à-dire ce qu'il y a de plus respectable au monde. Il l'accuse d'avoir trompé son peuple, en lui faisant des promesses de réformes qu'il n'a point exécutées, quoique le contraire soit prouvé. Il fait voir dans l'administration de ses finances des abus horribles qui n'existent pas. Il veut faire passer pour cruel et tyrannique ce gouvernement, qui est le plus paternel au monde. Enfin il ne voit dans son système judiciaire qu'un corps mort qu'il faut abattre à coups de hache et jeter au feu, quoique ce système soit ce qu'il y a de plus equitable . . .*

N'êtes-vous pas maintenant, Messieurs, à vous étonner que Le Pays *soit monté sur de si hautes échasses, pour essayer de cracher à la face du Souverain Pontife, des Cardinaux qui l'entourent et par contrecoup de 200,000,000 de catholiques qui se trouvent nécessairement insultés des outrages que l'on fait à leur Père en Dieu? Ne seriez-vous pas les premiers à rougir des principes erronés, des faits mal représentés, des mensonges impudents dont* Le Pays *se sature et sature ses lecteurs? Ne seriez-vous pas les premiers à regretter d'avoir donné votre concours, votre*

*influence et votre argent, pour soutenir un journal qui fait honte au catho-
lique Canada, au point que l'on se voit réduit à la pénible nécessité de le
rayer du nombre de nos feuilles catholiques? Vos abonnés, ceux du moins
qui demeurent catholiques, ne seront-ils pas profondément affligés et
peinés, en pensant qu'ils ont payé* Le Pays *pour l'encourager à être l'écho
des journaux impies de l'étranger, dont la mauvaise doctrine fermente
aujourd'hui, comme un levain empoisonné, dans le monde entier, et qui
met toute l'Europe comme sur un volcan?*

Les quatrième, cinquième et sixième lettres portaient sur l'administration financière des Etats romains. D'après Mgr Bourget, le rédacteur du
Pays se réclamait uniquement de *faits officiels,* qu'il empruntait aux "journaux piémontais." Mais le prélat récusait cette source de renseignements:
"S'il n'a pour prouver ses allégués," écrivait-il, "que ses journaux piémontais ou son *Siècle* ou d'autres autorités de cette espèce, je suis tout décidé
d'avance à n'en faire nul cas. Car un gouvernement qui ment habituel-
lement comme fait celui de Turin, ne mérite aucune confiance."

D'approche en approche, le prélat en arrivait au principal responsable
du gouvernement des Etats romains, le cardinal Antonelli, secrétaire
d'Etat. C'est une figure énigmatique à propos de laquelle les historiens n'ont
pas dit leur dernier mot, car ses papiers sont demeurés jusqu'ici inacces-
sibles. Le jugement de Roger Aubert est sévère:

*Ce prince de l'Eglise qui resta diacre toute sa vie fut l'un des derniers
représentants d'une lignée largement représentée à la cour pontificale
durant l'époque moderne, un de ces prélats tout laïques de sentiments,
pour qui les intérêts de ce monde comptaient plus que ceux de l'autre, mais
dont les moeurs faciles allaient de pair avec une foi sincère. Fils d'un
marchand de biens, Antonelli resta toute sa vie un parvenu avide d'argent,
dominé par l'idée très italienne de* fare una famiglia, *que l'opinion publique
accusait "d'avoir remplacé le népotisme des papes par le népotisme des
secrétaires d'Etat" et qui devait effectivement laisser une belle fortune à
ses enfants naturels.*[93]

Pour avoir osé critiquer la famille Antonelli, le *Pays* se voyait rabroué
d'importance par Mgr Bourget:

*Sans en faire un article de foi pour ses lecteurs, il leur fait remarquer
que les frères Antonelli, qui étaient pauvres il y a dix-huit ans, sont aujour-
d'hui de gros millionnaires. N'est-ce pas là faire planer sur une des plus
honorables familles de Rome un soupçon très grave et souverainement
injurieux? A-t-il des preuves que ces hommes si haut placés auraient mis
leurs mains sacrilèges dans le trésor de l'Eglise . . . ?*

*Mais il a beau faire, il est trop bas et trop petit pour pouvoir cracher
ainsi à la face du Cardinal Antonelli, qui a mérité par ses éminentes qualités
une réputation européenne; qui est le fidèle ministre de l'immortel Pie IX.*

D'après l'évêque de Montréal, c'était un parti pris de la part du rédacteur du *Pays* que de censurer l'entourage pontifical pour pouvoir atteindre

le pape lui-même. Mais le même journaliste, qui traitait si mal le cardinal Antonelli, n'avait que des éloges pour

le prince Napoléon, qui a soulevé, en France, tout le parti religieux par son trop fameux discours, dans la Chambre des Pairs [sic], contre le Souverain Pontife. Le Pays trouve qu'il n'a pas trop mal parlé, et que nous avons bien mal fait, à Montréal, de n'avoir pas été plus courtois envers ce prince généreux, qui a bien récompensé l'Institut Canadien pour le beau compliment qu'il lui avait adressé, en le félicitant d'avoir été assez courageux pour dire du Pape ce qu'il en avait dit. Car il lui a envoyé des volumes de 40 pouces de largeur sur 18 de hauteur, éblouissants par la magnificence extraordinaire des reliures et l'éclat des dorures. Ces beaux livres vont donc briller dans les rayons de la bibliothèque de l'Institut Canadien. Malheureusement, quelque beaux et bons qu'ils soient, ou puissent être, ils ne pourront pas faire lever l'interdit porté par l'autorité de l'Eglise contre cette bibliothèque qui, à cause de ses livres contraires à la foi et à la morale, est une sentine puante qui infecte notre ville.

Dans la septième lettre, datée du 24 février 1862, Mgr Bourget écrivait:

Je pense vous avoir prouvé dans mes six lettres précédentes que Le Pays *est* anti-chrétien, anti-catholique, anti-social *et* calomniateur *du gouvernement pontifical. Il me reste à vous faire voir, dans cette septième lettre, qu'il est* immoral, *et pour cette raison dangereux surtout à vos enfants, comme à toute la jeunesse canadienne, sur qui repose nécessairement l'avenir de notre belle et chère patrie.*

Après avoir analysé la nocivité d'un roman de Dumas que le *Pays* avait reproduit en feuilleton, le prélat développait encore une fois la théorie gaumiste que les "révolutions" étaient surtout provoquées par les "mauvais livres":

Pouvez-vous douter des maux affreux que causent les mauvais journaux, en voyant aujourd'hui de vos yeux l'horrible désolation de l'Italie en proie à la fureur de la révolution? Car c'est là le fruit amer des mauvaises lectures. Or le mauvais journal est sans contredit pire que le plus mauvais des livres. . . . C'est lorsque les masses ont été ainsi empoisonnées par les mauvais journaux, que le vertige s'empare de toutes les têtes. Ce levain des mauvaises doctrines fermente alors au sein des nations entières pour y produire ces affreuses convulsions que vous voyez régner aujourd'hui dans la malheureuse Italie. Ce qui arrive à l'Italie, ce qui arrive à la France trois ou quatre fois par siècle, nous arrivera infailliblement. Puisse cette prédiction être fausse! Puisse notre heureux Canada n'être jamais bouleversé par ce terrible ouragan! Il ne le sera pas si le journalisme ne l'empoisonne pas; et il le sera certainement si on y lit des mauvais journaux, des mauvais romans.

En terminant, il faisait part aux destinataires de ses lettres de sa détermination à continuer une lutte à outrance, si leur journal ne prenait pas une autre orientation: "Vous me trouverez donc toujours à la brèche, tant que j'aurai un souffle de vie, si *Le Pays* n'abandonne pas cette mauvaise voie."

* * *

Dès le dimanche 2 mars 1862 Dessaulles écrivait au chanoine Paré,[94] pour lui apprendre que la longueur des lettres épiscopales n'avait pas permis aux propriétaires du *Pays*, lors de leur réunion, de prendre une décision ferme: "Onze sur treize des propriétaires présents étaient *en faveur* de la publication." Lui-même la souhaitait vivement: "Inutile de vous dire, je suppose, que je me suis donné beaucoup de peine pour amener tous nos amis à consentir à l'insertion."

Je crois pour ma part, poursuivait Dessaulles, que la démarche de Monseigneur est profondément regrettable, parce que, dans une société mixte comme la nôtre, plusieurs des prétentions de Sa Grandeur feront revivre l'hostilité contre nous comme catholiques; parce que Monseigneur ne peut que diminuer, au lieu de l'augmenter, le respect dont il jouit à juste titre; enfin parce qu'il est d'une excessive inconvenance que l'on se serve des colonnes même d'un journal pour inviter ses abonnés à cesser d'y souscrire.

Ce furent les directeurs du *Pays*, Wilfrid Dorion et Cie, qui communiquèrent à l'évêque de Montréal, le 4 mars, leur décision de ne pas reproduire ses lettres dans leur journal.[95] Ils le firent avec une telle hauteur de vues, une si remarquable fermeté de pensée et de style, que la reproduction intégrale de ce texte inédit s'impose. C'est peut-être le document le plus significatif à verser au dossier de l'histoire du libéralisme canadien- français:

Monseigneur,

Les Directeurs du "Pays" ont pris en leur plus sérieuse considération les sept lettres que Votre Grandeur leur a fait l'honneur de leur adresser avec la demande de les publier dans les colonnes de ce journal, et ils sollicitent la permission d'exprimer respectueusement à Votre Grandeur le regret qu'ils éprouvent de ne pouvoir se rendre à Son désir.

En même temps, les Directeurs du "Pays" sentent que la nature même de ces lettres, et la position élevée de celui qui les a écrites, leur imposent le devoir de motiver leur décision un peu plus longuement qu'ils ne l'auraient fait dans une circonstance ordinaire.

Le "Pays" représente dans la presse canadienne un parti politique formé en dehors de toute controverse religieuse, et dont la sphère d'action n'embrasse que les intérêts matériels et moraux de notre commune patrie. Jamais il n'a eu la prétention de s'ériger en tribunal dogmatique, laissant aux autorités compétentes le domaine entier des doctrines religieuses et de la foi, ne s'adressant qu'à l'intelligence, à la raison et à la conscience du peuple dans les matières qui concernent la régie et l'administration de ses affaires temporelles.

Les institutions libérales dont nous jouissons, la forme de notre gouvernement, autorisent et justifient cette attitude, quel que soit, d'ailleurs, le sens politique dans lequel se manifeste cette liberté d'examen et de discussion qui forme l'un des plus précieux apanages des gouvernements constitutionnels. Nous avons toujours cru, et nous croyons encore, que cette position se concilie parfaitement avec le caractère de chrétien, de catholique et de bon citoyen.

Imbus de ces principes et de ces notions sur les devoirs et les droits de la presse, sous l'empire d'institutions libres, la direction que nous avons imprimée au "Pays" s'en est nécessairement ressentie. Dans un but et pour des motifs que nous ne voulons pas approfondir, on n'a pas assez tenu compte de cette réserve de notre part; aussi, dans les luttes que nous avons eu à soutenir, avons-nous plus d'une fois déploré que nos adversaires aient méconnu leur position et la nôtre jusqu'au point de faire intervenir la religion et sa divine autorité dans une polémique où elles se trouvaient singulièrement déplacées.

Le "Pays," loin de s'engager sur un terrain qui n'est pas le sien, a protesté hautement contre cet abus des choses saintes, et le public éclairé lui a donné raison, en l'entourant d'un patronage de plus en plus marqué. Or, c'est pour ne pas nous départir de cette règle de conduite, adoptée dès la fondation du "Pays"; c'est pour maintenir intacte la ligne de démarcation qui sépare les choses de l'ordre spirituel de celles que Dieu a livrées aux disputes du monde que nous désirons éviter une discussion avec Votre Grandeur sur des matières qui ne sont pas, à la vérité, du domaine du dogme et de la foi, mais dans lesquelles Votre Grandeur apporte la dignité et l'autorité d'un Pontife de l'Eglise.

Nous disons que nous désirons ne pas discuter, car il n'a pu entrer dans la pensée de Votre Grandeur que le "Pays" publierait, sans songer à se défendre, sept longues lettres dans lesquelles des accusations, aussi graves qu'imméritées, sont accumulées contre lui.

Du reste, nous déclarons en toute sincérité que nous ne pouvons voir à quel but profitable et utile conduirait une discussion de ce genre avec Votre Grandeur. En effet, il s'agit principalement de faits qui se passent sous les yeux de tout le monde en Europe, et plus immédiatement dans la péninsule italienne: ce sont les pages de l'histoire contemporaine qui se déroulent une à une et qu'il s'agit de recueillir pour la postérité. Toutes les discussions du monde ne pourraient empêcher que ces événements ne se passent, que ces faits n'existent.

En publiant le discours du Roi du Piémont et la circulaire du Baron Ricasoli, le "Pays" a consigné des documents authentiques que l'on peut également trouver dans les colonnes de tous les journaux qui tiennent à renseigner leurs lecteurs sur le mouvement de la politique européenne. Pour le même motif le "Pays" a également publié diverses allocutions de Sa Sainteté et autres documents officiels émanant de la Cour de Rome. Des feuilles locales, à tort ou à raison classées parmi ce qu'on appelle journaux religieux, n'ont pas craint de publier précisément les mêmes pièces que Votre Grandeur nous reproche d'avoir publiées et bien d'autres encore du même caractère et sur le même sujet; personne n'a songé à les en blâmer, que nous sachions.

La révolution italienne est l'un de ces faits graves qui prennent une large place dans les annales des nations; à l'heure qu'il est, c'est l'immense foyer autour duquel se groupent mille craintes, mille espérances, mille intérêts divers. Or, il arrive presque toujours, dans ces grandes perturbations où les événements marchent avec une rapidité qui déjoue les calculs de la sagesse humaine, que ce qui était vrai hier ne l'est plus aujourd'hui, parce que les situations changent, soit par le sort des armes, soit par un retour soudain de l'opinion. C'est ce qui explique des erreurs comme celles dans lesquelles sont tombées certains journaux légitimistes, en France, quand ils affirmaient que le Roi de Naples était victorieux sur toute la ligne, au moment même où ce dernier prenait la route de l'exil et où Garibaldi entrait, presque seul et sans armes, à Naples aux acclamations de la multitude accourue sur son passage.

Les sources auxquelles nous puisons nos renseignements pourraient, comme les autres, être exposées aux mêmes déceptions, mais tôt ou tard la vérité se fait jour, et jusqu'à présent le "Pays" peut se flatter que, sur les faits importants, les informations qu'il a données ont été pleinement confirmées.

Ce n'est pas trop dire assurément que d'affirmer que les autorités sur lesquelles s'appuie Votre Grandeur, pour former Son opinion sur le caractère et les progrès de la révolution italienne, peuvent être, pour la même raison, induites à dénaturer ou du moins à exagérer les faits. Car il ne faut pas perdre de vue que l'esprit de parti est fortement dessiné, et qu'il produit là ce qu'il produit ailleurs. Ainsi donc, jusqu'à ce qu'il soit démontré d'une manière satisfaisante que les faits en question ne sont pas tels que le "Pays" les a représentés, que la réaction est victorieuse dans le Royaume de Naples et ailleurs; que l'Italie est prête à rappeler ses rois et ses ducs; que les populations repoussent avec horreur le gouvernement de Victor-Emmanuel, nous n'avons rien à retrancher de ce qui a été dit là-dessus.

Maintenant, pour ce qui regarde le gouvernement temporel de N.S. Père le Pape, l'état de ses finances, la manière dont la justice criminelle y est administrée, les réformes promises et non accomplies, nous sommes bien aises de voir que Votre Grandeur n'a pas songé à dénier au "Pays," ni à nous comme catholiques, le droit d'examen et de critique, et nous en prenons acte. Ce dont Votre Grandeur se plaint, c'est que dans cet examen le "Pays" a outragé la vérité à un tel point que Votre Grandeur a cru pouvoir, sans manquer au respect qu'Elle se doit, dire qu'il a proféré "d'impudents mensonges."

Si nous jugions convenable d'entrer en discussion avec Votre Grandeur, sur ce point comme sur les autres, il nous serait facile de justifier par les témoignages les moins suspects et par l'autorité même de Princes de l'Eglise, la position prise par le "Pays." Dès que l'on nous reconnaît le droit de discuter de tels sujets, et qu'en les discutant, le "Pays" s'appuie sur des documents officiels et cherche sincèrement à s'inspirer d'autorités non suspectes, quelle que soit la conclusion à laquelle il en arrive, il ne peut être raisonnablement classé parmi les journaux anti-chrétiens, anti-religeux *et* anti-catholiques. *Prétendre le contraire, ce serait fermer la porte à toute discussion libre, bâillonner la presse et inaugurer un système de surveillance et de censure auquel nous ne pouvons ni ne voulons nous soumettre.*

Profondément convaincus que nous sommes dans les limites du droit, de la morale et d'une religion éclairée, nous ne pouvons renoncer à des privilèges qui nous sont garantis par les lois divines et humaines, et le "Pays," avec cette fermeté et cette modération qui ont caractérisé sa carrière, continuera, comme par le passé, à discuter sans crainte, comme sans colère et sans prévention, toutes les questions politiques et sociales qui se présentent tant ici qu'ailleurs.

Nous aurions pu donner, pour ne pas publier les lettres de Votre Grandeur, d'autres raisons de moindre importance: en premier lieu, la longueur de ces lettres; les inconvénients d'une discussion prolongée pendant cinq à six mois et l'effervescence de passions qui ne pourraient manquer de s'allumer dans la lutte; en second lieu, l'appel explicite fait par Votre Grandeur à nos abonnés de refuser désormais au "Pays" leur appui moral et matériel, appel que nous n'aurions pu, sans manquer au respect que nous nous devons à nous-mêmes, publier sans une protestation formelle dans tous les cas.

Mais nous nous en tenons aux premières objections, afin d'écarter tout ce qui pourrait revêtir l'apparence d'une question de forme.

En terminant, nous demandons la permission de dire à Votre Grandeur que nous ne reconnaissons point la distinction qu'Elle fait entre les Directeurs et la rédaction du "Pays" et d'assurer à Votre Grandeur que la solidarité la plus entière est acceptée par les Directeurs et les Propriétaires dans la direction du journal.

Enfin, nous prions Votre Grandeur de croire que, quelles que soient les conséquences de la position que nous avons cru devoir prendre, nous trouverons dans notre conscience, dans les traditions que nous ont laissées les hommes les plus distingués de notre histoire et dans l'approbation de nos concitoyens, la force nécessaire pour maintenir intacts la liberté de discussion, les droits de la presse et notre propre dignité.

Nous avons l'honneur d'être (etc)
Dorion et Cie
Propriétaires et Directeurs du journal "Le Pays."

*   *   *

Comme la décision à laquelle s'étaient arrêté les directeurs du *Pays*, privait Dessaulles de répondre à l'évêque de Montréal par la voie du journal, il le fit, le 7 mars, dans une lettre privée,[96] sous les mots de laquelle vibre encore, après plus d'un siècle, l'indignation véhémente où l'avait plongé la lecture des lettres épiscopales: "Les affirmations plus que hardies, les interprétations singulièrement hasardées qu'elles accumulent contre le *Pays* m'ont paru tellement extraordinaires que je me demandais réellement, en les lisant, si je possédais bien tout mon bon sens pour y trouver de pareilles choses."

Puisqu'il était le rédacteur en chef du *Pays* depuis le 1er mars 1861 et que les articles cités par Mgr Bourget avaient été publiés durant les derniers mois de la même année, Dessaulles se voyait directement pris à partie par l'évêque de Montréal:

. . . je suis en conséquence forcé de regarder comme s'adressant à moi personnellement les incroyables expressions que Votre Grandeur n'a pas craint d'employer en reprochant au Pays *d'impudents mensonges.*

Cette injure, Mgr, adressée à un homme qui a la certitude de n'avoir pas avancé un seul fait *qui ne soit appuyé sur des documents dont l'authen-cité est incontestable ne fait guère naître chez moi l'idée d'un* avertissement paternel, *pour employer le mot de Votre Grandeur.*

Je ne puis comprendre, Mgr, comment V. G. a cru pouvoir, j'ose me permettre de dire, abuser de sa haute position jusqu'à exprimer une pareille insulte, certainement imméritée par celui sur qui elle tombe. Avec tout le respect que je continue d'entretenir pour V. G., je crois avoir le droit de lui rappeler que ce n'est pas là le langage d'un Evêque, surtout quand j'ai la certitude absolue que, sur les points de fait, c'est moi qui suis dans le vrai.

Car il n'avait pas "commis l'étourderie de juger le gouvernement romain par les écrits et même les *pièces officielles*" qu'il aurait "pu puiser chez ses adversaires directs." La source principale de ses renseignements était l'*Annuaire des Deux Mondes*: "C'est là, Mgr, que l'on trouve des données nombreuses et exactes sur les finances romaines, et c'est le seul ouvrage que je connaisse en Canada où elles existent aussi complètes."

L'affirmation épiscopale que "les écrits du *Pays*" ne respiraient que "*mépris, insultes* et *outrages,*" lui paraissait donc dénuée de tout fondement: "Si j'avais l'honneur d'avoir quelques moments d'entretien avec V. G. je suis persuadé, Mgr, qu'Elle serait grandement embarrassée pour me citer un mot qui justifie ce grave reproche."

C'est surtout l'accusation réitérée de Mgr Bourget que le *Pays* voulait "amener jusqu'en Canada la révolution avec tout son cortège d'horreurs," qui offrait à Dessaulles l'occasion de donner à l'évêque une leçon d'histoire politique. Il la saisit au vol:

Il y a, Mgr, une raison bien simple pour que le Pays *ne veuille pas de la révolution ici; c'est que nous avons des institutions politiques qui, quoiqu'encore très imparfaites, permettent leur propre modification sans*

révolution. Ici les abus ne peuvent pas s'éterniser et immobiliser complète-
ment le progrés national ou les réformes administratives. Il suffit d'attendre,
et les hommes qui ont mal administré le gouvernement sont tôt ou tard
chassés par le seul fonctionnement régulier du système politique. Dans un
pareil pays, Mgr, les révolutions n'ont pas de raison d'être! Il n'y a que les
gouvernements qui veulent être éternels, qui forcent les peuples de recourir
aux révolutions! Ce sont les gouvernements qui veulent refouler l'opinion
publique qui sont brisés. Ceux qui marchent avec elle ne le sont jamais;
preuve qu'elle est la vraie souveraine. Il n'est donc pas un homme sensé qui
ne voie avec chagrin, avec une douloureuse surprise, des prévisions aussi
inapplicables, aussi dénuées de tout à-propos et de toute plausibilité que
celles que Votre Grandeur exprime. Elle parle pour le peuple, je le vois
parfaitement, pour le peuple qui est ignorant. Or c'est précisément parce
que le peuple est ignorant qu'il a le plus besoin de vérité, et la vérité n'est
certainement pas dans les épouvantails que lui présente Votre Grandeur.

Mais il est un sentiment qui perce constamment dans toutes les lettres
de Votre Grandeur, c'est l'hostilité instinctive contre tout ce qui ressemble
à un droit populaire, à la participation d'un peuple à son propre gouverne-
ment. Ainsi, dans l'opinion de V. G., les élections ne font que du mal, ne
produisent que de la démoralisation; on les voit toujours arriver avec
frayeur. *Votre Grandeur ne dit pas sans doute: donc il faut les abolir; mais*
quelle autre conclusion tirer de pareilles prémisses? L'absolutisme est bien
plus commode, en effet, pour ceux qui ne veulent pas que les nations
pensent et lisent, et qui ont toujours mis la pensée humaine à l'index. *Mais,*
Mgr, n'est-ce pas une chose remarquable que, sous nos institutions, on
puisse, sans danger pour soi-même ou pour l'ordre public, parler contre
les institutions du pays, pendant que, si dans les Etats romains, on eût
osé dire quelque chose de beaucoup moins grave contre les institutions
locales, on eût été de suite non seulement mis sous la surveillance de la
police, mais bien logé préventivement en prison pour y croupir pendant
2, 3, 5, 10 années, pour, au bout de ce temps se voir rendre à sa famille
sans avoir subi de procès, quelquefois même en ignorant totalement la
vraie cause de son emprisonnement.

Quand Mr Papineau était en Italie, il y avait des centaines de détenus
politiques écroués, quelques-uns depuis un grand nombre d'années, sans
qu'on leur eût jamais dit pourquoi on les retenait en prison.

Insensiblement, au cours de sa lettre, Dessaulles arrivait à la ligne
essentielle de démarcation entre les deux familles spirituelles représentées
par les ultramontains et les libéraux. Il rejoignait, d'une part, l'observation
de l'abbé Maret, à savoir que le système théocratique constituait le point
d'aboutissement normal des tendances ultramontaines; de l'autre, il mettait
l'accent sur ce qu'on appelle aujourd'hui "l'autonomie du temporel," et
dont il faissait un progrès libéral.

Après avoir fait part à Mgr Bourget de l'impression que la lecture de ses lettres avait produite sur des personnes qui ne pouvaient, à aucun titre, être classées parmi les *exagérées,* il ajoutait:

La conclusion la plus générale, Mgr, que l'on en tire, c'est que V.G., sans l'émettre explicitement, maintient et veut réaliser pratiquement l'idée "que comme il n'y a aucun ordre de pensée qui ne puisse avoir quelque point de contact avec l'idée religieuse, il n'y a conséquemment aucun ordre d'idées qui ne doive être jugé au point de vue absolu de l'idée de la suprématie de la religion; que conséquemment il n'y a pas de principe social et politique dont l'application, le fonctionnement pratique ne doive être subordonné à la censure ecclésiastique, conséquemment à la surveillance du Clergé."

Votre Grandeur veut mêler intimement les domaines spirituel et temporel pour diriger et dominer celui-ci au moyen de celui-là; nous laïques, (même ceux qui flattent aujourd'hui V. G. dans un but d'ambition politique et d'égoïsme) nous voulons éviter la confusion de ces deux ordres d'idées et nous voulons que l'ordre spirituel soit entièrement distinct de l'ordre temporel. En un mot, Mgr, dans l'ordre purement social et politique nous réclamons notre entière indépendance du pouvoir ecclésiastique. . . .

Si les lettres de Votre Grandeur deviennent publiques, elles convaincront beaucoup de gens qui en doutent encore que le Clergé n'abandonne rien de ses prétentions à régir directement le monde là où il peut s'emparer de cette direction.

*   *   *

Les prises de position de Dessaulles et de l'évêque de Montréal se situaient aux antipodes l'une de l'autre; aucune entente n'était possible entre deux adversaires aussi déterminés. Le dialogue reprit bientôt, mais ce fut un dialogue de sourds.

Comme il allait s'embarquer, le 19 mars 1862, afin d'assister à Rome à la canonisation de martyrs japonais, Mgr Bourget pensa écrire à son clergé pour le mettre au courant du refus d'insérer ses lettres qu'il venait de subir de la part des directeurs du *Pays.* Mais la circulaire resta à l'état d'ébauche et ne fut jamais expédiée.[97]

Ils (les directeurs du Pays*) s'y sont refusés, comme vous le verrez par leur réponse dont je crois devoir vous envoyer copie ainsi que de celle que vient de m'adresser Mr Dessaulles. Avec ces deux pièces, vous pouvez encore mieux juger ce Journal et comprendre le mal qu'il fait. Je me borne à intercaler, comme vous le verrez, quelques réflexions dans le texte. Je pense que cela suffit; et d'ailleurs je n'ai plus le temps d'entreprendre un plus long travail.*

A la fin du mois, les lettres épiscopales adressées au *Pays* n'avaient pas encore paru, même dans d'autres journaux, comme se l'était proposé l'évêque de Montréal, s'il se heurtait à un refus du journal libéral. Le vicaire général du diocèse, l'abbé A.-F. Truteau, cousin de Dessaulles, en donnait les raisons à son supérieur ecclésiastique dans une lettre datée du 30 mars:

Nous n'avons pas encore commencé à faire publier les lettres de Votre Grandeur contre le Pays. *Le Chapitre, après avoir entendu la lecture de la lettre des Directeurs du* Pays *ainsi que celle de Mr Dessaulles à Votre Grandeur, a cru qu'il valait mieux retarder. L'on est sous l'impression qu'il peut y avoir une poursuite judiciaire contre Votre Grandeur. D'un autre côté, comme ces gens-là, surtout Mr Dessaulles, sont d'un violence extrême, et qu'armés de tous les mensonges qu'ils peuvent tirer des mauvais journaux, ils peuvent mettre bien en peine pour les réponses à leur faire, Votre Grandeur n'étant pas sur les lieux pour y répondre Elle-même, toutes ces raisons ont porté le Chapitre à suspendre la publication de vos lettres jusqu'à nouvel ordre. Enfin l'on a craint qu'une discussion ouverte sur les journaux par le moyen de ces lettres, pendant l'absence de Votre Grandeur, n'occasionnât aux adversaires, qui sont si violents et si peu respectueux, de dire bien des choses désagréables contre l'autorité ecclésiastique. L'on a donc cru que, pour le moment, il valait mieux réfuter indirectement sur la* Minerve *et l'*Ordre *les erreurs et les faussetés que le* Pays *publie contre la* Religion *et le* St-Siège. *Cependant, si malgré ces représentations, Votre Grandeur nous dit qu'il faut publier ces lettres, nous sommes prêts à le faire.*[98]

Dans sa réponse datée du 26 avril suivant,[99] Mgr Bourget ne faisait aucune allusion à cette requête de son vicaire général. Il n'en fut pas davantage question dans la suite. C'est ainsi que ces lettres, encore toutes brûlantes d'ardeur ultramontaine, sont restées inédites jusqu'aujourd'hui.

*   *   *

L'âpre polémique Bourget-Dessaulles ne fut donc pas connue du grand public, à la différence de la controverse Fabre-Dessaulles,[100] qui dura trois mois, de décembre 1861 à mars 1862, entre le *Pays* et l'*Ordre*, et au cours de laquelle Dessaulles défendit vigoureusement l'attitude de l'Institut canadien contre Hector Fabre, qui avait été l'un des principaux sécessionnistes de 1858. Aussi l'Institut canadien, désireux de lui manifester sa reconnaisance, lui offrit-il, le 26 juin suivant, un encrier d'argent avec plume et porte-plume en or! Cette manifestation amicale permit à Dessaulles de faire le point dans la lutte ardente où s'affrontaient libéraux et ultramontains: "Messieurs, ce que l'on veut détruire ici, c'est moins un foyer d'étude et d'instruction qu'un foyer d'idées franchement libérales. Si nous étions partisans du droit divin, on serait moins actif dans la propagande contre nos livres. Cessons d'être libéraux en politique, cessons de proclamer l'indépendance de la pensée humaine et vous verrez la tactique changer à notre égard."

Pour sa part, il était persuadé que "les principes" qu'incarnait l'Institut canadien finiraient "par triompher ici comme ailleurs": "L'intolérance succombera nécessairement devant une attitude énergique et persévérante.

Le droit et la raison doivent finir par l'emporter sur une malveillance que rien ne justifie et sur l'esprit persécuteur."[101]

En sa qualité de président, Dessaulles reprit avec plus d'ampleur et de force la même thèse, le 23 décembre suivant, lors de la réunion qui marquait le dix-huitième anniversaire de l'Institut.[102] Il exalta, d'une part, "les résultats généraux réalisés dans le monde par la raison humaine," et voua au mépris ses adversaires, qu'il voyait, "à ce mot de raison," "prendre leur moins gracieux sourire,"[103] mais qui devaient "admettre que quelques-unes des grandes découvertes scientifiques modernes" s'étaient faites "un peu malgré eux";[104] de l'autre, il vitupéra l'intolérance, qui excluait d'une bibliothèque "les trois quarts des esprits éminents qui ont élevé si haut la raison de l'homme et illuminé le monde,"[105] et d'un institut les hommes qui professaient un autre culte que le culte catholique: "Ou il ne faut pas admettre de protestants, ou il leur faut montrer, une fois admis, la considération qu'ils méritent comme honnêtes gens."[106]

L'évêque de Montréal se voyait trop directement pris à partie, ses pastorales de 1858 trop manifestement visées quand Dessaulles mentionnait les "attaques" dont l'Institut était l'objet depuis quatre ans "dans la presse" et "souvent même dans l'intimité de la famille,"[107] pour ne pas riposter. Le dimanche 18 janvier 1863, les curés de Montréal lisaient en chaire les lignes suivantes d'une "Annonce" que Dessaulles était fondé de croire comme le concernant de très près: "Nous allons donc prier pour que ce monstre affreux du rationalisme, qui vient de montrer de nouveau sa tête hideuse dans l'Institut et qui cherche à répandre son venin infect dans une brochure qui répète les blasphèmes qui ont retenti dans cette chaire de pestilence, ne puisse nuire à personne."[108]

Le 9 février suivant, Dessaulles écrivait à Mgr Bourget pour lui apprendre qu'il était prêt à rétracter les "blasphèmes" de sa brochure, à condition qu'on les lui indiquât. Il recourait à l'exemple du pouvoir temporel pour faire, encore une fois, la distinction des deux domaines, spirituel et temporel: "C'est sur ce sujet, Mgr, et sur plusieurs autres qui ne touchent qu'à l'ordre temporel, que je réclame pour l'Institut et ses membres le droit de penser et de discuter."[109]

Deux mois plus tard, le 16 avril, n'ayant pas reçu de réponse, Dessaulles écrivait à Sa Grandeur pour "la supplier de nouveau de vouloir bien au moins condescendre à m'indiquer les *blasphèmes* qu'Elle me reproche d'avoir *répétés* dans ma brochure."[110]

Le but que se proposait Dessaulles dans son discours du 23 décembre 1862, il l'indiquait en clair dans une lettre qu'il adressait, le 13 octobre 1863, à un ami parisien, le libraire Hector Bossange, en lui transmettant un exemplaire de sa brochure: "C'est un véritable plaidoyer écrit pour combattre l'intolérance enragée dont l'Institut est l'objet." Dans cette conférence, il voulait "parler raison et bon sens avant tout":

Je voulais protester contre la prétention à laquelle l'on n'a pas encore renoncé de vouloir conduire des hommes faits comme des enfants qui ne doivent pas toucher un livre sans la permission du maître d'études. Voilà ce que l'on veut et ce que je combats. Voilà surtout pourquoi je suis noté comme impie *dans le clergé.*

Je tiens à ce que notre bibliothèque ne soit pas absolument veuve d'ouvrages philosophiques, et l'Evêque n'en veut pas entendre parler.

Dans ma derière conversation avec lui je lui demandai comment nous passer des traités d'économie politique, dont un si grand nombre sont à l'Index.

– Mais, s'ils sont à l'Index, comment puis-je les permettre?

– Votre Grandeur veut donc que les hommes politiques renoncent à étudier la science qui leur est, de fait, la plus nécessaire pour l'administration d'un pays?

– Je vois sans doute là une difficulté, mais, moi, mon devoir est d'obéir à l'Eglise avant tout.

Ceci peut vous donner une idée de la terrible pression qu'exerce le clergé de ce pays sur son développement intellectuel.

Si l'on ne jure pas par Veuillot ou l'abbé Gaume, la géhenne du feu est notre seule perspective avec un Monseigneur comme le nôtre.

Au reste, je dois dire que nombre de catholiques très zélés m'ont franchement avoué qu'ils ne pourvaient trouver de mal dans ma brochure.

Deux ou trois prêtres même me l'on dit, mais en ajoutant: "Ne nous nommez pas, car ce serait une terrible mauvaise note sur notre compte."[111]

Aux lettres, qui restaient sans réponse, succédèrent deux entrevues, l'un en octobre 1863, l'autre en mai 1864, grâce auxquelles Dessaulles et ses amis espéraient amener leur interlocuteur épiscopal à composition. Ce fut peine perdue. Finalement Dessaulles fit une dernière tentative, qui ne fut pas plus heureuse que les précédentes, si l'on en juge par la lettre qu'il écrivait à Mgr Bourget le 16 novembre 1864:

L'entretien que j'ai eu l'honneur d'avoir avec Votre Grandeur me fait voir une fois de plus ce que l'on peut attendre de l'autorité ecclésiastique, quand elle se croit toute puissante. . . . Il faudra tôt ou tard que la liberté individuelle puisse être respectée et que l'autorité ecclésiastique comprenne qu'il est aussi pernicieux d'exiger trop que pas assez. . . . la tactique d'écrasement suivie avec tant de parti pris par Votre Grandeur n'emporte pas nécessairement les conséquences qu'Elle en espérait.[112]

Désespérant de fléchir leur évêque et de faire lever les censures qui les concernaient, dix-sept membres de l'Institut canadien décidèrent d'en appeler au Saint-Siège. Ils lui adressèrent une supplique datée du 16 octobre 1865. Mais on pouvait déjà prévoir le résultat de cette démarche. En effet, le 8 décembre de l'année précédente, Pie IX avait publié l'encyclique *Quanta Cura* qu'accompagnait le célèbre *Syllabus des erreurs*. Mgr Bourget, dans une circulaire au clergé datée du 1er janvier 1865, annonçant ces lettres apostoliques, écrivait: "Vous comprenez, comme moi, que ces Lettres arrivent bien à propos, car il est visible que plusieurs des faux principes qui y sont réprouvés, se sont déjà infiltrés par les mauvais journaux et les discours de nos libéreaux jusque dans nos heureuses et paisibles campagnes."[113]

L'évêques de Montréal songeait évidemment au "libéralisme" avec lequel, selon la proposition 80 du *Syllabus*, le pape ne pouvait pas "se réconcilier," mais aussi très certainement à la proposition 76, qui résumait "l'erreur" de ceux qui avaient attaqué le pouvoir temporel, et qui était ainsi libellée: "L'abrogation de la souveraineté civile dont le Saint-Siège est en possession, servirait, même beaucoup, à la liberté et au bonheur de l'Eglise."

*   *   *

La conclusion de cette étude s'impose d'elle-même. L'affrontement idéologique et doctrinal entre libéraux et ultramontaine canadiens fut une illustration, à l'échelle locale, du grand drame qui déchira le dix-neuvième siècle: révolution ou contre-révolution. Il fallut attendre la fin du siècle pour que l'Eglise, sous le règne de Léon XIII, fût amenée à repenser des principes permettant, grâce aux distinctions nécessaires, d'intégrer au christianisme les idées de liberté et de démocratie qui, nées en dehors de l'Eglise, s'étaient développées dans un esprit hostile à celle-ci.

De même, faute de faire "le départ nécessaire entre le pouvoir temporel pontifical et l'intégrité de la foi," les catholiques ne virent trop longtemps dans le Risorgimento qu'une entreprise contre la papauté et l'Eglise – ce qu'il n'était pas.[114] L'avenir allait donner raison aux libéraux, qui reconnaissaient la nécessité de garantir l'indépendance du pape à l'égard de tout pouvoir temporel dans l'exercice de sa mission spirituelle, mais qui niaient la nécessité de lier le pouvoir spirituel pontifical à la possession et à l'exercice effectif d'une souveraineté temporelle sur une partie plus ou moins considérable de l'Italie. Si ce qui subsistait de l'Etat pontifical s'effondrait en septembre 1870, c'est que "la Providence" en avait "de longue main préparé la chute," comme écrivait Dessaulles trois ans plus tard, non sans impertinence, à l'adresse de Mgr Bourget et des ultramontains: "Ils nous disent chaque jour que rien en ce monde n'arrive que par elle. Qu'ils acceptent donc la conséquence du principe qu'ils posent et qu'ils admettent que c'est elle qui a dû permettre la chute du pouvoir temporel, puisqu'il est tombé."[115]

Les ultramontains livraient donc une bataille perdue d'avance: en rejetant en bloc les "conquêtes du monde moderne," ils devenaient "sans discernement les adversaires du monde dans lequel l'Eglise est appelée à oeuvrer."[116] Il faut donc admirer la sagacité d'un abbé Maret, qui, dès 1857, à l'époque où Veuillot était à l'apogée de son talent et de son influence, voyait dans l'ultramontanisme un "colosse," mais "un colosse aux pieds d'argile": "Les tendances rétrogrades, écrivait-il, n'ont pas d'avenir;

et toute opposition au cours légitime, nécessaire, providentiel d'un siècle, est vaine."[117]

Les deux documents pontificaux auxquels les ultramontains ne cessaient de se référer, l'encyclique *Mirari vos*, où Grégoire XVI, "dans la hantise de voir les Etats pontificaux décomposés par les idées modernes," s'était dressé "contre elles avec une énergie décuplée"[118]; mais surtout le *Syllabus* de Pie IX, s'inspiraient d'une "système de philosophie politique où l'Eglise d'aujourd'hui a cessé de reconnaître sa pensée profonde": c'est la partie caduque de l'enseignement de ces deux papes, "celle où une lente maturation de la pensée catholique a eu pour conséquence un progrès de la doctrine, qui va des encycliques de Léon XIII au schéma sur la liberté religieuse présenté à Vatican II en passant par certains discours de Pie XII et telle déclaration de l'encyclique *Pacem in terris*."[119]

Notes: Libéralisme et ultramontanisme: II

ABRÉVIATIONS:
ACAM *Archives de la chancellerie de l'archevêché de Montréal.*
MDM *Mandements . . . diocèse de Montréal.*
RLB *Registre des lettres de Mgr Bourget,* ACAM.

1. Bazin, op. cit., 34-35.
2. RLB, XI, 450.
3. MDM, III, 364-365.
4. Jean-Joseph Gaume, *La Révolution, recherches historiques sur l'origine et la propagation du mal en Europe depuis la Renaissance jusqu'à nos jours* (12 vol., Paris, 1856-1859). Les volumes I à IV sont consacrés à la Révolution française.
5. MDM, III, 366.
6. *Ibid.,* 368.
7. *Ibid.,* 371.
8 *Ordre,* 12 février 1862.
9. L.Petit, *L'Index, son histoire, ses lois, sa force obligatoire* (Paris, 1908), 479.
10. *Ordre,* 17 mars 1862.
11. Cité par Paul Théodore-Vibert, *La Nouvelle-France catholique* (Paris, 1908), 479.
12. *Ordre,* 17 mars 1862.
13. Le prélat écrivait, le 4 octobre 1858, au sulpicien Granet, supérieur du séminaire de Montréal, à propos des membres du nouvel Institut canadien-français: "On ne peut se dissimuler que ces Messieurs ne veulent pas être sous l'influence du prêtre; et ils savent s'unir pour s'en passer." RLB, X, 357.
14. *Ordre,* 17 mars 1862.
15. *Minerve,* 24 avr. 1858.
16. MDM, VI, 30.
17. ACAM 295.101-856.6.
18. ACAM 295.101-856.10.
19. MDM, VI, 37.
20. *Pays,* 13 mars 1862.
21. *Ordre,* 1er fév. 1859.
22. MDM, III, 382, 383, 393, etc.
23. A.Simon, *L'hypothèse libérale,* 12.
24. *Ibid.,* 14.

25. MDM, III, 398-399.
26. *Moniteur canadien,* 3 août 1854.
27. *National,* 19 fév. 1858.
28. MDM, III, 398.
29. *Ibid.,* 398-400.
30. *Ibid.,* 383-392.
31. *Ibid.,* 392.
32. *Ibid.,* 393.
33. Bazin, *Vie de Mgr Maret,* II, 27.
34. Charles Langelier, *Souvenirs politiques de 1878 à 1890. Récits études et portraits* (Quebec, 1909), 12-13.
35. Roger Aubert, "Les réactions belges devant les événements d'Italie de 1859 à 1861," *Risorgimento,* 3 (novembre 1960), 124.
36. Roger Aubert, "Les catholiques français, de 1815 à 1870," *Rassegna storica toscana,* 4 (juillet-décembre 1958), 345.
37. Maurice Vaussard, "L'attitude des catholiques français en face du Risorgimento italien," *Civitas,* 12 (1961), 115.
38. Alfredo Comandini, *Il Principe Napoleone nel Risorgimento italiano* (Milano, 1922), 137.
39. Jacques Droz, "L'anticléricalisme français et la question italienne en 1860," *Rassegna storica toscana,* 6 (1960), 273.
40. Pham-Nang-Tinh, "La réaction de la Belgique devant l'invasion des Etats Romains," *Risorgimento,* 3 (novembre 1960), 84.
41. Pierre Frédérix, *Un siècle de chasse aux nouvelles. De l'agence d'information Havas à l'agence France-Presse, 1835-1957* (Paris, 1959), 78.
42. *Ibid.,* 69.
43. *Courrier du Canada,* 2 nov. 1859.
44. *Journal de l'instruction publique,* 1 (jan. 1857), 14.
45. Notice nécrologique dans l'*Ordre,* 3 déc. 1860.
46. *Courrier du Canada,* 17 juin 1859.
47. *Ordre,* 4 nov. 1859.
48. *Pays,* 19 mai 1859.
49. *Courrier du Canada,* 13 juin 1859.
50. *Ibid.,* 10 août 1859.

51. *Pays,* 13 et 16 août 1859.
52. *Ordre,* 23 août 1859.
53. *Courrier du Canada,* 7 sept. 1859.
54. *Ordre,* 29 nov. 1859.
55. Henry Cochin, *Augustin Cochin, 1823-1872, ses lettres et sa vie* (2 vol., Paris, 1926), I, 220.
56. J.Maurain, *La politique ecclésiastique du Second Empire,* 357.
57. *Courrier du Canada,* 17 fév. 1860.
58. *Ordre,* 17 fév. 1860.
59. MDM, IV, 61.
60. Maurain, *op. cit.,* 402.
61. Jacques Godechot, "La France et les événements italiens de 1860," *Atti del XXXIX Congresso di storia del Risorgimento italiano,* Palermo-Napoli, 17-23 ottobre 1960 (Roma, 1961), 380.
62. Maurain, *op. cit.,* 427.
63. Manlio Mora, "Gli eventi politici del Risorgimento italiano, illustrati al Senato francese dal Principe Napoleone nella seduta del 1° marzo 1861," *Archivio storico per le Province Parmensi,* 4ª serie, 13 (1961), 107-119.
64. Comandini, *Il Principe Napoleone,* 211-212.
65. Maurain, *op. cit.,* 506-508.
66. Frédéric Masson, "Lettres inédites de George Sand et du Prince Napoléon," *Revue des Deux Mondes,* 93e année (15 août 1923), 864.
67. Pierre Guiral, "Les libéraux français et la fondation du Royaume d'Italie," *Atti del XL Congresso di storia del Risorgimento italiano,* Torino, 26-30 ottobre 1961 (Roma, 1963), 374.
68. *Mémoires de la Société royale du Canada,* 4e série, tome II, section I (juin 1964), 105-127.
69. Ernest d'Hauterive, "Voyage du prince Napoléon aux Etats-Unis et au Canada (1861)," *Revue de Paris,* 40e année (15 septembre 1933), 243-272; (1er oct. 1933), 549-587.
70. *Courrier du Canada,* 5 mars 1860.
71. Cité par Ferdinand Boyer, "La presse progaribaldienne à Paris en 1860," *Archivio storico messinese,* 60-61 (1959-1961), 227.
72. *Ordre,* 6 juil. 1860.
73. MDM, IV, 188.
74. *Ordre,* 5 oct. 1860.
75. *Courrier du Canada,* 3 oct. 1860.
76. *Ibid.,* 5 nov. 1860.
77. Bazin, *Vie de Mgr Maret,* II, 70.
78. Cité par Jean Leflon, "Le Royaume d'Italie et l'opinion catholique française," *Atti del XL Congresso di storia del Risorgimento italiano,* 214.
79. Aubert, *Le pontificat de Pie IX,* 83.
80. L'un des propriétaires du *Pays,* Wilfrid Dorion, écrivait à son cousin trifluvien Napoléon Bureau, le 11 mars 1861: "Je pense que tu apprendras avec plaisir que Mr Dessaulles en a entrepris la rédaction." *Papiers Dorion,* Archives du séminaire de Trois-Rivières.
81. J'ai reproduit intégralement dans "La visite du Prince Napoléon au Canada," Mémoires de la Société royale du Canada, 4e série, tome II, section 1 (juin 1964), 119, l'adresse de l'Institut canadien et la réponse du prince Napoléon.
82. *Pays,* 19 déc. 1861.
83. *Annuaire des Deux Mondes,* 16 vol., Paris, 1850-1866.
84. *Annuaire des Deux Mondes, Histoire générale des divers Etats.* Année 1850 (Paris, 1er sept. 1851), v.
85. ACAM 901.135-862.9.
86. RLB, XII, 328.
87. MDM, IV, 313.
88. ACAM 901.135-862.13.
89. ACAM 901.135-862.1 à 862.7.
90. MDM, VIII, 208-214.
91. R.Aubert, "Pie IX et le Risorgimento," *Risorgimento,* 4 (nov. 1961), 74.
92. *Ibid.,* 67.
93. Aubert, *Le pontificat de Pie IX,* 85.
94. ACAM 901.135-862.12.
95. ACAM 901.135-862.8.
96. ACAM 901.135-862.9.
97. ACAM 901.135-862.11.
98. ACAM 420.005-862.2.
99. ACAM 901.057-862.1.
100. Voir mon étude "La visite du Prince Napoléon au Canada," 123-126.
101. *Pays,* 1er juil. 1862.
102. *Discours sur l'Institut Canadien prononcé par l'Hon. L.A.Dessaulles, président de l'Institut, à la*

séance du 23 décembre 1862, à l'occasion du dix-huitième anniversaire de sa fondation (Montréal, 1863).

103. *Ibid.*, 10.
104. *Ibid.*, 13.
105. *Ibid.*, 10.
106. *Ibid.*, 7.
107. *Ibid.*, 13.
108. Cité par Dessaulles, *L'Index*, 55.
109. ACAM 901.135-863.1.
110. ACAM 901.135-863.3.
111. *Collection Gagnon*, Bibliothèque municipale de Montréal.
112. ACAM 901.135-864.3.

113. MDM, V, 39-40.
114. A.Simon, *Catholicisme et politique* (Wetteren, 1958), 20.
115. Dessaulles, *La grande guerre ecclésiastique*, 50.
116. Yves M.-J.Congar, *Vraie et fausse réforme dans l'Eglise* (Paris, 1950), 609.
117. Bazin, *Vie de Mgr Maret*, II, 30.
118. A.Simon, "Vues nouvelles sur Grégoire XVI." Cité par Roger Aubert, "La liberté religieuse, de "Mirari vos" au "Syllabus," *Concilium* 7 (15 sept. 1965), 82.
119. Aubert, *ibid.*, 92.

Viceregal Influences on Canadian Society

R. H. Hubbard, *The National Gallery of Canada*

For the Right Hon. Vincent Massey, C.H.,
on his eightieth birthday,
20 February 1967

The writing of Canadian social history, a relatively new field of study, is not unnaturally coloured by the social thinking of our own day. The existence and general acceptance of a social hierarchy in the nineteenth century tend to be minimized if not overlooked. Where it has been recognized, the social structure has sometimes been interpreted in borrowed and distorted terms – of class against class, the upper aping the English aristocracy, the lower bravely defending North American democracy.[1] In actuality, the fabric of society in Victorian Canada was somewhat finer than this oversimplified view would indicate. The influence of England was admittedly most evident among the upper ranks of society (who in any case were the more vocal element); but loyalty to the mother country and to the Crown were far from being the preserve of any one class.

Canadianism, as it developed in the years following Confederation, was not confined to the inhabitants of forest, field, and village. None could have been more enthusiastic Canadians than two early Governors General, Lord Dufferin and Lord Lorne. It is doubtful whether the first wave of national feeling that swept the country in the seventies and eighties could have gained momentum without their impetus behind it. Governors General provided the stimulus for the first national movements in the arts, letters, learning, and social welfare. Their residences at Rideau Hall in Ottawa and the Citadel in Quebec were the natural, if not the only, centres where Canadians of all provinces, of both cultures, and from many walks of life could meet on common ground.

These notions have suggested themselves to me in the course of my recent studies of Rideau Hall and its occupants in Victorian and Edwardian times.[2] Though Governors General from Lord Monck to Lord Grey formed a collection of very different individuals, they were linked by a common pursuit of Canadian unity and identity. As we know so well today, nine men over a period of forty-four years could hardly begin the gigantic task of binding a loose formation into a nation; but it is vastly to their credit that they took up their work with such energy and zeal.

The example set in these matters by their predecessors the Governors General (sometimes called Governors-in-Chief) of British North America was not overly impressive. British North America before Confederation was a collection of separate provinces, each more or less self-governing and cherishing its own local traditions. Even in the case of Canada, the East and West sections had different languages and cultures. The Governor General, though he held primacy over the lieutenant governors of the provinces, was only effectively Governor of Canada. His direct influence upon society, owing to the limitations of travel before the railways, was largely confined to his small capital city. Though the capital of Canada after 1840 sojourned briefly in Kingston, Montreal, and Toronto, it was situated in Quebec for the greatest length of time.

Early governors were of necessity military men and colonial administrators with but little time to spare for other pursuits. They were, however, the natural leaders of society and of all its amusements in the capital. They inherited from the French régime such traditions as the levée on New Year's Day and the right to visit the old convents of Quebec; and their wives inevitably became involved in the local charities. A few made active contributions to the intellectual life of the city: Lord Dalhousie founded the Literary and Historical Society of Quebec, Canada's first learned society. Like so many others of their period and station in life, the governors and their wives habitually made water-colour drawings of the picnics and sleighing parties to Montmorency Falls and of the scenery through which their travels took them. Lady Elgin's water colours, along with an Indian portrait by Théophile Hamel, some Indian relics, and a large sleigh collected by Lord Elgin are still preserved at the family seat, Broomhall in Fife. Lord Elgin also lent his patronage to the publication of four lithographs after paintings by Cornelius Krieghoff.[3]

The next-to-last governor before Confederation, Sir Edmund Head, was a typical mid-Victorian amateur of art. Having taken a personal interest in the "Norman" design of the University of Toronto (now University College), one of the major architectural monuments of its period, he used his influence to have the site-plan altered in order to accommodate a magnificent elm tree. "I am sure you can never put up anything half so pretty," he declared in a letter to the Vice-Chancellor, John Langton.[4] Lady Head, like Lady Elgin, painted Canadian landscapes, and it is said that one of these, representing Barrack (Parliament) Hill in Ottawa, was responsible for Queen Victoria's choice of the lumbering town as capital of Canada.

In 1860, during Head's governorship, the young Prince of Wales made the first important royal tour of Canada. On this visit, as on the many that were to follow, opportunity was taken to parade Canada's achievements in public. Not only the material, but also the cultural, resources of the country claimed attention: the universities through the honorary degrees they conferred on the Prince; and the artists of the day, such as William Armstrong, for the records they made of the tour.[5]

The actual year of Confederation, in spite of the First-of-July celebrations in all parts of the New Dominion, saw no immediate flowering of Canadian culture. Much less did the first Dominion Day create a nation of four provinces so widely separated geographically and socially. If the fruits of unity were not at once apparent, the first two Governors General of the Dominion did relatively little to force them to ripeness. Yet their period (1867-72), even if only by default, was fairly happy in the social sense. Though the city of Quebec was deserted by the government, and though the quelling of the Red River rising gave French Canada its first serious setback, the little society of the old capital remained the most homogeneous and cultivated in Canada. Lord Monck's reluctance to leave it for Ottawa in 1866 attests to its pleasantness.

Monck, the last Governor General of British North America and the first of the Dominion, is rightly assessed today as deserving an honoured place among the Fathers of Confederation, by virtue of his advocacy of union, of the erection of Canada into a kingdom, the elevation of the governorship into a viceroyalty, and the establishment of a Canadian system of honours. But he was not a colourful figure. A minor Irish peer, he cherished his quiet family life at his semi-rural residence, Spencer Wood at Quebec, with all the amusements traditionally associated with his office: the tobogganing and skating, the cricket and indoor tennis, the country rides and the fishing down river. In his over-cautious way he performed his duties on the 1st of July 1867 in plain clothes and with a deliberate lack of ceremony, perhaps waiting to see whether the government would really stay in Ottawa. He made little secret of his annoyance at having to move into little Rideau Hall at "t'other end of nowhere." He seems to have been unpopular with Members of Parliament, perhaps because his entertaining was restrained and confined to the minimum required. Yet Monck was responsible for setting in motion not only the coach of state but the painful process of transforming Ottawa into a capital.

A motion in Parliament near the end of his term to reduce his stipend made the appointment of a successor difficult. Several nominees refused the post before it was accepted by another Irishman and unspectacular colonial administrator, Sir John Young who was created Lord Lisgar while in Canada. He and his wife were elderly and in poor health and made little impression on Canadian society during the years from 1868 to 1872. They continued the Moncks' practice of quietly (too quietly to please the diarist E.A. Meredith[6]) entertaining Senators, Members of Parliament, and officials. None the less a few traditions associated with the Governor General were established. The New Year's levée, transplanted to Ottawa, and the noon gun on Nepean Point gave the capital its first small touches of ceremony. In addition to a few short tours of Ontario, Lisgar made the first official visit of a Governor General to the United States, meeting President Ulysses S. Grant at Portland for the opening of the railway to Saint John and Fredericton in October 1871.

The first royal visit to the Dominion was made by the young Prince Arthur (later Duke of Connaught and a Governor General of Canada) between August 1869 and January 1870. Like that of his elder brother in 1860, this visit proved to be a minor stimulus to various pursuits in the social sphere. The Prince took part in curling matches, went shooting along the Ottawa, attended balls, and was invested publicly with the Order of St. Michael and St. George by Lisgar in Montreal. The Montreal painter, Otto Jacobi, and the rising photographers of the day, William Notman of Montreal and W.J. Topley of Ottawa, recorded various phases of the tour and made reputations in the process. The Canadians who assisted the royal party, and indeed the crowds who gathered in the cities from the surrounding countryside, provided some of the necessary groundwork for the rise of national feeling. The royal tour was on its way to becoming an institution. As an expedient in the absence of a resident sovereign it helped to form the Canadian attitude towards the Monarchy, which has been characterized by the alternation of short outbreaks of impassioned loyalty during the tours and mingled doubt and idealization in the intervals between them.

Owing to the British government's refusal, for fear of adverse American reaction, to elevate the governor generalship into a viceroyalty as advocated by Monck, the office remained in an unformed state until 1872. In that year, to breathe life into it, there appeared on the scene one of the remarkable figures of the late nineteenth century. Lord Dufferin was then in training for a long career of diplomacy which was to lead to the viceroyalty of India and ambassadorships in Rome and Paris. He was Irish, the grandson of Richard Brinsley Sheridan and the son of the Helen of *Helen's Tower*;[7] and from these two he inherited great charm and energy and a sense of drama. His wife came from another Irish family and was equally well endowed to become the first wife of a Governor General to play a leading part in Canadian life.

Appalled by the regional, religious, and social chasms that separated Canadians of various communities, and perceiving the urgent necessity to bind the new provinces of Manitoba, British Columbia, and Prince Edward Island into the national fabric, the Dufferins eagerly took up their first great task. Their work was not made easier by the prolonged economic depression of the seventies nor by the political scandals which blighted their period. In addition, Dufferin was obliged to come to grips with the realities of responsible government in the Dominion. After a period of conflict with Sir Alexander Mackenzie and Edward Blake (for the sagacious Macdonald was denied him after the Pacific Scandal), he reluctantly gave over the effective authority to the Ministry. He retained, however, as did his successors for many years to come, real powers as an official of the Colonial Office in the conduct of Imperial and foreign affairs. Dufferin was the first to make Imperialism of the late Victorian variety felt in Canadian affairs, though not in the extreme form it assumed at the turn of the century. But he eagerly espoused Canadianism as the complement of Imperialism. His blend of Imperial and national interests set the trend for all his successors until well after the First World War.

Thus the Dufferins breathed life not only into the office of Governor General but also, through it, into the whole idea of a united Canada within the Empire. From the first they divided their time between Ottawa and the rest of the country. During sessions of Parliament they spent most of their time in the capital. After enlarging Rideau Hall by the addition of a large ballroom with a stage, and a "Tent Room" which ingeniously combined supper room and indoor tennis court, they were able to accommodate guests at the rate of fifteen hundred at a time. Here, from 1872 to 1878, a widely representative number of Canadians took part in the furious round of activities which are recorded in Lady Dufferin's spirited *Journal*.[8] Besides the numerous luncheons, teas, concerts, receptions, and dinners (including state dinners in the ballroom) they introduced such typically Victorian entertainments as private theatricals, musical plays, and historical costume balls complete with "singing quadrilles." Every Saturday there was a garden party in summer and a skating party in winter. Occasional winter carnivals with elaborate lighting and decorations were held in Montreal as well as in Ottawa. The winter amusements proved so popular that Dufferin at his own expense built a giant toboggan slide and an indoor curling-rink at Rideau Hall. All events were faithfully recorded in photographs by Notman and Topley, which in turn were reproduced in wood-engravings in the illustrated papers. Dufferin was the first Governor General to receive full press coverage of his activities.

The number of foreign visitors whom the Dufferins received increased sharply over previous periods. These included literary men like Charles

Kingsley; scientists like Sanford Fleming, Colonel Casimir Gzowski, and those who demonstrated in a talking-machine in 1878; and artists like the wide-ranging Albert Bierstadt (whom Dufferin induced to present a picture to the Art Association of Montreal). Bierstadt, whose pictures of the American West had caught Dufferin's attention in New York, was periodically invited to paint in Canada and to encourage Canadian painters to record their own country. In 1877, in a speech in Toronto, the Governor General called for the founding of a National Gallery of Canada.

When Parliament was not sitting, and sometimes when it was, the Dufferins travelled far and wide, covering the entire territory of Canada as it then was. Besides their numerous and extended official tours of central Canada, the Maritime Provinces, Manitoba and British Columbia – on all of which they both sketched the scenery – they spent considerable periods of time in Toronto, Montreal, and Quebec. In the latter city Dufferin was the first to establish a viceregal residence in the historic Citadel, Spencer Wood having become the lieutenant-governor's house. Here, with their growing family, the Dufferins spent a part of each summer entertaining Quebeckers and many visitors. The rest of the summer they passed fishing at Tadoussac or in the Gaspé. Everywhere they went they inspected every institution, educational, charitable, and artistic, and met Canadians by the thousands. The fall fairs of rural Ontario also had their turn. The truly popular nature of their receptions in the small towns is symbolized by the huge cheese which greeted them at Ingersoll, Ontario, and which when opened was found to contain numerous bottles of champagne. In each town they found a welcome arch constructed of local produce. In a speech at Brockville in 1874 the Governor General enumerated all the arches he had seen:

There was an arch of cheeses – (laughter) – an arch of salt – an arch of wheels, an arch of hardware, stoves, and pots and pans – (great laughter) – an arch of sofas, chairs, and household furniture – (laughter) an arch of ladders laden with firemen in their picturesque costumes – an arch of carriages – (laughter) – an arch of boats, a free trade arch, a protectionist arch – (great laughter) – an arch of children, and last of all, an arch – no, not an arch, but rather a celestial rainbow – of lovely young ladies. (Great laughter and applause.)[9]

Dufferin's eloquence found ample outlet on these occasions. He spoke easily not only in English and French but also, on academic occasions, in Latin and Greek.

The Dufferins also maintained Canadian contacts abroad. When they returned to England on home leave he made numerous public addresses on Canada. He and his wife paid several visits to the United States. In New York they sought out writers and artists, attended the theatre, and witnessed an early demonstration of the "cinematograph." In Boston they met all the literary lights including, Emerson, Longfellow, Lowell, Oliver

Wendell Holmes, and Richard Henry Dana. In Washington Dufferin called on President Grant at the White House and in Philadelphia visited the Centennial Exposition of 1876, at which the Canadian exhibits filled him with pride for both Canada and the Empire. In Chicago it was the wonderful new Palmer House Hotel and in San Francisco the Chinese theatre.

He could not, however, be content with the Canada he found in the seventies. His aspirations for her led him to set afoot in Quebec such major projects as the preservation of the walls and to propose to the Queen the gift of the Kent Gate as a memorial to her father. Also begun at his urging was Dufferin Terrace, one of the outstanding achievements of urban design of its century. In Ottawa he was the first to press for the replacement of the muddy streets and ramshackle buildings which so disfigured the capital.

Dufferin's many activities, carried on tirelessly and partly at his own expense, left an indelible mark on Canadian society. Perhaps the most permanent legacy he and his wife left was the new social equilibrium they established in the country. This they did by making the viceregal presence felt very widely among Canadians. Though some people at the time found their entertainments too "mixed," they successfully avoided the extremes of English formality and American laxity. The new system[10] was admirably suited to the Canadian temperament, and Canadian society at its best has preserved it ever since. More importantly, however, they transformed the role of the Governor General from one of governing to one of serving the national interest by promoting unity and national feeling and by instituting good works and cultural pursuits on a national scale. They were quick to sense that the prestige of the Crown could be used to foster movements which were desirable but difficult for local auspices to set in motion. Their work was further developed by the succeeding Governor General.

The Marquess of Lorne's viceroyalty was lent enormous dignity by the presence in Canada of his wife, the Princess Louise, the beautiful and talented daughter of Queen Victoria. The appointment was made by Disraeli in order to employ the Crown "as an instrument to proclaim the greatness and unity of the Empire."[11] Canadians of all classes, at a time when economic prosperity was returning, swelled with pride at the prospect of royalty in residence at Rideau Hall and the Citadel. Preparations for their arrival resembled those for a royal visit. Souvenir articles in china and pressed glass bearing their portraits were in wide popular demand. The *élite* of society were thrown into a state of excited anticipation of a "court" at Ottawa. As it turned out after their arrival late in 1878, the Lornes' household and its activities were far from "royal," in the sense of being exclusive and formal. Instead, they followed the pattern established by the Dufferins in nearly every respect. Rideau Hall (furnished with their own pictures and tapestries) in the winter and the Citadel (where a ballroom was added) became the Meccas of high society more than previously; but the democratic side of the Governor General's activities continued in full force. He made long and frequent tours of all regions and paid visits to the principal cities and all their institutions.

The Lornes' personal interests were artistic and literary. As amateurs of painting and writing, they let enormous prestige to these pursuits in the young nation. In England their circle of friends included the best known artists and authors, and in Canada they came to know virtually every creative and learned person in the country. Like the Dufferins they met the leading American writers and artists and continued to receive visits from Albert Bierstadt. At the same time Lorne did not scorn the popular attractions of the day such as the football matches, Buffalo Bill shows, and concerts of Negro spirituals by the Jubilee Singers.

The only real hindrances the Lornes experienced were the constant though unpublicized threats of Fenian action against Princess Louise's life. These threats not only made everyone nervous (especially on tours through the United States) but also doubtless caused Louise's "melancholy" and her long absences from Canada. However, the injuries she sustained from a sleighing accident in March, 1880, were the official reason given for her being forbidden, presumably by the Queen, from spending another winter in Canada.

In spite of this the Governor General, alone or with his wife, worked hard for Canadian unity and nationhood. Proclaiming himself "so enthusiastic a Canadian," he embarked on arduous journeys to the remoter parts of the country. In 1881, considerably in advance of the Canadian Pacific Railway, and accompanied by reporters from English newspapers, he crossed the prairies on horseback and by river steamer from railhead at Portage la Prairie to Calgary, where he held a great pow-wow with the Indians. The following year he and Louise visited British Columbia, travelling through the United States on the outward and homeward journeys. Both took a keen interest in French Canada, which is reflected in their long periods of residence at their beloved Citadel and in the Princess's reputed preference for the vivacious ladies of Quebec over their more strait-laced English-speaking sisters.

Lorne was fascinated by everything Canadian. Soon after his arrival he was excitedly discovering Canadian plants, birds, animals, and fishes. He entered into the winter sports, especially the tobogganing and skating, with great gusto. Of these amusements the photographers prepared masterpieces of the Victorian composite photograph, in which the many blanket-coated figures at toboggan parties were photographed individually and then assembled on a painted background.

Like the Dufferins, both Lorne and Louise painted water colours of Canadian scenery. A number of Lorne's were published in his various books, and the National Gallery of Canada possesses several albums of

Princess Louise's, including charming views of the St. Lawrence, the Gaspé, and British Columbia, as well as of the southwestern United States and Bermuda.

In an address to the Art Association of Montreal in 1879, the Governor General expressed his pride in Canadian achievements in the arts, singling out the great operatic soprano Emma Albani and the photographers as examples. He also called for the development of a school of landscape painters. By this time, in fact, he was already conferring with the Toronto painter Lucius Richard O'Brien on the founding of a Royal Canadian Academy of Arts on the plan of the Royal Academy in London. The Academy quickly came to fruition. Lorne and Princess Louise nominated the first academicians from the painters, sculptors, and architects of the day, with O'Brien as president. They also chose the diploma works the academicians would deposit in the National Gallery which was inherent in the Academy's charter. Early in 1880 Lorne persuaded Sir John Macdonald to purchase the Clarendon Hotel in Ottawa, where on the evening of March 6 he inaugurated the Academy. The Ottawa newspapers reported every detail of the proceedings, not omitting to remark that there was somewhat more promenading than looking at pictures, and describing a massive jumble of hats and galoshes at the end of the evening.

Some journalists of the period branded the Academy as premature by a century or more, but the Governor General succeeded where others could not have done in establishing the arts on a professional and national basis.[12] He also encouraged Principal G.M. Grant of Queen's University in the ambitious venture of publishing the two volumes of *Picturesque Canada*,[13] for which O'Brien served as editor of the many wood-engravings illustrating the scenery of the entire country. Finally, in an address to the Ontario Society of Artists in Toronto in 1883, Lorne made proud reference to the federal government's first important art commissions, the large canvas of *The Fathers of Confederation* by Robert Harris (placed in the Parliament Buildings in 1886 and destroyed in the fire of 1916) and the statue of Sir George-Etienne Cartier on Parliament Hill by Louis-Philippe Hébert.

Lorne's "other Canadian child" besides the Academy was the Royal Society of Canada. Stung by an encounter in the Canadian west with an expedition from the Smithsonian Institution in Washington, he determined to found a scientific and learned society in Canada on the plan of the Royal Society in London. After conferring with Principal William Dawson of McGill, and following some preliminary bickering among the scholars of the country, he inaugurated the Society in the Senate Chamber on May 25, 1882. It was the first body to bring together the learned men of the whole Dominion and to publish their works.

A few days after this occasion the Governor General visited the

National Gallery on the first day of its opening in the old Supreme Court building on Parliament Hill. This latter building was the first of a series of temporary homes for the Gallery down to the present day.

By early 1880 (to return to that year) Lorne had written his "Dominion Hymn" as a proposed national anthem for Canada:

> God bless our wide Dominion,
>> Our fathers' chosen land;
> And bind in lasting union
>> Each ocean's distant strand;
> From where Atlantic terrors
>> Our hardy seamen train,
> To where the salt sea mirrors
>> The vast Pacific chain:
>
>> *O bless our wide Dominion,*
>>> *True freedom's fairest scene;*
>> *Defend our people's union;*
>>> *God save our Empire's Queen!*
>
> Fair days of fortune send her;
>> Be thou her shield and sun,
> Our land, our flag's defender:
>> Unite our hearts as one.
> One flag, one land! upon her
>> May ever blessing rest;
> For loyal faith and honour
>> Her children's deeds attest:
>
>> *O bless our wide &c.*
>
> No stranger's foot insulting
>> Shall tread our country's soil,
> While stand her sons exulting
>> For her to live and toil;
> She hath the victor's nurture,
>> Hers are the conquering hours;
> No foeman's stroke shall hurt her,
>> This Canada of ours!
>
>> *O bless our wide &c.*[14]

In February Lorne induced Arthur Sullivan, who was accompanying the American tour of *The Pirates of Penzance*, to spend a few days at Rideau Hall to compose the music. Sullivan arrived on a Wednesday and by the Saturday the hymn had its première performance by the band of the Governor General's Foot Guards. The words, the last line of which, "This Canada of Ours," was a phrase used by Dufferin, never caught on.

Nor could the "rumtitum" tune compete with "O Canada," the music of which, by Calixa Lavallée, Lorne heard performed for the first time at a Saint-Jean-Baptiste Society gathering in Quebec in June, 1880.

Yet further evidence of his avid Canadianism is found in his pleading with the British government for a purely Canadian system of honours, the "Star of Canada"; but in this he was as unsuccessful as Lord Monck before him, and for the same reason. In order to foster an interest in Canadian history he took up Dufferin's cause of the preservation of historic Quebec. In June 1879 he presided over the inauguration of Dufferin Terrace and Louise laid the foundation stone of Kent Gate. He and his wife patronized the opera, music, and theatre in English and French. Both of them spoke and read French and German, and Lorne made a public address in the latter language on a visit to Berlin (now Kitchener), Ontario, in 1879.

Lorne's books on Canada, written during and after his stay which ended in 1883, reveal a deep and abiding love of the country. In his later writings,[15] dating from the years when he and Princess Louise lived quietly at Kensington Palace, his interest in Imperial Federation came to the fore.

Following the "high noon" of the Lorne period, the remainder of the eighties saw new political and economic difficulties in Canada, the Saskatchewan rebellion, and fresh episodes in the never-ending dispute with the United States over boundaries and fisheries. The appointment of Lord Lansdowne as Governor General in 1883 caused Sir John Macdonald to fear further Fenian Raids because of the criticism of Lansdowne in Ireland over his vast estates in that country. Though the troubles never materialized, the new Governor General felt constrained to write to the Colonial Secretary in London of regional and cultural conflicts in Canada which endangered Confederation.

Unlike Lorne, Lansdowne felt no instinctive response to the wilds of Canada. Though he joined in the national sports and attended a prototype of the Calgary Stampede, he wrote privately to his mother of his homesickness for England. His official activities reflect the growth of British interest in Imperial Unity, a cause which was eventually to cause irritation in Canada. As a cultivated man (who spoke good French and used "real gestures") he took an interest in learning in Canada and lent his support to the holding of meetings of the British Association for the Advancement of Science in Montreal in 1884. On his departure he could report on the "peaceful progress of industry, education, and art" in the Dominion.

So far as the role of the Governor General in Canadian society was concerned the Lansdowne period was one of quiet consolidation. The Lansdownes continued the activities of their predecessors, though they were able to furnish their residences grandly from their stores at Bowood, the family seat in Wiltshire, and to entertain in style. A spirited account of Canadian life in the eighties is found in the reminiscences of Lady

Lansdowne's brother, Lord Frederic Hamilton. In *The Vanished World of Yesterday* he describes the winter sports at Rideau Hall in all their varied movement and colour and notes the "unaffected simplicity" of Canadians and the charm of the little capital, Ottawa. One of his anecdotes reflects a perennial if minor Canadian reaction to English members of viceregal households. It concerns one of the aides-de-camp who was unwise enough to disguise himself as Romeo at a winter carnival in Montreal and was knocked over on the ice by some masked young men.[16] Lord Frederic also records the introduction of skiing into Canada in January, 1887.

The period of Lord Stanley of Preston, who arrived in 1888 and succeeded as Earl of Derby before he left in 1893, was unmarked by important political or social developments. The Governor General's prestige was fully assured in the stable society of the late eighties and early nineties. From the records, including family papers, the Stanleys' life would seem to have been arcadian indeed. Their one important innovation was the annual transcontinental tour of Canada by train, which had been made possible by the completion of the Canadian Pacific Railway. A special railway carriage *Victoria*, furnished with electric-blue seats with lace edges, was built for the Governor General at this time.

Stanley is best known today for his interest in Canadian sports. His now famous trophy for hockey recognized a game which was then only beginning its rise to popularity. A keen fisherman, he built a house in the Gaspé to which the family went each summer. After passing through several hands in the intervening years Stanley House at New Richmond, Quebec, has recently been presented to the Canada Council for use as the headquarters of summer conferences. Lady Stanley left her monument in Ottawa in the Lady Stanley Institute for Trained Nurses.

At the Citadel, during other parts of the summers, a series of parties was held for residents of the ancient capital. On hot evenings the rooms were cooled with blocks of ice, and on one splendid occasion when Prince George paid his second visit to Canada,* a row of little tents for "spooning" was arranged on the long platform overlooking the St. Lawrence.

The end of the nineteenth century saw vast new vistas opening up for Canada. The settlement of the prairies gave reality to the concept of a Dominion from sea to sea. Responsibility for many of the social advances of the period lies with Lady Aberdeen, the wife of the new Governor General. She brought to Canada a social conscience which had been developed in the England of the uneasy eighties, as well as her own immense energy. In the space of their five years in Canada she achieved amazing results. Her voluminous *Canadian Journal*,[17] recently published in large part by the Champlain Society, is described as the best social

---

*Prince George, later Duke of York, Prince of Wales, and eventually King George V, had first visited the Lornes at Rideau Hall in 1883.

portrait of Canada of its period. She felt no compunction whatever in using her exalted position to further a series of humanitarian schemes in Canada.

The handsome and warm-hearted Lady Aberdeen was the dominant partner of the two. She and her gentle husband, the Earl of Aberdeen, had been influenced by the liberal and evangelical teachings of their friend Henry Drummond, the Scottish theologian who wrote a famous book in which he attempted to reconcile Christianity and evolution. They were friends also of Gladstone and admirers of his "high idealism." All this had directed them towards good works on a large scale. On their own estates in Aberdeenshire they had instituted Saturday classes, Sunday Schools, cottage hospitals, and district nursing for the tenants, and, in their own home, the Haddo House Club which scandalized many by its "socialistic" treatment of servants. The short period at Dublin Castle, during which Aberdeen was Lord Lieutenant of Ireland, saw Lady Aberdeen deeply immersed in welfare work and the fostering of Irish arts and industries. On their first visit to Canada in 1890, undertaken after her health had broken down under the strain of work, she founded the "Lady Aberdeen Association for Distribution of Literature to Settlers in the West," thus giving a foretaste of what she would do from Rideau Hall. On their subsequent travels round the world they made a host of friends, particularly amongst influential and philanthropic Americans such as President Charles W. Eliot of Harvard, Bishop Phillips Brooks, Andrew Carnegie, Susan B. Anthony, Frances Willard, Jane Addams, and Dwight L. Moody. As president of the International Council of Women she was in touch with all the social movements of her day in Britain, Europe, and the United States.

Aberdeen's appointment by Gladstone as Governor General of Canada was made in 1893. Immediately on arrival at Quebec Lady Aberdeen inspected all the institutions in that city concerned with the reception of immigrants. She also arranged for lessons in French and in Canadian dance steps for her entire family. In Ottawa, between trips to Chicago to superintend the Irish Pavilion at the World's Columbian Exposition, she organized the servants at Rideau Hall into a Household Club on the lines of the Haddo House Club in Scotland, with classes in French, music, art, Canadian history, and other subjects designed for their edification. Many of the visitors to the house, including the Rev. Charles Gordon ("Ralph Connor"), were asked to address the Household Club.

Her first great task was the National Council of Women of Canada, which was founded in 1893 for the promotion of women's status and work. She became its first president and organized local councils of women wherever her constant travels took her in Canada. Far from being exclusively Presbyterian, Protestant, or even Christian in her sympathies, she managed in a short space of time to persuade French-speaking Roman Catholic, Unitarian, and Jewish ladies to join the N.C.W. This, however, gave rise to a deadlock within the organization as to the form of prayer that would be used to open the meetings. This was resolved when her friend, the Toronto newspaperwoman, Mrs. Emily Cummings, had the inspiration to suggest silent prayer!

Other forms of social work became the serious concerns of Lady Aberdeen. She fostered the Canadian branch of the Boys' Brigade which was to embrace Protestants, Roman Catholics, and Jews; organized the Ottawa Y.W.C.A.; urged prison reform; and brought the Ottawa Maternity Hospital into being in the face of opposition from the doctors who resented her intrusion into their strictly male precinct of medicine. She held the first May Queen's Court of Ottawa, a garden party at Rideau Hall at which young women raised money for hospitals; pleaded the cause of Sir Wilfred Grenfell's Labrador Mission and that of Father Lacombe to the western Indians; attempted, unsuccessfully at the time, to found a public library in Ottawa; and took a keen interest in the first stirrings of the Church Union movement in Canada.

Art and learning were not so much her métier, though she found time to patronize the theatre, musicians, and Canadian artists like Wyatt Eaton, Frederic Bell-Smith, and Tait McKenzie. She sponsored the Queen's University extension courses in Ottawa and organized a series of extravagant historical pageants in Ottawa, Montreal, and Toronto in order to interest Canadians in their own history. When the Royal Society of Canada met in Ottawa on one occasion she arranged "An Evening with the Canadian Poets," at which Archibald Lampman, Duncan Campbell Scott, Wilfred Campbell, and Pauline Johnson were present. On another occasion, however, the main attraction for the scholars was a troupe of performing dogs. In the midst of all these special events the traditional cycle of activities at Rideau Hall continued unabated, with its garden parties, skating masquerades, theatricals, and numerous hockey, curling, cricket, and lacrosse matches. Like their predecessors the Aberdeens pressed upon the government the necessity of improving the capital by providing parks and driveways.

Lady Aberdeen's greatest monument is the Victorian Order of Nurses, the noble female organization devoted to the care of the sick in their own homes. She conceived it as a fitting memorial of Queen Victoria's Diamond Jubilee of 1897. At the outset it met with fierce opposition from the medical profession. To overcome this she enlisted the aid of Dr. Alfred Worcester of Boston, a noted pioneer of nursing-training. By this time resentment of the Aberdeens was widespread, especially among the Conservatives, because of the Aberdeens' ill-disguised partiality to Sir Wilfrid Laurier in the Manitoba School Question. At a stormy session in Toronto the doctors accused Worcester of being Lady Aberdeen's paid agent. He however turned the tables on them by suggesting that opposition to the V.O.N. implied disloyalty to the Queen. This was too much for loyal

Toronto, which in the end felt obliged publicly to acknowledge its debt to Lady Aberdeen in the newspapers and in a great farewell banquet in 1898.

Lord Minto, shortly after succeeding Aberdeen, truthfully reported to his brother in England that the Aberdeens had "absolutely upset society" in Canada. Lady Aberdeen had indeed administered it a shock from which it never recovered. After her, Canadians could never be satisfied with their water-tight provincial societies and with resistance to ideas from the outside world. The immediate result of her assaults, however, was the embitterment of the various "establishments" over her invasion of their preserves. In her impetuousness she antagonized both sides of any given question – both Roman Catholics and Protestants over the National Council of Women, both temperance ladies and the more convivial over her entertainments; but shock tactics were needed in the Canada of her day. The "better folk" of the nineties particularly resented her inviting all and sundry to Rideau Hall; and her attempt to cast her net more widely by having the tram line extended to the very door of Rideau Hall was narrowly foiled. Her activities eventually reached the ears of the aged Queen who voiced her disapproval in an admonition to Lady Minto to avoid getting "mixed up in any new venture which might be criticized."

The unsubtle tactics of the Aberdeens provoked the inevitable reaction. The period which followed theirs saw a return to the conventions of society. Lord Minto resolved in 1898 that only persons entitled to official recognition should be invited to Government House. Minto, who had been Lansdowne's Military Secretary in the eighties and chief-of-staff to General Middleton during the second Riel Rebellion, was a soldierly and straightforward, if genial man. He was a staunch advocate of Imperial Unity, and his period saw new stress laid on Canada's ties with England. He and his wife and family moved in exalted circles in England. In Canada their chief contacts were with magnates like Lord Strathcona and in the United States with such leaders as Theodore Roosevelt.

It is characteristic of the period that the American influence in Canada, down to small details such as the Stars and Stripes flying over the summer cottages of Americans, should become a cause of concern to the Governor General. At the same time, however, another Imperialist ambition for a grand union of Anglo-Saxons caused Minto to welcome many an influential American to Rideau Hall. Imperial honours for Canadians took up a considerable amount of his time. In his period Sir Donald Smith was created Lord Strathcona and Mount Royal and, among others, two Canadian artists, Louis-Philippe Hébert and Robert Harris, received C.M.G.s in the Edward VII Coronation honours.

The principal event of Minto's period was the transcontinental tour of Canada which the Duke and Duchess of Cornwall and York (the future King George V and Queen Mary) undertook in 1901 just after Queen Victoria's death and during the Boer War. For this occasion the Canadian

Pacific built two new railway carriages, *Cornwall* and *York*, which were afterwards used by the Governor General. They were very splendid with their electric lights, internal telephones, and decorations in the style of Watteau. All along the route of the royal tour demonstrations of loyalty took place, and there can be no doubt that the Imperial cause was furthered. But also involved in the tour was a strong element of Canadianism. In addition to the stately processions through the cities there were other occasions like the tree-felling, folk-singing, luncheon of pork and beans that took place at a lumbermen's shanty near Ottawa, and the welcome interval of duck-shooting in Manitoba, which the Cabinet was loath to approve.

Minto in spite of Imperialism was anything but blind to Canadian aspirations. He fully understood the French Canadian lack of instinctive response to the mystique of Imperialism and Anglo-Saxonism. And when two successive British officers commanding the Canadian Militia acted independently of the Ministry he suppressed his personal feelings in the matter sufficiently to sanction their dismissal. His keen interest in things Canadian led to his presenting a trophy for the game of lacrosse, successfully advocating a permanent building for the Public Archives, and founding the first Canadian association for the prevention of tuberculosis. The Ottawa Improvement Commission formed in his period crystallized his and his predecessors' ambitions for a better capital. Lady Minto worked hard at the establishment of cottage hospitals in various parts of the country.

Minto's Canadianism was nowhere more apparent than in his visit to the Yukon in 1900, the first by a Governor General to the Far North. Arriving at Dawson City in August after a long journey by rail, sea, and river boat, he and his wife inspected working and living conditions among the gold-miners. He was thoroughly shocked by the high prices asked for food and by the misrule and corruption he saw, and on his return he bore down heavily on the government to provide education and welfare services. What he saw along the route, especially in British Columbia and the prairies, inspired in him a love of the natural beauties of Canada and led to his urging the conservation of wild lands and of Indian art and folklore. At a time when Canadians were not greatly interested in their primitive art he helped the British Museum to collect examples from the west coast.[18]

When Minto departed in 1904, to be appointed Viceroy of India, he was succeeded by his brother-in-law Lord Grey. One of the extreme imperialists of his time – "The British Empire appears to me to be the religion of righteousness itself" – he was a childhood friend of King Edward VII and a disciple of Cecil Rhodes. He arrived in Canada at a time when the Governor General's prestige was at its apogee. Though he used his position to the fullest to promote Imperial Unity, and at times became discouraged with the slow progress of the cause, national feeling became even stronger in him than in his predecessors. The confluence of the two streams of Imperialism and Canadianism at their flood lent his period its distinctive flavour. In spite of resistance from various quarters, especially French Canada, the idea of Canada as a partner in the Empire gained currency and generated pride amongst Canadians. Yet he too deeply appreciated the attitudes of French Canadians and cherished the cultural variety they lent the country. He once expressed the hope that English-speaking Canadians might "allow a little French sunlight to warm and illuminate their lives."

Grey's years in Canada embraced a period of prosperity and expansion, of immigration on a large scale, and an optimistic nationalism of which Sir Wilfrid Laurier was the presiding genius. To this period the new Governor General was well suited by his cosmopolitanism, sparkling wit, energy, and fulsome oratory. Though by some in England he was regarded as a wind-bag and a faddist, and though his enthusiasms were suspected by some in Canada like Sir Robert Borden,[19] his love of the country was undeniable. His personal charm is attested by the host of friends he had throughout the world. Rudyard Kipling, Lord Bryce, Sarah Bernhardt, and Andrew Carnegie were but a few who visited him at Rideau Hall; and on his endless travels through Canada he gained many more. His eloquence qualified him as Canada's premier advertising agent. He coined a new slogan for every place he went. Toronto had its "beautiful Mediterranean Sea," Hamilton boasted its "Bay of Naples," and Hudson Bay became another Mediterranean! Every city and town clamoured for a visit. His appeal to business men was immense. Addressing them in their clubs, the conjured up visions, which have very largely come true, of British Columbia exporting great quantities of fruit and electric power and of Manitoba becoming "a gigantic colossus" which would feed the entire world.

He devoted the same energy to the promotion of non-material ends. Hardly a day went by without his importuning his long-suffering Prime Minister to embark on some far-sighted project which sounded wildly impractical at the time. For the cities of Canada he recommended commission government, the establishment of juvenile courts, and the building of concert halls. For the nation at large he called for national parks, urged the restoration of Louisbourg, and invited foreign landscape designers to plan the Ottawa of the future. In the latter connection he had the satisfaction of seeing the first of Ottawa's famous driveways, Lady Grey Drive, come into being before the end of his term.

His actual achievements, as distinct from the schemes which have required the intervening fifty years for realization, fell into the categories of sport, the arts, and Canadian history. In sport, though he donated a cup for golf competitions, his name is chiefly remembered today by the Grey Cup for football. In the arts, he persuaded the government to appoint the Advisory Arts Council, which in 1907 assumed responsibility for official art commissions and for the National Gallery, thus separating it from the

Royal Canadian Academy and setting it on the road to its modern development. He also instituted competitions and trophies for music and drama; the drama festivals, abandoned during the First World War, were re-established by Lord Bessborough in the thirties.

His greatest single contribution was in the realm of history. Beginning two years ahead of time in 1906, he prepared the Quebec Tercentenary celebrations, which he visualized as serving both national and Imperial ends simultaneously. At his urging the federal government purchased the Plains of Abraham and appointed the Battlefields Commission to administer them. Early in 1908 rehearsals began for a series of elaborate military ceremonies and pageants of Canadian history involving folk-singing and dancing. The actual celebrations in the summer culminated in the review of the entire proceedings by Prince George, now Prince of Wales.

Associated with the Tercentenary was Grey's most ambitious scheme of all. It was for a colossal statue of the "Quebec Angel of Peace," which was to be slightly larger than the Statue of Liberty in New York. It was to be set upon the cliff above Quebec to welcome newcomers to Canada and to "clasp the whole of the old world to her bosom." Into this bosom a lift was to take visitors to see the book in which were recorded the names of thousands of school children of the Empire who had contributed their sixpences for its construction. The children's part foundered when the Royal Family showed no eagerness to have their children publicized by patronizing the fund, and the entire grandiose scheme came to naught. The Angel of Peace was never to spread her wings over Quebec.

Grey's prophetic vision of Canada nevertheless gathered up the ideals of all his forerunners in Victorian and Edwardian times. Too grand for realization in their own periods, these have very largely come true in recent years. Only the Monarchy as represented by the nine Governors General of Canada from 1867 to 1911 could have done or even projected as much as they. They were responsible for setting up standards that helped to guide the development of national feeling in a large and then underdeveloped country. They were equally responsible for adding some of the flavour of life that distinguishes Canada from her powerful neighbour the United States. Social conditions have changed drastically since their times, mainly as a result of two World Wars and the Depression of the thirties. Political and economic developments have taken place which were undreamt of by them, and Imperial Federation became a dead issue. The position of the Governor General has likewise changed greatly, especially since the Statute of Westminster in 1931. But later Governors General continued to open up new avenues of service to Canada, and Canadian nationhood reached new stages of maturity thanks to their efforts. Though the goal of unity still eludes us, we have been helped immeasurably along the difficult road towards it by our Governors General.

Notes: Viceregal Influences

1. A.R.M.Lower, *Canadians in the Making*, Toronto, 1958; see also Alan Gowans, *Building Canada*, Toronto, 1966, 39 ff., 77 ff., 163 ff.
2. As the greater part of the material in this chapter will appear in fuller form in my forthcoming *Rideau Hall, an Illustrated History of Government House, Ottawa* (Queen's Printer, 1967) the notes here for the most part comprise references to material not to be found in the book.
3. Marius Barbeau, *Cornelius Krieghoff, Pioneer Painter of North America*, Toronto, 1934, 126.
4. R.H.Hubbard, "Canadian Gothic," *Architectural Review*, Vol. 116 (1954) 126.
5. J.R.Harper, ed., *Everyman's Canada* (exhibition catalogue), Ottawa, 1962.
6. Private journal of Edmund Allen Meredith, Under-Secretary of State; MS in the possession of Colonel C.P.Meredith, Ottawa, by whose kind permission I was able to consult it.
7. Harold Nicholson, *Helen's Tower*, London, 1937.
8. Lady Dufferin, *My Canadian Journal*, New York, 1891.
9. George Stewart, Jr., *Canada under the Administration of the Earl of Dufferin*, Toronto, 1878, 350-351.
10. W.S.MacNutt, *Days of Lorne*, Fredericton, 1955, 16-17.
11. *Ibid.*, 8.
12. R.H.Hubbard, "The Early Years of the National Gallery of Canada," *Transactions of the Royal Society of Canada*, 4th ser., Vol. 3, Sect. 2, 1965, 121-129.
13. G.M.Grant. *Picturesque Canada*, Vol. 2, Toronto, 1882.
14. Marquis of Lorne, *Memories of Canada and Scotland*, Montreal, 1884, 14; *Yesterday & To-day in Canada*, London, 1910, xvi.
15. *Yesterday & To-day in Canada*, for example.
16. Lord Frederick Hamilton, *The Vanished World of Yesterday*, London, 1950, 265.
17. J.T.Saywell, ed., *The Canadian Journal of Lady Aberdeen, 1893-1898*, Toronto, Champlain Society, 1960.
18. Public Archives of Canada (microfilm), Minto Papers, Minto to Sir Maunde Thompson, 23 Apr., 1903.
19. Sir Robert Borden, *Memoirs*, Toronto, 1938, 320.

L'Immigration Française au Canada vue par les Représentants de la France de 1859 à la Fin du 19e Siècle

Pierre Savard, Université Laval

La question de l'immigration de Français de France au Canada a toujours constitué un problème capital au Québec. L'afflux d'immigrants francophones représente, avec l'accroissement naturel, la solution toute trouvée pour équilibrer la balance démographique et conserver aux Canadiens français leur importance relative dans la Confédération. Cette immigration compte des effets incalculables sur la mentalité canadienne-française: la langue, les moeurs traditionnelles, la pensée canadienne-française sont remises en question. Enfin, l'image de la France qui informe si profondément la psychologie collective et individuelle des Canadiens français est confirmée ou infirmée par ce que chaque émigrant de l'ancienne métropole apporte avec lui.

Certes, l'immigration ne constitue qu'un filet des échanges franco-canadiens d'hommes, de biens et d'idées, de ce va-et-vient ininterrompu depuis l'arrivée de Cartier dans le Saint-Laurent. Echanges surtout culturels depuis 1760, la France ayant reçu étudiants et artistes, fourni des modèles littéraires et modelé l'âme religieuse canadienne par ses congrégations, alimenté le courant libéral et radical – surtout dans les années 1830 et 1840 – mais plus encore, nourri l'idéologie conservatrice traditionnelle. Le thème de l'abandon par la France constitue aussi depuis 1850 un thème privilégié de l'éloquence québécoise; et au delà des phrases, il y aurait sans doute une belle étude de psychologie collective à entreprendre sur cette attitude qui cherche à "culpabiliser" la France comme pour mieux se la rendre accessible et clémente. L'analyse des récits de voyages de

Français au Canada et de Canadiens en France aident également à remonter aux sources des tendances d'éloignement et de rapprochement.

L'histoire de l'immigration française proprement dite reste à faire. Le rôle de nos agents en France et l'action des gouvernements français, canadien et britannique sont encore mal connus. Nous savons bien peu de chose de l'origine sociale et de la mentalité des émigrants. Les rares documents utilisés jusqu'ici consistent dans quelques récits de voyageurs et dans quelques romans. Une quantification précise du courant apparaît même impossible. Les sources les plus utiles sont les recensements décennaux canadiens. Ces documents nous révèlent le nombre des habitants du Canada – naturalisés ou non – nés en France. Comme le remarque un représentant de la France en 1883, "des individus nés en France peuvent être originaires de parents étrangers." "Au Canada," ajoute-t-il, "suivant la tradition britannique, les autorités n'exigent du nouvel arrivant la production d'aucune pièce d'identité." Les ressortissants français ne s'inscrivent au consulat que lorsque les affaires les y obligent. C'est pourquoi il est impossible non seulement de déterminer le chiffre exact des entrées annuelles au Canada, mais même de connaître le nombre des Français habitant le pays.[1]

A l'aide des données bien limitées fournies par les recensements, nous pouvons cependant esquiver un profil grossier de l'immigration et de sa distribution géographique. Le recensement de 1861 fait dans les Haut et Bas-Canada révèle qu'il y a dans l'Ontario actuel 2,389 "Français" sur 1,396,091 habitants tandis qu'on n'en trouve que 672 sur 1,110,664 habitants dans le Bas-Canada (le Québec actuel). Dix ans plus tard, les quatre provinces de la Confédération canadienne comptent 2,899 "Français". On trouve alors au Québec 723 "Français" nés en France et, en Ontario, 1,751. En 1881, la somme des Français s'établit à 4,389 pour les sept provinces et territoires. Le Québec avec 2,239 habitants nés en France, dépasse l'Ontario qui en compte 1,549. Dix ans plus tard, les 5,381 "Français" se répartissent comme suit: 2,882 dans le Québec, 1,294 en Ontario, 474 au Manitoba et en Colombie-Britannique. C'est à partir de 1900 surtout que le nombre des Français s'accroît dans l'Ouest. Au recensement de 1901, on en trouve 1,470 au Manitoba (contre 1,254 en Ontario et 3,183 au Québec). En 1911, sur 17,619 Français dans le Dominion, l'Ouest (Manitoba, Saskatchewan, Alberta et Colombie-Britannique) en compte 9,175; près de 6,000 vivent au Québec et un peu moins de 2,000 en Ontario.

L'immigration française représente une fraction bien mince de l'ensemble des entrées. Il entre environ cinq fois plus d'Allemands que de Français durant les deux dernières décennies du dix-neuvième siècle. En 1881, il y a 1 Français né en France pour 110 habitants originaires des Iles Britanniques. En 1911, malgré la remontée dans l'immigration venue de France, il y a encore au Canada 46 habitants originaires des Iles Britanniques pour 1 Français de France. La France vient longtemps après l'Autriche-Hongrie, la Russie, la Norvège-Suède, l'Allemagne et l'Italie pour ne prendre que des états européens.

Enfin, rappelons que de 1820 à 1910, le Canada aurait admis 50,000 Français alors que les Etats-Unis en recevaient 470,868 pendant la même période.[2]

L'examen de la correspondance commerciale et politique des représentants de la France à Québec et puis à Montréal au siècle dernier peut apporter quelques pièces nouvelles au dossier de l'immigration française. Certes, la valeur de ces documents reste limitée par la qualité de chacun de leurs auteurs. On y trouve de tout, allant de la lettre de routine du fonctionnaire ennuyé jusqu'aux dépêches solidement informées qui livrent parfois des jugements éclairants. Un connaisseur des archives consulaires, monsieur Georges Dethan, n'a-t-il même pas pu écrire que ces documents rédigés par des observateurs plus proches de la vie quotidienne, rendent parfois des services que ne peuvent rendre les archives diplomatiques proprement dites.[3] Les archives consulaires constituent au surplus d'excellentes séries si chères à l'historien, à notre époque d'histoire structurale et conjoncturelle.[4]

Au dix-neuvième siècle, le principal représentant de la France dans les colonies britanniques de l'Amérique du Nord puis au Canada réside à Québec de 1859 à 1894, alors que le consulat est déménagé à Montréal.[5] Le premier consul en titre, le baron Gauldrée-Boilleau, inaugure à la fin d'août 1859 le consulat de l'empereur Napoléon III. A partir de ce moment, les consuls et les chargés du consulat adressent régulièrement des lettres au quai d'Orsay. Ces documents sont classés dans deux séries. La correspondance politique, accessible jusqu'à 1914, compte onze forts volumes de 300 folios chacun environ pour la période allant de 1859 à 1895. La correspondance commerciale, plus considérable, compte 16 volumes classés sous le poste de Québec (jusqu'à 1894) et 6 volumes relevant de Montréal (1894-1901).[6]

* * *

Le maire de Québec, qui vient accueillir avec chaleur le nouveau consul de France à son débarquement à la fin d'août 1859, aborde d'emblée le problème de l'immigration. Dans son "adresse" de bienvenue, le maire lance un appel au consul pour activer la venue sur les bords du Saint-Laurent de "cultivateurs" français. Dans le climat de rivalité démographique entre le Haut et le Bas-Canada, la préoccupation apparaît obsédante chez les chefs politiques. Prudent, le consul remercie le maire de ses bonnes paroles, mais ne promet rien.[7] L'attention qu'il porte dans ses dépêches au problème révèle que d'autres voix lui ont sans doute redit la demande de collaboration. De 1855 à 1880, d'ailleurs, les relations France-Canada, à en juger par les récits de voyageurs français au Canada connaissent un stade idyllique de "retrouvailles" de cousins.[8]

Sans les reprendre tous pour son compte, le consul énumère les arguments que font valoir les Canadiens français. Ceux-ci semblent bien préoccupés de l'avenir de leur nationalité. Ils espèrent trouver en France (surtout en Normandie, en Bretagne et en Vendée), en Belgique et en Suisse les émigrants catholiques qui leur permettront de rétablir l'équilibre entre le Bas et le Haut-Canada qui, lui, s'accroît grâce à l'immigration. Au Québec, le français recule dans les villes. Le Bas-Canada perd plus par l'émigration aux Etats-Unis qu'il ne gagne par l'immigration. Les Québécois prétendent n'avoir pas reçu plus de vingt familles françaises depuis 1759. Pour eux, le rétablissement des relations commerciales directes entre le Canada et la France n'est qu'une étape en vue de créer un mouvement d'émigration. Ils se plaignent volontiers que la France les a oubliés et qu'en ne leur envoyant pas d'émigrants, elle refuse de contribuer à leur survivance. Lorsqu'en 1862, on ouvre à la colonisation une nouvelle portion du comté de Dorchester, le ministre fédéral Hector Langevin signale le fait au consul. Celui-ci écrit à son gouvernement qu'on pourrait au moins s'efforcer de détourner vers le Canada une partie du courant d'émigration qui se dirige sur les Etats-Unis "perte de force sans profit, pour la nationalité française."

Le consul se rend vite compte des difficultés de l'entreprise. Les Canadiens sont loin d'être unanimes sur la question de l'immigration française. Les Canadiens anglais protestants voudraient qu'on attirât au Canada que des émigrants de même croyance qu'eux. Les Irlandais plaident en faveur des catholiques de langue anglaise. Les Canadiens français eux-mêmes sont divisés. Gauldrée-Boilleau écrit deux ans après son arrivée: "Au fond, on ne croit pas dans les régions officielles à la possibilité d'attirer au Canada une large immigration française et je ne m'avance pas en disant qu'on de la désire point." En 1870, son successeur, Frédéric Gautier, voit trois courants d'opinions chez les dirigeants du Québec: un groupe croit que les efforts et l'argent consacrés à l'immigration sont peine perdue car l'accroissement naturel de la population suffit (le Québec est alors la province de la Confédération depuis trois ans); un autre groupe continue de chercher à recruter des colons catholiques français, belges ou suisses; un troisième groupe enfin, soutient qu'il faut chercher à rapatrier les Canadiens passés aux Etats-Unis. Et c'est ceux-ci, suivant le consul, qui sont dans le vrai.

Gauldrée-Boilleau ne laisse pas de remarquer que le Français émigre peu, et que, quand il part, c'est rarement pour le Canada mais plutôt pour les Etats-Unis ou les rives de la Plata. D'ailleurs, soutient le consul, "si le goût de l'émigration . . . venait à naître," il trouverait des avantages à se développer en Algérie mieux qu'ailleurs.

Les Canadiens français qui semblent souhaiter une émigration française ne font rien de concret pour attirer celle-ci. Gauldrée-Boilleau explique que cela est dû à leur manque d'esprit d'organisation. Cet esprit, les Canadiens anglais le possèdent à un haut degré. Et le consul ajoute qu'ils "trouvent chez les capitalistes du Royaume-Uni des facilités que les Canadiens français sont loin de rencontrer."

Il passe cependant des Français au Québec (le recensement de 1861 en dénombre 672, nous l'avons vu). Mais ces immigrants "n'entendent rien aux travaux des champs et réussissent mal dans un pays pauvre, imparfaitement peuplé, où l'agriculture, l'exploitation forestière et peut-être la pêche maritime paraissent être les seules branches de l'industrie profitables à des étrangers." Pour les fonctions publiques, les professions libérales et les petits emplois de la banque et du négoce, les Canadiens leur font une sérieuse concurrence . . . ." Les consuls répètent que les immigrants qui viennent au Canada doivent, sous peine de s'exposer à de sérieux mécomptes, apporter des fonds pour le défrichement, la mise en culture de la terre et le premier établissement. D'ailleurs, le gouvernement du Bas-Canada ne pourra attirer des colons qu'en consacrant des sommes plus considérables à cette fin et en augmentant les dons gratuits de terre.[9]

Les événements politiques de 1870 et 1871 entraînent l'exil ou la fuite de Français, dont plusieurs viennent se réfugier au Canada. Le Canada semble avoir attiré fort peu d'Alsaciens malgré une propagande faite en allemand pour eux.[10] Par contre, près de trois mille Français, "écume" des "événements de la Commune," écrit un publiciste français quelques années plus tard, passent dans la vallée du Saint-Laurent.[11] On sait bien peu de chose de ces "Communards". Réfugiés pour la plupart à Montréal, un club qu'ils y ont formé aurait été dispersé par la police. Le curé périgourdin Cyprien Polydore, qui parcourt le Québec vers 1874, retrouve parmi eux des compatriotes.[12] A l'automne de 1873, le consul Martial Chevalier estime qu'il y a dix mille Français dans le Dominion dont quatre mille dans la seule ville de Montréal.[13]

Ce courant s'accompagne d'un effort sérieux de la part du gouvernement canadien pour attirer des émigrants de France. En Angleterre, le recrutement d'émigrants était organisé depuis 1839 alors que lord Sydenham avait nommé le Dr. Thomas Rolph agent d'immigration suivant une recommandation de lord Durham. En 1861, on voit apparaître dans les comptes publics le nom d'un A.H. Verret, agent chargé de l'Europe occidentale.[14] En 1873, Gustave Bossange tient à Paris une salle de lecture où l'on trouve des journaux canadiens et un registre pour l'inscription des Canadiens. La première d'une série de brochures de propagande célébrant le Canada a paru en 1871.[15]

Le consul de France à Québec ne tarde pas à subir les contrecoups de ce réveil quelque peu inattendu de l'immigration. Dès l'automne de 1872, Martial Chevalier constate que les nouveaux arrivants appartiennent surtout à la classe ouvrière, alors que l'émigrant le plus utile serait celui des campagnes. Six mois plus tard, il souligne que certaines catégories bien déterminées de Français seulement peuvent émigrer avec profit, à savoir les manoeuvriers employés au chargement et au déchargement des navires, les ouvriers d'élite et les commerçants habiles et expérimentés. Pour les autres, l'émigration au Canada ne peut se solder que par une aventure sans profit. A l'automne de 1873, le consul souligne que la crise commerciale et financière qui s'abat sur les Etats-Unis entraîne un retour d'émigrants canadiens dans ce pays. L'année suivante, le nombre des émigrants qui retournent en Europe dépasse celui de ceux qui entrent au Canada.[16]

Le consul et son vice-consul à Montréal se retrouvent avec des ressortissants au bord de la misère et prêts à la révolte. Misère aggravée par le fait que la Province de Québec, contrairement à ce qui se fait à New-York n'aide en aucune façon les sans-travail. Plusieurs Français demandent leur rapatriement et parlent même de provoquer une interpellation du Ministre des Affaires Etrangères sur les faits et gestes des agents d'émigration à Paris. Le consul a une piètre opinion des meneurs, des "socialistes", des "ivrognes", des "gens déclassés", des "réfractaires à la loi militaire". Un de leurs chefs est Humbert d'Abrigeon, ex-rédacteur du *Père Duchêne* sous la Commune.[17]

Non seulement ces Français parlent haut au consul, mais il soulèvent les Canadiens contre la France et contre les immigrants français. Pendant l'été de 1874, ils attaquent "les principes sur lesquels repose l'ordre social dans toute société civilisée." "Ces gestes sont néfastes, car la population canadienne," au dire du consul, "est loin d'être sympathique aux Français," et "elle est trop disposée à rejeter sur la masse les fautes de quelques-uns."[18]

Le représentant de la France au Canada dénonce périodiquement la propagande "coupable" des agents d'émigration à Paris, en particulier, de Gustave Bossange, propagande responsable en grande partie de ces difficultés. Chaque émigrant rapportant vingt francs aux agents, on comprend, soutient-il, que ceux-ci soient portés à abuser de la classe ouvrière. Le consul va jusqu'à parler de "traite de nos compatriotes." Il expédie au Ministre un spécimen de feuillet de propagande rempli de demi-vérités et d'exagérations grossières. On y décrit avec optimisme le climat canadien dont l'été est comparable à celui de Toulouse ou de Marseille, l'hiver étant "un peu plus rigoureux qu'en France" mais sans humidité, tout au plus "composé de froids secs, gelées et neiges." Dans la même feuille, on lit que "les divers gouvernements de la Confédération offrent gratuitement à chaque adulte de 18 ans au moins, un lot de 50 hectares de bonnes terres, et lui font des avances du matériel nécessaire pour monter une ferme." Quelques mois plus tard, Chevalier transmet au Ministre la copie d'une lettre qu'il a envoyée à un propriétaire français d'Oran intéressé au Canada. Le consul décourage nettement l'impétrant. Il lui rappelle que les Canadiens eux-mêmes émigrent aux Etats-Unis. Il résume la situation en déclarant que si le commerce est "assez florissant," l'agriculture connaît des difficultés, et l'industrie, dans la province de Québec est "peu avancée".[19]

Albert Lefaivre, qui succède à Chevalier en avril 1875, et qui restera six ans à Québec, a laissé la réputation méritée d'un ami sincère et dévoué des Canadiens. C'est à ses efforts, conjugués à ceux de son ami le premier ministre québécois Adolphe Chapleau, qu'on doit l'établissement du Crédit foncier franco-canadien, première tentative sérieuse faite pour intéresser les capitaux français au développement du Québec. Lefaivre travailla aussi beaucoup mais sans succès à la conclusion d'un traité de commerce entre la France et le Canada sans l'intermédiaire de Londres. Ce projet ne sera réalisé qu'en 1895.

Les perspectives pour l'immigration française que brosse le nouveau consul apparaissent bien plus favorables que les commentaires de son prédécesseur. Les paysans canadiens vivent dans l'aisance: on en trouve un signe dans leurs familles nombreuses. Les Français qui émigrent ont tout intérêt à préférer le Canada aux Etats-Unis, car la vallée du Saint-Laurent offre une "image vivante de la mère-patrie par sa langue, ses coutumes, ses traditions nationales." D'ailleurs, "que peut-on reprocher à cette terre fécondée depuis trois cents ans par des mains françaises?" lance le fonctionnaire, littérateur à ses heures. On a exagéré, continue-t-il, la misère des émigrants. La plupart des Français qu'il a rencontrés "gagnent leur existence." La moitié seulement des personnes qui étaient susceptibles d'être rapatriés aux termes des instructions du ministre en réponse aux demandes de certains Français, s'est prévalue de ce droit.[20]

A ces lignes écrites dans l'euphorie des premiers mois succèdent des commentaires moins optimistes. Le consul se voit obligé d'organiser des sociétés d'assistance mutuelle entre les Français vivant au Canada. En avril 1876, il en existe deux établies à Montréal et à Québec avec des succursales aux Trois-Rivières et à Ottawa. A Montréal plus de cent chefs de famille sont à ce moment sans travail. Un millier d'anciens soldats et officiers de la Commune qui se sont enfuis pour se soustraire au conseil de guerre, continuent de se distinguer par "leurs tendances anarchiques et leur fanatisme religieux." Plusieurs dénoncent le cléricalisme dans des conférences publiques. Un groupe nombreux appuie bruyamment la campagne entreprise par Charles Chiniquy, ex-prêtre catholique canadien-français passé au presbytéranisme.[21] Ils publient des articles incendiaries dans le *Witness,* organe du "chiniquysme." Lefaivre regrette "des faits si publics et si compromettants pour notre dignité nationale." Et le consul soupire: "L'effet en est d'autant plus malheureux que les Canadiens sont restés français de coeur et que les scandales causés par notre colonie française troublent chez eux le culte de l'ancienne mère-patrie.[22]

La crise industrielle et commerciale qui continue de sévir entraîne une baisse nette dans le nombre des immigrants qui tombe de moitié entre 1873 et 1878, suivant les calculs de Lefaivre.[23]

Durant le reste du siècle, on trouve peu à glaner sur l'émigration dans la correspondance consulaire. Léon Duchastel de Montrouge, en charge du consulat d'avril 1883 à juillet 1885, consacre une de ses missives au problème. Il rappelle principalement que "l'émigration reste sans profit pour le pays qui la fournit." Les Français s'établissent au Canada sans esprit de retour, ils s'y marient et leurs enfants deviennent des Canadiens sans aucune attache à la patrie de leurs parents.[24]

En 1885, la question de l'immigration française revient pour un moment à l'ordre du jour. En 1884, à Québec et à Paris, Frédéric Gerbié a publié un gros ouvrage de 448 pages sur le Canada et l'émigration française. L'auteur, qui a séjourné pendant cinq ans au Canada, vante le pays et invite ses compatriotes à garder leur regard fixé vers le Rhin mais à ne pas perdre de vue les rives du Saint-Laurent.[25]

Les Canadiens français souhaitent alors l'établissement d'une ligne directe de commerce avec la France. Un groupe d'hommes d'affaires français conduit par le curé Labelle et reçu aux frais de la "Halifax Steam Navigation Co. Ltd.," se promène à travers le Canada jusqu'à Winnipeg.[26] Le prélat, sous-ministre de la Colonisation du Québec, cherche à promouvoir à cette occasion la cause de l'immigration française et de la colonisation dans sa province.[27] Le consul à Québec, le marquis de Ripert-Montclar, voit d'un bon oeil le resserrement des liens commerciaux entre le Canada et son ancienne métropole, mais il déclare qu'il faut lutter énergiquement contre l'idée même d'une émigration française au pays. Ripert-Montclar, qui a occupé le poste de consul à Montevideo, croit que l'Amérique du Sud (en particulier la région de la Plata) constitue un lieu d'émigration plus favorable que le Canada. Mais avant tout, l'intérêt bien compris de la France est de diriger ses émigrants vers ses colonies. Et il rappelle que ses prédécesseurs Chevalier et Duchastel ont déjà abondé dans le même sens. Il souligne aussi nettement qu'aucun émigrant pauvre venu en 1872 n'a "prospéré." Le consul revient à la charge quelques semaines plus tard, le 9 octobre 1885, en soulignant que l'affaire Riel, qui élargit le fossé séparant Canadiens français et anglais, risque de compromettre les projets d'entente commerciale avec la France. Le voyage des "excursionnistes français métamorphosés en *délégués* pour les besoins de la cause, sous laquelle se cache une nuée de spéculations particulières," a eu le bon effet de ramener l'attention sur les relations commerciales franco-canadiennes. Mais il a aussi malheureusement attiré l'attention des émigrants sur "une région désolée par un climat meurtrier, et où le travail et les ressources matérielles manquent beaucoup plus qu'en France même." Le consul a noté depuis quelques semaines un accroissement dans le nombre des arrivées d'émigrants de France. A sa suggestion, le Ministre des Affaires étrangères demande par lettre, le 12 octobre 1885, à son collègue du Commerce, que le *Moniteur du Commerce* encourage les travailleurs français à se diriger vers les colonies françaises plutôt que vers le Canada.[28]

Les consuls cessent à peu près de parler du problème de l'émigration après 1885. Le 29 juillet 1892, le comte de Turenne d'Aynac fait rapport d'un voyage commandé dans le "Nord-Ouest" et jusqu'en Colombie-Britannique. Il prévoit un accroissement considérable de la province du Manitoba qui pourra devenir une province française plus importante même que le Québec. L'Ouest canadien compte déjà 800 familles d'agriculteurs français. Turenne suggère qu'on établisse un vice-consulat à Winnipeg.[29]

*　　*　　*

Commencé bien avant 1859, le mouvement d'immigration française au Canada reste réduit durant la seconde moitié du siècle. Ce n'est qu'à partir de 1900 qu'il connaît un accroissement relatif; et il se dirige alors surtout vers l'Ouest canadien. Au début des années 1860, des dirigeants canadiens-français espèrent une immigration française et catholique qui viendrait consolider les positions démographiques du Bas-Canada. Ce sentiment s'estompe progressivement avec la création de la province de Québec en 1867. La France, pour sa part, ne peut envoyer les types spécifiques d'émigrants dont le Canada a besoin. L'afflux de réfugiés politiques appelés "communards," vers 1872, qui se révèlent des émigrants mal préparés et turbulents, favorise une poussée de francophobie, et accentue le repli des Canadiens français sur eux-mêmes. La politique anticléricale de la République à partir de 1880, et le réveil du colonialisme français avec Jules Ferry, ne contribuent pas pour peu à éloigner de leur ancienne mère patrie les Canadiens français de la vallée du Saint-Laurent. Autour des années 1885-1890, les efforts du curé Labelle pour attirer des colons français au Québec remportent un bien maigre succès. Ce n'est qu'après 1890, et dans le Canada de l'Ouest, que l'émigration française connaîtra une carrière vraiment intéressante.

Les consuls de France à Québec et puis à Montréal ont tous eu à faire face à ce délicat problème. Leur attitude apparaît commandée non seulement par la conjoncture et les structures matérielles et mentales, mais aussi par leurs sympathies personnelles. On constate toutefois que même les plus préjugés d'entre eux en faveur du Canada et des Canadiens – un Albert Lefaivre, par exemple – finissent, devant les difficultés et les obstacles, par décourager l'immigration de Français dans les vallées du Saint-Laurent, ou tout au moins cessent d'en parler. Faut-il, pour faire comprendre ces prises de position, rappeler que les consuls ont été envoyés au Canada pour promouvoir les liens commerciaux, et qu'ils se sont vite rendu compte que ces relations ne postulaient pas une présence française. Les consuls savent également bien que le Canada est un pays d'émigration (vers les Etats-Unis) durant toute cette période, et ils ne manquent pas de le rappeler à l'occasion. Au surplus, c'est au consul qu'aboutissent les problèmes découlant d'une émigration mal contrôlée: fausse représentation des agents d'émigration en France, difficultés matérielles et morales d'adaptation des émigrants au Canada, mauvaise image de la France projetée par des membres de colonie française. Les obstacles rencontrés sur ces points par les consuls de France au Canada au siècle dernier aident à comprendre le peu d'ardeur qu'ils manifestèrent à favoriser l'immigration de leurs compatriotes au Québec.

Notes: L'Immigration Française au Canada

1. Archives du Ministère des Affaires étrangères, Paris. Correspondance commerciale et consulaire, Québec, 11, fol. 395. Lettre de Léon Duchastel de Montrouge, en charge du consulat, du 18 juillet 1883.

2. Rosaire Morin, *l'Immigration au Canada* (Montréal, 1966), 138. La plus récente vue d'ensemble. Les quelques considérations historiques qu'on y trouve s'appuient sur des données bien fragmentaires.

3. "De la valeur pour l'historien de la correspondance consulaire de Stendhal" dans *Mélanges Pierre Renouvin* (Paris, 1966), 167. Voir du même auteur: "Les archives des Affaires étrangères," invitation aux historiens américains dans *French Historical Studies* IV (1965): 214-218.

4. Sur les possibilités inexploitées de ce type de document, voir Huguette et Pierre Chaunu, "Le climat des relations franco-espagnoles à Cadiz dans la seconde moitié du XVIIe siècle. Histoire sérielle et psychologie collective: problèmes de méthode" dans *Mélanges offerts à Marcel Bataillon* (Paris, 1962), 19-29.

5. Sur les consuls, voir Francis-J. Audet "Les représentants de la France au Canada au XIXe siècle" dans *Les Cahiers des Dix,* 4 (Montréal, 1939), 197-222.

6. Deux volumes de correspondance politique contiennent aussi des dépêches émanant d'autres consulats (années 1866 et 1867). Les volumes, après 1895 pour la correspondance politique et après 1901 pour la correspondance consulaire, étaient à la reliure au moment de nos recherches (été 1966).

7. *Le Canadien* du 31 août 1859. La France cherchait essentiellement à établir des relations commerciales comme en font foi les instructions données à de Belvèze, commandant de *la Capricieuse* en 1855. Dans son ouvrage fantaisiste *Le Canada reconquis par la France* (Paris, 1855) le Canadien Joseph-Guillaume Barthe, après avoir évoqué une reconquête armée, se rallie à l'idée d'une reconquête pacifique par l'émigration massive.

8. Armand Yon, "Les Canadiens français jugés par les Français de France, 1830-1939" dans *Revue d'Histoire de l'Amérique française,* XVIII (1964-65): 321-342 et livraisons suivantes (en cours de parution).

9. Correspondance commerciale en consulaire (désormais citée CC), Québec I, fol. 14, I, fol. 169, fol. 180, fol. 320vo et 321, 2 fol. 20, fol. 92, 93 et vo, 6, fol. 68; Correspondance politique des consuls (désormais CP), Angleterre, 35, fol. 31, fol. 78, fol. 104, 42 fol. 404.

10. Yon, *op cit., RHAF,* XIX (1965-66): 446.

11. Frédéric Gerbié, *Le Canada et l'émigration française* (Québec, 1884), 400-401. Dans sa dépêche du 15 octobre 1875, le consul Lefaivre donne comme chiffres d'entrées de Français au Canada 1,366 pour 1872, 2,634 pour 1873 et 1,632 pour 1874 (on observe une baisse générale dans tous les groupe cette année-là) (CC Québec, 7 fol. 281vo). Ces chiffres d'entrées sont les seules que nous avons retrouvés pour la période.

12. Yon, *op. cit., RHAF,* XIX (1965-66): 73.

13. CC, Québec, 6, fol. 440; CP, Angleterre, 46 fol. 272.

14. Lionel Groulx, *Histoire du Canada français depuis la découverte* (Montréal, 1960) II: 260-261.

15. Yon, *op cit., RHAF,* XIX (1965-66): 443. On sait que la commissariat du Canada à Paris ne sera fondé qu'en 1882 avec comme premier titulaire Hector Fabre.

16. CC, Québec 6, fol. 305, fol. 403vo et 404, 7, 208vo et 209, Angleterre, 46 fol. 271 et 272, fol. 387.

17. Alphonse Humbert, condamné aux travaux forcés passe en Amérique puis revient à Paris; il est élu conseiller municipal de Javel (15e arrondissement) contre le candidat gouvernemental en octobre 1879.

18. CP, Angleterre, 46 fol. 387, CC, Québec, 6, fol. 440, fol. 466. Sur l'opinion québécoise envers la France de 1875 à 1905, voir notre thèse *Jules-Paul Tardivel, la France et les Etats-Unis* (Québec, 1967).

19. CC, Québec, 6 fol. 440, 466vo, fol. 43, fol. 83, fol. 150 à 154vo., fol. 207vo.

20. CC, Québec, 7, fol. 283 et vo et 284.

21. Sur le retour offensif de Chiniquy à Montréal de 1875 à 1878 voir Marcel Trudel, *Chiniquy* (Trois-Rivières, 1955), 247-251.

22. CP, Angleterre, 50, fol. 94 à 99vo.

23. CC, Québec, 8, fol. 113. La chute est plus sensible encore aux Etats-Unis, révèle Lefaivre.

24. CC, Québec, 11, fol. 486.

25. F. Gerbié, *op. cit.,* 443.

26. Sur l'expédition, voir Léopold Lamontagne, "Le Roi du Nord et sa suite française à Winnipeg en 1885" dans le Rapport 1954 de la Société historique du Canada *(Canadian Historical Society, Report, 1954)*, 36-44.

27. Labelle réussit à attirer un nombre restreint de colons français qui s'installeront surtout dans la Beauce et les Cantons de l'Est (Yon, *op. cit., RHAF,* XIX (1965-66): 448).

28. CP, Angleterre, 85, fol. 31vo, 32, CC, Québec, 12, fol. 360, 364vo et 347vo. En France, la cause de l'émigration au Canada continue de rallier des suffrages. En 1886, à l'occasion de la mort de Paul Bert à Hanoï, Henri Rochefort s'écrie "Vous voulez des colonies salubre? Laissez donc le Tonkin et allez au Canada." Le même auteur écrit un "drame canadien" intitulé *Home Rule.* Onésime Reclus préfère à l'Argentine la vallée du Saint-Laurent où les Français conserveront leur langue et connaîtront une merveilleuse fécondité. L'hebdomadaire *Paris-Canada* poursuit sa propagande pour attirer des colons. Charles Gailly de Taurines qui a visité le Canada de part en part, célèbre le pays d'émigration dans *La Nation canadienne* (Paris, 1894). Voir Yon, *op. cit.,* XIX (1965-66): 262-263 et 446-447.

29. CP, Angleterre, 99, fol. 178 et vo. En 1891 les chanoines réguliers de l'Immaculée Conception viennent de fonder Notre-Dame de Lourdes (Manitoba) sous la direction de dom Paul Benoît; cinq ans plus tard, ils fondent Saint-Claude.

Duncan of Metlakatla: the Victorian origins of a model Indian community

Jean Usher, National Museum of Canada

> *"There is a happy spot of busy life*
> *Where order reigns where hushed the din of strife,*
> *Harmonious brethren neath paternal rule,*
> *Ply their glad tasks in Metlakatla's school,*
> *There Duncan holds supreme his peaceful throne,*
> *His power unquestioned, and their rights his own.*
> *Anvil and hammer, saw and wheel resound,*
> *And useful arts of industry abound*
> *While faith and knowledge find an altar there."*[1]

The inspiration for such a eulogy was Metlakatla, a Christian Indian village established in 1862 not far from the mouth of the Skeena River in British Columbia. By 1876 under the direction of William Duncan, an Anglican lay missionary, this settlement of some nine hundred Tsimshian Indians had begun to attract marked attention both in Britain and Canada as an outstanding example of missionary endeavour, and of the industrial potential of the American Indian.

The Earl of Dufferin after a vice-regal visit to Metlakatla in 1876 spoke of the "neat Indian Maidens in Mr. Duncan's School at Metlakatla, as modest and as well dressed as any clergyman's daughter in an English parish" and advised British Columbians that "what you want are not resources but human beings to develop them and consume them. Raise your

30,000 Indians to the level Mr. Duncan has taught us they can be brought, and consider what an enormous amount of vital power you will have added to your present strength."[2]

With its parallel rows of neat white houses, gardens and picket fences, its school, store, street lamps, gaol, and dominated by a church reputed to be the largest west of Chicago and north of San Francisco, the village presented an imposing picture of civilized life in the wilderness. The society developed within this environment was hardly less impressive, particularly when seen in contrast to the life of the heathen Indians of the area. Rank and class had apparently been abolished, as had liquor, potlatching and other heathen customs. Church attendance and family prayers had become the rule, whilst day schools, evening schools and Sunday schools were well attended by adults and children. Government was by a council of elders and enforcement of law and order was carried out by a corps of native constables. Besides encouraging the traditional pursuits of hunting and fishing, Duncan claimed to have introduced such trades as coopering, weaving, rope making, printing and had built a variety of workshops and a saw mill for the Indians' use. European clothing and cleanliness marked the appearance of the Metlakatla Indians, who spent their leisure time in hymn singing, playing football or participating in the activities of the village fire brigade and the Metlakatla brass band. The introduction of Christianity to the Tsimshian Indians of British Columbia had meant not only were they offered new spiritual ideas and beliefs, but an entirely different kind of life was opened for them at the Christian village of Metlakatla.

Before Duncan's arrival at Fort Simpson in 1857, the Tsimshian had had a varied and lengthy contact with European culture. From 1775 to 1825 the maritime fur trade introduced many goods and techniques to the coastal Indians with few disruptive effects.[3] Similarly the North West Company, and after 1821 the Hudson's Bay Company posts, established among the Tsimshian served mainly to give impetus to a new growth of arts, technology and social and ceremonial life.[4] The Hudson's Bay Company had had extensive experience in dealing with Indians and aimed generally by a strict but just policy, to keep the peace that was necessary for successful trade relations. The trader, in most cases, had no desire to change native society. The Indians were asked only to accept that part of white culture they desired, and on this basis reasonably harmonious relations could be maintained. But, whereas the process of cultural diffusion in the trader-native contact situation is one of imitation, the missionary attempts to inculcate his values into the native society and asks that the native accept all the values and beliefs that he offers.[5] The missionary is of necessity a reformer and likely to make a far greater impact on native societies than other Europeans. The kind of influence he exerts and the demands he makes of prospective converts will be largely characterized by his own cultural background, mores and social position.[6]

William Duncan began his mission to the Tsimshian Indians in 1857 under the auspices of the Church Missionary Society, the evangelical missionary society of the Church of England. Born in Beverley, Yorkshire in 1832 the year of the great Reform Bill, he grew up in an era of great ferment in English society, in an age of reform where Evangelical and Utilitarian alike were challenging old institutions, and attempting to ameliorate or change the social conditions that industrialization had produced. "Reform-political, religious social, artistic – was more deeply a part of the early Victorian temperament than was the complacency of which it has been consistently and smugly accused."[7] In later years the Church was to claim that Duncan had been no more than a far-sighted social worker. Yet in fact he was primarily a Christian protestant missionary, but one espousing a nineteenth century Christianity, formed in the religious, humanitarian and middle class framework of mid-Victorian England.

*   *   *

Duncan's own cultural background is found in the larger sphere of Victorian attitudes and reform movements and in the more particular policies and ideals of the Chuch Missionary Society and of Henry Venn. Duncan himself received little formal education and like most children of working class parents was sent out to work at the age of thirteen. For nine years he was employed by the leather firm of Cussons in Beverley, spending seven years as an apprentice clerk and two years as a clerk and commercial traveller. A serious and earnest young man, Duncan appears to have shunned frivolous activities and to have spent most of his time working, reading, singing in the Church choir and teaching a Sunday School class at Beverley Minster. In his late adolescence he developed close relations with his employer Mr. G. Cussons and with his minister the Reverend E. Carr. Carr conducted a weekly bible study and prayer meeting for young men, at which Duncan was a devout and regular attendant. He received particular and fond attention from Carr and it was under his influence that Duncan decided to devote part of his life to missionary work.

Duncan seems to have had no close family ties, and although from a working class background himself, derived most of his attitudes from these middle class men with whom he was most familiar. As an ambitious young clerk too, it was understandable that he should try to pattern himself after his employer.

The Victorian middle classes, the small manufacturers, retailers, independent businessmen, saw their society as a dynamic one where a man was judged on his abilities and where progress and advancement depended upon the exertions and skills of the individual. The Gospel of Work was eminently suited to their own social and economic position.

Samuel Smiles' doctrine of Self-Help embodied this middle class view of the road to individual success and progress, but was itself directed at the working classes. Smiles, like many of the middle class, feared the growth of proletarian radicalism and sought to make it unnecessary by exhorting the worker to educate himself, to find a joy in work, to persevere, to be thrifty, dutiful and of strong character; to change himself rather than society. Smiles emphasised in his lectures to working men in Leeds the value of discipline and drill "Wonderful is the magic of drill! Drill means discipline, training, education."[8] Although faith in education was characteristic of much of Victorian thinking, Smiles was less interested in the formal education of the schoolroom than in the industrial training of the workshop and the moral training of a Christian home.[9] In essence, Smiles recognized the condition of the working classes and aimed not to change society, but to elevate the mass of the proletariat to the level of the middle class. Yet only by the elevation of the individual could the mass be raised. He fully accepted the Victorian ideal of a free and independent labourer, and felt that the improvement of the individual should be initiated by a personal, moral desire rather than by government pressure, "Whatever is done *for* men and classes to a certain extent takes away the stimulus and the necessity of doing for themselves."[10] The dominance of middle class values and mores over a large part of Victorian society meant that Self-Help ideas were prevalent in the attitudes of many of the Victorian reformers.

The values of Victorian society were derived from the humanitarian tradition of evangelical protestantism and from the economic needs of the middle class. A dominant feature of the era was the close relationship amongst religious, economic and social ideas. Samuel Smiles' emphasis on thrift was based on the fact that individual savings were the foundation of the nation accumulation of wealth, essential to that continued economic growth and progress which so enthralled the Victorians. A thrifty worker received moral accolades too, since his savings guaranteed his independence and reinforced the Victorian faith in the idea of the free labourer. The gospel of work, like the protestant gospel, saw idleness as a sin, "an abrogation of God's will and a dangerous opportunity to move downwards to hell."[11] Poverty too was seen as a moral failing, since by individual action the worker could improve his position and hence improve society. Failure in this social duty was a moral offence.

The religious revival of Wesley had made Victorian religion acutely aware of the constant inner struggle with temptation and the strong necessity for leading a disciplined Christian life. This emphasis on discipline and authority is evident in many aspects of Victorian society and the continuous efforts of Christians to discipline themselves in the struggle with evil led to a concern for self improvement in secular life which gave added impetus to the ready acceptance of the doctrine of Self-Help.

The Victorian reform movements "arose from the intense feelings of a few individuals acting on the sensibilities of a governing class increasingly accustomed to change, increasingly persuaded of the possibility of progress and increasingly alarmed by industrial and urban misery . . . [it] found its most energetic expression in the Evangelicals and Utilitarians."[12] The early Victorian reformers Evangelicals like Ashley, or Utilitarians like Edwin Chadwick and Kay-Shuttleworth, saw poverty as dependent upon the indolent disposition of the individual. Like Samuel Smiles they felt that the interests of the individual would best be served by freeing him from the corrupting relief and making him a free and independent agent. Such was the general philosophy behind the New Poor Law which rationalised and centralized the administration of relief.

Although they recognised the need to alleviate the overcrowding and poor sanitation they found in English cities, the reformers maintained that social conditions only reflected the moral destitution of the people. "The absence of any sound moral training, said numerous inspectors in countless reports, caused the intemperance, pauperism and crime which threatened English society."[13] Such ideas were eminently suited to the backgrounds of the reformers. Many Evangelicals felt that prosperity was the earthly reward for living a moral life and that poverty must thus be a reflection of immorality. Social evils were seen as due primarily to ignorance of religious and moral principles.

The emphasis of the reformers on the ignorance of the population as a general cause of social problems, meant that a corresponding stress was laid on the necessity for more universal education. Education was seen by E.C. Tufnell, a government inspector as "the universal remedy," the panacea for all ills. Like many Victorians, the inspectors saw education as the agent of progress and held optimistic, rational views of its power to mould human nature. Men such as Dr. James Kay-Shuttleworth also believed the school had a responsibility to develop a child's skill, and encouraged schools to introduce their pupils to a wide variety of subjects such as science and music. Under the influence of Swiss educators such as de Fellenberg, the school inspectors encouraged industrial training and farming as a means of reforming pauper children. Just as Samuel Smiles encouraged thrift to produce moral, independent workers, the school inspectors advocated gardening to teach the future workers the forethought and economy that would ensure their independence.

The commissioners themselves who so influenced the social life of England in these years were endowed, as so many Victorians were, with an un-ending zeal and energy. Their reports reflected the enthusiasm they felt for their work. "Across the length and breadth of England, assistant commissioners reported miraculous regeneration. Their communications read like letters from missionaries describing the conversion and rebirth of the heathen."[14] Throughout the 1840's and 1850's the steady work of the reformers resulted in sanitary and prison reform, new approaches to the treatment of lunacy, regulation of merchant shipping, mines, smoke and burial grounds. The initiation of reforms owes much to the humanitarianism, paternalism and conscience of the Evangelicals. But the extensive investigation of conditions, the exhaustive research, writing, inspecting and interviewing that characterised the work of the inspectors was a product of the rational, utilitarian ideas of Chadwick and Kay-Shuttleworth.

The number of small utopian movements in the mid-nineteenth century is evidence of the growing realization that human life and human societies were malleable and that their form and structure could be changed as desired. Historians have tended to treat these social experiments as forms of retreat from the realities of the world. In fact they should be considered in the context of the general movement for reform in the early and mid-nineteenth century. The utopian reformers sought to exert an influence on society as a whole, to produce reform and change.[15] They established separate communities and hoped to prove the efficiency and practicality of their ideas in this microcosm of society.

In England the Moravian Brethren had several community settlements which lasted into the nineteenth century. The unity of the group in secular as in religious life was emphasised, and before admittance to the community, the individual signed a "brotherly agreement" declaring willingness to abide by the rules and discipline of the community. A council of elders was the ruling body and had general control of economic life, education and social welfare. The rules were read loud once a year and those guilty of disobedience were expelled from the settlement.[16] Impressed by the Moravian groups, John Minter Morgan in the 1840's proposed a similar scheme for self-supporting villages under the auspices of the established church. The Church of England Self-Supporting Village Society was formed, and aimed at "those benefits resulting in the Moravian settlements from a more intimate connection between secular and religious affairs."[17] The economic basis of the communities was to be mainly agricultural (like the school inspectors, Morgan encouraged gardening) with some industrial and handicraft work. A committee of management was to direct the community affairs, and Morgan introduced a "strongly authoritarian note, in his emphasis on "codes of conduct!"[18] The community as a whole was intended to be a practical demonstration of Christian brotherhood and unity, "wherein each labouring for all, the exertions of each will receive their due and proper reward – wherein the weak shall be aided and supported by the strong."[19] Although there was little implementation of these proposals on an extensive scale, the Church of England Self-Supporting Village Society did in fact receive wide attention in the press, and Morgan and his adherent, James Silk Buckingham, spoke at many meetings throughout England. The *Illustrated London News* in 1850 commented on Morgan's proposals for a model town, "It reminds us of Bridewell or some contrivance for central inspection. . . . The idea is obviously borrowed from the unsuccessful efforts of the State to correct the people by Bridewell's workhouses and prisons – substituting a gentler kind of control for diet, ships, dungeons and fetters . . . . Mr. Morgan does not conceal his desire to organise the "destitute people" and the whole society in Reductions (formal villages) similar to those by which the Jesuits drilled the Indians in Paraguay."[20]

"The 1840's was an age of models; model villages, model apartments, model lodging houses and even model beds."[21] Perhaps the most spectacular model was the industrial town of Saltaire, fifty miles from Duncan's home in Beverley. Titus Salt, a former mayor of Bradford, a woollen manufacturer and himself a hero of Self-Help, alarmed by a serious cholera outbreak in Bradford, began in 1851 to build a model manufacturing town for his workers. Residential and industrial areas were separate, and schools, shops and a literary institute were established. The mill itself, a huge structure with unusually large windows for light and ventilation was a model of industrial architecture. Though moved by humanitarian ideals, concern for the health and welfare of his workers, Salt, a Congregationalist felt like many Victorians that the evils of society were not all environmental. The sign across the entrance to the town read "All Beer Abandon Ye that Enter Here." As in many model communities the element of discipline and authority was evident at Saltaire too.[22]

Early Victorian social work was endowed with a strong missionary zeal. Apart from the building trusts, the alleviation of hunger and care of orphans, its main efforts were directed at the moral failings of the individual. Drunkenness and lust were seen as the basic problems of the working class and temperance societies and prostitution reform movements were active and well supported. The Church sisterhoods were active in the 1850's in establishing homes for penitent and wayward ladies. The sisters had strong faith in education and example and hoped to change the character of the girls by love, prayer and the example of a religious and pious life. By work and training in laundry and domestic work they tried to prepare the women to make an honest living for themselves.[23]

Thus although Duncan's role as a missionary to the heathen would lead him inevitably into attempts at social reform, his own cultural background was also one where reformers and their ideas had captured the imagination of many people. The nature of Victorian reform and the values which determined it were to play an important part in establishing the Christian Indian Society of Metlakatla.

There was however, a more particular influence evident, in the formation of Duncan's attitudes towards the Indians and to his conception of his task as a missionary. As an agent of the evangelical Church Missionary Society, he was directly influenced by their ideas and practices, through personal contacts, correspondence with the secretaries of the

Society and through accounts of other missionary work in the various journals of the Church Missionary Society.

That body was dominated in these mid-Victorian decades by the energetic and vigorous ideas of Henry Venn, whose "Native Church" policy established the guidelines for C.M.S. missionaries until the late 1870's. Venn's "Minute on the Native Pastorate and Organisation" first published in 1851, recognised that European and American missionaries could not, even in the distant future, hope to reach all the heathen of the world. He advocated that the European missionary act purely as an evangelist, and hoped to maintain a clear distinction between the missionary who preached to the heathen and the pastor who ministered to the congregation of native Christians.[24] The role of the missionary was to establish a self-supporting and self-governing congregation of Native Christians, and when this had been effected, the mission would have "attained its euthanasia and the Missionary and all the Mission agency can be transferred to the regions beyond."[25] From the beginning the missionary was to train a native pastor and helpers who would be capable of taking eventual control of the congregation. "The main underlying principle which appears to have guided Mr. Venn . . . is that foreign missions to the heathen must always be treated as a transition state."[26]

The man who did not train up a native clergy was building on an insecure foundation and Venn warned particularly that the skills and technology possessed by the European would tend to make him indispensable to his converts and this might unnecessarily prolong his work among them. "It may be said to have been only lately discovered in the science of missions, that when the missionary is of another and superior race than his converts he must not attempt to be their pastor; though they will be bound to him by personal attachment, and by a sense of benefits received from him, they will not form a vigorous, native Church, but as a general rule they will remain in a dependent condition, and make but little progress in spiritual attainments. The same congregation under competent native pastors, would become more self-reliant, and their religion would be of a more manly, home character."[27]

Like Samuel Smiles, Venn appeared to see an intrinsic value in encouraging Self-Help and independence among the native Christians. Converts should not become dependent on a foreign mission but should become members of a native church as soon as possible. Nor should they be allowed to fall into the habit of thinking that everything should be done for them. From the beginning of the mission they should be encouraged to contribute to a native church fund and at each stage of development of the mission, the missionary should inculcate the values of self support, self government and self extension.

Although influenced by the problems of personnel, the climatic difficulties for Europeans in tropical climates, and the vast field of work to be covered, Venn was also idealistically concerned that the result of missionary endeavour should be the establishment of national native churches. As the church in each nation assumed a national character, he hoped it would ultimately supersede the denominational distinctions introduced by foreign missionary societies, which divided the church of Christ in Europe and America.

It was important to Venn too, that this national church be an expression to some extent of the native people themselves. Unlike Roman Catholic missions, the C.M.S. under Venn, was to make Christianity indigenous and not exotic, with many centres instead of one.[28] The missionaries when forming a national church were enjoined to avail themselves of national habits, of Christian headmen and of a church council. "Let every member feel himself doubly bound to his country by this social as well as religious society."[29] It is interesting to note that many of Venn's ideas were directly influenced by Rufus Anderson, the Secretary of the American Board of Commissioners for Foreign Missions. Both Venn and Anderson emphasised the importance of the work of the Apostle Paul, whose task had been the gathering and forming of local churches, and putting the power of self-government and organisation in the hands of each Christian community.[30]

Detailed plans were laid out by the C.M.S. to guide the formation of native churches. Each district brought under missionary action would have its converts formed into companies where they could receive daily instruction in Christianity and make regular contributions towards a church fund, a system comparable in many ways to that of the Methodists in England. These companies aimed at providing mutual support and encouragement for new converts. Each company was to have an elder or Christian headman, approved of or selected by the missionary. Weekly company meetings were to be held under him and to a large extent the converts were to be dependent on these headmen for their Christian instruction. The missionary was to hold monthly meetings of headmen at which reports would be presented on the moral and religious conditions of companies. Subscriptions would be handed over and the headmen would receive spiritual counsel and encouragement from the missionary.[31]

The first step in the organisation of a native church would be the formation of one or more companies into a congregation, having a schoolmaster or native teacher amongst them and supported by their own funds. Secondly, a native congregation would be formed under an ordained native pastorate paid by a native church fund; and the final phase would be when the district conferences would come together to organise the future of the national church.

Venn was interested however, not only in the expansion of Christianity but in the kind of native Christian that was to be created. He instructed his lay agent embarking for Abeokuta in 1853 to study the resources of the country in marketable products and to direct the attention of the converts towards them, so that "these parties may rise in social position and influence while they are receiving Christian instruction and thus form themselves into a self-supporting Christian Church and give practical proof that godliness hath promise of the life that now is, as well as that which is to come."[32]

Sir Thomas Fowell Buxton, writing in 1841,[33] recommended not only that British naval force be used to blockade the slave trade, but that Christian England should invest in Africa and attempt to stimulate agriculture and commerce and produce an industrial class of African. "These Africans, protected by Britain, guided by the missionaries, and working with capital from European merchants would . . . move inland and man factories at every strategic spot living together in little colonies, little cells of civilisation from which the light would radiate to the regions around."[34] Venn like Buxton, his colleague and friend, wanted to find a substitute for the profits from slave trading, and also needed to make the Christian converts self-supporting. It was thus under the influence of Venn that the Moravian ideal of a mission station catering for education, trades, agriculture, industry and medicine besides the teaching of Christianity became the pattern upon which many Anglican missions were founded.[35]

Although in the early years of the evangelical revival there had been little concern for secular problems, the idea of taking the gospel and civilization to the heathen was no novelty in the history of the C.M.S. The Reverend Samuel Marsden, a missionary in Australia and New Zealand in the early decades of the century, continually pressed the C.M.S. to find employment for the Maoris. Lacking the arts of civilization, the Maoris were not "so favourably circumstanced for reception of the Gospel as civilized nations are . . . since nothing can pave the way for the Gospel but civilization."[36] He was able to persuade the C.M.S. to send not ordained men but mechanics; a carpenter, a blacksmith, a twinespinner and a man able to teach the cultivation of sugar cane, cotton, coffee and other marketable products. An essentially practical man, Marsden himself was active in New South Wales in cattle-rearing, growing grain and improving the breed of Australian sheep. This was the kind of man that Venn needed for his Christian settlements in West Africa. At least as important as the ordained missionary in the life of the Christian villages were the lay schoolmasters, carpenters, the men who taught the mechanics of civilization which not only enabled the village to become self-supporting but elevated the Christian African above his heathen counterpart.

Venn aimed to create an African middle class, though not necessarily in the image of its Victorian counterpart. His great insistence on the learning and transcribing of native languages, and on the toleration of native customs and systems of law were strongly felt throughout the C.M.S. Venn realised how difficult it was for Englishmen to show respect for national peculiarities different from their own, yet advised the missionary to "study the national character of the people among whom you labour and show the utmost respect for national peculiarities . . . from your first arrival in the country [it is best] . . . to study and respect the national habits and conventionalities, till it becomes a habit with you and second nature."[37] Yet he advocated no immediate or drastic changes in the form of native societies and recommended that although the wielding of authority in native society might seem absurd or unjust to a European that "nevertheless they are the framework of society and till they are replaced by a more enlightened system they must be respected."[38] Missionaries, indeed, were to utilize the present structure of the society to further their own ends. In attempting to evangelise a nation they were exhorted to follow the example of St. Paul and to concern themselves particularly with men of influence and the leaders of national thought.

As a true Evangelical, Venn did not concern himself only with the children of a nation. In fact, the conversion of the adult was of utmost importance for the future of a mission, for here was evidence to his neighbours that Christianity came not merely by habit or force of education. The adult was aware, too, of the idolatry and native customs he must renounce and not only was he often also imbued with a missionary zeal himself but "he has some idea of the obloquy and danger to which he is exposed."[39]

Education was to be the means to full conversion. Sunday school and religious instruction were of course of primary importance but the arts of civilization must also be taught. Venn advised that the missionary was not to develop a highly educated élite, but was to attempt to build self-supporting educational institutions by combining book learning and industrial labour. "The separation of scholastic life and manual labour is a refinement of advanced civilisation. It may be doubted whether even in this case it is desirable, but certainly it is not desirable in a mission school or according to the example of the Apostle of the Gentiles."[40] Venn's ideal native Christian, a man of strong but simple faith, able to read and understand the Bible and economically self-supporting, bore a strong resemblance to the Victorian ideal of Samuel Smiles' independent Christian working man.

Samuel Smiles would have found much to admire in William Duncan. Although *Self-Help* was not published until 1859, Smiles had already popularized his ideas in lectures to working men and many books for young men concentrated on similar ideals. Duncan himself was impressed by such books[41] and from a *Young Man's Own Book* copied out such homilies as "Nothing is so valuable as a good stock of information . . . Success depands on having fixed principles . . . be accustomed to studying your own self, for all other knowledge, without a knowledge of yourself is but splendid ignorance . . . to have a good memory you must be temperate in both eating and drinking and sleeping . . . ."[42] Energetic and ambitious, Duncan's "lists of things to learn" ranged from Grammar, Histories of Great Men,

Navigation, Law, Astronomy, and Farming to Manners and Politeness."[43] Recognizing that "one of the great lessons I have yet to learn is to be diligent and spend well the present moment," Duncan disciplined his life strictly, allocating twenty-seven hours a week to religion, twenty-seven hours to education, fifty-four to business activities, ten hours for exercise and healthful pursuits, and allowing fifty-four hours a week for sleep. Years later Cussons commented that "besides discharging his duties to myself most faithfully and effectually, he planned out his spare time for self-improvement and laboured most industriously to make up for his want of earlier education."[44]

Duncan had no doubt been a model employee, and in fact in 1854 turned down Cusson's offer of double salary to go to London to train as a schoolmaster in the Highbury College of the Church Missionary Society. Besides expanding his own basic education in Arithmetic, Grammar, History, and Geography, Duncan continued formal studies in Liturgy and Church History. This was combined with the practical application of pedagogical techniques and school management. Several weeks each term were spent in teaching at the model school attached to the college and students were marked on their lesson plans, their use of illustrations, their ability to keep a class attentive and whether examination of the children had been animated, judicious and patient.

It was at Highbury too that Duncan came into contact with the mission field, through his teachers, the missionary magazines and meetings and through his fellow students. In 1856 he commented that his close friend at the college "Mr. Kirkham, a missionary student, leaves this month for Abeokuta, I have learnt a good deal by being here with him."[45] Kirkham's impressions of Abeokuta, a model C.M.S. mission, must have been instructive for Duncan. "The natives are naturally industrious but our converts much more so: in one corner of the yard you will see a carpenter's shop, in another a cotton cleaning establishment and in another a printing press busy at work. In the school are about sixty children receiving a sound elementary education. I have school hours from nine to two and then from three to five they, the pupils, work at agriculture, carpentry and book-binding."[46]

The C.M.S. at this time was mainly active in West Africa. It was conditions in Africa which had influenced the ideas of Henry Venn and several Highbury students, including Duncan, anticipated a missionary career there. Captain James Prevost's offer of a free passage to a missionary to the North Pacific coast meant that not only was Duncan unable to finish his final third year at Highbury, but that instead of following his friend Kirkham to a Christian village in West Africa, Duncan was expected to be the first bearer of the gospel to the Indians of British Columbia. In such a context, perhaps it is less surprising that within four years Duncan had established a Christian self-supporting industrial village among the Coast Indians.

Impressed by the life and work of Samuel Marsden, after whom he named his first convert, and like many Victorian missionaries, Duncan was convinced that civilization and Christianity were inseparable. The savage condition of the aborigines was seen as due to the free operation of the power of original sin, and it was felt civilization could only be reached by means of Christian moral teachings and the development of industrious and sober men.[47]

* * *

The Tsimshian Indians had had a lengthy, and in some cases a close contact with white civilization. The maritime fur trade and the Hudson's Bay Company had so stimulated their desire for European artifacts that when the Hudson's Bay Company established a post at Fort Simpson in the 1830's, the neighbouring tribes moved from their ancient home of Metlakatla to take up residence outside the gates of the fort. Thus for twenty years the Tsimshians had been able to observe and learn the daily operations of civilized life, from people whom they held in great respect, yet such an example had apparently made no mark on their own lives. The contrast between life in the fort and in the Indian camp struck the young missionary forcibly. "Here in the Fort steady industry marks the hours from morn till night while forethought ever directs the shortest way to the desired goal: And what is more, hundreds of Indians, in the course of the year, being employed about the Fort come within these regulation; yet in the Camp the people are content with their sloth and all its train of evils."[48]

Indeed, Duncan saw no reason for the Indians to imitate the life of the Hudson's Bay Company, for here was civilization without the gospel. White civilization shaped the exterior of the fort but ungodliness was the rule within. Here was the answer for those who felt that if civilization were disseminated among the heathen, they would cast away their heathenism and adopt the virtues of white men. "I think this instance alone to the contrary is sufficient to explode such an absurdity. No civilization apart from Christianity has no vitality – how then can it impart life? It is the fuel without the fire, how then can it radiate heat? Civilization appears to the eye and to the hand but not to the heart. It may prove the muscles but it cannot reach the hidden springs of life."[49] In Duncan's eyes, the godlessness of the Company not only rendered it unable to civilize the Indians, but by exhibiting such a poor example of Christian civilization, was in fact likely to retard his own civilizing and religious mission. The desire to lessen the influence of the Hudson's Bay Company played no small part in Duncan's decision to move from Fort Simpson and establish a Christian Indian Village at Metlakatla.

The influx of miners into the region, almost immediately after Duncan's establishment at Fort Simpson, made the worst aspects of civilization available to the Indians. Liquor, disease and prostitution had a devastating effect on the native population and strongly influenced Duncan's determination to establish a settlement where not only a greater control could be maintained over converts, but alternative forms of wealth and diversion could be offered to them. A self-supporting industrial village, ruled by Duncan and other Christian missionaries would provide the society necessary for the Christian life. "One effect the mission must have upon the Indian will be to make them desire social improvement. How necessary therefore it is that the Mission be established where social improvement is possible. But at Fort Simpson it is *not* possible."[50]

Duncan soon recognized the difficulties facing his few converts at Fort Simpson. Open to all the temptations offered by their old way of life, they needed also to withstand the taunts and challenges of their fellows, and scattered through the various tribes they could develop no sense of group cohesion which might have helped them to bear their burden. As early as 1859, in reply to an old chief and his sons who had complained about drunkenness in the camp, Duncan mentioned "the probability of some day dividing them. The Good going away to some good land and establishing a village for themselves where they could be free from the drunkenness and the bad ways."[51]

Thus there were pragmatic and immediate reasons for wanting to isolate the native Christians in their own village. But as we have seen, the idea of a Christian self-supporting settlement was by no means novel and was in fact the mode of operation for C.M.S. missionaries in other parts of the world, particularly in West Africa. The Church of England Self-Supporting Village Society had also promulgated similar ideas in England, whilst the idea of Metlakatla bore striking similarities to the cells of civilization advocated by Fowell Buxton for Africa.

Contemporaries also saw Metlakatla as a small utopian movement. "Many, both whites and Indians were ready to ridicule our scheme. They felt sure it was Utopian and could only end in failure."[52] To the extent that it was a gathering of converts into a communitarian society, espousing specific principles of behaviour and attitudes and attempting to find a way to reform the Indian society as a whole, Metlakatla certainly should be considered in the context of utopian movements of the mid-Victorian era.

Lord Dufferin, like other visitors to the settlement, had been most impressed by the secular industrial work undertaken at Metlakatla. Besides developing a large scale program of public works and a thriving trading business, Duncan was constantly searching for new industries to establish in the village. Initially the purpose of the industries was to offer an alternative form of employment and means of gaining wealth to Indians who had previously gone to Victoria and had there been exposed to the evils of liquor and disease. It was in effect a means of physically preserving the Indians and was a necessary concomitant of the policy of isolation.

Duncan, like Venn, was interested in increasing the wealth of the converts so that their capital position might be elevated over that of their heathen counterpart. He realized that the adoption of civilization might tend to impoverish the Indians by "calling for an increased outlay in their expenses without augmenting their income."[53] A Christian Indian needed to clothe, wash and house himself in a civilized manner and this demanded capital which was not generally available to the individual Indian.

In the early days of Christianity, evangelism had been the main means of spreading the gospel, but Duncan pointed out that "the early days can hardly be said to apply to this Mission. The people amongst whom the early Christian Churches were first established were civilized and very differently situated socially and civilly from the poor Indians. Christianity and civilization must go on together. I think and [I mean] . . . to get both fairly established at Metlakatla."[54] He strongly advocated that the missionary should become everything to his converts. The North American Indians in particular "are a race of people found without means or appliances necessary for advancement to civilized life, and whose labours are hunting and who are but barely able to supply their daily needs . . . how can such a people as this if they become Christian be expected ever to maintain their own Church and Schools unless fresh industries are introduced amongst them and markets opened to them for what they can produce."[55] Here again is evident the strong influence of the policies of Henry Venn. The development of native churches necessitated that the body of Christians be self-supporting and financially independent of European help. The C.M.S. reminded those engaged in new missions that "self-support and self-government are far more easily introduced when the first groups of Converts are formed than when the Native Christians have become accustomed to the faulty system of helpless dependence and blind subordination."[56] The sooner a congregation became self-supporting in fact, the sooner the euthanasia of the mission could be effected and the missionary be transferred to other fields.

The industrial establishment at Metlakatla was also useful to Duncan in inculcating the social and moral attitudes desirable in a native Christian. Sabbath observance was strictly enforced and, like Samuel Smiles, Duncan stressed the moral value of honest toil. The influence of the miners was felt to be particularly pernicious for the Indians were "being jostled by rolling stones and reckless gamblers; hence unless we can catch up and utilise their energies and bend their backs to the yoke of steady and profitable industry, they will become at best mere hangers-on among the whites."[57] Duncan was, in fact, creating an environment in which Victorian values of industriousness, thrift and self-help would have relevance and could be systematically taught.

Victorians concerned with the problems of native peoples were generally convinced that cultural change necessitated economic development.[58] The alliance between the Bible and the plough has been seen as the main feature of Canadian policy from the seventeenth century.[59] and there were many Victorian theorists such as Fowell Buxton who advocated this policy. But others, like Venn, saw the possibilities of developing commercial societies, and it was under such influence, and putting to use his own mercantile talents that Duncan chose commerce as an agent of acculturation for the Indians of the North Pacific.

Having left Fort Simpson, there were urgent practical reasons for finding a convenient method of supplying the new settlement with trade goods. By taking control of trade into his own hands, Duncan was able not only to satisfy this need, but to make it an integral part of his civilizing mission. He saw that many of the drawbacks to civilization among the Indians were traceable to the way they were treated by traders and set himself "the task of removing away some of those drawbacks . . . I saw and felt persuaded that intoxicating drink is the bane of the Indian population and the root of nearly all the crime amongst them. Hence I longed to set up a trade in this new settlement in which liquor should find no countenance."[60] Not only would he be able to control the supply of liquor, but he could also determine the type of goods available to the new converts, "ensuring a supply of such things (many which the traders never bring) as their new habits and tastes demand."[61] Within the store Duncan demanded quietness and courtesy and hoped to teach the Indians the just and honest business principles of Victorian England.

Besides having such an important educational function, the village store with its cheap, good quality articles, attracted groups of Indians from surrounding tribes, who thus came into contact with Christianity and religious teachings. By purchasing a schooner for the trade and selling shares in this to the Metlakatla Indians, Duncan aimed to encourage Self-Help and eventually enable them to move into independence. Practically speaking, the most important effect of the trade was its financial success, which enabled Duncan to spend considerable sums of money on "objects conducive to the public benefit, in the erection of public buildings and in subsidies to the people in aid of improving their wharves and canoes."[62]

The fur trade had been long established among the coastal Indians and it was this which became the basis of Duncan's trade at Metlakatla. Following Venn's advice on adaptation to native customs, Duncan also turned to the traditional pursuits of fishing and crafts to find marketable exports. Attempts were made to export kippered, salted and smoked fish and barrels of oolachan oil were sent to the Victoria market. The Tsimshian were reputed to be particularly skilled in the working of metals and wood and, besides exporting numbers of curios, Duncan re-introduced old crafts such as hat-making which might find a market locally or as curios in Victoria. Several Indians were taught coopering so that casks could be made for the export of salt oolachan and salmon; soap making was introduced, the product being mainly for local use to stimulate habits of cleanliness among the Metlakatlans and neighbouring tribes; and the women were encouraged to sew their own clothes and in some cases taught to spin yarn and weave blankets. Such activity aimed to encourage not only industrious habits, but taught thrift, and was to keep the Indians honestly occupied for large parts of the day. Like the school inspectors of England, Duncan also encouraged gardening to develop the forethought and economy that could maintain the independence of the individual that was so highly prized by the Victorians.

On a communal basis, Duncan introduced a saw mill and in later years a salmon cannery. Both were significant in introducing a wage labour system and regular work hours into the settlement, whilst the saw mill was particularly important in providing the means to initiate an ambitious building programme.

Metlakatla was to be a model town which would provide the environment necessary for Christianity and would stimulate others to follow the Metlakatla system. Religious reform in Victorian eyes was inextricably entwined with social and moral regeneration. A man's social condition was seen as a reflection of his moral state, which was itself dependent upon the strength of his religion. Not only would the improvement in dwellings and physical conditions greatly facilitate the moral and religious improvements of the Indians, but the physical appearance of the civilized settlement would provide a significant contrast to that of the Indian camps, and would prove a constant testimony to the effect of Christian religious and moral teachings.

In building the new village Duncan's main concerns, like those of Titus Salt, were order, uniformity, health and morality. At Abeokuta, Kirkham had commented that "the houses are built without any regard to order, nay confusion seems to be studied for you will scarcely find two houses in the same continuous line."[63] He noted too that much of the sickness in the settlement was caused by ill ventilated houses and unsanitary conditions and advised Duncan that "your determined habits of cleanliness would be very useful here."[64] At Metlakatla, order and regularity were most apparent. Formal streets were constructed, and neat rows of identical Indian houses were built according to a rational plan, determined jointly by Duncan and the new converts.

In designing the basic plan for the model houses, Duncan was undoubtedly influenced by the many model dwellings proposed in the 1840's. Perhaps he had seen the Prince Consort's own model apartments for the working classes at the Crystal Palace Exhibition; or perhaps he had been familiar with some of the philanthropic building trusts in London. His aim at Metlakatla was to "combine the accommodation necessary for the Indian as a Christian without offering impediment to his love of hospitality and conflicting with his habits of life."[65] Just as he had incorporated the traditional economic activities of the Indian into the life of the new settlement, so were the house plans adapted to the traditional needs of the Indians. The old communal house, with the extended family living in one room, had provided an important form of social control, and Duncan was faced with the problem of reconciling this with his need to provide the privacy demanded by Victorian morality. The Reverend Edward Cridge noted that though "the houses are after the European model and the habits of the people proportionately improved . . . they have not forsaken the habit of living more than one family in a house, for the sake of fuel and company, they are beginning to build their houses with small apartments at each end and a common room in the centre and thus to reconcile the difficulties of their situation with a due regard to the decencies of life."[66] In an almost romantic manner Duncan also wanted to see the Indians surrounded by all the trappings of the Victorian home. "I wanted to see each house possessed of a stove and have chairs and tables and a clock in it and also see the walls papered and floors well matted, etc."[67]

Education in its broadest sense was the major function of the Metlakatla settlement. As an Evangelical, Duncan was concerned with the teaching of religion through the knowledge and understanding of the word of God. The C.M.S. desired to make Christianity indigenous, and Venn was particularly insistent on the necessity for missionaries learning and transcribing native languages. Working with the British and Foreign Bible Society the C.M.S. had encouraged the translation and publication of the Scriptures in many languages and dialects. Duncan's first task at Fort Simpson had been to master the Tsimshian language and to translate portions of the prayers and the gospels. Besides being trained and sent out as a schoolmaster, the Evangelical's need to teach a convert to read and understand his Bible, would have perforce made formal education a major undertaking for this first missionary to the Tsimshian people.

For many years a Sunday School teacher at Beverley Minster, and trained in pedagogical techniques in the model school attached to Highbury College, Duncan was an enthusiastic and conscientious teacher.

His children's day school at Metlakatla, assembled by the ringing of a school bell, and composed at times of over a hundred children, was redolent of the many schools organised on the Lancaster system both in England and abroad. As in the Lancaster schools children were divided into classes and taught by monitors who were themselves instructed by the master. Duncan noted "I took the first class almost exclusively in the afternoon — because I employ them as teachers in the morning."[68] The monitorial system was well adapted to the problems of instructing large numbers, with no other help, but it also conformed to the C.M.S. aims of encouraging the development of native teachers and evangelists. As in their English counterparts, competition was encouraged among pupils, prizes were given for advancement and the use of slates and tickets for each child was in accordance with Lancaster's practices.[69]

As a Sunday School teacher Duncan had aimed, in teaching others, to "Instruct, Delight, Overcome or bend the will" and this became essentially his approach to the education of the Tsimshian. Discipline was strict and often involved corporal punishment which Duncan defended as being a very ancient mode of correction used frequently by officers of Her Majesty's Navy, and one not entirely obsolete in England. Reading, writing and Scriptural knowledge formed the basis of the curriculum, but a conscious effort was made, particularly in the adult evening school to widen the experience of the Indian and to stimulate his curiosity about a larger world and to attempt to get rid of what Duncan felt to be his superstitious beliefs. Systematic lectures were given on history, geography, and the physical basis of the universe and arithmetic and composition were also taught.

The Metlakatla School however was also to inculcate the attitudes and values desirable in native Christians. Duncan commented proudly on the achievements of his first pupils. "They can sing hymns and are learning God Save the Queen . . . they know the consequences to us of both courses of conduct, bad and good. They have learnt what are the proper expressions in prayer. They can count alone to 100 . . . . They have learnt how to speak in terms of civility to their fellow men and have had several of their ways corrected."[70]

One of the purposes in establishing Metlakatla had been to gather a community whose moral and religious training might render it safe and proper to impart secular instruction. The moral lesson of their secular learning was most important in Duncan's instruction. "After reading and writing lessons were over I gave them a lecture on perseverance illustrating by . . . George Stephenson the great Engineer."[71]

Like Venn, Duncan believed that it was undesirable to separate labour and learning. Industrial training in its most practical form was an integral part of a Metlakatla education. Unless the Christian Indian were taught a useful and profitable trade he would not rise in status above the heathen, nor could he in future contribute to the support of a native Church. If the Christian Indian were "obliged to go back to the Indian mode of getting a living . . . [he would be] little better off than the Indian who have had no such education."[72] So earnest was Duncan to encourage the Victorian habits desirable in Christian converts that he decided in 1872 that only the girls and small boys were to attend the day school. "Let the big boys earn their bread in daylight and come to school at night, will be my rule."[73] Perseverance, industriousness, thrift and Self-Help were to be as important to the Metlakatla Indian as they were to William Duncan.

As in Victorian England the atmosphere of a Christian family home was seen as vital to the education of the Indian child. This was partly why the C.M.S. was insistent upon reaching all generations of natives. Not only were there individual souls to be saved, but men like Venn recognised the value of the influence of Christian parents and saw how difficult it was to isolate one generation within a community. In the training of native pastors, Venn recommended that training be given to the men and their wives not only in Scripture but in Christian habits, "For this purpose an establishment is required rather partaking of the character of a Christian settlement than of a collegiate institution."[74] Such was the settlement at Metlakatla.

To further his aim of producing moral Christian homes, Duncan, like Samuel Crowther at Lagos and many other missionaries of the mid nineteenth century, established a boarding home for young girls at the Mission House. Hoping not only to eliminate some of the promiscuity in the village but to train the girls in domestic pursuits and Christian habits, Duncan tried to create a strict but kindly family atmosphere within the house. The Reverend A.J. Hall noted that "there is a marked contrast between the women who were trained in the Mission house and others. The former are quite domesticated, many of them have clean homes and they exercise a good influence throughout the village. The girls enter the Mission House when about sixteen years of age and remain, if their conduct is good, until they are married. The training of these girls keeps a check upon the young men who are all anxious to obtain a wife from the house and are aware that good conduct is necessary to obtain such a prize."[75] Redolent of the female homes of the Anglican sisterhoods in England, this was one of the most forceful and successful forms of acculturation and one which considerably extended the personal influence and control of the missionary.

The Metlakatla system was all-embracing. Duncan's belief that the missionary should become everything to his people meant that he was concerned with all aspects of their life including their leisure hours. The seasonal nature of the Tsimshian economy meant that traditionally the winter season had been devoted to medicine practices and ceremonial dances. Having eliminated these from Metlakatla, the missionary had to attempt to replace such activities with those considered more conducive to the life of a Christian Indian. Thus, the education of a Metlakatlan included the informal learning of English games such as football. Duncan reported the Indians were delighted. "They had never seen the game before. The village is in two wings east and west. So it was easy to get sides."[76] A playground was built for the children who were also introduced to sack races, and "hunt the hare." The year was punctuated with Christmas and Boxing Day feasts, whilst the Queen's Birthday was always celebrated with canoe races and magic lantern shows. Duncan himself was particularly interested in music, having as a boy been a noted chorister in Beverley Minster. Regular choir practices were held at Metlakatla, and the hymn singing in church was noted by visitors to be most pleasant and hearty. In the 1870's after Duncan's return from a visit to England, a brass band was begun at Metlakatla. It is interesting to note that the "Brass Band" is a peculiarly British institution and one which had its origin and found its most enthusiastic reception in that northeastern part of England from which Duncan came.[77]

As in the north of England, where works bands and village bands flourished, the Metlakatla brass band was an object of pride for the whole group, and served also to constructively utilise the time and energies of the young men.

Community life at Metlakatla as in other utopian ventures had a clearly defined framework and the formal laws were strictly enforced. Liquor, medicine work, gambling, face painting and potlatching must be renounced by all prospective residents. Once established, the new settler must send his children to school, attend all Divine services, settle all quarrels by civil process, pay the village tax, build himself a neat house, cultivate a garden and endeavour to be cleanly, industrious, orderly, peaceful and honest.[78]

All ranks and class had been abolished and each Metlakatlan became equal in the eyes of the law and in the sight of God. In such a context it was almost inevitable that Duncan's authority would become supreme. He was, however, supported by the establishment of a corps of twenty uniformed native constables. With remarkable insight and perhaps influenced by Venn's ideas on the development and civilizing of native societies, Duncan felt that the proper persons for constables in Indian villages were the natives themselves. "The results may not be satisfactory at first but such an office is good training for the natives – tends to enlist their sympathies on the side of the law – is less expensive to the Government and ultimately will afford a better guarantee of the preservation of the peace than if held by white men in their midst."[79]

By becoming a magistrate himself, Duncan was also able effectively to control the lawlessness and liquor trade in the area, which might have threatened the success of Metlakatla. Although the C.M.S. itself did not generally approve of its missionaries taking such posts, there were many and indeed distinguished precedents in English history for the combination of the offices of vicar and justice of the peace. Lacking any legal training, Duncan administered the law in a common sense manner and with a firm sense of justice.

One of the aims of Metlakatla had been to set up the supremacy of the law, teach loyalty to the Queen and conserve the peace of the country, and it was in this aspect that Duncan felt the most striking progress of the Metlakatlans was evident. "From a great number of lawless and hostile hordes, we have gathered out and established one of the most law-abiding and peace loving communities in the province."[80] So vital did he feel this aspect of his work to be, that when advising an American acquaintance on the treatment of the Alaskan natives, Duncan recommended that the missionary be immediately given magisterial powers. "Let him choose a few Indian constables and be occasionally visited and supported by a ship of war and all will go well both for the Indian and the Country too."[81]

Visitors found the internal organization of Metlakatla particularly fascinating. The men of the village were divided into ten companies, each having two constables, a Sunday School teacher and an elected Elder, the latter forming a Native Council. Although unique in the Canadian mission scene at the time, these companies were in fact similar to the classes advocated by Henry Venn in his plans for native church organization. Sunday School work, the explaining and teaching of Scriptural texts, was carried out in the mature years of the settlement, almost entirely by native Christian teachers within each company. The constables were specifically enjoined to be responsible for the conduct of their company members, to promote their industry and improvement and to report annually to the missionary on their progress. This was very similar to the system in practice in Sierra Leone, where to develop native leadership a portion of the Church members were entrusted to the care of a Christian Visitor who was "required to assist the Minister in seeking out every case of sin, want and need and report to him."[82]

Similarly the Native Council at Metlakatla which under Duncan's guidance administered the laws of the settlement, may be compared to the Native Council in Lagos. The Reverend J.A. Lamb noted that the system was most useful for "if any member needs reproof for carelessness or improper behaviour or has been guilty of conduct which requires suspension, the case comes before the meeting for united decision. Thus personal responsibility is thrown off me, and our people are taught to respect their own people when put in a position of authority in the Church."[83] And in such a manner did the Council function at Metlakatla.

Historiographically, Duncan has been seen as a man with exceptional talent and insight into the problems of handling native peoples. There can be no doubt of his ability to understand Indian needs and society, or to lead and control the people. But he was hardly the daring innovator and social theorist that has been portrayed. Following the advice of Henry Venn to study and adapt to the native society, to utilize as much of it as was valuable, to develop leadership, independence and industriousness among his converts, Duncan was moving along a well trodden path. The problems facing the Tsimshian Indians in coping with the impact of white civilization were not unique. Similarly the solutions proposed by their Victorian missionary had their origin in the ideas of men with the same ideals, who had faced similar problems in other parts of the world. For Will Duncan the cultural reference was always London, not Victoria or Ottawa. Metlakatla was not in essence a response to the wilderness or the Canadian frontier, but a systematic attempt to establish a community where Victorian values and ideals could shape the future of the Indians of the North Pacific.

Notes: Duncan of Metlakatla

The major primary sources for the study of William Duncan are to be found in the William Duncan Papers referred to here as WD/C and the Church Missionary Society papers, referred to here as C.M.S./A.

1. WD/C 2156, Reverend G. Mason, *Lo! The poor Indian*: Read before the Mechanics' Literary Institute, Victoria, Oct. 28, 1875.
2. WD/C 2156, Earl of Dufferin, *Speech in Victoria B.C.*, Sept. 20, 1876.
3. J.A.Wike, *The Effect of the Maritime Fur Trade on Northwest Coast Indian Society* (Ph.D. Thesis, Columbia, 1951), 3.
4. W.Duff, *The Indian History of British Columbia*, Vol. I: *The Impact of the White Man* (Victoria: Provincial Museum of Natural History and Anthropology, Memoir No. 5, 1964), 53.
5. V.D.Annakin, *The Missionary, An Agent of Cultural Diffusion* (Ph.D. Thesis, Ohio State University, 1940), 50.
6. R. Gordon Brown, "Missions and Cultural Diffusion," *American Journal of Sociology*, L (Nov., 1944), 214.
7. J.W.Dodds, *The Age of Paradox* (New York: Rinehart and Company Inc., 1952), 348.
8. Asa Briggs, *Victorian People* (London: Odhams Press Ltd., 1954), 137.
9. *Ibid.,* 139.
10. *Ibid.*
11. W.E.Houghton, *The Victorian Frame of Mind* (New Haven: Yale University Press, 1957), 254.
12. David Roberts, *The Victorian Origins of the British Welfare State* (New Haven: Yale University Press, 1960), 88.
13. *Ibid.,* 214.
14. *Ibid.,* 221.
15. A.E.Bestor Jnr., *Backwoods Utopias. The Sectarian and Owenite Phases of Communitarian Socialism in America: 1663-1829* (Philadelphia: University of Pennsylvania Press, 1950), vii-viii.
16. W.H.G.Armytage, *Heavens Below: Utopian Experiments in England, 1560-1960* (London: Routledge and Kegan Paul, 1961), 55.
17. *Ibid.,* 57.
18. Asa Briggs, *Victorian Cities* (London: Odhams Press Ltd., 1963), 71.
19. Armytage, 211.
20. *Ibid.,* 221.
21. Briggs, *Cities,* 70.
22. Many of the Utopian movements of the nineteenth century were derived to some extent from the practices and writings of Robert Owen. The fame of New Lanark was widespread but Owen's atheism did not endear his humanitarian ideas to the Victorian middle class. The ideas of Charles Fourier had less influence in England than in the United States. A major aim of the organization of his phalanxes was to make work enjoyable and attractive. Such ideas were unlikely to find a sympathetic audience in a Victorian England which saw a moral worth in toiling at unenviable tasks.
23. A.F.Young and E.T.Ashton, *British Social Work in the Nineteenth Century* (London: Routledge and Kegan Paul, 1956), 218.
24. W.Knight, *The Missionary Secretariat of Henry Venn B.D.* (London: Longmans, Green and Co., 1880), 305.
25. E.Stock, *A History of the Church Missionary Society* (London: Longmans, Green and Co., 1899), Vol. II, 83.
26. Knight, *Venn,* 210.
27. Henry Venn to the Bishop of Kingston, London, January 1867. Cited in Knight, *Venn,* 216.
28. Knight, *Venn,* 210.
29. Henry Venn, *On National Church-*

es. Cited in Knight, *Venn,* 285.

30. Rufus Anderson, *Foreign Missions: Their Relations and Claims* (New York: Charles Scribner and Company, 1869), 47ff.

31. Henry Venn, *On National Churches.* Second Paper, 1861. Cited in Knight, *Venn,* 312.

32. C.M.S. CA/2L1, Final Instructions to Dr.E.Irving, London, Dec. 23, 1853; cited in J.F.A.Ajayi, *Christian Missions in Nigeria. 1841-1891. The Making of a New Elite* (London: Longmans, Green and Company Ltd., 1965), 81.

33. T.F.Buxton, *The African Slave Trade and its Remedy* (London: 1841).

34. Cited in Ajayi, *Christian Missions,* 7.

35. Peter Hinchcliff, *The Anglican Church in South Africa* (London: Darton, Longman and Todd, 1963), 45.

36. S.M.Johnstone, *Samuel Marsden. A Pioneer of Civilization in the South Seas* (Sydney: Angus and Robertson Ltd., 1932), 71.

37. Henry Venn, *On Nationality*; cited in Knight, *Venn,* 282.

38. Henry Venn, *Memoir on the Character of the Reverend Edward Bickersteth*; cited in Knight, *Venn,* 166.

39. Henry Venn, *Memoir of the Character of the Reverend Edward Bickersteth,* Knight, *Venn,* 166.

40. C.M.S. CA/L2, Instructions of the Parent Committee to Mr.W.Kirkham, Schoolmaster, Jan. 29, 1856; cited in Ajayi, 144.

41. The public library at New Metlakatla, Alaska (Duncan's second settlement) possessed multiple copies of all the works of Samuel Smiles.

42. WD/C2157, Notebook, Apr., 1852.

43. WD/C2157, Notebook, n.d.

44. C.M.S./A124, G. Cussons to the C.M.S., Beverley, Jan. 2, 1866.

45. WD/C2154, Journal, Jan. 16, 1856.

46. WD/C2143, W.Kirkham to Highbury Friends, Lagos, July 19, 1856.

47. P.Curtin, *The Image of Africa. British Ideas and Action, 1780-1850* (Madison: University of Wisconsin Press, 1964), 420.

48. WD/C2154, First Report From Fort Simpson, Journal, Feb., 1858.

49. *Ibid.*

50. C.M.S./A80, William Duncan to the C.M.S., Metlakatla, Oct. 25, 1860.

51. WD/C2154, Journal, June 2, 1859.

52. C.M.S./A81, William Duncan to the Hon. D.Laird, Minister of the Interior, n.p., May, 1875.

53. *Ibid.*

54. WD/C2154, William Duncan to Mrs.W.J.Macdonald, Metlakatla, Sept. 6, 1869.

55. WD/C2154, Journal, Statement in Reference to Metlakatla, n.p., n.d.

56. WD/C2145, The C.M.S. to William Duncan, London, Sept. 8, 1876.

57. WD/C2148, William Duncan to the C.M.S., Metlakatla, Dec. 5, 1871.

58. Curtin, *Image of Africa,* 431.

59. G.F.G.Stanley, "The Indian Background of Canadian History," *Canadian Historical Association Annual Report,* 1952, 14-21.

60. WD/C2144, William Duncan to W.F.Tolmie, Metlakatla, May 9, 1866.

61. WD/C2155, Journal, Aug. 5, 1863.

62. C.M.S./A105, Rev. E.Cridge to the C.M.S., Metlakatla, Sept. 27, 1867.

63. WD/C2143, W.Kirkham to Highbury Friends, Lagos, July 19, 1856.

64. WD/C2143, W.Kirkham to William Duncan, Lagos, Mar. 20, 1856.

65. C.M.S./A81, William Duncan to the C.M.S., Metlakatla, Jan. 29, 1874.

66. C.M.S./A105, Rev. E.Cridge to the C.M.S., Metlakatla, Sept. 27, 1867.

67. WD/C2155, Journal, Nov. 17, 1863.

68. WD/C2155, Journal, Nov. 11, 1867.

69. Joseph Lancaster, *The British System of Education* (Georgetown: Joseph Mulligan, 1812), 58 ff.

70. WD/C2154, Journal, Feb. 18, 1859.

71. WD/C2155, Journal, Dec. 22, 1864.

72. C.M.S./A80, William Duncan to the C.M.S., Fort Simpson, May 14, 1861.

73. WD/C2155, Journal, Oct. 2, 1872.

74. Henry Venn to the Bishop of Kingston, London, Jan., 1867; cited in Knight, *Venn,* 218.

75. C.M.S./A106, Rev. A.J.Hall to the C.M.S., Metlakatla, Mar. 6, 1878.

76. WD/C2155, Journal, Dec. 26, 1864.

77. John F. Russell and J.H.Elliot, *The Brass Band Movement* (London: J.M.Dent and Sons Ltd., 1936). The first brass band contests were held in the 1840's at Burton Constable, twelve miles from Duncan's home.

78. WD/C2158, Notebook, Laws of Metlakatla, Oct. 15, 1862.

79. WD/C2149, William Duncan to the Provincial Secretary, Metlakatla, Jan. 27, 1875.

80. C.M.S./A81, William Duncan to Hon. David Laird, Minister of the Interior, May, 1875.

81. WD/C2154, William Duncan to Mr.N.Colyer, New York, Feb. 28, 1870.

82. WD/C2156, Rev. J.Johnson to the C.M.S., Sierra Leone, Apr. 15, 1869.

83. WD/C2156, Rev. J.A.Lamb to the C.M.S., Lagos, Apr. 17, 1869.

Victorian Canada

W. L. Morton, Trent University

The portrait of the Victorian Age in Canada is not yet to be drawn; the features are too faint, the traits too undetermined. There may, nevertheless, be place for an essay in reconnaissance of the ideas that formed and the sentiments that moved the lives and actions of Canadians between 1837 and 1901; some attempt may be made to state those ideas and take note of those sentiments. Victorian Canada has now receded into perspective; detail has fallen away but main contours are rising into view.

The essential achievement of the Age was that of pioneering – the replacement of wilderness by civilization, forest by field, river by road, a cluster of wigwams by the pattern of towns. Victorian men marched, however, to various tunes, and the ear of the historian must strain to catch the drum beats and bugle calls carried on winds dying out of the past. The most audible and most continuous strain, the re-current motif of Canadian history, is that of the External Ties: Victorian Canada, for all its seeming isolation, no more lived of itself then than Canada to-day.

The second loudest strain was Limited Politics; the state, so far as it existed, was secondary to more compelling pre-occupations – religion, business, and personal freedom. Because the External Ties were two, and because the state was weak and provisional, there were in Canada two nationalisms, British and French, which moved after the 1860's on diverging courses.

Yet there were more cheering, more robust airs shared by both the marching columns. One was the re-assuring idea of Providence, and another, the idea of Progress. Yet another was the Rural Myth, the idea that the basis of welfare and virtue was the land and its cultivation. To British Canadians the Myth was a blend of Arthur Young, William Cobbett, and Thomas Jefferson; to French Canadians, it was an equally odd mixture of rural clericalism and Jean-Jacques Rousseau. Its great strength was that, however traditional its origins, it was justified throughout the era because clearing and breaking land were the occupations of most Canadians. The stone-fenced fields of eastern Ontario, the clearings on the shoulders of the Laurentians reveal how strong the Myth was, and what sweaty labour it confirmed. The clearing and cultivation of the land were the main tasks of Victorian Canada, as they had been those of mediaeval Europe. Thus was Canada made.

The Rural Myth carried with it resentment and envy of the townsman, not a resentment of class, but rather of privilege. The Myth reinforced, therefore, the Age's dogmas of Democracy and Nationalism, but it left no place for the rise or acceptance of proletariat. Most men might vote, all men have the attributes of nation and of class; but the important fact was that all Canadians worked. The landed base of Canadian society was, however, the foundation for a society that defined its own purposes. One was the Pursuit of Respectability, another the Cult of Manliness. These two cults were the principal cultural features of Victorian Canada, the chief expression of a "middle" class that absorbed almost all the former social grades of the maternal societies from which Canadians took their origins.

Yet the chief and central task remained that of the creation of a habitat; the land had to be made livable. From this necessity arose the Canadian fixation on the Pioneer, a belief that the supreme act of history was to be the first, first in the conversion of wilderness to civilization.

Amid so many, the chief trait of the age remained that of the External Ties. There were two, simply because the people of Victorian Canada were British and French; because two languages, English and French, were in use, both privately and publicly; and because each community had different concepts of society and of a society's expression and behaviour – of its civilization.

There was thus in Canada neither a traditional common heritage, as in England and France, nor a fusing ideology, as in the United States. And this duality of cultures was, in the Victorian era, to be underlined and exaggerated by the duality of the External Ties. One was the tie of British Canada with the Empire, and the other, the tie of Canada with the Papacy. The former was to give way after Confederation to the movement for Imperial Federation which inflamed the British character of British Canada; the latter was to provoke, with the unification of Italy as a liberal nation state from 1859 to 1866, that fierce contest of *rouge* and ultramontane from which French Canadian *nationalisme* was to come. One sentiment raised and sent the Canadian 100th Regiment to Gibraltar during the Indian Mutiny; the other raised and sent the French-Canadian Papal Zouaves to Rome when the troops of the Second Empire were withdrawn from guarding of the Papacy. The two nationalisms, British and French , clashed in the Manitoba School Question of 1890, and the clash ended the hope that British and French might find in Confederation, as planned in 1867, a commodious political nationality that would contain and nourish both British and French cultural inheritances.

The hope was by no means an idle one. The French were a North American offshoot of French society, and as community were determined to remain French. As such, they inherited and practised the peculiar trait of the French character that makes the French artisans, indeed artists, of culture. To the French manners, ideas, and aspirations were matters of conscious cultivation and deliberate aim. Descendants of those who had wrought God's deeds and civilized Europe could hardly think otherwise. And by responsible government in the union of the two Canadas they had found the means to be themselves.

The British, it is true, had no such consciousness of culture. Themselves the creation, rather than the creators, of culture, they tended to think of culture as something added to family upbringing and personal decency, as refinement rather than formed behaviour. Moreover, they lacked (being as they were of four national groups, English, Irish, Scots and Welsh, and two religious confessions, one endlessly fragmented) the coherence and the kinship of the French. And they were both interspersed with one another in little communities and widely scattered over great distances. English Canada was therefore socially catholic and individually self-directed, while French Canada was religiously Catholic, and socially self-contained.

Both communities, of course, were exposed to the same environment: both had to struggle with a severe climate and an often gruelling terrain. Both, in consequence, were Canadian, having much in common in their response to a common country. It was this possession and experience of a common environment, rather than the historical accident of the Conquest, that made political union necessary, despite the blood-stained snow of Saint-Eustache and the cold utilitarian arrogance of British superiority, inflamed by Scots and Orange fervour. It was also this that made their fruitful partnership in the great staple trades – and in politics – both necessary and possible.

How intensive the partnership had become any close study of the Union of the Canadas reveals. The decade of the forties, with its elaboration of responsible government, provided the means to place French beside British Canadians in the public service. Place had been made for the rising French middle class. The new political conventions allowed both communities to carry those measures of reconciliation and reform, the Rebellion Losses Act, the creation of the school and local government systems, the abolition of seigneurial tenure and the clergy reserves – the institutions and principles of government each community desired. It was their organic development of a British-French community that made Confederation possible as a means of expansion for a society equipped with complete resources of self-government. Confederation made no fundamental change in Canadian life; it merely opened the way to the wider growth of communities that had already realized themselves.

Because this was so, it was tragic irony that the Imperial and Papal connections should, in their diverse ways, have so guided the lives of thought and heated the emotions of Canadians, both British and French. It would be a nice judgement to decide whether Victoria herself, or Pio Nono, had more lasting influence on Victorian Canada.

The reason for this situation was simply that religion – not wealth, and not politics – was the chief concern, the main ideal occupation of Canadians, both British and French. The Age is indeed to be comprehended only in terms of the idea of Providence, that God and His Church were very present actors in the World. The fact indeed even transcended the differences between French and English. The great gulf actually lay between Catholic and Protestant, and much of the difficulty of co-existence of British and French arose from the Protestant creeds of the former, the Catholic faith of the latter. If the importance of religion in Victorian Canada seems surprising now, it is only necessary to recall that both the great confessions had undergone recent and major revivals. The reaction to the French Revolution had driven conservative Catholic thinkers, led by Joseph de Maistre, to revive the ultramontane spirit of the great ages of the Church. By the beginning of Victoria's reign, ultramontane influences were active in French Canada with the election of Bishop Bourget of Montreal in 1840 and the return of the Jesuits to Canada in 1842. In England, the late eighteenth century had seen the flowering of Methodism outside the Church of England, and the great Evangelical revival within the Church itself, the revival that was to set the moral tone of Victorian life. Even in the Presbyterian Church of Scotland the same evangelical fervour was to lead to the disruption of 1843, and the founding of the Free Church of Scotland. The latter brought to Canada and had as its champion and statesman, George Brown. Religious life in Canada was touched, indeed infused, by all these surges of religious ardour; and in Canada they were if anything more fervid than in Europe. Religion was thus the chief guide of life for most Canadians; it touched all matters from personal conduct to state policy. All politics were indeed sectarian, the explanation of the perfervid spirit of Canadian partisanship; *odium theologicum* was also *odium politicum*; the assured Old Presbyterian in Macdonald could not but dislike the thrusting Free Kirkman in Brown, the *rouge* Laurier distrust the clerical Langevin.

A common element ran through these religious feelings and commotions; the relations of church and state. This was perhaps to be the central issue of Victorian Canada – central certainly, if it was religion rather than nationality which made the relations of British and French Canada so distant in their enforced intimacy.

That it should be vexatious, even if not central, was assured by two things. One was that Canada was a colony, and could not, by an act of revolution, as in the United States, declare Church and State separate as a matter of fundamental law. Both British and French were bound by history to states in which the church was established as a partner of the state, as in England and Scotland, or claimed public equality with the state, as in France. Religion and the church, or churches, could not be declared private and a matter of public indifference.

The other vexing factor was the views held of the place of religion in society by the Canadian churches themselves. The Roman Church in Quebec was at once a missionary church (of which the role was to create a Catholic and French society) and also a domestic, an autochthonous church, or at least clergy (of which the function was to maintain the Catholic faith and a French society in America). The Church of England and Ireland at the beginning of the era, so far as it accepted the lead of Bishop John Strachan, had the mission to provide, as partner of the state which maintained public order, the means and opportunity for public worship, public observance of the place of religion in birth, marriage and death, and for private decency and private charity. So also did the Church of Scotland. Even the dissenting churches, despite their tendency to withdraw from the world, saw religion and its agencies, the congregations of the faithful and their pastors, as the arbitrators of social morals and public conduct.

That a society so religious could be so divided and so tumultuous is an arresting thought. That of men so religious, some could so readily seek to isolate the state from the church is more so. They assumed, however, that the state would be kept Christian by a Christian society. The ultramontane, read in the experience of Europe, had no such easy faith. Nearly all, however, from Catholic ultramontane to Protestant voluntaryist, were at one in assuming the existence, the imperative need, of a Christian society with Christian beliefs and institutions. Only a few, the extreme *rouges* and Grits, contemplated a secular state indifferently serving a society part secular and part Christian. Few but the ultramontanes foresaw – and almost none would have welcomed – the effect of a century of liberal thought, of discoveries by science, and of teaching separated from religion in the common schools.

It was indeed the question of the part of religion in education that prevented the absolute separation of church and state in any of the provinces. The neutral state and the neutral school never quite came to birth in Victorian times. The churches had, after all, been the first patrons and the constant supporters of education, not only in Quebec but in all the other provinces – the education of the laity as well as of the clergy. The state was a latecomer to the field, and was often not welcome because it was suspected of not being neutral. As it moved more resolutely into the area, it found itself occupying a position already partly held by the churches. It had therefore either to co-operate with the churches or to replace them. And in the middle of the century neutrality was not desired. It is instructive that the first Superintendent of Education in Upper Canada was a clergyman, as was the second, Egerton Ryerson and that in Quebec and Newfoundland the schools remained confessional, that in the other provinces, they were "separate" with religious teaching, or allowed religious exercises and even time for religious teaching. The ghost of religion was never completely exorcized from the school. Not until the last decade of the age were politicians to appear who willed the exclusion of religion from the school desired – when Joseph Martin and Clifford Sifton drafted the Manitoba School Act of 1890.

Where the separation was made, it was done in the name of the "common" schools, which were in fact necessary for economy, and not in the name of the separation of church and state. The truth was that the "state" in Canada was not dominant, and neither was it ideological: it was a practical convenience, not an expression of the community; the schools were the community's and jealously cherished as such. Thus it was that all Canadian politics were sectarian politics. Church and state could not really be separated because religion dominated the state.

Nor was politics subordinate only to religion, it was secondary in addition to the economic activities of the community. It was, in short, the Limited State. This limited and subordinate character of government became one of the main traits of Victorian life: a belief that politics was an agency of social interests; that its functions were derivative, not original; and that the discharge of its responsibilities could be left to secondary people, in particular, to country lawyers. As Elgin remarked, "public life is ruin to men in these Countries."[1] It is interesting to observe that the one considerable political discussion in Canada, that on the federation of British North America (which rivals the Federalist papers in its perception) was conducted very largely by men who were not politicians. Thus was prepared a shoddy legacy for the next century, when the return to the positive welfare state was made without the supremacy of politics and the service of first class men necessary to that new order.

Nor did politics suffer only from the usual consequences of the negative, liberal state. Victorian politics also failed to become completely responsible, sophisticated and mature. (The outstanding quality of the Victorian, John A. Macdonald, was that he was all those things.) The reasons were evident. One was the British connection. It was true that the colonies had had for two generations self-government in abundant measure for small and provincial communities. And when this measure was increased by "responsible government" in the 1840's, it was at least as much thrust upon the colonies by an impatient and distracted mother country as struggled for by petulant and demanding children. The second reason was American influence. This had been powerful, indeed fundamental, down to 1837, for the old colonial governments were basically the same as those of the revolted colonies and as those of the independent states. They were made British by degrees after 1830. But the new conventions, such as cabinet government, were still operated by men used to the old forms. Much of the customs and practices of that old American system remained, to be reinforced by the constant example of the vigorous society near-by. Canadian political practice, then, became British in dress but remained American in spirit, as in matters of patronage and in the provision of chairs and desks instead of benches for legislative chambers. Canadian politics of the Victorian age were very like Canadian football of the present; politicians could play by British or American rules with little difficulty.

None the less, the great political decision of Canadian politics in the Victorian Age was not to confederate but to be British rather than American. The decision was made at bottom in the crushing of the rebellions of 1837, and in the Colonial Office's resolution to give Canada, as Simcoe had not, a "very image and transcript" of the British constitution, the most efficient, modern and prestigious of the day. Nowhere is this decision seen more clearly than on the career of John A. Macdonald, an apt student of British political life, the eager and unabashed pupil of the younger Pitt and the impressive Peel. Steadily, year after year for nearly fifty years in Victorian politics, Macdonald moulded the usages and the spirit of Canadian political practices in British forms, even to the extent of creating in Canada a living and powerful Treasury Board on the British model, a model which existed in name only! In Victorian Canada, the Canadian imitation often outdid the British imitated.

Less superficial was the parallel response to the same needs, rather than the conscious following of established forms, by the legislation of the colonies and of Confederation. The development of Canadian politics was not only a following of British precedent; it was also a study and clarification of British current practice. What was the institution of responsible government, after all, but a revelation of the nature of cabinet government in England, one that preceded by a quarter of a century Bagelot's brilliant essay, published in Confederation's year, 1867? And the winning of responsible government has been allowed to hide the fact that the more important British novelty was not cabinet government but utilitarian legislation.

Canada had no Edwin Chadwick but rather had scores of his disciples. Just as the needs of British society in the Victorian Age produced new technologies, new professions,[2] new modes and agencies of government, general and local – so the needs of the fantastically rapid growth of Canadian society produced a profound change in the purposes and behaviour of government. Philosophers and economists might propound, and business-men and politicians accept, the utility and moral value of *laissez-faire* and Limited State, but the steady drift of legislation and action was against such surface waves. Even responsible government itself, so much an academic exercise in itself, meant more government; for it was preceded by, and based upon, the development of rationally organized departments of government. The creation of the school systems was a massive interference by the state with one of the most basic and most cherished of human rights, the right of parents to determine the education of their children. The new systems of local government were acclaimed as an advance of democracy, but they meant in fact more action by government, more services, more taxes. The poor and the mentally ill claimed the benevolent thought and action of the government even in the Victorian hey-day of the 1850's. A Civil Service was created by the legislation in 1857, three years after the introduction of competitive examinations in England. It might take Canada sixty years to complete the same advance, but the legislation was enough to make it clear that the positive state must be a rational organization acting through a bureaucracy of qualified persons appointed for life. The growth of cities and of manufacturing only accelerated the swelling of the utilitarian state beneath the eighteenth crust of political patronage and minimial state action.

The growth of the positive, powerful state, however, was still only a minor current in the stagnant waters of a liberal society. It was fully under-stood, and clearly enunciated in Victorian Canada that the business of politics was to set men free, and leave them free – however convenient an aid it might be in railway construction or by tariffs – to pursue the great ends of life, the exploitation of resources and the increase of capital. No-where in the world, not even the United States, was the supremacy of economics more clearly understood, or more religiously upheld. The pure doctrine of Adam Smith was subscribed to by practical men and thinkers alike, challenged neither by religious nor positivist utopians, nor by intellec-tuals, and not even by the advocates of tariff protection. A doubting intellec-tual like the poet Archibald Lampson might touch on his qualms, but a radical bard like Archibald Maclachan could assert nothing more daring than "Jack is as good as his master"[3] – mere radical democracy hostile to privilege but not to individualism or the Limited State. Even the caution the British Canadian inherited from his ancestors, even the peasant conserva-tion of the rural society of Quebec, did not challenge the fundamentals of classical economics or even of liberal society.

Central to this acceptance of autonomous interests, of the belief that competing individuals co-operate to produce general welfare, was the Idea of Progress. This was the on-going idea thrown off by the Enlightenment, the assurance that the individual, if left free of controls based on fear and superstition, would reveal an unspoiled goodness and develop a better social order. In Victorian Canada there was little disposition to assume that such progress came only from a natural but perverted goodness that once freed would of itself better man and society. The iron teachings of its churches forebade any such easy optimism. There remained a large and central place for self-discipline and self-help both by traditional rites or by self-improvement. Indeed, those popular doctrines might even redeem the heathen, as William Duncan demonstrated at Metlakatla.[4] Providence and Progress went hand in hand in Canada. The intellectual optimism of the Enlightenment and the cautious hope of the creeds were thus pragmatically reconciled; all the evidence of daily life – the forests felled, the fields cleared, the roads made and the canals dug – lay before men's eyes as emphatic evidence of progress. Moral progress and material, none could doubt, advanced together.

Such was the essence of the liberal creed in Victorian era, the creed of men like A.A. Dorion and Alexander Mackenzie, men who combined active membership in their respective churches with liberal optimism, and saw themselves justified by professional and business success. Man liberated was man progressing.

The liberal creed, however, was to be drastically challenged in the third quarter of the century by the ultramontane beliefs of the Catholic bishops of Montreal and Three Rivers, the Roman prelate Bourget, the missionary priest Laflêche. At first sight this seems to have been a powerful and clear-sighted challenge of the whole liberal creed of secular redemption in a free society nourished by science. So indeed it was. But as a controversy it was a challenge by the church to the power of the state. It was, in modern terms and over current issues, the mediaeval conflict of the swords spiritual and temporal, rather than the concussion of incompatible creeds. What was at issue was not what kind of society man should inhabit, or what destiny he should move toward, but what counsellors should guide him, ultramontane priests or liberal politicians. At bottom, both accepted the Idea, or at least the reality, of Progress. The ultramontane protested only that progress was not, and could not be enough of itself to satisfy man's nature, the liberals only that men must have freedom sufficient to allow them to judge themselves what was enough.

That this grapple for power was actually another instance of the subordination of politics in Canada – to theology, in this instance – is revealed by a glance at still another aspect of the Idea of Progress, one particularly affirmed by Canadian experience. That was the concept of the conquest of nature. To the Canadian this meant replacing forest by field, turning rapids by canals, diminishing distance by railway, bridging the St. Lawrence with the engineering science of Robert Stephenson. Nothing in this concept was inacceptable to the ultramontane, still less to French Canadians. The arrogance of the phrase was, of course, repugnant to the Christian temper.

Only to the agnostic intellectual was nature brute and antagonistic. It was, to the believer, part of God's universe in which man was to prove himself, partly by learning its mysteries.

It was indeed, not at the level of appreciation of progress wrought by science that French and English Canadians differed; in that they were pretty much at one. It was on the level of culture, or rather, cultivation, that they diverged. The point was made concrete by the differing characters of the *Institut canadien* and the Canadian Institute, founded in 1847 and 1849 respectively; and for the same general purposes, the extension of knowledge. But the *Institut* became at once an assembly of professional men and lovers of literature, philosophical and political, and a focus of radical political thought. The Institute, on the contrary, was founded by practical men, engineers, surveyors, architects, John Stoughton Dennis, F.W. Cumberland, Sandford Fleming. Its concern was with science, technology and the useful arts. When it widened its scope on re-organization in 1851, it was into related fields like archaeology and history, specific history, such as the history of the horse. Politics was ignored. Its principal aim is revealed in its President's, W.E. Logan, geological survey of the western peninsula of Ontario in 1854,[5] followed by the oil strike and rush of 1857. The *Institut* on the one hand provoked the outpourings of ultramontane wrath; the Institute on the other hand set running the oil wells of Petrolea, oil which might well have smoothed the stormy waters of Lower Canada.

The difference between the French and English American subjects of Victoria, however, could not have been removed by the oil wells' being in Lower rather than in Upper Canada. French Canadian society was in the Latin mould, Catholic, classical, ideological. Its better minds went into the professions, not into business. And the Conquest had deprived this society of most of the external stimuli by which a colonial society is galvanized. French Canadian society was, until the 1840's and the return from exile of Papineau, isolated. It was up to that decade engaged in survival, an endeavour carried out by the sacrifice of intellectual daring and general enterprise. A society doubtful of survival could not give much effort to progress. The return of Papineau broke this trauma. The Second Empire of Louis Napoleon and the threat to the Papacy once more involved French Canada in the affairs of the world. But the involvement was ideological and the cult of survival remained dominant in Quebec for the remainder of the Victorian era. Combined with the Latin cast of thought, it prevented French Canada from overtaking English Canada in the acceptance of the Idea of Progress until 1960.

The instinct of survival, moreover, by its very nature was defensive. British Canadians as members of a brilliant and confident Empire which still led the world in industry and science, which could send the *Great Eastern*, the world's largest iron steamship, with troops to Quebec in 1861, whose engineers and navies had built the Grand Trunk Railway and the Victoria Bridge at Montreal, could be less cautious, and were indeed confident and aggressive. Their dominant cult, the general popular attitude, can only be termed the Cult of Manliness. The assertion of British character, constantly incited by the proximity and flamboyance of the United States, the pioneer drive and the engineering power released in canal and railway building; the Protestant temper kept burning by the political union with French Canada and the French Catholic pressure for separate schools in Ontario, the garrison and ascendancy mentality brought by the Orange lodges from Ireland, the public dogma of physical courage and self-defence; all these combined to produce a moral temper and a code of conduct that made the Victorian British Canadian a highly masculine, athletic, outdoor man, independent of mind and trained in the habit of authority. In men like Frank Rhodes, the mighty hunter of Quebec and George T. Denison, the soldier-author of Toronto, the type was fulfilled; in others it existed in lesser degrees, but it was a dominant stereotype in Victorian British Canada.

In that Canada, accordingly, the ground was laid for sharing the social temper produced by Darwin's theory of evolution. This curious distillation of statistics and competitive struggle appealed at once to the Victorian mind, intoxicated with the strange fantasies of the new science of statistics and prepared by its upbringing to accept the idea that struggle was a fit determinant of survival. Victorian Canada, too, was to be touched by the crudities of Social Darwinism, but was saved from the worst excesses by its continuing religious habits, by its preoccupation with internal expansion and social formation rather than imperial aggression and class struggle. Thus the Cult of Manliness and the spirit of Social Darwinism, channelled into Imperial Federation, were turned against Catholic and ultramontane Quebec in the feverish last two decades of the Age, rather than against the proletariat, or against any external foe – except the unhappy Boers, whom the Canadian volunteers would have understood readily enough at closer than Lee-Enfield range.

In the Cult of Manliness is apparent one expression of two other ideas, perhaps the most prevailing and influential of the age, Democracy and Nationalism. Manliness was simply the expression of the drive to prove oneself in an individualistic and competitive society, and to do so with some style and *éclat*. The style was necessarily in that age drawn from the Idea of Nationalism, the belief that common language and common institutions created – or sprang from – a kinship of mind, a shared set of assumptions and manners, a collective loyalty to defined ideals. Here again British and French differed, the British by stressing the competitive and the material, and the French, the collective and the cultural. In both communities, however, the two ideas were powerful within the biases of each community.

Democracy was, of course, a mid-Victorian and even a late Victorian gospel. It had little part in the coming of responsible government which simply transferred from appointed office holders, British and Canadian, to Canadian middle class professionals and businessmen the power to govern the colonies in domestic matters. It had itself nothing to do with democracy, but only with representative government.

The secular Cult of Democracy, indeed, came into Canadian life by side and often secret entrances. The idea itself was at mid-century abhorred as a particularly repulsive aspect of American ideology, upheld by a few extremists, the more pronounced *rouges* of Canada East and Clear Grits of Canada West. It came rather in nationalistic, or sectional guise, as in the demand for representation by population, and some of the opposition to rep. by pop. derived from fear of its inherent democratic bent.

There was indeed no demand for the extension of the franchise itself until the 1880's. The reason was that the wide, almost universal dispersion of landed property already enfranchised the great majority of Canadian males, and might easily enfranchise the remainder. When Canada indeed adopted a wider franchise, it was at the lead of a Conservative government and after the great extension of the English franchise by Gladstone in 1884. The measure was at bottom a manoeuvre by Macdonald, the shrewd forestaller of the Grits, to check the tendency already strong in the province to put the franchise on the democratic principle of one man, one vote. The Dominion Franchise Act of 1885 kept property franchises, but they were almost as fragile as Disraeli's unfortunate fancy franchises.

Much more significant was the temper of the growing democracy of the last quarter of the century. Suppressed by the Liberal-Conservative coalition from 1854, smothered by the broadened coalition that carried Confederation, the democratic principle had, except for the sparse reforms of the bleak Mackenzie régime, to find expression in the provinces. Here it did so from the New Brunswick School Act of 1871 and the abolition of dual representation in Ontario in 1872 until the Liberal accession to federal power in 1896. The temper of this provincial, sectional, sectarian democracy was parsimonious in finance, mean in its concept of public interest, hostile to style and elegance in either life or the arts. Mean in its aims, it was mean in all it did. Lavish only in its parsimoniousness, it was ungenerous, though liberal, and intolerant, though boastful of freedom. It was ungenerous because its sectarian bases gave it assurance of righteousness and intolerant because it believed its power came from the sovereign people. Its character was betrayed by the lack of libraries in the Canadian provinces, the studious depression of the arts, and even of joy itself, in Canadian life. Its character is betrayed finally in the shabby little churches, in which God perforce died, through the Eastern Townships and across Ontario and the West. More evident, though less important, was its persistent and concerted undermining of the original national constitution of Confederation until it was converted into a federal state as near republican the American model as possible, and rested on provinces made sovereign by the democratic idea. One man, one vote had become one province, one sovereign state.

The *rouges* in Quebec escaped the principled meanness of the Grits, and were never themselves able to obtain power except in alliance with extreme conservatives and ultramontanes. One result was that they produced a man of cultivation and magnanimity in Wilfrid Laurier. Another was they prepared that combination of democrats and theocrats, resting on the basis of provincial democracy, which was under Honoré Mercier ended the régime of LaFontaine – Cartier moderate conservatism in Quebec. This was the *nationalisme* of the next century – ethnic, cultural, democratic.

These different outcomes of the democratic idea among French and English explain the different character of their nationalism. English Canadians thought their nationality to be British, much as the French thought theirs French. To the former, however, nationality was a matter of sentiment and allegiance. To the latter, it was a matter of birthright and culture. The effect of democracy was to make the one open and assimilative, the other closed, except by marriage. The democratic idea in Canada therefore, by its insistence on being of the people, impaired the readiness of both English and French to accept the idea of nationality proclaimed at Confederation, a political nationality based on common political institutions and not on sentiment, language, or kinship.

The sense of kinship was, however, exceedingly strong among Canadians, and not only those of French descent. The family was for all the centre of life a place not only sanctioned by religion but required by economic necessity. Marriage was a religious before it was a civil ceremony; divorce was rare and scandalous, paternal authority was unquestioned and maternal influence great and usually decisive. The family were therefore still the focus of duty, and more often than not of affection. It was the chief influence in moral education, and an economic unit of the first importance. Children were engendered and reared not only in love, but for their labour. Particularly was this true of farming families, the major part of the population in all the colonies but Newfoundland. This need of children for farm work, and then of land for the young folk when they themselves married, was in fact the basic dynamic of Canadian life in the Victorian Age. From it came that expansion both into the West and into industry of which Confederation was the political agent.

So important, Canadian family life can be known only scantily by its external features. No Canadian novel of the time adequately depicts its internal life. The hints from private letters and diaries, as yet so little published, are few and scattered. George Brown's letters to his wife, Egerton Ryerson's to his daughter, Antoine Gérin-Lajoie's *Jean Rivard le défricheur,* are examples of the sparse, if revealing evidence.

The family, then was private, but much of its quality was evident in external aspects of social life, the festivities, the sports, the social pastimes. The Canadian festival year ended with Christmas and began with New Year. Christmas was still a religious and a family holy-day, predominantly the former in French Canada. The Catholic Irish and the Presbyterian Scots and Ustermen seem not to have given Christmas the same reverence; the sterner Presbyterians of course rejected it as popish. As a family festival, then it was still an English, a Dickensian affair, with stockings at the mantel-piece, perhaps a Yule log, mistletoe, plum pudding and much cheer. The German-American Christmas of St. Nicholas and Christmas trees was only beginning towards the end of the Age to influence Canadian custom. In this private and intimate festival the strong British influence on the Con-federation and post-Confederation generation may be seen.

New Year's Day was rather the day of the French and the Scots, although all Canadians were moving towards the later practice of two equal celebrations. The governor's New Year's levée, taken over from the French régime, was in Quebec, Ottawa and Manitoba a day of calls on his Excellency. The New Year's call, made by gentlemen and received by ladies, was a widespread social habit among the well-to-do. With these and with the less prosperous a great deal of the riot of the Scottish Haugmannay continued and became general among the population, well-to-do and not so well. The two great feasts were of the first importance in creating social ties among the various elements of the population, and the two festivals a punctuation of the great psychological stress of the long Canadian winters when travel was hazardous and difficult, and young and old, and the women, were housebound much of the time.

The festivals broke the winter for such. For the more vigorous, how-ever, winter was eagerly seized opportunity for sport. Sleigh-riding was not only a necessity of travel, it could in parties in a bob-sleigh, or in couples in a cutter, be made a pleasure, whether rowdy, as when youngsters sleighed in dozens, or decorous, when a sober citizen drove his wife, or a young officer his "muffin" (girl friend) in a cutter on the streets or on the smooth snow of the frozen rivers. Ponds and lakes made curling from at least the 1840's a pastime of adult men, skating a pursuit of both young and old, and both sexes; ice hockey from the 1880's the sport – the most Canadian of sports – of the boys and young men. Quieter, but not less strenuous, was snow-shoeing for sport, a natural – as ski-ing was not – Canadian pastime brought out of the woods from the trapline.

Nor was the summer less enjoyable. Public holidays such as the Queen's Birthday, on the twenty-fourth of May, or *la fête de Saint-Jean-Baptiste*, on the twenty-fourth of June, or, as the age waxed, Dominion Day, were celebrated with fireworks, parades in the streets, and "pic-nics" in parks by lakes and rivers. And the religious banners and panache of Saint-Jean-Baptiste was matched by the throbbing of the drums on the Glorious Twelfth of July, when the Orangemen walked in memory of King

William and the Boyne. These lusty expressions of ancestral memories betrayed the uncut umbilical cords of Canada, the British, the Roman and the Protestant ties. But they also, by becoming familiar and festive rather than commemorative, did something to unite as well as divide.

For private pleasure, there were rowing, canoeing, sailing on the many waters. Among Canadian oarsmen, the peerless Edward Hanlan advanced to the championship of the world from 1880 to 1884. Here and there, out from the growing cities, there were the beginnings of the summer vacations. Farmers were going into the Muskoka county and the Laurentides in the 1850's, and summer cottages followed. The cooler summer of the lower St. Lawrence had long been known, especially to salmon fishermen, as were the Miramichi and the Restigouche, and Prince Edward Island had drawn summer holidayers to the cool waters of the Gulf before the Fathers of Confederation made their memorable September jaunt in 1864.

With fall came the hunting season for waterfowl, partridge and wood pigeons. Indeed, shooting was a year round sport for country dwellers, not yet made seasonal to preserve the birds and keep some for city folks. Later came the deer and moose hunting in the sombre woods of New Brunswick, and the lone lakes of the Shield. In this as in the summer vacation, Canadians were re-immersed in the perpetual wilderness of the country's rugged hinterland, the wilderness they were so busily converting to field and road and town in the river valleys and the great Ontario peninsula. It was timeless, daring land, and these sports lay at the root of the Cult of Manliness.

In that cult also was escape from the sometimes heavy burden of the formal social rites of the age, rites the well-to-do had to observe, and from which the less respectable escaped only by rites almost as demanding if much less formal. Church-going, weddings, funerals, banquets public and private, were governed by elaborate and costly conventions. And the chivaris, the barn-raisings, the wakes, and the drinking sprees at the end of the timber runs, were even more personally and socially demanding than their respectable counterparts. Even abstention from ostentation in dissipation, practised by a growing number of Canadians as sectarian fervour became more respectable and grim with the passing of the Age, and as the transformation of grace into respectability went on, was even more demanding.

Common to all these social rites, even in the alleviated form of sherry at respectable funerals, was the use of wine, beer and spirits. Canadians of all stocks had inherited from their ancestors an uninhibited use of drink. But the inheritance had been greatly increased by the plentiful supply of cheap rum from the West Indies in the Atlantic provinces and cheap *whiskey blanc* and rye in the Canadian. The effect of lack of transport in leading to the distilling of grain to increase sales and decrease transport costs, added to the weight of the legacy. It was one thing to drink wine and beer freely, quite another to be equally free with cheap and potent spirits. Canadians were in general heavy drinkers, a trait perhaps increased among the less well-to-do by their grinding labour in the bush, or at sea, by the exacting heat of summer and cold of winter, by the gravity and dourness of their social and religious life. Certainly it was increased by Canadian drinking habits; spirits were often drunk neat, and the treating habit at the bars made the practice often disastrous. Like their Indian brethren, all too many Canadians drank, not regularly for a mild stimulus, but in bouts to get drunk.

The drunkenness, the wild battles, the absences from work, and the wife-beating to which such intemperance led among the rougher sort of course provoked its opposite, as it did in Great Britain and the United States. It did so even in French Canada and among the Catholic Irish, where cultural traditions might have been expected to lead to greater differences of behaviour. The land and its customs were again making for an unconscious uniformity of attitudes. By the 1840's there were strong temperance movements in all the provinces. The great drive to impose temperance by law as well as precept had set that current running which was to affect the legislation of the provinces and distort the constitution of Confederation, and in the next century was to bring women into politics and prohibition to North America. Formidable indeed was the geni which emerged from the demi-john of rye, and great as the evil wrought by the Demon Rum, as great at least was wrought by his opponents in the disrespect for law and temperance that resulted from prohibition.

*   *   *

Historians of Canada are only beginning to discuss the place of class in Canadian history, and have been criticized for not doing so.[6] The criticism would have puzzled Victorian Canadians. They were well aware of class, indeed took it for granted. What they did not include in their thinking was the concept of class conflict. Marxist thought did not penetrate to Canada until near the end of Victoria's reign, and then seemed alien to Canadian thought and experience.

The reasons for this seeming indifference to class are probably simple enough. The foundation of the outlook of many Canadians, and certainly of the conservative, was the older view that society by its nature required rank and subordination. Class, that is, was an inevitable part of social order. The result, however, in a free and constitutionally governed society, was not class conflict but social harmony. That society was more likely to be seen in this way from the top than from the bottom was shown by the rebellions of 1837, which were social to some degree as well as political and economic, and by the moderating effects produced by the coming of responsible government. By the 1850's champions of the old Tory view of society had fallen silent much through that concept, sustained by the Imperial connection and the presence of British garrisons to 1907, continued to be cherished and privately practised. Canadian girls married British officers, Canadian young men were confirmed in their devotion to the gentlemanly code of rank and honour.

It was not at once replaced by a professedly democratic regime, still less by avowed class conflict. The churches continued to play their unifying role across class divisions and the growth of towns and individual wealth made for social stability and transmitted respectability. But the releasing of the last areas of land for settlement and the annexation of the West, together with the beginnings of industry, increased the dissolution of class structure, the erosion of rank and subordination, that the economic opportunities of North America, as well as the growth of democratic ideals in the United States and the British Isles, had always caused. The Victorian Age saw the sweeping away of the last barriers to the flood of land occupation, economic growth and class fluidity. The flood now ran unvexed to its fulfilment in the highly mobile society of the first half of the twentieth century.

Class structure and class conflict were, however, no prominent part of Victorian Canadian thinking. There was social order, there was even social structure, but it was not fixed in a country of no great fortunes, no great families, few public honours. What there was of class were, first, the respectable and well-to-do, then those who aspired to respectability, and finally those who did not, by choice or through indifference. Every community had its élite of professional and prosperous men, its middle class of small merchants and artisans; its "working" people, hired hands, hired men and hired girls. There were wide areas of rural poverty, and sometimes squalid misery, in the north reaches of the Pre-Cambrian counties of eastern Ontario, the North Shore of New Brunswick, the new parishes in the Laurentides and the Gaspé. There was the numerous proletariat of the canal and railway navies, and of the lumber camps, of the fishing outports of the Atlantic provinces.

None of this was fixed, however, except in the rural areas where poverty was so deep as to prevent removal, or in the outports where debt and habit bound the fisherman in peonage. But respectability waxed and waned over the generations. Comparatively rare were the families like the Papineaus, the Chipmans, the Robinsons, and Lotbinières, the Macaulays, the Mac-Nutts, to name only some, that continued not only to be respectable but generally known to be so. And families could arise, like the Masseys, the Booths, the Siftons, from simple origins. The working people, except for the fugitive proletariat from Quebec in Massachusetts, could hope to rise as foremen and contractors, or take their wages to establish themselves on new, cheap land, as many did. Many indeed were sons of farmers earning wages they could not win at home. It would be absurd to imply that the mass of them escaped poverty after an industrious youth. Many did not, and many died in the breaking of log jams and the blasting of railway cuttings; many became permanent labourers, alternating between the Spartan life of the lumber camp and the "drunk" in riverside taverns. The point is that they did not think of themselves as a fixed element in society, permanently dispossessed. They were, in short, often exploited; they suffered social and economic injustice from which they had little protection in law or through union organization, but they did not think themselves a proletariat. No more than the respectable and the well-to-do, did they think in terms of class and class struggle until the second generation of the Age, and then only some of them, the new industrial workers and members of the first labour unions, especially the Knight of Labour. The union, moreover, not only recognized the working class as a fact of social life, they created in Canada that very Victorian thing, the working class mentality.

To be able to know what people really thought – or precisely, assumed – about the society in which they lived, one must be able to state their social ideals. Victorian Canadians certainly did not think of social or economic equality; they possessed no utopians and few ideologues. They had perhaps three such ideals, that of the gentlemen, respectable, industrious, well bred and well read; the honest businessman and honest worker; the prosperous farmer. The common element was that of respectability, the possession and evidence of those personal and social traits that were generally commended. These ideals left room for injustice and for its resentment, but they were open to all, they were not competitive or exclusive, and they took little account of class conflict, or class envy. It was the prevalence of these ideals, and the economic opportunity to realize this, that account for the absence of "class" in Victorian Canadian society, and for the Canadian distrust of concept of class war as something "unCanadian."

That there should be a feeling that something was not Canadian implies a feeling of what it was to be Canadian. What was there, one may ask, of private or public expressions in areas other than political behaviour or social prejudice, in the arts and letters, for example, that was Canadian? That theme in Victorian Canada was, even more than in other aspects of its life, derivative and colonial is not of great importance. That a colonial society should be derivative in its style, mind and taste was only to be expected. Indeed, the need of a new country was not to be original but to prove the old possible in the new, to re-affirm accepted modes in new conditions. The task was not creative, but re-creative.

Canadians of course did participate during the Victorian era fully in the thought and action of the world. Its newspapers from the first brought to the literate something, and by the end of the era, nearly all that was of current importance. The reporting of political debates and the wars was full and detailed. And periodicals were stocked by the booksellers and widely read from the beginning of the thirties.[7] In particular, British Canadian readers were kept abreast with British thought by two New York papers, the *Albion* and the *New York Spectator*[8] and Canadian writers not only initiated the poetry and novels of the day, they published periodicals of intellectual interest and not inconsiderable lengths of life. The *Canadian Journal* of the Canadian Institute in the 1850's, the *British American Magazine* in the early 1860's, the *Canadian National Magazine,* of the 1880's revealed a capacity for literary discourse that befitted men of the world.

In the world of action the Victorian Canadian also easily transcended the limits of Canada. George T. Denison winning the Czar's prize for a text book on cavalry tactics is perhaps the more surprising, and his account of the difficulty of collecting the prize money in St. Petersburg as good a description as any of Russian bureaucracy in that age.[9] Fenwick Williams defending Kars in the Crimean War, A.R. Dunn charging with the Light Brigade at Balaclava, and emerging a live hero to receive the Victoria Cross,[10] the boatmen with Wolseley on the Nile, are known examples of such immersion in the world of which Canada was a part. The return of Louis-Joseph Papineau from his Parisian exile brought French liberal thought into the bloodstream of French Canada to transform the intellectual tenor of its life. So also is the Pickswicksian scene of the Fathers of Confederation on the road to Epsom Downs on Derby Day; the suggestive but unannotated attendance of John A. Macdonald at London play entitled "The Strike." In the high noon of Victoria's reign Canadians, not yet committed by Confederation to the occupation of their own West, were easy and accustomed members of the world civilization of Western Europe.

It is indeed surprising that Canada was as distinctive and original as it was, surprising both because it sought to be neither, and also because a country still clearing land and building cities should have the energy and resolution to found educational systems and cultivate at all the arts and letters. The truth was, however, that Canada, like other colonial societies between 1814 and 1914, passed with great speed, usually in less than a generation, from wilderness to fully-equipped communities, often the better equipped for being new. The equipment, it is true, was often more material than intellectual, more organized than cultivated. Yet there was no community that had not some knowledge of and contact with the chief ideas and main currents of sentiment and taste in the great world. The actual enemies were those any community not metropolitan but provincial suffered, distance and diffusion. Only a metropolitan community can have that concentration of talents and exchange of ideas which make possible any considerable performance in literature or the arts.

The true criterion of achievement of the Victorian Age is thus not really the comparative performance of Canadian writers and artists with those of France, England, or the United States. It is not even the judgment of them in their own terms. It is to measure the degree to which the prevalent ideas of the Age, the main styles, the currents of thought, were active in Victorian society, were indeed imposed upon, not drawn from that experience. For the original and creative work of Victorian Canada was not to invent, but to apply, not to bring forth new things, but to make old, and contemporary things, live and move in new conditions.

On this point of view is taken, then the Canadian achievement is considerable, indeed surprising. That for example, the main styles and fashions in architecture from the Georgian to the Victorian electic should have flowered, sometimes to excellent effect, was in itself a major triumph. That painting and sculpture should have been representational, as in Kreighof, was only contemporary; domestic as in Harris, was only because the respectable family was the vital organism of Canadian society, romantic, as in Hébert, because the romantic was contemporary reaction to the past, picturesque, as in Kane, or William Hind, because the artist saw that a primitive and disappearing way of life was to be caught only in his time. That Canadian verse and prose should have been much like that of contemporaries was to be expected, because Canadians were building with main force a contemporary society which they willed should without deviation be as much like that of the old lands as possible. The imperative was to reproduce, the triumph was not to alter.[11] Not until the twentieth century in the West was any element of utopianism to enter Canadian life and bring to Canada the belief that a new country called for new ways.

Nor need one be troubled that the heights of artistic performance not reached. Statistics alone would account for that. Canadian art and letters compare favourably with that of any provincial society of equivalent population which had not the happy accident of an Ibsen or an Olive Schreiner.

Perhaps, to follow the same lines of thought, the real proof of Canadian artisic achievement lies in its pattern of towns, Quebec grey and gentle on its rock, Toronto shaping itself to its ridges and ravines, in its farmsteads of stone house and boarded barn, in the tree-lined roads and the blue rigour of the great canals. Here was nothing, or little, that was subtle or refined. But here was the conscious, deft and masterful creation of human environment, the transforming of a wilderness, often harsh, often sparse, into a cultivated landscape, a human abode, waterways to carry commerce, roads to be followed along hillside and over rivers without jar or stay. To create a Human Habitat, to make the land habitable, and responsive to human needs, that might be articulate and sensitive, was to work a gigantic masterpiece, to draft a very Shield of Achilles.

The point must, of course, not be pushed too far. Not only was such work utilitarian, the spirit in which it was done was overwhelmingly utilitarian. There was little of this that was of the intellect, although the humanizing of the land was the chief Victorian achievement. The true intellectual achievement of Victorian Canada was neither in literature nor theology but in the sciences.

The study of the sciences had long been established in Europe when the Age of Victoria began. It was, indeed, an easy and integral part of European culture, natural philosophy alongside moral philosophy in the map of knowledge, a particular mode of cultivation, even a gentlemanly hobby. The sciences had taken their place in human learning, but there were as yet no scientists. The lore of science could, indeed, be expressed in verse, as Erasmus Darwin had shown, and scientific enquiry to the believer was but another way of revealing God's providence and purpose to man.

If there was any hint as yet of the cultural rift that was later to appear, it lay in the utilitarian trend of the sciences. The study of the natural world was part of that new learning that Mr. Christopher Hill traced so skilfully as the antecedents of the plain practical world of eighteenth century whiggery.[12] Those who introduced the sciences to Canada were in that tradition, men such as the Honorable Peter Russell studying for their minerals the stray boulders from the Shield in the fields near Toronto,[13] or William Logan tracing the strata of Nova Scotia, or Sir Charles Bagot creating the Geological Survey of Canada in 1842. The last, of course, was the first and greatest scientific achievement of Canada, and a natural undertaking to meet the need of understanding the grotesque structures of a titanically glaciated and most ancient terrain, and finding the minerals that would broaden the simple economy of pioneering days.

Thus it was that when the Canadian Institute was founded in Toronto in 1849, the founders were practical men, engineers, surveyors, architects and when the Institute was refounded in 1851 the same men made up its core, only adding William Logan and J.H. Lefroy, two scientists, at the top and broadening the interests of the Institute to include archaeology, history, and even literary sketches. But they "eschewed nationality" and it may be added, politics, unlike the *Institut canadien*. Quebec, indeed, was to linger behind English Canada in the cultivation of the sciences, except in the universities of Laval and McGill. Science remained in that province of the classical tradition very much a matter of personal cultivation, as W.M. LeMoine with his ornithological museum and his historical and literary interests at Quebec exemplified.

Yet it was in the sciences as in the arts. Results were sought by the application of known principles and practices, rather than the discovery and cultivation of new. The arts were concerned to assist the creation of a humane environment, the sciences to create a progressive one. The great scientific feats, apart from the geologists' revelation of the structure of the country, were engineering works, such as the Victoria Bridge, the longest in the world when built, the even deepening channels of the Welland Canal's majestic scaling of the Niagara escarpment.

Similar was the peculiar dedication of many of the best Canadian minds to the profession of medicine. Not only did the study open to the way to respectability and give a similar outlet to the sacrifical mood of Canadian Christianity; it was also the most direct means of using science for human benefit. Such was the background out of which was to come William Osler,

Frederick Banting and Charles Best in the last years of the Age. And in it one may see, not fancifully, the rolling impetus from the Canadian creation of the "man scape" of Canada. As the axe and plough, the surveyor's chain and the engineer's transit, had cleared the forest and opened the canals and railways, so the surgeon's delicate skill and the physician's trained mind would drain the swamps of disease and open the paths to health. Science thus became not just an instrument of power; it was a more sensitive and perceptive humanity.

Strange it was, indeed, that the old Queen's reign should have ended in the pomp of the Jubilee, and the wild clamour of Mafeking night. In this heavy pomp and circumstance, in this frantic-feeble jubilation, British – not French – Canadians took part in spirit. The tide of Empire, the long accumulation of British immigration, British investment, British manners, had carried Victorian Canada far into waters alien to many of its people and to its collective destiny.

It may indeed, be doubted whether in this imperial sentiment is to be found the true character of the Victorian era. Already the tide was running the other way, as the loyal but reluctant participation of Laurier in the pageantry of 1897 revealed. The Empire to Canada was only a blazed trail to union; unity it must make by and within itself. What the Victorian era did was to give Canada the means to unity; the Pax Britannica, responsible government, Confederation, the concept of political nationality; the railways; the sciences; many steady men and women, their ideas and their ideals. The task of the Age was to assimilate these things to the Canadian experience, the fierce grapple with circumstance in the Atlantic waters, in the forests, in the six months isolation from the sea before the railways linked settlement to settlement and sea to sea.

How was this done, what came out of it, still awaits study and definition. Certainly to those of the age it seemed but part of the general march of progress. They did not study its particularities or record its subtleties. Canadian experience, Canadian art, Canadian history, have always suffered and suffer still, from the pioneering trauma, the Cult of the Pioneer. Too often these are not statements of social or individual experience; they are a scripture, a recording, of when the first settler arrived, the first road was opened, the first child born. Truly Canadian history is an epic, but one that has as its model the Book of Genesis.

Yet Victorian Canada was actually a highly sophisticated and cultivated age. It was neither a by-way nor a backwater in the spread and development of Victorian civilization. It was a wilderness which had become a country in two generations of men. The work of civilization was rapid and complete. Canada was not only politically united, it was physically transformed from sea to sea under the placid gaze of the Queen. What had been wild land had become tilled field; what had been nameless was named; what had been unresponsive wilderness had been made a familiar and possessive landscape with which men lived in harmony. The royal and unruffled gaze might well have shown some astonishment, were it not that the marvel of Victorian Canada was only one marvel of those wondrous years, with their troubled spring, fecund summer, and golden troubled autumn.

A more discerning vision than that of the bland Hanoverian eyes might have seen much more, and not only the girdle of civilized country bound across the continent. Men always work to greater results than they know, society always lives to more purpose than it is aware. The great heartbeat of humanity dilates and contracts in pulse-strokes felt only over time. What was done in the Victorian era was to realize in Canada by peaceful growth and social harmony the pulsation of liberation and progress set running in the Renaissance and Reformation, and to create in the mid-Victorian years and in Confederation a society free as no contemporary society was, without slave, chattel or wage, and yet ordered in local peace and in a political structure that was one of the greatest of men's devising. This vast throb was to run on to the completion of liberal democracy in the next century.

Then, in the late Victorian years, with the rise of business corporations, like the Canadian Pacific Railway, the growth of trade unions and farmers' organizations, the revival of imperialism in English Canada, and the union of the *rouges* and the *ultramontanes* in the *nationalisme* of Quebec, came the contraction which set the blood flowing fast away from the Limited State and individual freedom of liberal thought, towards the organic, and positive state of which the ideal was social welfare rather than individual prosperity. This was more than pioneering, more than observing Providence, more than responsible government, more than the re-creation of received and honoured models. Canadians had lived out, to its ultimate consequences, their particular version of the fate of western men. With Mill on their lips, they had moved into the world of Marx: insisting on individual freedom, they had brought forth a society of which co-operation was the essence. Such was the Victorian dialectic in Canada as elsewhere, that man freed would forge himself new bonds of social obligation.

Notes: Victorian Canada

1. PAC Publications, *Elgin-Grey Papers* 1, 228.
2. W.J.Reader, *The New Professions,* London, 1966.
3. J.P.Matthews, *Tradition in Exile,* Toronto, 1962, 127 and 137.
4. See above "Duncan of Metlakatla," p. 319.
5. Toronto Public Library, Canadian Journal, August and Oct., 1854.
6. See S.R.Mealing, *Canadian Historical Review,* XLVI, 1965: "The Concept of Social Class and the Interpretation of Canadian History."
7. F.N.Walker, *Sketches of Old Toronto,* Don Mills, 1965, 181.
8. Henry Scadding, *Toronto of Old,* Toronto, 1873, 282.
9. G.T.Denison, *Soldiering in Canada; Recollections and Experiences,* London 1900, Chaps. XIV-XVI.
10. Scadding, *Toronto of Old,* 342.
11. Matthews, *Tradition in Exile,* 118, on the Canadian "Academic Tradition."
12. Christopher Hill, *The Intellectual Origins of the English Revolution,* Oxford, 1965.
13. Walker, *Sketches,* 69.